Living and Working in the
Far East

A Survival Handbook

by
Graeme Chesters

SURVIVAL BOOKS • LONDON • ENGLAND

First published 2004

Survival Books Limited, 1st Floor,
60 St James's Street, London SW1A 1ZN, United Kingdom
☎ +44 (0)20-7493 4244, ▤ +44 (0)20-7491 0605
✉ info@survivalbooks.net
💻 www.survivalbooks.net
To order books, please refer to page 444.

British Library Cataloguing in Publication Data.
A CIP record for this book is available
from the British Library.
ISBN 1 901130 97 5

Printed and bound in Finland by WS Bookwell Ltd

ACKNOWLEDGEMENTS

M y sincere thanks to all those who contributed to the successful publication of this book, in particular David Hampshire (for commissioning the book and directing its content), Joe and Kerry Laredo (for editing, proof-reading and desktop publishing), Louise Chesters (for her patience and tolerance) and the many people in the Far East who provided help and information, particularly Patrick Koh in China, Michael Leung in Malaysia, Neil Morrison and Srimuang in Thailand, and Lenny Page in Japan. Finally a special thank-you to Jim Watson for the superb cover and cartoons.

OTHER TITLES BY SURVIVAL BOOKS

Living and Working Series

Abroad; America; Australia; Britain; Canada; France; Germany; the Gulf States & Saudi Arabia; Holland, Belgium & Luxembourg; Ireland; Italy; London; New Zealand; Spain; Switzerland

Buying a Home Series

Abroad; Britain; Florida; France; Greece & Cyprus; Ireland; Italy; Portugal; Spain

Other Titles

The Alien's Guide to Britain; The Alien's Guide to France; The Best Places to Live in France;The Best Places to Live in Spain; Buying, Selling & Letting Property; How to Avoid Holiday & Travel Disasters; Renovating & Maintaining Your French Home; Retiring Abroad; Rioja and its Wines; The Wines of Spain

Order forms are on page 444.

WHAT READERS & REVIEWERS

When you buy a model plane for your child, a video recorder, or some new computer gizmo, you get with it a leaflet or booklet pleading 'Read Me First', or bearing large friendly letters or bold type saying 'IMPORTANT – follow the instructions carefully'. This book should be similarly supplied to all those entering France with anything more durable than a 5-day return ticket. It is worth reading even if you are just visiting briefly, or if you have lived here for years and feel totally knowledgeable and secure. But if you need to find out how France works then it is indispensable. Native French people probably have a less thorough understanding of how their country functions. – Where it is most essential, the book is most up to the minute.

LIVING FRANCE

Rarely has a 'survival guide' contained such useful advice. This book dispels doubts for first-time travellers, yet is also useful for seasoned globetrotters – In a word, if you're planning to move to the USA or go there for a long-term stay, then buy this book both for general reading and as a ready-reference.

AMERICAN CITIZENS ABROAD

It is everything you always wanted to ask but didn't for fear of the contemptuous put down – The best English-language guide – Its pages are stuffed with practical information on everyday subjects and are designed to complement the traditional guidebook.

SWISS NEWS

A complete revelation to me – I found it both enlightening and interesting, not to mention amusing.

CAROLE CLARK

Let's say it at once. David Hampshire's *Living and Working in France* is the best handbook ever produced for visitors and foreign residents in this country; indeed, my discussion with locals showed that it has much to teach even those born and bred in l'Hexagone. – It is Hampshire's meticulous detail which lifts his work way beyond the range of other books with similar titles. Often you think of a supplementary question and search for the answer in vain. With Hampshire this is rarely the case. – He writes with great clarity (and gives French equivalents of all key terms), a touch of humour and a ready eye for the odd (and often illuminating) fact. – This book is absolutely indispensable.

THE RIVIERA REPORTER

A mine of information – I may have avoided some embarrassments and frights if I had read it prior to my first Swiss encounters – Deserves an honoured place on any newcomer's bookshelf.

ENGLISH TEACHERS ASSOCIATION, SWITZERLAND

Have Said About Survival Books

What a great work, wealth of useful information, well-balanced wording and accuracy in details. My compliments!

THOMAS MÜLLER

This handbook has all the practical information one needs to set up home in the UK – The sheer volume of information is almost daunting – Highly recommended for anyone moving to the UK.

AMERICAN CITIZENS ABROAD

A very good book which has answered so many questions and even some I hadn't thought of – I would certainly recommend it.

BRIAN FAIRMAN

We would like to congratulate you on this work: it is really super! We hand it out to our expatriates and they read it with great interest and pleasure.

ICI (SWITZERLAND) AG

Covers just about all the things you want to know on the subject – In answer to the desert island question about the one how-to book on France, this book would be it – Almost 500 pages of solid accurate reading – This book is about enjoyment as much as survival.

THE RECORDER

It's so funny – I love it and definitely need a copy of my own – Thanks very much for having written such a humorous and helpful book.

HEIDI GUILIANI

A must for all foreigners coming to Switzerland.

ANTOINETTE O'DONOGHUE

A comprehensive guide to all things French, written in a highly readable and amusing style, for anyone planning to live, work or retire in France.

THE TIMES

A concise, thorough account of the DOs and DON'Ts for a foreigner in Switzerland – Crammed with useful information and lightened with humorous quips which make the facts more readable.

AMERICAN CITIZENS ABROAD

Covers every conceivable question that may be asked concerning everyday life – I know of no other book that could take the place of this one.

FRANCE IN PRINT

Hats off to *Living and Working in Switzerland*!

RONNIE ALMEIDA

THE AUTHOR

Graeme Chesters was born in the north-west of England in 1963, obtained a degree in philosophy at Bristol University and worked in the City of London for ten years. He has lived in Spain since 1995. He's a columnist for a Spanish newspaper, contributes to British newspapers and magazines, and writes wine, travel and children's books. He is the author of *Living and Working in the Gulf States & Saudi Arabia, How to Avoid Holiday and Travel Disasters* and *The Wines of Spain,* all published by Survival Books (see page 444).

CONTENTS

4. HEALTH 131

5. FINANCE & INSURANCE 157

6. EDUCATION 181

7. TRANSPORT 199

8. MISCELLANEOUS MATTERS 241

9. COUNTRY PROFILES 309

10. ARRIVAL & SETTLING IN 399

APPENDICES   423

INDEX   437

ORDER FORMS   444

IMPORTANT NOTE

This book covers 11 Far Eastern countries (including Hong Kong), which are spread over a huge area and encompass a myriad ethnic groups, religions, languages and customs. Rules, conventions and lifestyles vary considerably between (and often within) countries and many are constantly changing. Factors such as political stability and health hazards are also subject to sudden change. **I therefore cannot recommend too strongly that you check with an official and reliable source (not always the same) before making major decisions or undertaking an irreversible course of action. However, don't believe everything you're told or read, even, dare I say it, herein!**

To help you obtain further information and verify data with official sources, useful addresses and references have been included in most chapters and in **Appendices A, B** and **C.** Important points have been emphasised throughout the book in bold print, some of which it would be expensive or even dangerous to disregard. **Ignore them at your cost or peril.** Unless specifically stated, the reference to any company, organisation, product or publication in this book doesn't constitute an endorsement or recommendation.

AUTHOR'S NOTES

- The countries covered by this book are Brunei Darussalam (referred to simply as Brunei), China, Indonesia, Japan, Malaysia, Philippines, Singapore, South Korea (referred to simply as Korea), Taiwan and Thailand. Although Hong Kong is now an administrative region of China, it's treated as a separate 'country' in this book. The ten countries and Hong Kong are sometimes referred to as 'territories' to avoid confusion.

- The capital of the Philippines is Manila, but this term properly applies to central Manila. The whole conurbation, comprising three 'cities' and 13 municipalities is called Metro Manila. However, Manila is used in this book to refer to the whole of Metro Manila, unless otherwise specified.

- Times are shown using the 12-hour clock, e.g. ten o'clock in the morning is written 10am and ten in the evening 10pm.

- Costs and prices are shown in US$ or local currency where appropriate (with US$ equivalents). They should be taken as guides only, although they were accurate at the time of publication.

- His/he/him/man/men (etc.) also mean her/she/her/woman/women (no offence ladies!). This is done simply to make life easier for both the reader and, in particular, the author, and isn't intended to be sexist.

- British English is used throughout, but American English equivalents are given where appropriate.

- Warnings and important points are shown in bold type.

- The following symbols are used in this book: ☎ (telephone), 🖹 (fax), 🖥 (internet) and ✉ (email).

- Lists of useful addresses, further reading and useful websites are contained in **Appendices A, B** and **C** respectively.

- For those unfamiliar with the metric system of weights and measures, conversion tables are included in **Appendix D**.

INTRODUCTION

Whether you're already living or working in the Far East or just thinking about it, this is **THE BOOK** for you. *Living and Working in the Far East* is designed to meet the needs of anybody who needs to know the essentials of life in the region, including temporary workers, business people, transferees, retirees and even tourists. However long your intended stay, you'll find the information in this book invaluable.

General information isn't difficult to find about the Far East, and a number of guide books are published for tourists and short-stay visitors. However, reliable and up-to-date information in English specifically intended for foreigners living and working in the Far East isn't so easy to find, least of all in one volume. Our aim in publishing this book was to help fill this void and provide the comprehensive practical information necessary for a relatively trouble-free life. You may have travelled to the Far East on holiday, but living and working there for an extended period is a different matter altogether; adjusting to a different environment, culture and language, and making a home abroad can be a traumatic and stressful experience.

You need to adapt to new customs and traditions and discover the local way of doing things, for example, finding a home, paying bills and obtaining insurance. For most foreigners, overcoming the everyday obstacles of life has previously been a case of pot luck. But no more! With a copy of *Living and Working in the Far East* to hand, you'll have a wealth of information at your fingertips – information that derives from a variety of sources, both official and unofficial, not least the hard-won personal experiences of the author and his researchers, family, friends, colleagues and acquaintances.

Adapting to living in a new country is a continuous process and, although this book will help reduce your 'beginner's phase' and minimise the frustrations, it doesn't contain all the answers (most of us don't even know the right questions to ask). What it will do is help you make informed decisions and calculated judgements, instead of uneducated guesses and costly mistakes. Most importantly, it will help save you time, trouble and money, and will repay your investment many times over.

Although you may find some of the information a bit daunting, don't be discouraged. Most problems occur only once and fade into insignificance after a short time (as you face the next half dozen!). The majority of foreigners living in the Far East would agree that, all things considered, they enjoy living there. A period spent in the region is a great way to enrich your life, broaden your horizons and, with any luck, please your bank manager! I trust this book will help you avoid the pitfalls of life in the Far East and smooth your way to a happy and rewarding future in your new home.

Good luck!

Graeme Chesters
January 2004

1.

CHOOSING THE COUNTRY

The countries covered by this book are Brunei Darussalam (henceforth referred to simply as Brunei), China, Indonesia, Japan, Malaysia, Philippines, Singapore, South Korea (henceforth referred to simply as Korea), Taiwan and Thailand. Although Hong Kong is now an administrative region of China, it's treated as a separate 'country' in this book.

Before deciding which of these countries to live in, or indeed whether to live or work in the Far East at all, it's important to do your homework thoroughly and investigate all the possibilities. It may be that you already know the country where you wish to live or work, but have you thought about the alternatives? Of course, if you're being posted to the region by your employer, you may have little or no choice about where you're going – and may not even be in a position to refuse! However, for anyone planning to retire in the Far East or who has a choice of countries where they can work, it's important to do exhaustive research before making a decision. **It isn't uncommon for people to regret their decision after some time and wish they'd chosen a different country.** Unless you know exactly where you want to live or work in the Far East, it's wise to spend some time getting to know the countries. This is particularly important if you're planning to retire or start a business in the region.

As when making any major decision, it's never recommended to be in too much of a hurry. Many people make expensive (even catastrophic) errors when moving abroad, often because they don't do sufficient research and fail to consider all the possibilities and the circumstances of each family member. **It isn't unusual for people to uproot themselves after a few years and wish they'd chosen a different country or even that they'd stayed at home (many people who emigrate return home within a relatively short period).**

The first question to ask yourself is exactly why you want to live or work in the Far East. If you've been offered a transfer to the region by your employer, the decision may be relatively straightforward, although you still need to take into account the wishes and considerations of your family. On the other hand, if you're seeking a new life or career (or career development) or planning to start a business, want to retire to a warmer climate, or simply wish to make more money (who doesn't?), the decision is much more difficult. If you're a young single person, the decision is usually easier than if you have a family. Families need to take into account such considerations as job opportunities for spouses and children, the availability of suitable accommodation (at an affordable price), security, education, family health, leisure and sports opportunities, culture shock, the cost of living and many other matters, most of which are covered by this book.

Having decided exactly why you want to live or work in the Far East, the next thing you need to do is choose the country – unless you're being transferred to the region by your employer. There is, of course, no perfect country for everybody, and each has its advantages and disadvantages.

When choosing a country there are numerous considerations to take into account. For example, if you're planning to work in the Far East, what are the prospects in your profession or trade? Can you freely change jobs if the job you've been offered doesn't work out? If you're planning to start a business, what opportunities are available and can you realistically expect to make a good living? Would you have to leave the country if the business folded? Can you speak the language or are you willing to learn? What is the cost of living? Do you wish to buy a home (which isn't permitted for foreigners or is prohibitively complicated or expensive in some countries) and could you sell at a realistic price should the need arise? Do you need or wish to be 'close' (measured in driving or flying time) to your home country or another country? How important is the climate?

Note that, in order to study or work in some countries, you need a 'sponsorship' letter, which is a letter from the organisation in that country responsible for your visit, e.g. a business, university or government agency by which you've been invited. The letter should briefly outline the reason for your visit, its duration and where you will be staying, and carries more weight if it's on official stationery, i.e. the company's or agency's letterhead.

You may already have some preferences, possibly influenced by where you've spent holidays or where you have family and friends. If you're planning to start a new life, you should choose a country that suits your family's personalities and tastes, as this will be a key factor in your future enjoyment. Before deciding on a country it's wise to do as much research as possible and to read books written about all aspects of that particular country. It will also help to read magazines such as *Resident Abroad* and visit expatriate websites such as ▣ www.escapeartist.com, www.expataccess.com, www.expataccess.com and www.ftexpat.com (see **Appendix C** for other useful sites). **Bear in mind that the cost of investing in a few books or magazines (and other research) is tiny compared to the expense of making a big mistake!**

PERMITS & VISAS

Before making any plans to live or work in the Far East, you must ensure that you will be permitted freely to enter and leave a particular country, live there as long as you wish and become a resident, and do anything else you have in mind, such as be self-employed, start a business or buy a home. **If there's a possibility that you or any family member may wish to live or work in the region permanently, you should enquire whether it will be possible before making any plans.** In many countries in the Far East, the rules and regulations governing permits and visas change frequently, so it's important to obtain up-to-date information from an embassy or consulate in your home country. **Permit infringements are taken seriously by the authorities in most countries and there are penalties for breaches of regulations, including fines and even deportation for flagrant abuses.** The following is a summary of the requirements in each of the eleven territories covered by this book.

Brunei

Entry to Brunei is usually refused to visitors holding passports with less than six months' remaining validity. Citizens of Belgium, Canada, Denmark, France, Germany, Indonesia, Japan, Liechtenstein, Luxembourg, the Republic of Maldives, New Zealand, Netherlands, Norway, the Philippines, South Korea, Sweden, Switzerland and Thailand can visit Brunei for up to 14 days without a visa. British, Malaysian and Singaporean citizens can stay up to 30 days without a visa, while US citizens can stay up to 90 days without one. Australians require visas for any length of stay. Fourteen days is the standard visa length, but they're sometimes issued for longer periods depending on circumstances and your reasons for visiting Brunei. Visas are sometimes issued on arrival at Brunei airport, but it's recommended to obtain one before arrival.

Types Of Visa

Visitor Visas: There are two types of Visitor Visa: a Professional/Business Visit Visa and a Short/Social Visit Visa. Each is valid for three months and is processed in around three days. A single entry visa costs BD$15 (US$26), a multiple entry visa is BD$20 (US$35). A Professional/Business Visit Visa must be sought personally from the visa section of the Immigration and National Registration Department in Brunei. You must provide a passport with at least six months' validity, two passport-size photographs and a 'sponsorship' letter from a company, business representative or government agency (see page 19). A Short/Social Visit Visa must be applied for in person at the Brunei Embassy or High Commission in your home country. You need to provide a passport with six months' validity and a return ticket.

Student Visa: This costs BD$15 (US$26) and you must apply through the Brunei Embassy or High Commission in your home country. You must take a passport with at least six months' validity, two passport-size photographs and an introductory letter from the Brunei Ministry of Education.

Other Requirements

All foreign workers must undergo a blood test and health screening at least one week after their arrival date. A yellow fever vaccination certificate is required by all visitors and travellers aged one year and over who have visited infected areas within the previous six days.

Work Permit: Citizens of all countries except Malaysia and Singapore need a work permit, known as a labour licence or employment pass, to work in Brunei. An labour licence is valid for three months, takes seven working days to process and costs BD$15 (US$26). Your employer obtains the visa prior to your arrival in Brunei, from the work pass section of the Immigration and National Registration Department in Brunei. He must first have a quota licence from the Labour

Department, then he must write an application letter to the Director of Immigration and National Registration, and take to the Department a work pass application form (Bur23), a visa form, a passport photo and a photocopy of your passport (which must have at least six months' validity). There's usually little difficulty in obtaining a permit, as Brunei needs foreign labour to satisfy the demands of the private sector, where some 75 per cent of employees are foreign. Employment visas for foreigners are issued only for three months and must be renewed for longer periods of employment.

Identity Card: Any foreigner staying in Brunei for more than three months must have a Green Identity Card or Green IC. It costs BD$2 (US$3.45) and is processed in 21 working days. You must apply in person at the national registration section of the Immigration and National Registration Department, taking your passport and a photocopy, and two passport-size photographs.

China

Visas are required to enter China, even as a transit passenger, and must be obtained prior to arrival. **Visas cannot be obtained on arrival in China.** Nobody suffering from a mental disorder, leprosy, AIDS, any venereal disease, contagious tuberculosis or any other contagious disease is allowed to enter China. For all Chinese visas, you must present the following:

- A passport with at least six months' validity remaining (12 months for Z and X visas – see below) and at least one blank page left in it;
- A completed visa application form (BG-O1), with one extra passport photograph (black and white or colour). If the form isn't filled in completely or some of it's illegible, this can delay the processing or even lead to denial of the visa.

Applicants should apply at the visa office of their nearest Chinese Embassy or Consulate. If you cannot go yourself, the task can be carried out by a relative, friend or travel/visa agent. The usual processing time is four working days. You can apply for expedited processing, with an additional fee of around US$30 for processing in one working day or US$20 for two to three working days. You cannot pay by personal cheque but must use cash, a money order or a bank cheque, which should be made payable to the Embassy or Consulate.

Visas are issued at the discretion of the consular officers and their decisions are based on the laws and regulations of the Chinese Government. Any application can be refused, with no reason given. All visa conditions, requirements and prices are subject to change without notice, at the discretion of Chinese Embassies and Consulates.

Visas are generally valid for 90 days from the date of issue. It's recommended to apply for a visa around 30 days before the planned date of departure.

Types Of Visa

Tourist/Family Visit (L Visa): This visa is issued to tourists and those on family or personal visits. In some circumstances (these aren't stated by the authorities), you must provide airline tickets showing your departure date from China and/or an invitation from relatives. A consular official will telephone you if additional information is required. Travel to Tibet is dealt with differently (contact the Tourist Bureau of Tibet Autonomous Region – see the telephone book). Fees are as follows:

Entry	Validity	Duration Of Stay	Americans	Others
Single	90 days	30 days	US$50	US$30
Double	90 days	30 days (each entry)	US$75	US$45

Business/Official Visit (F Visa): This visa is issued to people coming to China for no more than six months for business, research, lectures, scientific or cultural exchanges, or short-term advanced studies or internships. Fees are as follows:

Entry	Validity	Duration Of Stay	Americans	Others
Single	90 days	30 days	US$50	US$30
Double	90 days	30 days (each entry)	US$75	US$45
Multiple*	6 months	30 days (each entry)	US$100	US$60
Multiple*	12 months	30 days (each entry)	US$150	US$90

* You require a letter from a Chinese government organisation, which has the authority to request the Embassy or Consulate to issue the visa. Based on this, the length of duration might be longer than 30 days.

Employment/Work (Z Visa): This visa is issued to people taking up employment in China and to accompanying family members. You must submit an official invitation issued by a Chinese government agency, which has the authority to request the Embassy or Consulate to issue the visa. In order to work on an academic or scientific research project or to provide technical and economic assistance, you must submit a Foreign Specialist's Licence issued by the Chinese Foreign Specialist's Bureau. Foreigners staying or working in China for more than a year must provide a Physical Examination Certificate for Foreigner (*sic*).

A Z visa is valid for 90 days and the duration of stay varies. Americans must pay US$50, other nationalities US$30.

Student (X Visa): This visa is issued to people studying in China for six months or longer. You must provide an approved Foreign Student Visa Application Form (JW201 or JW202) issued by the State Education Ministry of China and an enrolment letter from the receiving university. Those who aim to study in China for less than 12 months and stay for not more than 180 days may qualify for an F visa. If staying for more than a year, you must provide a Physical Examination Certificate for Foreigner. An X visa is valid for 90 days and the duration of stay varies. Americans must pay US$50, other nationalities US$30.

Transit (G Visa): This visa is issued to those who pass through China. You sometimes need to provide a valid visa for the country of destination or an invitation to visit, and an airline ticket showing transit through China. Fees are as follows:

Entry	Validity	Duration Of Stay	Americans	Others
Single	90 days	7 days	US$50	US$30
Double	90 days	7 days (each entry)	US$75	US$45

Other Visas: Other types of visa are the C Visa (issued to aviation workers and crew members), the J-1 Visa (issued to foreign correspondents resident in China), the J-2 Visa (issued to foreign correspondents temporarily in China) and the D Visa (issued to those wanting to reside permanently in China).

Other Requirements

To work and live in China on a long-term basis (i.e. for more than 12 months) you need a work or business visa, a health permit and a residence permit (see below). Each family member must also obtain a residence permit and visa. You might also need a foreign expert's certificate (a maroon booklet), depending on the nature of employment.

Work Permit: All foreign nationals require a work permit, which can be difficult to obtain, as Chinese nationals take priority. To obtain a work permit you must have an official invitation from a Chinese Government Agency or a government authorised company, as well as a Foreign Specialist's Licence from the Chinese authorities for some jobs. These documents must be attached to your work visa application.

Health Certificate: You must be able to prove that you're in good general health and free of any communicable diseases, including HIV, which requires a Health Permit. First, you must obtain a Physical Examination Certificate. A health examination can be performed in China or in your home country. If it's in the latter, you need to provide a doctor's letter stating that you're healthy, original copies of the chest X-ray, HIV test and STD (sexually transmitted diseases) tests. You must take your Physical Examination Certificate to the local Health and Quarantine Verification Office in China, with a Health Permit application form (available from the same office), your passport, two photographs and your work visa. When you receive your Health Permit, submit it with your passport to the local health officer for approval. You will then be registered at the local Public Security Bureau and submitted for a residence permit.

Hong Kong

British passport holders don't require a visa or entry permit to enter Hong Kong for any purpose for stays of up to six months. Nationals of over 170 countries and territories can visit Hong Kong visa-free for between 7 and 180 days (see 🖳 www.immd.gov.hk for a full list): for example, Australians, Canadians, New Zealanders and Americans may stay for 90 days, and South Africans for 30 days. Everyone entering Hong Kong must have a passport valid for at least six months and must be able to show evidence of sufficient funds to support themselves during their stay.

If you need to apply for a Hong Kong visa for employment, investment, education, training or residence, complete an application form ID812 or the new form ID(E)936A (available from Chinese Embassies and Consulates) in block capitals, affix a photograph of yourself and send it to your 'sponsor' in Hong Kong (a Hong Kong business, institution or resident who acts as your guarantor during your stay) along with photocopies of your passport, an additional identical photograph of yourself, and the appropriate sponsorship form (ID428B for employment, ID428D for education or ID428A for residence). Your sponsor must submit the application to the Hong Kong Immigration Department. The visa is issued to your sponsor, who sends it on to you. The process takes between four and six weeks, and the fee is generally HK$135 (US$17.35), varying according to nationality, nature of visit and type of visa. Visas are usually valid for three months and can be extended.

Other Requirements

Anybody who enters and is permitted to stay in Hong Kong for more than 180 days must register for a residence permit (called a Hong Kong identity card) within 30 days of arrival. You can telephone a 24-hour line to make an appointment to register (☎ 2598-0888) or book online (🖳 www.esd.gov.hk).

Work Permit: Work permits are required by all foreign nationals and may be difficult to obtain, as the authorities have a policy of recruiting from the local workforce whenever possible. Alternatively, the employer must show that the employee will contribute substantially to the economy.

Indonesia

Indonesia takes a particularly dim view of anybody flouting its entry requirements. Holders of British, Australian, Canadian, New Zealand and US passports can enter Indonesia for tourist visits of up to 60 days without a visa. South Africans and Israelis need to apply for a visa and seek special approval from the Immigration Department of Indonesia prior to travelling. Those entering Indonesia require at least six months' validity on their passports. You must show that you have sufficient funds in cash and/or travellers' cheques to support yourself during your time in Indonesia. Credit cards are no longer acceptable as proof of financial status because of the widespread misuse of credit limits.

Visas should be obtained from your nearest Indonesian Embassy before travelling to the country. In addition to the fees listed below, there's sometimes a fee of US$8.50 imposed for each visa, although it's unclear why! Journalists wishing to come to Indonesia need to seek approval from the Indonesian Immigration Office.

In the case of personal applications, visas are usually issued within two or three working days. Postal applications take seven working days. Any applications that require referral to Indonesia can take up to two months, occasionally longer.

Types Of Visa

Tourist Visa: To apply you need a passport with at least six months' validity from the date of entry to Indonesia, an application form, a passport-size photograph, evidence of sufficient funds to cover your stay, onward or return tickets, a travel itinerary, a pre-paid delivery envelope for postal applications and the fee (payable only in cash or by postal order), usually US$60. Visas are valid for three months from the date of issue and are for a maximum stay of 60 days.

Social Visit Visa: To apply, the requirements are the same as for the business visa below, except that the last requirement is replaced by a letter of invitation from your family or friends in Indonesia stating the reason for and duration of the visit, and providing details of your accommodation while in Indonesia.

Business Visa: You need a passport with at least six months' validity from the date of entry into Indonesia, an application form, a passport-size photo, evidence of sufficient funds to cover your stay, onward or return tickets, a pre-paid delivery envelope for postal applications, the fee (payable only in cash or by postal order), usually US$60, and two supporting letters from your company in your home country and your sponsor/counterpart company in Indonesia, stating the reason for and duration of the visit, and accommodation details. A visa is usually valid for three months from the date of issue and is for a maximum stay of 60 days.

Multiple Entry Business Visa: To apply, conditions are as per the business visa, but the visa is valid for 12 months, costs US$210 and you need to secure approval from the Indonesian Immigration Office.

Other Requirements

Work Permit: In order to work in Indonesia for more than 60 days, a one-year work permit is usually required – and you must have patience to get through the tortuous administration procedure. You need an employer in Indonesia to 'sponsor' your application and the process takes around a month. However, if time is pressing (and you need to begin work immediately) or if your work project will last less than six months, you can apply for a temporary work permit (even this is an involved process). This is done in Indonesia at the Department of Manpower and you must already have secured a business visa. Temporary work permits are valid for three months and can be extended for an additional month. If your regular work permit isn't received by the time it expires, you can apply for a second temporary work permit. This necessitates your applying for another business visa outside Indonesia (usually in Singapore).

The following are required to apply for a temporary work permit:

- A detailed CV;
- Three passport-size photographs;
- A sponsorship letter from your Indonesian employer;
- A copy of your business visa.

Approval usually takes around a week and you must then get a permit stamp in your passport from an Indonesian consulate abroad (usually Singapore). In order to get this stamp at the foreign consulate, you must present an application form in duplicate, two passport-size photographs and your original passport. For jobs below the rank of director, you might be charged a fee of US$150 per month for the temporary work permit by the Department of Manpower.

To apply for a standard work permit in Indonesia, you require the following documents **in addition to those required for a temporary permit (see above)**:

- An organisation chart of the company in Indonesia;
- The registration number of the company in Indonesia;
- An 'expatriate utilisation plan' (RPTKA);
- An approved application for a recommendation to employ an expatriate (TA-O1).

Once the TA-O1 has been received, your employer must apply for a Temporary Stay Visa (VITAS) from the Directorate General of Immigration. This is then issued by a consulate of the applicant's choice. Next you must apply to the Directorate General of Immigration for a Temporary Stay Permit (KITAS) for yourself and your family. This permit is valid for a year and can be extended on request. The work permit is then processed. When issued, it's valid for one year and can be extended on request.

Once the KITAS is received, you must register with the local police and municipal government and obtain the following documents:

- *Surat Tanda Melapor Diri* (STMD) – a registration book issued by the Aliens' Supervisory Division of the Indonesian Police Headquarters or the local regional police office;

- *Surat Tanda Melapor* (STM) – a report from the local sub-district police office in your area of residence;
- *Surat Kependudukan* – a resident's registration issued by the local municipal office;
- An immigration book, issued by the Directorate General of Immigration.

Both the STM and the immigration book stipulate that any change in information (e.g. change of address) must be reported to the appropriate authorities. **You can be arrested for not doing so.** Your dependants must follow the same registration procedures, but they make their initial entry to the country as tourists.

Japan

Nationals of Austria, Germany, Ireland, Liechtenstein, Mexico, Switzerland and the UK can stay in Japan for up to six months without a visa, although they cannot work without a visa. They're initially granted a stay of three months and can then apply when in Japan to the local Immigration Department to have this extended by another three months (which is at the discretion of the authorities). Nationals of all other EU countries, Australia, Canada, New Zealand and the US can stay in Japan for up to 90 days without a visa. South Africans must obtain a visa for a stay of any duration.

Whether or not you need or have a visa to enter Japan, entry can be denied if you don't have visible means of support for the duration of your stay, onward or return tickets and documentation necessary for your next destination.

Visas should be applied for in person at a Japanese Embassy or Consulate in your home country. Applications usually take around five working days for those that don't need referral to the Ministry of Foreign affairs in Tokyo, when processing can take up to four weeks. If you possess a Certificate of Eligibility (see below), processing might be only three working days. Unusual or complex visa applications can take three or more months. Validity of visas varies greatly, according to nationality and purpose of visit. Most single-entry visas are for three or six months, double-entry or multiple-entry visas are usually for 12 months. Work visas are usually for between one and three years. Visa fees are around ¥700 (US$6.40) for a transit visa, ¥3,000 (US$27.50) for a single-entry visa and ¥6,000 (US$55) for a double-entry or multiple-entry visa.

When applying for a visa, the following documents are always required:

- A passport;
- Two passport-type photographs taken within the previous six months;
- Two official visa forms (available from embassies and consulates);

> ● Documents certifying the purpose of the visit, e.g. an offer of work from an employer or confirmation of acceptance from a university.

For a full list of the current requirements for the many categories of Japanese visa and residence status, see 🖳 www.mofa.go.jp.

Types Of Visa

Japan has seven types of visa, including two for short-term stays; working visas are issued for 14 residence statuses, as shown in the table below:

Visa Category	Residence Status
General Visa	Engaged in cultural activities*
	College student*
	Pre-college student*
	Trainee*
	Dependant*
Work Visa	Professor
	Artist
	Religious activities
	Journalist
	Investor/Business manager
	Legal/Accounting services
	Medical services
	Researcher
	Instructor
	Engineer
	Specialist in humanities/international services
	Intra-company transferee
	Entertainer
	Skilled labour
Temporary Visitor's Visa	Temporary visitor*
Transit Visa	Temporary visitor*
Diplomatic Visa	Diplomat
Official Visa	Official
Specified Visa	Engaged in designated activities+

Spouse or child of Japanese national

Spouse or child of permanent resident

Long-term resident

*work not permitted

+permission to work depends on circumstances

Other Requirements

Certificate Of Eligibility: When applying for any of the work or long-term stay visas, it's recommended to obtain a Certificate of Eligibility first, as it facilitates the visa process, making referral to Japan much less likely (although it isn't a guarantee that a visa will be issued). The Certificate is issued by a regional immigration authority in Japan and is evidence that the applicant fulfils the conditions of the Immigration Control Act. There are two ways to obtain a Certificate of Eligibility: one is for a proxy in Japan to make the application at the nearest immigration authority, using the proxy's home address in Japan; the other is for applicants who are in Japan to apply personally and then leave the country to apply for a visa.

Alien Registration Card: If you're in Japan for more than three months, you must apply for a residence permit, known as an Alien Registration Card (also called a *gaigin* card). You must go to your local city hall and take two passport photographs and around ¥3,000 (US$27.50). You're fingerprinted and given a sheet confirming that you've applied and the card is issued a couple of weeks later – displaying your fingerprints! The card must be carried at all times and the police will want to see it if they stop you.

Work Permit: All foreign nationals require a work permit, which is issued only if you have a firm offer of work or a contract from a Japanese employer/sponsor, who must apply on your behalf. Once the Ministry of Justice has issued a Certificate of Eligibility, this is sent to the Japanese consulate or embassy where you make your application for a work visa. Note that you can only obtain a work visa from outside the country, even if you're in Japan when an offer of employment is made.

Korea

Your passport must be valid for at least six months in order to gain entry to Korea. Nationals of Australia and EU countries can stay up to 90 days without a visa (except those from Italy and Portugal, who can stay up to 60 days). Nationals of Canada can stay up to 180 days, but US citizens can stay only for up to 30 days. Most visas are valid for three months, although they can be extended. Costs vary greatly (from around US$30 to US$80) according to the type of visa (see below) and the nationality of the applicant and must be paid in cash or by postal order. Full details are available from embassies and consulates, where you apply for visas.

Application requirements vary according to the nationality of the applicant and the type of visa, but for tourist and visitor visas, they're usually as follows:

- A passport valid for at least six months;
- A completed application form;
- One or two passport photographs (depending on your nationality and the purpose of your visit);
- A stamped, self-addressed envelope (if applying by post);
- Proof of sufficient funds (a bank statement or company letter – ask at the consulate or embassy what is currently required).

Types Of Visa

The three main types of visa are tourist, visitor and work visas. For a work visa, you require all of the above except the proof of sufficient funds. Instead, you need a letter of invitation on headed notepaper from a company in Korea, including the purpose of the visit, the duration of the stay and a contact address and telephone number in Korea. Visas usually take five working days to be processed, but more complex work visas can take up to a couple of months.

Other Requirements

If you intend to stay in Korea for longer than 90 days, you need to apply for a residence permit from the Immigration Office in Seoul (☎ 650-6212). Documents required are usually the same as for visa applications.

Work Permit: All foreign nationals require a work permit, which must be applied for from outside Korea, even if you're offered a job while visiting. The process is long and complicated requiring a lot of paperwork, which includes a firm offer of employment from a Korean sponsor. All paperwork must be signed by representatives from various government agencies in Seoul.

Malaysia

Entry to Malaysia is forbidden for nationals of Israel and Serbia and Montenegro and to foreign women who are six months or more pregnant, unless they're in transit and remain within the airport. People of scruffy appearance are sometimes denied entry. Your passport must be valid for at least six months at the date of entry and it must have sufficient pages for the embarkation stamp given on arrival. You also need evidence of sufficient funds to support yourself during your stay and an onward or return air or sea ticket.

Nationals of EU countries can stay in Malaysia for social or business visits for up to three months without a visa, except nationals of Ireland, who can stay only for up to two months, and Greek and Portuguese nationals, who can stay for just one month. Nationals of Australia, Canada, New Zealand, South Africa and the US can stay for up to three months. Travellers in transit to another country can usually stay up to five days without a visa, if they have a confirmed ticket via a Malaysian airport.

Visas usually cost around US$15 (US$25 for Indian passports), payable in cash or by postal order, but prices are subject to change. Visas are usually for between one and three months' duration, and extensions are usually possible from the Malaysian High Commission.

In order to apply for a visa in your home country or in Malaysia, the following documents are required:

- A passport valid for at least six months;
- Two passport-size photos;
- Two completed and signed application forms (around 40¢ each);
- Proof of sufficient funds (the original and a photocopy of your most recent bank statement usually suffices);
- An onward or return ticket;
- A yellow fever vaccination certificate if you've come from an infected area;
- If appropriate, a letter of introduction (and a copy) from your employer, college or university in Malaysia.

Visas are usually available for collection after 3.30pm the same day if applied for before midday.

Work Permit

If you're coming to work in Malaysia, your employer must apply for a Professional or Employment Pass (sometimes called a work permit) from the Malaysian Immigration Head Office in Kuala Lumpur (☎ 2094-5096). This is invariably done when the employee has arrived in the country. Your monthly salary must be at least RM2,500 (US$660) and the post must be approved for at least two years. If the post is for less than two years, a Visit Pass (Temporary Employment) is granted instead. If the post is for less than six months, a Visit Pass (Professional) is issued. These Passes take between four and six weeks to be issued. Fees, which are payable to the Immigration Department, invariably by your employer (although you should check), are RM300 (US$80) per annum for key posts and RM200 (US$52) per annum for mid-ranking posts. There's also a RM50 (US$13) processing fee per application.

Documents required for work permits are as follows:

- A copy of your passport;
- Three passport-size photographs;
- Academic certificates;
- A CV from head office overseas (if there is one);
- Your employment contract with your Malaysian employer.

If family members are coming to Malaysia with you, they need a Dependant Pass, requiring a passport, three passport-size photographs and a marriage certificate (birth certificates for children).

The East Malaysian states of Sabah and Sarawak have their own immigration procedures and work permits.

Philippines

Visitors from most EU and western countries can enter the Philippines for up to 21 days without a visa, provided they have an onward ticket and a passport with at least six months' validity. Single entry visas are usually valid for 59 days, multiple-entry visas for between six and 12 months from the date of issue. Visa extensions are at the discretion of the Bureau of Immigration. Fees (in cash or by postal order only) are around US$22 for a three-month single-entry visa, US$43 for a six-month multiple-entry visa and US$65 for a one-year multiple-entry visa. You should apply for a visa at a Philippines Embassy or Consulate in your home country, with the following documents:

- An application form;
- A passport valid for at least six months beyond the intended period of stay;
- A passport-size photograph signed on the reverse;
- Proof of means of support for the duration of the stay (a recent bank statement or letter of employment);
- If applying by post, a stamped, addressed envelope and a notary's signature on the application;
- Onward or return tickets;
- For business travellers, a letter from your sponsoring Filipino company or from your employer, stating the purpose of the visit.

Visas usually take two working days to be processed.

Types Of Visa

Employment Visa: Foreigners who will be working in executive, technical, managerial or 'highly confidential' positions for between one and five years may apply for employment visas under section 9(g) of the Philippine Immigration Act. The prospective employer must first establish that nobody within the Philippines can be found who's competent and willing to do the job. Because the application process can take several month, a three-month work permit can be issued in the interim. The visa, if granted, is for the same period as the job and functions as a work permit.

Trader & Treaty Visa: Trader and Treaty visas are available to those who have or intend to invest at least P300,000 (US$5,400), among other conditions, and are granted for a year.

Other Visas: Other types of visa include Special Resident Retiree's Visas (SRRV), Special Investor's Resident Visas (SIRV) and Subic Bay Freeport Residence Visas, which require certain investments and incomes in order to qualify (current details and requirements are available from your nearest embassy or consulate).

Singapore

Visas aren't required to enter Singapore for nationals of Australia, Canada, Western Europe, New Zealand or the US, but a passport with at least six months' validity is mandatory and you must provide evidence of sufficient funds to support yourself and have an onward or return ticket.

Work Permits

Professional Visit Pass: Those visiting Singapore for a specific, short-term assignment need a Professional Visit Pass. It costs S$50 (US$29) for periods of under three months and S$100 (US$58) for three months. If you also need a visa, this costs an additional S$20 (US$11.60). Apply at a Singapore Embassy or Consulate or the Visitor Services Centre, 10 Kallang Road, Singapore 208718 (☎ 6391-6100). You need the following:

- Two copies of Form 14, completed and signed;
- Two passport-size photographs;
- Two copies of a letter from a Singapore-based organisation acting as a local 'sponsor' for the assignment.

Processing takes between two and four weeks.

Some people applying for a Professional Visit Pass also require a Public Entertainment Licence and/or a copy of the contract of employment. Requirements vary slightly for different types of employment and full current details are available on the Immigration and Checkpoints Authority website (🖥 http://app.ica.gov.sg), as well as downloadable application forms.

Work Permit: Those wanting to work in Singapore for a long period but who aren't permanent residents are divided into two categories: those whose basic monthly salary is more than S$2,500 (US$1,450), who must apply for an Employment Pass (see below), and those whose salary is below S$2,500 (US$1,450), who must apply for a Work Permit.

For a Work Permit, your prospective employer must place a S$5,000 (US$2,900) security deposit (unless you're from Malaysia), which is refunded when your job finishes and you leave Singapore. Depending on the type of employment, the employer must also pay a levy of between S$200 (US$116) and S$400 (US$232) to the Ministry of Manpower. Application forms are available from Counter 1, Level 2 of the Work Permit Department (☎ 6538-3033) and from Singapore Immigration and Registration, 10 Kallang Road, Singapore 208718 (☎ 6391-6100). To apply for a Work Permit you need the following:

- Two passport-size photos taken in the previous three months;
- A local Singapore sponsor (invariably your employer);
- A certificate from a registered Singapore doctor confirming that your general health is good;
- Four completed copies of Form 8 signed by you and an authorised officer from your sponsor and endorsed with the company's stamp or seal;
- One copy each of your professional qualifications;
- Employment testimonials.

Employment Pass: Those wanting to work in Singapore for long periods (who aren't permanent residents) whose basic salary is more than S$2,500 (US$1,450) must apply for an Employment Pass. There are four main types of Employment Pass, which are generally issued only to foreigners who hold acceptable degrees, professional qualifications or specialist skills:

- A **P1 Pass** is issued if the applicant's basic monthly salary is over S$7,000 (US$4,065).
- A **P2 Pass** is issued if the applicant's basic monthly salary is between S$3,500 (US$2,032) and S$7,000 (US$4,065).
- A **Q1 Pass** is issued to foreigners whose salary is between S$2,500 and S$3,500 (US$1,450 to US$2,032).
- A **Q2 Pass** is issued in exceptional circumstances to foreigners who don't automatically qualify as above.

The following documents are required for an Employment Pass (and should be submitted to the Employment Pass Department, Ministry of Manpower, 9 Maxwell Road, 03-01, Singapore 069112):

- A completed Form 8 signed by the applicant and the sponsoring local company;

- A passport-size photograph taken during the previous three months;
- A copy of the applicant's qualifications and employment testimonials.

When you collect the Pass, you must present your passport, a completed medical report confirming that your general health is good and the fee, around S$30 (US$17.40). Check the website of the Ministry of Manpower for current requirements and prices (💻 www.mom.gov.sg).

Dependants' Pass: The spouse and unmarried children under the age of 21 of those requiring a work permit or Employment Pass must apply for Dependant's Passes, for which you must submit the following:

- Two passport-size photographs of each applicant taken within the previous three months (but photos aren't required for children under 12);
- Two completed and signed copies of Form 12;
- One copy of your marriage certificate;
- One copy each of the children's birth certificates or court papers relating to custody of the children.

Taiwan

Taiwan isn't recognised as separate from China by most countries and therefore doesn't have embassies or consulates. Visas and details about entering Taiwan can be obtained at 'pseudo-embassies' (also called representative offices), which are often trade offices, travel companies or friendly associations.

Types Of Visa

Landing Visa: Nationals of Australia, Canada, the EU (except Denmark, Finland and Ireland), New Zealand and the US don't need visas to enter Taiwan for stays of up to 14 days. People from these countries can apply for a Landing Visa on arrival at CKS International airport or Kaohsiung International airport if they have onward tickets and don't have a criminal record. A Landing Visa is valid for 30 days and cannot be extended. You must provide a passport-size photo and pay a fee of NT$2,000 (US$58.75).

General Visa: A general visa is required by all foreigners except those listed above for stays of up to 14 days and by all foreigners for longer stays (up to six months), irrespective of the purpose of their visit. A single-entry visa costs around US$42 and is valid for up to 60 days (depending on your nationality and the purpose of your visit), and you're allowed up to two extensions of 60 days each (apply at your local police station). A multiple-entry visa costs around US$85 and is valid for six months. Fees are payable in cash or by cheque or postal order. Apply at Taiwan 'embassies' with the following documents:

- Two passport-size photos;
- A passport valid for at least six months;
- Documents verifying the purpose of the visit or a letter from a Taiwan 'sponsor' if appropriate.

Resident Visa: If you want to stay in Taiwan for more than six months, you must apply for a Resident Visa in your home country. You need a passport valid for at least six months, an application form and a photograph. If you're intending to work in Taiwan, you must also provide documentation from your employer to this effect; the visa will state that you're allowed to work. Make sure that a Resident Visa has been obtained **before** leaving for Taiwan, as it isn't unknown for people to begin the application process and arrive in Taiwan to find that their employer has been unable to arrange a visa. **It's illegal to work for somebody other than the employer who sponsored your Resident Visa.**

Other Requirements

Holders of Resident Visas must apply for an Alien Residence Certificate (ARC) within 15 days of arrival in Taiwan or within 15 days of the issue of the visa. Apply at the nearest county police headquarters. You're required to carry the ARC card at all times. ARC holders must apply for a re-entry permit before leaving Taiwan if they intend to return.

Those wanting to stay in Taiwan for more than three months need to pass an AIDS test. **The rules and requirements for foreign workers change frequently in Taiwan and it's recommended that you check the latest regulations at a Taiwanese representative office.**

Work Permit: All foreign nationals wishing to work in Taiwan require an employment authorisation or work permit. Employers must fulfil certain conditions in order to obtain work permits for foreign personnel. Note that foreigners cannot be self-employed in Taiwan.

Thailand

Nationals of Australia, Canada, the EU, South Africa, the UK and the US (among others) can stay in Thailand for up to 30 days without a visa, provided their passports have at least six months' validity beyond the end of their intended stay in Thailand and they have a dated return ticket. Entry is sometimes refused to people with long, untidy hair or who are dressed in 'hippy style'. Nationals of Afghanistan are closely scrutinised before being allowed entry, and passports issued by the Palestinian government aren't recognised. If you want to stay for longer than 30 days, you must secure a visa before arriving in Thailand.

For all visas, you must apply at Thai consulates with the following:

- A passport valid for at least six months from the date of application;
- Two recent passport-size photos;
- Proof of sufficient funds to cover your stay;
- A confirmed onward or return ticket;
- A registered, stamped, self-addressed envelope if applying by post;
- A valid international health certificate for yellow fever (usually only for people from affected countries);
- If applying for a non-immigrant visa (see below), a letter from your employer in your home country and from the business partner in Thailand detailing the nature and purpose of the visit.

Fees (see below) are payable in cash or by postal order only. Visas are usually processed within two working days. **Note that the Thai authorities are constantly changing the requirements for and costs of visas and work permits and it's recommended to check with a consulate or embassy immediately before applying.** If they're unhelpful, speak directly to the Royal Thai Foreign Ministry, Sri Ayudha Road, Bangkok 10400, (☎ 662) 643 5000.

Types Of Visa

Tourist Visa: Tourist Visas are usually valid for three months from the date of application, for stays of up to 60 days, and cost around US$42 for single entry.

Non-Immigrant Visa: Non-Immigrant Visas are normally required for business trips and are a pre-requisite for a work permit (see below). They cost US$68 for single entry and US$153 for multiple entry. Unless you know that you will require only a single entry, it's recommended to apply for the latter so that you don't have to reapply every few months, which is a time-consuming and expensive business. A Non-Immigrant Visa can be obtained in your home country before your arrival or after you arrive in Thailand, although you must then leave the country and arrange it through a Thai Consulate or Embassy in a neighbouring country.

A Non-Immigrant Visa is valid for a year, but it's reasonably straightforward to extend it by a further year. You must take the following to the Immigration Department:

- Your passport and copies showing the picture page and entry stamp;
- Your work permit (see below);
- A copy of your employment contract (or a company letter including your salary and length of employment);
- A passport photograph;

- A Tax ID Card, which is required in order for your salary to be paid – apply at the Revenue Department, Phaholyothin Road, Bangkok 10400 (☎ 662-272 9387/8, 💻 www.rd.go.th, which includes an English version);
- Copies of your last six months' tax forms;
- Your bank book (not always required);
- The fee of Bht1,900 (US$47.60).

You must be accompanied by a Thai staff member from your company to help to translate or clear up any queries.

Transit Visa: Transit visas cost US$25 for single entry.

Other Requirements

Work Permit: If you want to work in Thailand, you need a work permit. Before you can apply for one, however, you need a Non-Immigrant Visa (see above). In order to obtain a Non-Immigrant Visa for the purpose of securing a work permit, you need a letter from your future employer on company headed paper confirming that you've been offered a job and that the company knows you to be reliable and law abiding, and requesting that you be given a non-immigrant visa so that the company can apply for a work permit for you. You must sometimes also provide registration documents for the company that you will be working for.

When you've obtained a non-immigrant visa, you can apply for a work permit. The following are required:

- A photocopy of your passport;
- A Non-Immigrant Visa;
- A copy of your degree certificate or CV (which must sometimes be certified by your embassy);
- A doctor's certificate stating that you're in good health;
- Two passport-size photos;
- The fee of between Bht3,000 (US$75) and Bht5,000 (US$125), which depends on the length of the permit.

Your employer must submit tax and legal documents concerning his business.

When you've submitted the papers for a work permit, you must not let your visa expire. If you don't receive the work permit before the visa expires, you must have it extended (see **Non-Immigrant Visa** above). **Note that work permits can take between several weeks and several months to be processed.**

When you receive your work permit, you must go to the Labour Department with your passport and sign a document acknowledging receipt. Your passport is stamped at the time of receipt. **Work permits allow you to work only at the named company and place. If either changes, you must obtain a new permit.**

Re-Entry Permit: With a visa and a work permit, you might think that the paper-chase is over. It isn't. If you wish to leave the country for any reason, you also need a Re-Entry Permit. If you leave without one, your visa and work permit are invalidated. You obtain a Re-Entry Permit from the Re-Entry window at the Immigration Department; if you need it that day, go before noon. You must submit a re-entry request form, your passport, three passport-size photos and the fee: Bht1,000 (US$25) for one re-entry, Bht3,800 (US$95) for multiple re-entry. You're given a receipt and must return later to pick up the permit and your passport.

HOLIDAY HOMES & RETIREMENT

If you wish to retire or spend long periods each year in the Far East (e.g. in a holiday home), you must check whether this will be possible before making any plans and ensure that you will be able to afford to live in the region. **Note that, if you don't qualify to live in a country by birthright or as a national of a country, it may be impossible to obtain a residence permit.**

Despite the bureaucracy and red tape encountered in some countries, an increasing number of people are retiring abroad and the number is expected to rise sharply in the future as more people choose early retirement. Many retirees seeking a home abroad are North Americans or northern Europeans, who can often buy a retirement home abroad for much less than the value of their family home. The difference between the money raised on the sale of your family home and the cost of a home abroad can be invested to supplement your pension, allowing you to live comfortably in retirement, particularly when a lower cost of living is taken into consideration.

Until recently, many northern Europeans chose the Spanish coasts and islands, Portugal or Cyprus, while North Americans headed for Florida, Arizona, New Mexico or California. But the increased availability and reduced prices of long-haul travel have opened up the Far East to many people and retirement to the region is now a possibility. The Philippines government is in the process of discussing visas and the rules applying to foreigners wanting to spend time in the country after their retirement, and Malaysia is also looking to attract long-stay visitors (see 🖳 www.tourism.gov.my/my2ndhome for further details of what is proposed). Nevertheless, of the 11 territories covered in this book, Thailand is currently the only one regarded as potentially attractive to foreign retirees (see below).

Before planning to live in the Far East permanently you must take into consideration many factors, including the cost of living, pension payments (some countries such as the UK automatically freeze state pensions when retirees move to certain countries), investment income and local taxes. In most countries it's necessary for retirees to have a minimum income to qualify for a residence permit, and in some countries they must also own a property (although a long-term lease on a property may be sufficient).

You should also ask yourself the following questions: Can you really afford to retire abroad? What of the future? Is your income secure and protected against inflation? There are both advantages and disadvantages to retiring abroad (see below).

Thailand: Thailand is beginning to see the potential of attracting wealthy retirees and has the warm climate and beautiful beaches to enable it to do so. As a result, the Thai government has considered the question of issuing visas to foreigners wanting to spend time in the country after retirement and the following are the current regulations. **Note, however, that these subject to regular change, so you should check the latest requirements at the Thai Embassy in your home country before making any irrevocable decisions.**

- Applicants must be at least 50.

- Applicants must not have a criminal record, either in their home country or in Thailand.

- Applicants must have at least 18 months remaining on their passports.

- You must present the following documents:
    - Evidence of sufficient funds, i.e. around Bht800,000 (US$20,000) in a bank account or proof of a monthly income of at least Bht60,000 (US$1,500) for at least a year;
    - Three copies of a health certificate issued no more than three months previously;
    - Three copies of a certificate issued by the local police within the previous three months confirming that you have no criminal record in your home country;

- The last three documents must be certified by a public notary.

- Three application forms must be filled in, with three recent passport-size photographs.

Retirement visas – usually called Non-Immigrant O-A Visas – are usually processed within a week (provided that all documentation is in order) and allow stays in Thailand of up to 90 days. Once in the country, you can apply (at Thai Immigration at Bangkok Airport) for a one-year stay. If this is granted, however, you must still report to the local Thai Immigration or local police every 90 days while you're in Thailand. People wanting to stay in Thailand for longer than a year must provide further evidence of having sufficient funds to Thai Immigration.

Advantages

The advantages of retiring to the Far East may include a more favourable climate, lower taxation, a lower cost of living, a higher standard of living, the reinvigorating effect of moving to a different environment and culture, and the availability of a wide range of leisure and sports activities at an affordable cost. For most people, one of the principal benefits is the improved health that results from living in a warmer climate (see page 242) and a more relaxing environment (provided you don't expect things to be done the same way as at 'home'). Those who suffer from arthritis, colds, influenza and other illnesses exacerbated by cold and damp may live longer and enjoy a better quality of life in a warm climate, while those who suffer from stress are often recommended to live in a country with a more relaxing way of life. However, if you're planning to retire to the Far East for health reasons, you should ask your doctor for his advice regarding suitable countries and locations (see also **Chapter 4**). Don't make the mistake of assuming that the entire region enjoys warm, sunny weather throughout the year (see **Climate** on page 242).

Disadvantages

The main disadvantages of retiring abroad may include separation from family and loved ones, language problems, boredom (what are you going to do all day?), dangers of disease and infection and poor medical facilities in some countries, the health risks of too much sun, humidity and alcohol, overeating and too little exercise, poor social services, e.g. little or no state support for the elderly and infirm, financial problems (e.g. high cost of living, high taxation, exchange rate fluctuations and poor investments), possible loss of pension indexation, homesickness (e.g. sadness or depression from missing friends and family) and culture shock (see page 414).

Before planning to live in the Far East you should also consider how you'd cope if your mobility was restricted (many countries provide inadequate facilities and support for those with disabilities). The time and cost involved in travelling back to your home country for visits (or for family and friends coming to visit you in the Far East) should also be taken into consideration. Older passengers tend to find long flights much more arduous than younger travellers.

WOMEN

While women are generally accustomed to being treated as the equals of men in most western countries in most areas of daily life and discrimination against women is gradually being eradicated, this is far from the case in many Asian countries, where women certainly aren't treated as equals and their daily lives can be severely restricted by western standards. Contrary to popular western belief, the constraints on women's lives aren't always imposed by religion – for example, Islam places great importance on the role of women, although some brands of Islam ignore this – but sometimes by social customs and tradition.

While some countries tolerate western attitudes and allow women to dress and behave as they would in their own countries, others impose strict restrictions on women, particularly Brunei and parts of Indonesia and Malaysia. Women should be aware of a country's attitude towards them and bear this in mind before making the decision to live abroad. You should also note that restrictions, which also apply to female children, are often legally enforceable and infringements may incur fines or even (in extreme cases) deportation. Restrictions may apply to various aspects of life, including those described below. For further details of restrictions in particular countries, see **Social Customs & Rules** on page 285.

If you think any of these restrictions would be unacceptable to you or that your lifestyle and well-being would be significantly eroded by them, you should seriously consider not moving to the country in question. However, before making a final decision it's recommended to talk to other women with similar experiences and, if possible, to women who have lived in the country you're thinking of moving to.

Dress

In most Muslim countries and regions, women are expected to dress modestly with their arms and legs covered, and in some countries or regions they must wear a long-sleeved, full-length dress (*kandoura*). Hair must usually covered by a scarf and in some countries and regions women must also cover their faces (many wear the traditional *chador*). At work, the dress code may be relaxed. In expatriate compounds, women can dress as they would in their home countries, but outside a compound dress restrictions apply.

Work

In many Muslim and Asian countries men retain the traditional view that the woman's place is in the home, although in some countries (e.g. Japan) women are encouraged to work. However, even where women work, their employment may be limited to professions traditionally regarded as 'appropriate', such as health care, teaching and banking. In some Muslim countries and regions, women aren't permitted to work alongside men.

Going Out

In some Muslim countries and regions it's unacceptable for women to go out unescorted and they must be accompanied by their spouse or a close male relative. Women travelling alone may be refused entry to public transport, or taxis may refuse to take lone female passengers. Women may even be subjected to verbal abuse by men. Single women may generally be subject to unsolicited attention from local men, many of whom regard all western women as 'available'. In certain countries, e.g. Japan, women are often excluded from nightclubs.

CHILDREN

Parents should never underestimate the effects a move to the region will have on children, particularly adolescents, and, if you feel that relocation is likely to affect a child negatively (in the long term) rather than positively, it's probably wise not to make the move. Bear in mind that children rarely have a choice about a move abroad, yet their needs must be considered as one of your priorities when making the decision. If a child has learning difficulties or disabilities, relocation shouldn't usually be considered unless you're certain that you will find experts in the Far East to help you cope with the situation. A possible alternative for teenagers may be for them to attend a boarding school in your home country or to stay with their grandparents and attend a local school while you're abroad. See also **Children** on page 410.

GETTING THERE

An important consideration when deciding whether to live in the Far East is communications (air and sea links) with your home country. How long will it take to get there, taking into account journeys to and from airports or ports? What will transport cost? How frequent are flights or boats at the time(s) of year when you plan to travel? Is it feasible to travel home for short periods, given the cost and travelling time involved? Note that scheduled airline fares are prohibitively expensive to some countries, while charter flight companies can be unreliable and over-booking is often a problem in the high season. If you need to take a flight at short notice, it can be prohibitively expensive, as you may be unable to get an inexpensive charter or APEX flight. Also bear in mind that in some countries, ferry services are severely curtailed outside the main holiday season and services are often cancelled altogether due to bad weather.

Note also that local airlines in some countries have a poor safety record and ferry accidents involving large losses of life are common in the waters of some Far Eastern countries.

If you intend to make frequent trips back home, it obviously makes sense to choose a country that involves a relatively short journey or isn't too expensive. If a long journey is involved, you should bear in mind that it takes most people at least a day or two to fully recover (some people take a week), particularly when a long flight (and possibly jet-lag) is involved.

On the other hand, regular travellers, e.g. with ferry companies and airlines, can take advantage of travel clubs, season tickets, discount schemes for shareholders and special deals for frequent fliers. Shop around for the lowest fares available. For some destinations it may be cheaper to fly via another country than to take a direct scheduled flight, assuming that this is possible. British readers should compare the fares listed in newspapers such as *The*

Sunday Times, Observer and London's *Time Out* entertainment magazine. In the US the best newspapers include the Sunday editions of the *New York Times*, the *Los Angeles Times* and the *Chicago Tribune*.

Useful publications for frequent fliers include the Official Airline Guides (OAG) *Worldwide Pocket Flight Guide*, *The Complete Sky Traveler* by David Beaty (Methuen), and *The Round the World Air Guide* by Katie Wood and George McDonald (Fontana). Regular air travellers may be interested in subscribing to *Frequent Flyer* magazine published by Official Airline Guides, PO Box 58543, Boulder, CO 80322-8543, US (☎ 1-800-323-3537).

Allow plenty of time to get to and from airports, ports and railway stations, particularly when travelling during peak hours, when traffic congestion can be horrendous. In many Far Eastern cities, it's horrendous most of the time!

KEEPING IN TOUCH

The availability, quality and cost of local services such as post, telephone (including mobile phones and the internet/email) and fax may be an important consideration when living and working in the Far East, particularly if you wish to keep in regular touch with family and friends or need to liase closely with business colleagues in other countries. The range of services and the reliability and speed of post deliveries varies considerably according to the country (see **Chapter 9**). In some countries airmail letters can take weeks to be delivered, even to neighbouring countries, and countless thousands of items of post go astray each year.

Telephone

Most countries in the region provide a good or excellent telephone service and a phone can usually be installed in days. The cost of international telephone calls varies considerably according to the country and can be very expensive. However, there are a number of ways to reduce the cost, including obtaining an international calling card, e.g. from an American telephone company, or using a callback or resale company (see below). Note that, if you will be absent from a home in the region for long periods, you should pay your telephone bill (and all other regular bills) by direct debit from a local bank or post office account. If you fail to pay a bill on time your service could be stopped and it can take weeks to have it restarted. For details of telecommunications services in each territory see the **Communications** sections in the Country Profiles chapter (**Chapter 9**).

Home Country Direct

Many countries subscribe to a Home Country Direct service that allows you to dial a number giving you direct and free access to an operator in the country you're calling. The operator will connect you to the number required and will also accept credit card and reverse charge calls. However, you should be wary of making international reverse charge calls to some countries using this scheme, as you will pay at least double the cost of using a local payphone. For a list of countries served by the Home Country Direct service, consult your telephone directory or call the local operator.

International Calling Cards

You can obtain an international calling card from telephone companies in most countries, which allows you to make calls (at local rates) from as many as 120 countries and charge them to your telephone bill in your home country. American long-distance telephone companies (e.g. AT&T, MCI and Sprint) compete vigorously for overseas customers and offer calling cards allowing customers to bill international calls to a credit card. The benefits of international calling cards are that they're fee-free, and calls can be made to/from most countries, usually from any telephone (including hotel telephones), and via an English-speaking operator in America (foreign-language operators are also available). Some companies offer conference call facilities that allow you to talk to a number of people in different countries simultaneously. Other features may include a 'world office' facility allowing you to retrieve voice and fax messages at any time, from anywhere in the world. Note that if you do a lot of travelling, it's wise to carry a number of calling cards, as the cheapest card often depends on the country you're calling from and to.

Callback Or Resale Companies

Callback and resale telephone companies buy international line time at a cheap rate from major telephone companies, thus enabling them to offer inexpensive international calls. Callback companies are so-called because you used to have to call a number, usually in the UK or the US, then hang up and be called back by the company, which then provided you with a line as if you were calling from the UK or the US. In this way you could bypass expensive local telephone companies. Nowadays this system has been replaced in most countries by a simple code that must be dialled before making a call, which connects you to the resale company's services. Using these companies may entail dialling a lot of numbers, although the 'effort' and time can be reduced if you have a phone with a memory facility (highly recommended). Calls must usually be paid for with a credit card, possibly in advance, or by direct debit each month from a bank account or credit card.

Mobile Phones

Many Far East countries provide a mobile phone service in the major population centres or countrywide in some countries. Note, however, that in some countries mobile phones are expensive to buy and operate and have high connection fees, standing charges and call rates. With so many products and services on the market, it's important (albeit confusing and sometimes frustrating) to shop around. International tariffs can vary by hundreds of per cent according to your network provider and your contract.

Digital mobile phones that subscribe to the Global System for Mobile (GSM) communications system can be used to make and receive calls in over 160 countries (called international roaming). For information about individual countries, see the internet (🖥 www.gsmworld.com/gsminfo/gsminfo.htm) or contact the GSM Association, 6-8 Old Bond Street, London, UK (☎ 020-7518 0530). Before using a GSM phone abroad you must contact your service provider to make sure that your tariff allows this facility. You must also ensure that your phone will operate in the country you're planning to visit.

When you take a GSM phone abroad, all calls made to your phone will go via the country where it is registered and you must pay for the call from that country to the country where you're located. For example, if your GSM phone is registered in the UK, a caller in the UK pays the standard call charge for calls to mobile phones and you pay for the call from the UK to where you're abroad. This is because callers have no way of knowing that you've taken your phone abroad. You can, however, divert all incoming calls to voicemail when abroad. Calls made from abroad are routed automatically via a local GSM service provider.

Internet 'Telephone' Services

If you have correspondents or friends who are connected to the internet, you can make international 'calls' for the price of a local telephone call (which is free in some countries) to an internet provider. Once on the internet there are no other charges, no matter how much distance is covered or time is spent on-line. Internet users can buy inexpensive software that effectively turns their personal computer into a voice-based telephone (both parties must have compatible computer software). You also need a sound card, speakers, a microphone and a modem, and access to a local internet service provider. While the quality of communication isn't as good as using a telephone and you need to arrange call times in advance, making international calls costs virtually nothing. The internet can of course also be used to send emails, which is the next best thing to a telephone conversation.

Fax & Telex

Fax machines are available in all countries, although the cost varies considerably. It may be possible to take a fax machine to the Far East, but you must check that it's compatible or that it can be modified at a reasonable cost. Public fax services are provided by main post offices in many countries, although they may only send faxes, not receive them. Telexes can also be sent via post offices, and telexes and faxes can be sent and received via major hotels, business offices (providing 'business services') and newsagents in many countries.

Other Services

In major towns and tourist areas in most Far Eastern countries there are offices (such as Mail Boxes Etc.) offering a range of communications services, which may include telephone, fax (transmission and receipt), postbox service, post-hold, post forwarding, call-in service and 24-hour access, stamps, envelopes, postcards, packing supplies, air shipping/receiving, postal metering, money orders and transfers, telegrams, voicemail, email, internet, telex, copy service, telephone message service and various other business services. For details of postal services in each territory see the **Communications** sections in the Country Profiles chapter (**Chapter 9**).

2.

FINDING A JOB
& WORKING

Before making any plans to work in the Far East, you must ensure that it will be possible and under what conditions. If you don't qualify to live and work in a country by birthright or as a national of a country that's a member of a treaty, obtaining a work permit may be impossible. Even when you don't require a permit, you shouldn't plan on obtaining employment in a particular country unless you have a firm job offer, special qualifications or experience for which there's a strong local demand. If you want a good job, you must usually be well qualified and sometimes need to speak the local language fluently. If you plan to arrive without a job (assuming it's permitted), you should have a detailed plan for finding employment and try to make some contacts before you arrive. Being attracted to a country by its weather, cuisine and lifestyle (etc.) is understandable but doesn't rate highly as an employment qualification! It's extremely difficult to find work in many countries, particularly in rural and resort areas, and can even be difficult in cities and large towns.

Before planning to work in the region, you should dispassionately examine your motives and credentials. What kind of work can you realistically expect to do? What are your qualifications and experience? Are they recognised in the Far East? How good is your local language ability? Unless you're fluent, you sometimes won't be competing on equal terms with the locals (you won't anyway, but that's a different matter!). Some employers aren't interested in hiring anyone without, at the very least, an adequate working knowledge of the local language. Are there any jobs in your profession or trade in the country and region where you plan to live? Could you work in a self-employed capacity or start your own business? How will you survive while looking for work? The answers to these and many other questions can be quite disheartening, but it's better to ask them before moving to the region rather than afterwards.

Further Information: There are numerous books written for those seeking a job abroad, including the *Directory of Jobs and Careers Abroad* and the *Directory of Work and Study in Developing Countries* (both published by Vacation Work), *Getting a Job Abroad* by Roger Jones (How To Books), *The Equitable Guide to Working Abroad* by William Essex (Bloomsbury), the *Guide to Working Abroad* by Godfrey Golzen and Helen Kogan (Kogan Page), *International Jobs* by Eric Kocher and Nina Segal (Perseus) and *What Color is Your Parachute?* by Richard Nelson Bolles (Ten Speed Press). There are also numerous magazines and newspapers, many of which are dedicated to particular professions, industries or trades (see **Appendix B**).

UNEMPLOYMENT

The local unemployment rate is generally an excellent guide to employment prospects, although a low rate is no guarantee that you will be able to find work with a reasonable salary, particularly if you have few qualifications and little experience. And bear in mind that a low average unemployment rate may mask particularly high rates in some regions of a country. When deciding where to live, you should check the economic forecasts for the region and whether unemployment is rising or falling. Areas that depend on one or two industries only, such as motor manufacturing, armaments and textiles, may not be the best choice from a long-term point of view. In today's ever-changing world, nobody is immune from unemployment and it's important for workers to have skills that are in demand and which are constantly updated with further education and training. The following list shows 2002 unemployment rates in the 11 territories covered by this book and seven western economies for comparison (US government figures):

Far East	
Country/Territory	Unemployment (%)
Brunei	10
China	10*
Hong Kong	7.5
Indonesia	10.6
Japan	5.4
Korea	3.1
Malaysia	3.8
Philippines	10.2
Singapore	4.6
Taiwan	5.2
Thailand	2.9

* This figure is for urban areas; unemployment is higher in rural areas.

Rest Of The World	
Country/Territory	Unemployment (%)
Australia	6.3
Canada	7.6
France	9.1
Germany	9.8
New Zealand	5.3
UK	5.2
US	5.8

QUALIFICATIONS

The ability to speak the local language is less important in most Far Eastern countries – where the language of commerce is often English – than it is for foreigners seeking work in some other countries. You should establish whether your trade or professional qualifications and experience are recognised in a particular country. If you aren't experienced, employers usually expect studies to be in a relevant discipline and to have included work experience (i.e. on-the-job training). Professional or trade qualifications are required for many types of job, although these are much more stringent in some countries than in others.

Most qualifications recognised by professional and trade bodies in Australasia, North America and EU countries are accepted throughout the Far East. However, recognition varies from country to country, and in some cases foreign qualifications aren't recognised by local employers or professional and trade associations. All academic qualifications should also be recognised, although they may be given less prominence than equivalent local qualifications, depending on the country and the educational establishment where they were gained. In general, qualifications earned in developing countries aren't as acceptable abroad as those from western institutions. Some professionals and tradesmen are required to undergo special training or work under supervision for a period (possibly a number of years) before they're permitted to work unsupervised or work as self-employed.

EMPLOYMENT AGENCIES

Most governments operate an official employment agency whose job is to provide assistance for the unemployed to find work, particularly the long-term unemployed, the disabled and the disadvantaged. It may also be responsible for paying benefit to the unemployed. Government employment services may place people directly in jobs and offer guidance and counselling so that you can find the best way to return to employment, e.g. through education or training. Most employment services have websites. Some countries provide 'job centres' where local companies advertise for employees.

In addition to government employment services, many countries also have private employment agencies, which generally fall into two main categories: recruitment consultants (or head-hunters) for executives and senior personnel, and staff employment agencies that may recruit full-time, part-time and temporary staff. These agencies are usually plentiful in major cities and towns. Most large companies are happy to engage consultants to recruit staff, particularly executives (head-hunters account for around two-thirds of all top level executive appointments in some countries), managers, professional employees and temporary office staff (temps).

Most agencies specialise in particular fields or positions, e.g. computer personnel, accounting, executives and managers, sales staff, secretarial and office staff, catering, engineering and technical, nursing, industrial recruitment and construction, while others deal with a range of industries and professions. Some agencies deal exclusively with temporary jobs such as office staff, baby-sitters, home carers, nannies and mothers' helps, housekeepers, cooks, gardeners, chauffeurs, hairdressers, security guards, cleaners, labourers and industrial workers. Nursing agencies are also fairly common (covering the whole range of nursing services, including physiotherapy, occupational and speech therapy, and dentistry), as are nanny and care agencies. Many employment agencies, both government and private, have websites (see page 66) where vacancies are advertised.

SEASONAL JOBS

Seasonal jobs are available throughout the year in some Far Eastern countries, the vast majority in the tourist industry. Many jobs last for the duration of the summer or winter tourist seasons, May to September and December to April respectively in all 11 territories, the peak holiday season being July and August (as well as late January to mid-February in China), although some are simply casual or temporary jobs for a number of weeks. Seasonal jobs include most trades in hotels and restaurants, couriers and travel company representatives, a variety of jobs in ski resorts (see **Ski Resorts** below), sports instructors, bar and club work, fruit picking and other agricultural jobs, and various jobs in the construction industry.

It's essential to check whether you will be eligible to work in your chosen country before making plans, and you may also need to obtain a visa (see pages 19). Check with a local embassy or consulate in your home country well in advance of your visit. Students studying abroad can usually obtain a temporary work permit for part-time work during the summer holiday period and school terms. The main seasonal jobs available in the Far East include those described below.

If you're a sports or ski instructor, tour guide, holiday representative or are involved in any job that gives you responsibility for groups of people or children, you should be extremely wary of accepting an illegal job without a contract, as you won't be insured for injuries to yourself, the public or accidents while travelling. **Bear in mind that seasonal workers have few rights and little legal job protection, and can generally be fired without compensation at any time.**

Further Information: There are many books for those seeking holiday jobs, including *Summer Jobs Abroad* by David Woodworth and *Work Your Way Around the World* by Susan Griffith (both published by Vacation Work). See also **Temporary & Casual Jobs** on page 56, **Holiday & Short-Term Jobs** on page 57 and **Working Illegally** on page 75.

Resort Representatives

Resort representatives' or couriers' duties include accompanying tourist groups to and from airports, organising excursions and social events, arranging activity passes and equipment rental, and generally providing a customer support service. A job as a courier is tough and demanding, and requires resilience and resourcefulness to deal with the chaos associated with the package holiday business. The necessary requirements include the ability to answer many questions simultaneously (often in different languages), to remain calm and charming under extreme pressure, and above all, to maintain a sense of humour. Lost passengers, tickets, passports and tempers are everyday occurrences. It's an excellent training ground for managerial and leadership skills, pays well and often offers opportunities to supplement your earnings with tips and commissions.

Couriers are required by many local and foreign tour companies in both winter and summer resorts. Competition for jobs is fierce and local language ability is sometimes required, even for employment with American or British tour operators. Most companies have age requirements, the minimum usually being 21, although many companies prefer employees to be older. In Far Eastern countries with a winter sports industry (see **Seasonal Jobs** on page 55), the majority of courier jobs are available during the winter season with ski-tour companies and school ski-party organisers. A good source of information is ski magazines, which contain regular listings of tour companies showing who goes to which resorts. It's wise to find out the kind of clients you're likely to be dealing with, particularly if you're allergic to children or yuppies (young urban professionals – similar to children but more immature and often drunk). Note that to survive the winter in a ski resort, it helps to be a keen skier or a dedicated learner; otherwise, you risk being bored to death by skiing stories!

Holiday Camps & Theme Parks

For those who like working with children, holiday camps offer a number of summer job opportunities, ranging from camp counsellors and sports instructors to administrative and catering posts. Note that summer school holidays vary according to the country. Some of the region's countries have a number of theme parks that rely to a large extent on seasonal staff. The larger parks may also provide on-site accommodation for employees (the cost is deducted from your wages). Positions range from maintenance and catering to performing in the shows and pageants that form part of the entertainment. Check local newspapers starting in January or February for job advertisements for the coming summer season. April is a popular month for parks to hold auditions for performing roles. Most theme parks have websites containing employment information.

Hotels & Catering

Hotels and restaurants are the largest employers of seasonal workers, from hotel managers to kitchen hands, and jobs are available year round. Experience, qualifications and fluent local language ability are required for all the best and highest paid positions, although a variety of jobs are available for the untrained and inexperienced. Note that if accommodation with cooking facilities or full board isn't provided with a job, it can be expensive and difficult to find. Ensure that your salary is sufficient to pay for accommodation, food and other living expenses, and allows you to save some money. The best way to find work is to contact hotel chains directly, preferably at least six months before you wish to start work.

Ski Resorts

Skiing is currently a growth industry in the region. Japan is the leader, with several hundred ski and snowboard resorts, the three largest concentrations being in Hokkaido (128 resorts), Nagano (108) and Gifu (41). South Korea has 13 resorts (six in Gangwon-do Province, five in Gyeonggi-do Province and one each in Chungcheongbuk-do Province and Jeollabuk-do Province). Even Taiwan (around half of which is south of the Tropic of Cancer) has several resorts, most in the Hehuan Valley, which enjoys snow depths of over a metre. The island - which has an abundance of mountains but relatively little snow except in the Hehuan area - is also promoting grass-skiing and sledding.

China has seen the region's biggest growth in the sport over the last decade and ski resorts are springing up in many parts of the country, attracting increasing numbers of foreign skiers (as well as domestic ones, usually from the burgeoning middle class) with their low prices. The best resorts (for facilities and snow) are currently in the north-east, e.g. Alshan, Beidahu, Changbaishan, Erlongshan and Yabuli, which are near the cities of Changchun and Ha'erbing. There are also over 110 resorts in north-west China, 60 in Heilongjiang Province, 15 in the area around Beijing and four in Sichuan (around Chungdu).

A seasonal job in a ski resort can be a lot of fun and very satisfying. You will get fit, improve your foreign language ability, make some friends, and may even save some money. Note, however, that although a winter job may be a working holiday to you (with lots of skiing and little work), to your employer it means exactly the opposite! Ski resorts require an army of temporary workers to cater for the annual invasion of winter sports enthusiasts. Besides jobs in the hotel and catering trades already mentioned above, a variety of others are available, including couriers, resort representatives, chalet girls, ski technicians, ski instructors and guides. As a general rule, the better paid the job, the longer the working hours and the less time there is for skiing. Employment in a winter resort usually entitles employees to a discounted ski pass.

Ski instructors and guides should contact tour operators, large luxury hotels, and ski rental and service shops. Start applying for work from May onwards. Interviews usually take place from early September through to early November and successful candidates are on the job by mid-December. If you miss the May deadline, you could still apply, as many applicants who have been offered jobs drop out at the last minute.

Sports Instructors

Sports instructors are sought for a variety of sports, including bungee jumping, canoeing, diving, golf, hang-gliding, horse riding, mountaineering, parachuting, rock-climbing, sailing, scuba diving, swimming, tennis and windsurfing. Whatever the sport, it's invariably played and taught somewhere in many Far Eastern countries. If you're a qualified winter sports instructor, you should contact winter resorts (see above).

TEMPORARY & CASUAL JOBS

Temporary and casual jobs are usually for a fixed period only, e.g. from a few hours to a few months, or work may be intermittent. In some countries, some two-thirds of companies use temporary staff at some time, mostly in the summer when permanent staff are on holiday, and usually in clerical positions. Employers usually require your national insurance number and sometimes a tax code, so it isn't usually easy for non-residents to obtain legal employment. For information regarding your legal obligations, contact the local tax or social security office. Many employers illegally pay temporary staff in cash without making any deductions for tax or national insurance (see **Working Illegally** on page 75).

Casual workers are often employed on a daily, first come, first served basis. The work often entails heavy labouring and is therefore intended mostly for men, although there's no bar against strong women. Pay for casual work is usually low and is almost always in cash. Those looking for casual, unskilled work in many countries must compete with locals and certain immigrant groups (possibly illegal), who are usually prepared to work for less money than anyone else, although nobody should be paid less than the minimum salary (if applicable). Temporary and casual work includes the following:

- Office work, which is usually well paid if you're qualified and the easiest work to find owing to the large number of secretarial and office staff agencies in most countries;

- Work in the building trade, which can be found through industrial employment agencies and by applying directly to builders and building sites;

- Jobs at exhibitions and shows, including setting up stands, catering (waitresses and bar staff), and loading and unloading jobs;

- Jobs in bars, restaurants, clubs and discotheques at busy times of the year;

- Jobs in shops during holiday and sales periods;

- Gardening jobs, both in private gardens and in public parks for local councils. Local landscape gardeners and garden centres are also often on the lookout for extra staff, particularly in spring and summer;

- Market research, which entails asking people personal questions, either in the street or house to house (excellent language skills are obviously required);
- Modelling at art colleges; both sexes are usually required and not just the body beautiful;
- Security work in offices, factories, warehouses and shopping centres, offering long hours for low pay;
- Nursing and auxiliary nursing staff in hospitals, clinics and nursing homes (who are usually employed through nursing agencies to replace permanent staff at short notice);
- Newspaper and magazine distribution;
- Courier work (own transport usually required, e.g. motorcycle, car or van);
- Labouring jobs in markets;
- Driving jobs, including coach and truck drivers, taxi drivers, and ferrying cars for manufacturers and car hire companies;
- Other jobs as cleaners, baby-sitters and labourers, which are available from a number of agencies specialising in temporary work.

HOLIDAY & SHORT-TERM JOBS

Holiday and short-term jobs are provided by numerous organisations in many countries, ranging from a few weeks up to six months. Before planning to travel to the Far East for a working holiday or short-term job, it's essential that you check that you're eligible and will be permitted to enter the country under the immigration and employment regulations. You may be required to obtain a visa or work permit (see page 19) and should check the documentation required with a local embassy or consulate in your home country well in advance of your planned visit. If you plan to study full-time in a Far Eastern country and to work during your holidays, you don't usually require a work permit, but you may need to obtain official permission and evidence from your school or university that the employment won't interfere with your studies.

Vacation Work, 9 Park End Street, Oxford OX1 1HJ, UK (☎ 01865-241978, 🖥 www.vacationwork.co.uk) publishes *Work Your Way Around the World*, which incorporates hundreds of first-hand accounts and provides authoritative advice on how to find work around the world in advance or on the spot. It covers working your passage, childcare jobs and voluntary projects worldwide, and explains how to become a barmaid, pineapple picker, film extra, jackaroo, ranch-hand, prawn fisherman, camp counsellor and many other jobs. Vacation Work also publishes *Taking a Gap Year* and books targeted at those working in particular fields and professions, including au pairs, accountants, animal carers, cooks, cruise ship staff, environmental workers, health professionals, nannies, ski resort staff and other tourism-related jobs. A database of seasonal and summer jobs is available on via internet (📖 www.summerjobs.com).

Many other holiday jobs are available in a range of occupations, including couriers and representatives (e.g. in holiday camps), domestic staff in hotels, farmhands, supervisors and sports instructors, teachers, youth leaders, secretaries, nurses and shop assistants. A wide range of contacts for these and other jobs are listed in the *Working Holidays* book mentioned above.

TRAINEES & WORK EXPERIENCE

Nationals of many countries, particularly developing countries, can work abroad as trainees or gain work experience under specific schemes, which are intended to give greater flexibility to companies 'to assist their international business and trading links whilst maintaining adequate safeguards for local nationals'. Many are designed 'to assist the emerging democracies of Eastern and Central Europe by helping their citizens gain valuable training or work experience abroad'.

Applications for training are often considered even if the training is available in the applicant's home country. Training usually applies to professions or occupations in which the training leads to the acquisition of occupational skills or professional qualifications. Trainees must usually be aged between 18 and 54, and work experience applicants, who must be at the start of their careers, between 18 and 35. The training or work experience must be for a minimum of 30 hours per week and for a fixed period, which is normally limited to a maximum of one year, although in exceptional circumstances it can be extended to two years. Trainees occupy full-time positions with a similar salary and conditions of employment as local trainees.

Work experience differs from training in that it doesn't usually result in a formal qualification, the worker doesn't fill a full-time position, and wages are paid in the form of pocket money or a maintenance allowance and are much less than would be paid to an ordinary employee (unless a statutory minimum wage is applicable). Applications are considered even when applicants have had no previous employment related to the intended work experience, provided they have relevant qualifications and the work experience is closely related to their intended career.

Although training and work experience schemes are intended to develop the applicants' industrial and commercial experience, a secondary objective is to improve their knowledge of the local language, although applicants must have an 'adequate knowledge' before they're accepted. Applicants may not transfer from training or work experience to full employment and aren't usually permitted to take a regular job for at least two years after the completion of their training or work experience. Trainees must sign an undertaking to return to their home countries once they've completed their training or work experience.

For further information about training and work experience schemes abroad, contact the government education or training authorities in your home country, or the local embassy of a country where you'd like to work.

AU PAIRS & NANNIES

Single people aged between 17 and 27 are eligible for a job as an au pair in many countries. Those under 18 need their parents' written approval. Men wanting to work as au pairs in the region might find that families are unwilling to employ them, as traditional attitudes to male/female roles prevail in all 11 territories, although this is changing, particularly in Japan. The au pair system provides you with an excellent opportunity to travel, improve your language ability, and generally broaden your education by living and working in the Far East.

Au pairs are usually contracted to work for a minimum of six months and a maximum of two years. You may work as an au pair on a number of separate occasions, provided the total period doesn't exceed two years. It's also possible to work for two or three months in the summer.

As an au pair, you receive free meals and accommodation and have your own room. You're required to pay your own fare to and from the country where you will be working, although some families contribute towards the return fare for au pairs who stay for six months or longer. You may also be entitled to a week's paid holiday for each six month period of service. Some au pairs holiday with the family or are free to take Christmas or Easter holidays off, but you must obtain permission before making arrangements to go home at these times. Most families prefer people with a driving licence and non-smokers; some won't accept smokers.

Working hours are officially limited to five hours per day (morning or afternoon), six days per week (a total of 30 hours), plus a maximum of three evenings per week baby-sitting. You should have at least one full day and three evenings per week free of household responsibilities and should be free to attend religious services if you wish. Au pairs are paid around US$60 per week (possibly more in major cities), which means you stand little chance of getting rich unless you meet a wealthy foreigner.

Au pair positions must usually be arranged directly with a family or through a private agency – there are no official government agencies. There are dozens of agencies in many countries specialising in finding au pair positions (both locally and abroad), and they're usually licensed and inspected. Some agencies offer a two-week trial period, during which either the au pair or the family can terminate the arrangement without notice. Write to a number of agencies and compare the conditions and pay offered. Agencies must provide a letter of invitation clearly stating your duties, hours, free time and pay (which must be shown to the immigration officer on arrival abroad). Agencies aren't permitted to charge au pairs a fee, which is paid by the family.

Unfortunately, abuses of the au pair system are widespread and you may be expected to work long hours and spend many evenings baby-sitting while the family is out having a good time. If you have any questions or complaints about your duties, you should refer them to the agency which found you the position (if applicable). You're usually required to give notice if you wish to go home before the end of your agreement, although this won't apply if the family has abused the arrangement.

It's possible for responsible young English-speaking women (even without experience or formal training) to obtain employment as a nanny in many countries. Duties are similar to those of an au pair, except that a position as a nanny is a 'proper' job with a reasonable salary – and therefore subject to any relevant work permit regulations (see page 19). For au pair positions, a work permit isn't usually necessary, but a letter of invitation from the family or agency must be produced. This letter doesn't provide entitlement to any other kind of paid work abroad.

A useful book for prospective au pairs and nannies is the *Au Pair and Nanny's Guide to Working Abroad* by Susan Griffith and Sharon Legg (Vacation Work). There are also numerous websites where further information can be found, e.g. 🖥 www. aupairs.co.uk and www.princeent.com/aupair.

VOLUNTARY WORK

The minimum age limit for voluntary work in most countries is between 16 and 18 (there's no upper age limit, provided you're physically fit). Many organisations require good or fluent spoken English and the minimum length of service varies from a month to a year (there's often no maximum length of service). Special qualifications may be required, depending on the position; in recent years, countries have been increasingly seeking qualified professionals in fields such as engineering, health, social services and teaching. Disabled volunteers are welcomed by many organisations. Voluntary work is usually unpaid, although meals and accommodation are usually provided, and some organisations also pay pocket money.

Before planning a trip abroad to do any kind of voluntary work, it's essential to check whether you're eligible and whether you will be permitted to enter the country under the immigration and employment regulations. You may be required to obtain a visa or work permit (see page 19), and you must check what documentation is required with a local embassy or consulate in your home country well in advance of your planned visit. The normal visa regulations usually apply to voluntary workers and your passport must normally be valid for at least a year. For voluntary work or temporary employment in international work or farm camps (see below), a work permit isn't usually necessary, but a letter of invitation from the voluntary organisation or your employer must be produced. This letter doesn't provide entitlement to any other kind of paid work abroad.

Further Information: Information about volunteering in most countries can be obtained from national associations and from a wealth of websites such as Voluntary Services Overseas (🖥 www.vso.org.uk), the Peace Corps (🖥 www.peacecorps.com), the Relief Web (🖥 www.reliefweb.int/vacancies/links.html) and World Service Enquiry (🖥 www.wse.org.uk/home.html). There are also a number of books published for volunteers, including *Green Volunteers* and the *International Directory of Voluntary Work*, a guide to 400 agencies and sources of information on short to long-term voluntary work worldwide, both published by Vacation Work (🖥 www.vacationwork.co.uk).

Work Camps

International work camps provide the opportunity for people from many countries to live and work together on a range of projects, including building, conservation, gardening and community projects. Camps are usually run for periods of two to four weeks between April and October. Normally, workers are required to work for six to seven hours per day, five or six days per week. The work is normally quite physically demanding and accommodation, which is shared, is usually fairly basic. Most work camps consist of 10 to 30 volunteers from several countries and English is generally the common language. Volunteers are usually required to pay a registration fee and pay for their own travel to and from the work camp, and may also be expected to contribute towards the cost of their board and lodging. An application to join a work camp should be made through the appropriate recruiting agency in your home country.

ENGLISH TEACHERS & TRANSLATORS

There's a high demand for English teachers, translators and interpreters throughout the Far East. These jobs are one of the most common types of employment for foreigners and there's a high turnover of teachers in language schools and a constant demand for translators (and sometimes technical authors and copywriters) from local companies.

Further Information: A useful book is *Teaching English Abroad* by Susan Griffith (Vacation Work). Useful websites include the Centre for British Teachers (🖥 www.cfbt.com), the British Council (🖥 www.britishcouncil.org) and 🖥 www.jobs.edufind.com.

Language Schools

There are literally hundreds of English-language schools in the Far East, many of which expect teachers to have a Teacher of English as a Foreign Language (TEFL) certificate or its equivalent. Some schools will employ anyone whose mother tongue is English provided they've had experience in teaching, while others have their own teaching methods and prefer to train their own teachers. Many of the best schools are members of a local association of English language schools, a list of which is usually available from the British Council (🖥 www. britishcouncil.org/cbiet) or local British or American Embassies.

Language schools generally pay less than you can earn giving private lessons, but they provide a contract and pay your taxes and social security contributions. However, you may be able to obtain only a short-term contract or freelance work. You're usually paid by the hour and so should ensure that you have a guaranteed number of hours per week, but not usually more than 25.

Private Lessons

Work giving private English lessons is easy to find in some countries, particularly in university cities and towns, as students must usually study English as part of their course work. Many foreigners teach English privately and are paid in cash by students. You can place an advertisement in local newspapers and magazines offering private English lessons, although you may receive some replies from men who think that 'English lessons' implies something other than language lessons! Most people find that, once they have one or two students, word gets around and before long they have as much work as they can handle. The going rate for private lessons varies and can be anywhere between US$7.50 and US$22.50 per hour (it's higher in major cities than in small towns).

Note that many Far Eastern students favour grammar-based teaching and many know a lot about English literature even if they can't speak a word of the language correctly! If you don't know your participles from your prepositions nor your Austen from your Hardy, you should stick to conversation classes or teaching children!

Translating & Interpreting

Many expatriates combine teaching with translating and/or interpreting. Professional translators and interpreters are in huge demand and are usually employed by agencies. For anyone speaking a foreign language fluently and wanting to work in a country where it's the national language, it may be worthwhile training as a translator or interpreter. Professional translators are paid by the page (or line) and the average rate is around US$15 per page, although this varies considerably according to the kind of translation. Translating is a slow and tiresome business, you must usually work to strict deadlines, the subject matter can be highly technical (requiring a specialised vocabulary) and translations must be precise. If you don't translate medical notes, legal papers or business documents accurately, any mistakes can have serious consequences and you should be insured accordingly! Interpreters are employed mainly for exhibitions, congresses and seminars, where you're paid a daily or an hourly rate.

University Teaching

English is taught in most universities throughout the region and positions for assistants in English-language departments are usually open to foreigners with university degrees. Applications should be made directly to the Rector of the university. There are also institutes of modern languages, foreign universities and special schools in many countries offering a range of job opportunities for qualified teachers.

JOB HUNTING

When looking for a job in the Far East, it's best not to put all your eggs in one basket, as the more job applications you make, the better your chances of finding the right job. Contact as many prospective employers as possible, by writing to them, telephoning them or calling on them, depending on the type of vacancy. Whatever job you're looking for, it's important to market yourself correctly and appropriately, which depends on the type of job you're after. For example, the recruitment of executives and senior managers is handled almost exclusively by consultants, who advertise in local newspapers (and also abroad) and interview all applicants before presenting clients with a shortlist. At the other end of the scale, manual jobs requiring no previous experience may be advertised at government employment centres, in local newspapers and in shop windows, and the first suitable, able-bodied applicant may be offered the job on the spot.

When writing for a job, address your letter to the personnel director or manager and include your curriculum vitae (CV) and copies of all references and qualifications. Note, however, that writing for jobs from abroad is a hit and miss affair. It can, however, be more successful than responding to advertisements, as you aren't usually competing with other applicants. Some companies recruit a large percentage of employees through unsolicited CVs. If you're applying from abroad and can attend interviews in the country, inform prospective employers when you will be available and arrange as many as you can fit into the allotted time. Note that, in order to work in some countries, you need a 'sponsorship' letter (see page 19).

Your method of job hunting will depend on your circumstances, qualifications and experience, and the sort of job you're looking for, and may include the following:

- Visiting local government employment offices abroad (see page 52). This is mainly for non-professional skilled and unskilled jobs, particularly in industry, retailing and catering.

- Visiting information centres for jobseekers, which exist in some countries to provide information about jobs, job hunting, education and training. Main libraries also provide a range of resources for jobseekers, although they may not specifically provide advice and assistance to the unemployed.

- Checking the internet (see page 66) and other bulletin boards, such as those provided by TV teletext services;

- Applying to international and national recruitment agencies (see page 52) and executive search consultants acting for companies in the country where you wish to work. These companies mainly recruit executives and key managerial and technical staff, and many have offices worldwide. Note that some agencies may find positions only for local nationals or foreigners with a residence permit (or the right to work in the particular country).

- Obtaining copies of daily newspapers, most of which have appointments sections on certain days. The quality daily and Sunday newspapers all contain appointments sections for executive and professional employees, and also contain job advertisements dedicated to particular industries or professions, e.g. the computer industry, teaching and the media. Local and national newspapers may be available in the reading rooms of local libraries. Jobs are also advertised in industry and trade newspapers and magazines. Major foreign newspapers are available abroad from international news agencies, trade and commercial centres, expatriate organisations and social clubs, although they don't always contain the appointments sections. Note that most major newspapers and magazines have websites where you can usually access appointments sections free of charge.

- Consulting professional and trade journals. Most professions and trade associations publish journals containing job offers (see *Benn's Media Directory Europe*) and jobs are also advertised in various English-language publications, including the *International Herald Tribune* and *Wall Street Journal Europe* and local publications (see **Appendix B**). You can also place an advertisement in the appointments section of a local newspaper in the area where you'd like to work.

- Visiting Chambers of Commerce in your home country, which usually maintain lists of their member companies doing business (or with subsidiaries) in the Far East and sometimes allow you to file your CV with them (for a fee). An advertisement may also be posted on their website and included in their monthly newsletter. Most countries also maintain Chambers of Commerce in the region, which are a good source of information.

- Applying directly to American, British and other multinational companies with offices or subsidiaries in the Far East and making written applications directly to companies. You can obtain a list of companies working in a particular field from trade directories, such as *Kelly's* and *Kompass*, copies of which are available at main libraries and Chambers of Commerce abroad.

- Putting an advertisement in the appointments section of a national newspaper or a local newspaper in an area where you'd like to work. If you're a member of a recognised profession or trade, you could place an advertisement in a newspaper or magazine dedicated to your profession or industry. It's best to place an advert in the middle of the week and avoid the summer and other holiday periods.

- Networking, which involves getting together with like-minded people to discuss business and make business and professional contacts. It can be particularly successful for executives, managers and professionals when job hunting, especially in countries where people use personal contacts for everything from looking for a job to finding accommodation. In fact, a personal recommendation is often the best way to find employment in the region (nepotism and favouritism are rife in many countries). It's difficult for most newcomers to make contacts among the local community and many turn to the expatriate community, particularly in major cities. You can also contact or join local expatriate social clubs, churches, societies and professional organisations.

- Asking relatives, friends or acquaintances working abroad whether they know of an employer looking for someone with your experience and qualifications;

- Checking notice and bulletin boards at large companies, shopping centres, embassies, clubs, sports centres and newsagents;

- Personal applications (see below).

Personal Applications

Your best chance of obtaining certain jobs in the Far East is to apply in person, when success is often simply a matter of being in the right place at the right time. Many companies don't advertise but rely on attracting workers by word of mouth and their own vacancy boards. Shops often put vacancy notices in their windows and newsagents may also display job advertisements from employers on a notice board, although these are generally only for temporary or part-time help.

It's recommended to leave your name and address with a prospective employer, and, if possible, a telephone number where you can be contacted, particularly if a job may become vacant at a moment's notice. You can give lady luck a helping hand with your persistence and enterprise by advertising the fact that you're looking for a job, not only with friends, relatives and acquaintances, but with anyone you come into contact with who may be able to help.

When leaving a job in the region, it's wise to ask for a written reference (which isn't usually provided automatically), particularly if you intend to look for further work locally or you think your work experience will help you obtain work in another country.

The Internet

The internet provides access to hundreds of sites for job-seekers, advertising millions of job vacancies, including corporate websites, recruitment companies and newspaper job advertisements. These can be found using a search engine such as Google. Millions of people use the internet to find a new job and many companies do the majority of their recruitment via their own websites, where they don't have to pay for advertising. The rapid development of the internet has also led to a big increase in the number of online recruitment agencies and job search sites. Some sites charge a subscription fee to access their vacancy listings, but most permit jobseekers to view and respond to advertisements free of charge.

It's possible to post your CV online (also usually free) but it's wise to consider the security implications of this. By posting your home address or phone number on the internet, you could be opening yourself up to nuisance phone calls or even worse. Some websites allow you to exclude certain companies, such as your present and previous employers. A selection of internet websites that list vacancies in a number of countries are listed below:

- Asia Net (⌨ www.asia-net.com);
- Big Blue (⌨ www.bigbluedog.com);
- Engineering Production Planning (⌨ www.epp.co.uk);
- Job World (⌨ www.jobworld.com);
- Jobs4u (⌨ www.jobs4u.com);
- Michael Page International (⌨ www.michaelpage.com);
- Monster Board (⌨ www.monster.com);
- New Monday (⌨ www.newmonday.com);
- Online Recruitment (⌨ www.onrec.com);
- Overseas Jobs (⌨ www.overseasjobs.com);
- People Bank (⌨ www.peoplebank.com);
- Planet Recruitment (⌨ www.planetrecruit.com);
- Reed (⌨ www.reed.co.uk);
- Riley Guide (⌨ www.dbm.com/jobguide);
- Robert Walters (⌨ www.robertwalters.com);
- Stepstone (⌨ www.stepstone.com);
- TAPS (⌨ www.taps.com);
- Top Jobs (⌨ www.topjobs.net);
- Total Jobs (⌨ www.totaljobs.com);
- University of London Careers Service (⌨ www.careers.lon.ac.uk/links).

It's worth noting that foreign language sites may not include an English-language version. However, if your foreign language skills are rudimentary, you can obtain a rough translation using the (free) Babel Fish translator provided by the search engine company Alta Vista (🖥 http://babel fish.altavista.digital.com – enter the address of the website that you wish to visit in the Babel Fish dialogue box that appears). Another useful site is 🖥 www.universe.com.

Curricula Vitae & Interviews

A curriculum vitae (CV) or résumé is of vital importance in many of the region's countries when looking for a job, particularly when jobs are thin on the ground and applicants are a dime a dozen. Never forget that the purpose of your CV is to obtain an interview, not a job, and it must be written with that in mind. This means that it must be tailored to each job application, paying particular attention to any useful skills you may possess (adaptability, tolerance), language ability (spoken and/or written), international experience (work, travel), etc.. If you aren't up to writing a good CV, you can employ a professional CV writer who will turn your humdrum working life into something that Indiana Jones would be proud of.

Covering letters should be tailored to individual employers and professionally translated if your language ability isn't perfect. Note that in some countries, companies request hand-written letters from job applicants and submit them to graphologists (employers may also use astrology, numerology and even wilder methods of selecting staff!). When writing from abroad, enclosing an international reply coupon may help elicit a response. In addition to a good CV, employers may require the names of a number of personal or professional referees (e.g. three), whom they will usually contact. It's also wise to provide written references if you have any.

Job interviews shouldn't be taken lightly, as interviewing and being interviewed for a job is a science, and making a good impression can make the difference between being on the ladder of success or in the unemployment queue. Dress smartly, even if the interview is for a lowly position (if they like the look of you they may offer you a better job!). The secret is in preparation, so do your homework thoroughly on prospective employers and try to anticipate every conceivable question (and then some) and rehearse your answers. Some employers require prospective employees to complete aptitude and other written tests.

Further Information: There's a wealth of books available detailing everything from writing a compelling CV to how to answer (or field) questions during an interview, including *The Perfect Résumé* by Tom Jackson, *The Damn Good Résumé Guide* by Yana Parker, *Sweaty Palms: The Neglected Art of Being Interviewed* by H. Anthony Medley, and *Knock 'em Dead With Great Answers to Tough Interview Questions* by Martin Yate. You may also wish to peruse some of the websites listed in this chapter, many of which contain useful advice and information. One website of particular interest is Labour Mobility (💻 www.labourmobility.com), which contains useful tips for international jobseekers.

SALARIES

It can be difficult to determine the salary you should command in the Far East and getting the right salary for the job is something of a lottery. Salaries can also vary considerably for the same job in different parts of a country. A decade or so ago, working in the region (particularly in Hong Kong, Japan, Thailand and Singapore) was very attractive mainly because of the very high salaries offered, particularly in countries with low personal taxation. Although this is still true to some extent, salaries and expatriate packages are now generally less generous.

The table below compares median gross salaries for six grades of profession in all the countries considered in this book except Brunei against those in Australia (source Mercer Human Resource Consulting 2003):

Country	Gross Annual Salary (US$)					
	Labourer		Professional		Manager	
	General	Skilled	Junior	Senior	Lower	Upper
Australia	20,165	25,153	31,089	38,666	48,887	63,063
China	-82.3%	-76.5%	-68.3%	-57.7%	-44.3%	-28%
Hong Kong	-9.7%	+4.7%	+22.5%	+42.5%	+63.1%	+83%
Indonesia	-90.1%	-86.5%	-81.3%	-74.4%	-65.4%	-54.2%
Japan	+65.3%	+67.6%	+71.5%	+74.5%	+74.6%	+71.2%
Korea	-12.1%	-10.7%	-8.4%	-6.7%	-6.5%	-8.2%
Malaysia	-78.5%	-73.8%	-67.8%	-60.7%	-52.7%	-44.2%
Philippines	-84.4%	-81%	-76.6%	-71.4%	-65.6%	-59.5%
Singapore	-38.2%	-29.5%	-18.8%	-7%	+4.7%	+15.6%
Taiwan	-33.7%	-27.3%	-19.5%	-11.5%	-4.3%	+1.4%
Thailand	-83.9%	-79%	-72.3%	-63.7%	-53.1%	-40.7%

Those working in major cities are usually the highest paid, mainly thanks to the higher cost of living (particularly accommodation), although if you're employed in a remote area you may receive a 'hardship' allowance.

Salaries are usually negotiable and it's up to you to ensure that you receive the level of salary and benefits commensurate with your qualifications and experience (or as much as you can get!). Salaries in some companies, trades and professions (particularly in the public sector) are decided by national pay agreements between unions and the government, and minimum salaries exist in some countries in many trades and professions, but generally it's every man (or woman) for himself.

There's usually a huge disparity between the salaries of the lowest and the highest paid employees, which is much wider in some countries than in others. If you work illegally (see page 75), you're likely to receive particularly low pay. At the other extreme, executive and managerial salaries have been increasing in leaps and bounds in recent years. The average salary of the chief executives of a multinational company is usually over US$1 million per year, plus performance-related bonuses, share options and perks such as chauffeured company cars. Salaries for some professionals have also soared in recent years, e.g. top commercial lawyers can earn millions of dollars per year! Private sector salaries generally increase at a much faster pace than those in the public sector and there's a growing pay gap in many countries. This has made it difficult for local authorities to recruit and retain staff, with the result that there are thousands of public sector vacancies in some countries.

Many employees, particularly company directors and senior managers, enjoy a 'salary' that's much more than what they receive in their monthly pay packet. Many companies offer a number of benefits for executives and managers, which may even continue after retirement. These may include a free company car (possibly with a chauffeur), free health insurance and health screening, paid holidays, private school fees, cheap or free home loans, rent-free homes, free train season tickets, free company restaurants, non-contributory company pensions, share options, interest-free loans, free tickets for sports events and shows, free subscriptions to clubs, and 'business' conferences in exotic places (see also **Managerial & Executive Positions** on page 81). The benefits of board members in some companies may comprise up 50 per cent or more of their total remuneration (to keep it out of the hands of the taxman). In addition, executives often receive huge golden handshakes should they be sacked or resign, which can run into US$ millions.

SELF-EMPLOYMENT

One route to working in the Far East is to be self-employed, although you may still need a work permit and it can be difficult to become established and make a good living. If you want to be self-employed in a profession or trade in many countries, you must meet certain legal requirements and register with the appropriate organisation, e.g. a professional must become a member of the relevant professional association. In many countries, the self-employed must have an official status and it's illegal to simply hang out a sign and start trading.

Members of some professions and trades must possess recognised qualifications and are sometimes required to take a written examination in the local language. You may also be required to attend a business administration course. You're subject to any professional codes and limitations in force, e.g. a medical practitioner must have his qualifications accepted by the medical association of the state or region where he intends to practise and by any other controlling bodies. You must also show that you're in good standing with the professional authorities in your home country. In certain professions, such as the law, it's unusual to be permitted to practise abroad without local qualifications.

As a self-employed person you don't have the protection of a limited company should your business fail, although there are certain tax advantages. It may be advantageous to operate a limited company. Obtain professional advice before deciding whether to work as a sole trader or form a company abroad, as it may have far-reaching social security, tax and other consequences. All self-employed people must register for income tax, social security and local taxes (such as sales, purchase or value added tax). Don't be in too much of a hurry to register, as from the date of registration you may be required to pay state social security, pension and health insurance payments and are also liable for income and other taxes. On the other hand, you should never be tempted to start work before you're registered, as there are harsh penalties that may include a large fine, confiscation of machinery or tools, and even deportation and a ban from entering a country for a number of years.

New businesses may enjoy a tax exemption for the first few years of trading, including sole traders. There are, however, drawbacks to being self-employed in many countries, which may outweigh any advantages. Social security contributions for the self-employed are usually much higher than for salaried employees and you receive fewer social security benefits. As a self-employed person you aren't entitled to unemployment benefit should your business fail and there may be no state benefit for accidents at work. It's wise to join a local professional or trade association, which can provide valuable information and assistance and may also provide insurance discounts. In some countries it's possible to register a company abroad in order to reduce your taxes.

STARTING A BUSINESS

One way (and the most expensive) to live and work in the Far East is to start your own business, although most foreigners spend less than five years in the region, which is hardly time to establish a business. However, investing in a business can be a profitable venture and in some cases is the only way to obtain a residence permit. The amount a business investor needs to invest varies considerably, e.g. from a few thousand to a million dollars or more (some countries 'sell' residence permits to wealthy investors). Businesses that create jobs are welcomed with open arms, particularly in areas with high unemployment, and a business licence may be conditional on the employment of a number of local citizens.

There are various ways to set up a small business and it's essential to obtain professional advice regarding the best method of establishing and registering a business abroad, which can dramatically affect your tax position. Companies cannot be purchased 'off the shelf' in most countries and it usually takes a number of months to establish a company. Incorporating a company in most countries takes longer and is more expensive and more complicated than in the UK or the US (those bureaucrats again!). There's a wide range of 'limited companies' and business entities in many countries and choosing the right one is important. Always obtain professional legal advice regarding the advantages and disadvantages of different types of limited companies.

Some people find doing business in the Far East exceedingly frustrating and the bureaucracy associated with starting a business is often onerous. The red tape can be almost impenetrable, especially if you don't speak the local language, as you will be inundated with official documents and must be able to understand them. It's only when you come up against the full force of local bureaucracy that you understand what it really means to be a foreigner! It's difficult not to believe that the authorities' sole purpose in life is to obstruct business (in fact it's to protect their own jobs). Patience and tolerance are the watchwords when dealing with foreign bureaucrats (and will also do wonders for your blood pressure!).

As any expert (and many failed entrepreneurs) will tell you, starting a business abroad isn't for amateurs, particularly amateurs who don't speak the local language.

Many small businesses exist on a shoe-string, with owners literally living from hand to mouth, and they certainly aren't what could be considered thriving enterprises. Self-employed people usually work extremely long hours, particularly those running bars or restaurants (days off are almost impossible in the high season), often for little financial reward. In most countries many people choose to be self-employed for the lifestyle and freedom it affords (no clocks or bosses), rather than the money. It's important to keep your plans small and manageable, and work well within your budget, rather than undertake a grandiose scheme.

Research

For many foreigners, starting a business in a foreign country is one of the fastest routes to bankruptcy known to mankind! In fact, many foreigners who start a business abroad would be better off investing in lottery tickets – at least they would then have a chance of receiving a return on their investment. Many would-be entrepreneurs return home with literally only the shirts on their backs, having learnt the facts of life the hard way. If you aren't prepared to thoroughly research the market and obtain expert business and legal advice, you shouldn't even think about starting a business in the Far East.

Generally speaking, you shouldn't consider running a business in a field in which you don't have previous experience. It's often wiser to work for someone else in the same line of business to gain experience than to jump in at the deep end. Always thoroughly investigate an existing or proposed business before investing any money.

If you're planning to buy or start a seasonal business based on tourism, check whether the potential 'real' income will be sufficient to provide you with a living. This applies particularly to bars, restaurants and shops in holiday resorts, especially those run by foreigners relying on the tourist trade, hundreds of which open and close within a short space of time. Don't overestimate the length of the season or the potential income and, most importantly, don't believe everything the person selling a business tells you (although every word may be true). Nobody sells a good business for a bargain price, least of all one making huge profits. In most areas, trade falls off dramatically out of the main holiday season and many businesses must survive for a whole year on the income earned in the busy months. The rest of the year you could be lucky to cover your costs.

Buying An Existing Business

It's much easier to buy an existing business than start a new one from scratch and it's also less of a risk. The paperwork for taking over an existing business is simpler, although still complex. Note, however, that buying a business that's a going concern is difficult, as most people aren't in a habit of buying and selling businesses, which are usually passed down from generation to generation. If you plan to buy a business, obtain an independent valuation (or two) and employ an accountant to audit the books. Never sign anything that you don't understand fully; even if you think you understand it, you should still obtain unbiased professional advice, e.g. from local experts such as banks and accountants. In fact, it's best not to start a business at all until you have the infrastructure in place, including an accountant, lawyer and banking facilities.

A New Business

Most people are far too optimistic about the prospects for a new business abroad and over-estimate income levels (it often takes years to make a profit) and under-estimate costs. Be realistic or even pessimistic when estimating your income and overestimate the costs and underestimate the revenue (then reduce it by 50 per cent!). While hoping for the best, you should plan for the worst and have sufficient funds to last until you're established (under-funding is the major cause of business failures). New projects are rarely, if ever, completed within budget and you need to ensure that you have sufficient working capital and can survive until a business takes off.

Banks are usually extremely wary of lending to new businesses, particularly businesses run by foreigners, and it's difficult for foreigners to obtain finance in the region without local assets. If you wish to borrow money to buy property or for a business venture in the Far East, you should carefully consider where and in what currency to raise finance.

Location

The location of a business is even more important than the location of a home. Depending on the type of business, you may need access to motorway (freeway) and rail links, or to be located in a popular tourist area or near local attractions. Local plans regarding communications, industry and major building developments, e.g. housing complexes and new shopping centres, may also be important. Plans regarding new motorways and rail links are usually available from local town halls.

Employees

Hiring employees shouldn't be taken lightly in the Far East and must be taken into account before starting a business. You must usually enter into a contract under local labour laws and employees often enjoy extensive rights. If you buy an existing business, you may be required to take on existing (possibly inefficient) staff who cannot be dismissed, or be faced with paying high redundancy compensation. It's expensive to hire employees in some countries, where, in addition to salaries, you may need to pay an additional 50 per cent or more in social security contributions, bonus months' salary, paid annual holiday, plus pay for public holidays, sickness, maternity, etc.

Types Of Business

The most common businesses operated by foreigners in the Far East include holiday accommodation, caravan and camping sites, catering, hotels, shops, franchises, estate agencies, translation and interpreting bureaux, language schools, and holiday and sports centres. The majority of businesses established by foreigners are linked to the leisure and catering industries. Some professionals such as doctors and dentists set up practices abroad to serve the expatriate community. There are opportunities in import and export in many countries, e.g. importing foreign products for the local and expatriate market, and exporting locally manufactured goods. You can also find niche markets in providing services for expatriates and others, which are unavailable locally.

Professional Help

Because of the difficulties in complying with (or understanding) local laws and bureaucracy, there are agencies and professionals in some Far Eastern countries that specialise in obtaining documents and making applications for individuals and businesses. They act as a buffer between you and officialdom, and will register your business with the tax authorities, social security, register of companies, Chamber of Commerce and other official bodies. A lawyer or notary can also do this but will be much more expensive. If you're a professional, you may have to take a routine examination before you can be included on the professional register with the Chamber of Commerce.

There are also business consultants and relocation agencies in many areas, which provide invaluable local assistance. International accountants such as

PricewaterhouseCoopers and Ernst & Young have offices in most countries and are an invaluable source of information (in English) on subjects such as forming a company, company law, taxation and social security. Most countries maintain Chambers of Commerce abroad, which are also a good source of information and assistance. It's important to employ an accountant to do your books.

Legal Advice

Before establishing a business or undertaking any business transactions in the Far East, it's important to obtain expert legal advice from an experienced lawyer and accountant (who speaks English or a language you speak fluently) to ensure that you will be operating within the law. There are severe penalties for anyone who ignores the regulations and legal requirements. Expert legal advice is also necessary to take advantage of any favourable tax breaks and to make sense of the myriad rules and regulations. It's imperative to ensure that contracts are clearly defined and water-tight before making an investment, because if you become involved in a legal dispute it can take years to resolve. Businesses must also register for local sales, purchase or value added tax. Most people require a licence to start a business abroad and no commitments should be made until permission has been granted. Among the best sources of local help and information are Chambers of Commerce and town halls.

Avoiding The Crooks

In addition to problems with the authorities, you may also come into contact with assorted crooks and swindlers who will try to relieve you of your money. You should have a healthy suspicion regarding the motives of anyone you do business with abroad (unless it's your mum or spouse), particularly your fellow countrymen. It's also generally best to avoid partnerships, as they rarely work and can be a disaster. In general, you should trust nobody and shouldn't sign anything or pay any money before having a contract checked by a lawyer.

It's a sad fact of life, but foreigners who prey on their fellow countrymen are commonplace in some countries. In most cases you're better off dealing with a long-established local company with roots in the community (and therefore a good reputation to protect) than with your compatriots. Note that if things go wrong, you may be unprotected by the law, the wheels of which grind extremely slowly in some countries – when they haven't fallen off completely!

Grants & Incentives

A range of grants and incentives is available for new businesses in many countries, particularly in rural and deprived areas. Grants may include central government grants, regional development grants, redeployment grants, and grants from provincial authorities and local communities. Grants may include assistance to buy buildings and equipment (or the provision of low-rent business premises), research and technological assistance, subsidies for job creation, low-interest loans and tax incentives. Contact Chambers of Commerce and embassies for information.

Wealth Warning

Whatever people may tell you, working for yourself isn't easy and requires a lot of hard work (self-employed people generally work much longer hours than employees), a sizeable investment and sufficient operating funds (most new businesses fail due to a lack of capital), good organisation (e.g. bookkeeping and planning), excellent customer relations and a measure of luck – although generally the harder you work, the more 'luck' you have. Don't be seduced by the apparent laid-back way of life in some countries – if you want to be a success in business you cannot play at it. **Bear in mind that some two-thirds of all new businesses fail within three to five years and that the self-employed enjoy far fewer social security benefits than employees.**

WORKING ILLEGALLY

Illegal working thrives in some Far Eastern countries and is most common in industries that employ itinerant workers such as catering (bars and restaurants), construction, farming, tourism and textiles, and in jobs such as domestic work and language teaching. In many countries, officials turn a blind eye, as the 'black' economy keeps many small businesses alive and the unemployed in 'pocket money'. In many countries, the long-term unemployed don't receive unemployment benefit and any other state benefits paid are usually too low to live on. Moonlighting by employees with second or third jobs is also widespread in many countries, particularly among those employed in the public sector, who are generally low paid. However, unscrupulous employers also use illegal labour in order to pay low wages (below the minimum wage) for long hours and poor working conditions.

Note that it's strictly illegal to work without a work permit or official permission in most countries. If you're tempted to work illegally, you should be aware of the consequences, as the black economy is a risky business for both employers and employees. If you run a business and use illegal labour or avoid paying taxes, you have no official redress if you run into difficulty. Non-payment of income tax or social security are criminal offences in many countries, and offenders are liable to large fines and imprisonment. Employees who work illegally have no entitlement to social security benefits such as insurance against work injuries, public health care, unemployment pay or a state pension. **A foreigner who works illegally is liable to a heavy fine and deportation, while businesses 'employing' staff illegally can be fined and closed down and the owners imprisoned.**

EMPLOYMENT CONDITIONS

Employment conditions in most countries are largely dependent on an employee's contract of employment and an employer's general terms of employment. Many aspects of employment conditions are set by governments and, although many employers' pay and conditions are more generous than the statutory minimum, employers in many countries offer pay and conditions that are illegal. In many countries there's a huge disparity between the conditions applying to hourly paid workers and salaried employees (i.e. monthly paid), even those employed by the same company. As in most countries, managerial and executive staff generally enjoy a much higher level of benefits than lower paid employees. Employees hired to work abroad by a multinational company may receive a higher salary (including fringe benefits and allowances) than those offered to local employees.

General terms of employment are usually referred to in employment contracts and employees usually receive a copy on starting employment (or in some cases beforehand). Certain subjects, such as health insurance and company pension plans, may be detailed in separate documents. Terms of employment may include rules, restrictions and benefits relating to the validity and applicability of your contract, your place of work, salary and benefits, extra months' salary and bonuses, working hours and flexi-time rules, overtime and compensation, and travel and relocation expenses, social security contributions and benefits, company pension plan, accident insurance, unemployment insurance, salary insurance, health insurance, miscellaneous insurance, use of company cars, notification of sickness or accidents, sick pay and disability benefits, annual and public holidays, compassionate and special leave of absence, allowances and paid expenses, probationary and notice periods, education and training, health and safety, pregnancy and confinement, part-time job restrictions, changing jobs and confidentiality, acceptance of gifts, retirement, discipline and dismissal, redundancy (severance) pay, and trade union membership.

Negotiating an appropriate salary is only one aspect of your remuneration, which for many employees consists of much more than what they receive in their pay packet. When negotiating your employment conditions for a job in the Far East, the checklists on the following pages should prove useful. The points listed under **General Positions** below apply to most jobs, while those listed under **Managerial & Executive Positions** (on page 81) may apply only to higher level appointments.

Working Hours: Your working hours in the Far East may be quite different from those in your home country and will vary according to your profession and employer as well as with the country you work in – see Country Profiles (**Chapter 9**). The Far East is notably work-oriented and, even where there are rules or guidelines regarding maximum working hours, breaks and holiday allowances, they're rarely adhered to. Many people work much longer than the standard 9 to 5, work through lunch and break times and don't take their full holiday allowance. This is particularly true in China, Hong Kong, Japan, Korea, parts of Malaysia, Singapore and Taiwan.

General Positions

- **Salary:**
  - Is the total salary adequate, taking into account the cost of living (see page 173)? Is it index-linked or protected against devaluation and cost of living increases? This is particularly important if you're paid in a foreign currency which may fluctuate wildly or could be devalued. Are you paid an overseas allowance for working abroad?
  - Does it include an allowance for working (and living) in an expensive area or a 'hardship allowance' for working in a remote or inhospitable region?
  - How often is the salary reviewed?
  - Does the salary include commission and bonuses?
  - Does the employer offer profit-sharing, share options or share-save schemes?
  - Is overtime paid or time off given in lieu of extra hours worked?
  - Is the total salary (including expenses) paid in local currency, or is it paid in another country (in a different currency) with expenses for living abroad? Many employers pay expatriate employees' salaries into an offshore bank account, possibly with living expenses paid locally, which can have considerable tax advantages.
- **Relocation:**
  - Are relocation expenses or a relocation allowance paid?
  - Do the relocation expenses include travelling expenses for all family members?
  - Is there a maximum limit and, if so, is it adequate?
  - Are you required to repay your relocation expenses (or a percentage) if you resign before a certain period has elapsed?
  - Are you required to pay for your relocation expenses in advance (which may run to thousands of US$ or GB£)?
  - If employment is for a fixed period, will your relocation expenses be paid when you complete or leave the job?
  - If you aren't shipping household goods and furniture abroad, is there an allowance for buying furniture locally?
  - Do relocation expenses include the legal and estate agent's fees incurred when moving home?

- Does the employer use the services of a relocation agent (see page 90)?
- Does the employer provide free briefing services before you leave?

● **Accommodation:**
- Will the employer pay for a hotel (or pay a lodging allowance) until you find permanent accommodation?
- Is subsidised or free, temporary or permanent accommodation provided? If so, is it furnished or unfurnished?
- Must you pay for utilities such as electricity, gas and water?
- If accommodation isn't provided by the employer, is assistance in finding suitable accommodation given? What does it consist of? Does it include an advance visit to find accommodation?
- What will accommodation cost?
- While you're living in temporary accommodation, will the employer pay your travelling expenses to your workplace?
- Are your expenses paid while looking for accommodation?

● **Working Hours:**
- What are the weekly working hours?
- Does the employer operate a flexi-time system? If so, what are the fixed (core time) working hours? How early must you start? Can you carry forward extra hours worked and take time off at a later date, or carry forward a deficit and make it up later?
- Are you required to clock in and out of work?
- Can you choose to take time off in lieu of overtime worked or to be paid for it?

● **Part-time Or Periodic Working:**
- Is part-time or school term-time working permitted?
- Are working hours flexible or is part-time working from home permitted?
- Does the employer have a job-sharing scheme?
- Are extended career breaks permitted with no loss of seniority, grade or salary?

● **Holidays & Leave:**
- What is the annual holiday entitlement? Does it increase with age or length of service?
- What are the paid public holidays?
- Is free air travel to your home country or elsewhere provided for you and your family, and if so, how often? Are other holiday travel discounts provided?

- Is paid maternity/paternity leave provided?
- Is compassionate or special leave permitted?

● **Insurance:**
- Is health insurance or regular health screening provided for you and your family? What does it include (see page 143)?
- Is free life assurance provided?
- Is accident or any special insurance provided by your employer?
- For how long is your salary paid if you're ill or have an accident?

● **Company Pension:**
- Is there a company pension scheme and what (if anything) is your contribution?
- Are you required or permitted to pay a lump sum into the pension fund in order to receive a full or higher pension?
- What are the rules regarding early retirement?
- Is the pension transferable (portable) and do you receive the company's contributions in addition to your own? If not, will the employer pay into a personal pension plan?
- Is the pension index-linked?
- Do the pension rules apply equally to full and part-time employees?

● **Employer:**
- Have you checked the prospective employer's status? Is it legal?
- What are the employer's prospects?
- Are his profitability and growth rate favourable?
- Does he have a good reputation?
- Does he have a high staff turnover?
- What are your promotion prospects?
- Will the employer guarantee to employ you at the end of your assignment, either in your home country or in another country? Will the employer pay your repatriation expenses?

● **Women:**
- What is the employer's policy regarding opportunities for women?
- How many women hold positions in middle and senior management or at board level (if the percentage is low in relation to the number of women employees, perhaps you should be wary if you're a career woman)?
- Does the employer have a policy of reinstatement after child birth (which may be a legal requirement)?

- **Family:**
  - Will the employer employ your partner or help her/him find a job?
  - Is private schooling for your children paid for or subsidised? Will the employer pay for a boarding school locally or in another country?
  - Does the employer provide a free nursery or subsidised crèche for children below school age or a day care centre for the elderly?
- **Training:**
  - What initial or career training does the employer provide?
  - Is training provided in-house or externally and will the employer pay for training or education abroad, if necessary?
  - Does the employer have a training programme for employees in your profession (e.g. technical, management or language)? Is the employer's training recognised for its excellence (or otherwise)?
  - Will the employer pay for the cost of non-essential education, e.g. a computer or language course?
  - Will the employer allow paid day release for you to attend a degree course or other study?
  - Are free or subsidised language lessons provided for you and your spouse (if necessary)?
- **Miscellaneous:**
  - Is a free or subsidised employee restaurant provided? If not, is a lunch allowance paid? Is any provision made for shift workers, i.e. breakfast or evening meals?
  - Is a travel allowance paid from your home to your place of work?
  - Is free or subsidised parking provided at work?
  - Are free work clothes, overalls or uniforms provided? Does the employer pay for the cleaning of work clothes (both workshop and office)?
  - Does the employer offer cheap home loans, interest-free loans or mortgage assistance? Note that a cheap home loan can be worth many thousands of US$ or GB£ per year.
  - Is a company car provided? What sort of car? Can it be used privately and, if so, does the employer pay for petrol? Does this affect your income tax liability?
  - Does the employer provide any fringe benefits such as subsidised in-house banking services, car discount scheme, cheap petrol, travel discounts, product discounts, in-house store, sports and social facilities, or subsidised tickets for social and sports events?
  - Do you have a written list of your job responsibilities?

- Have your employment conditions been confirmed in writing?
- If a dispute arises over your salary or employment conditions, under the law of which country will your contract be interpreted?

Managerial & Executive Positions

- Is a 'golden hello' (similar to a 'golden handshake' when made redundant) paid, i.e. a payment for signing a contract?
- Is there an executive (usually non-contributory) pension scheme?
- Is a housing allowance paid or a rent-free house or company apartment provided?
- Are paid holidays provided (perhaps in a company-owned property) or 'business' conferences in exotic places?
- Are the costs incurred by a move abroad reimbursed? For example, the cost of selling your home, employing an agent to let it for you or for storing household effects.
- Will the employer pay for domestic help or towards the cost of a servant or cook?
- Is a car provided? With a chauffeur?
- Are you entitled to any miscellaneous benefits such as club membership, free credit cards, or tickets for sports events and shows?
- Is there an entertainment allowance?
- Is extra compensation paid if you're made redundant or fired? Redundancy or severance payments are compulsory for all employees in many countries, but executives often receive a generous 'golden handshake' if they're made redundant, e.g. after a take-over.

EMPLOYMENT CONTRACTS

In many countries, a 'contract of employment' exists as soon as an employee confirms his acceptance of an employer's terms and employment conditions, e.g. by starting work, after which both employer and employee are bound by the terms offered and agreed. The contract isn't always in writing, although employers must usually provide employees with a written statement containing certain important terms and conditions of employment and additional notes, e.g. regarding discipline and grievance procedures. A written contract of employment should usually contain all the terms and conditions agreed between the employer and employee.

You usually receive two copies of your contract of employment (which may be called a 'statement of terms and conditions' or an 'offer letter'), both of which you should sign and date. One copy must be returned to your employer or prospective employer, assuming you agree with the terms and want the job, and the other (usually the original) is for your records.

There are generally no hidden surprises or traps for the unwary in a contract of employment provided by a bona fide employer, although, as with any contract, you should know exactly what it contains before signing it. If your knowledge of the local language is imperfect, you should ask someone to explain anything you don't understand in simple English (employers rarely provide foreigners with contracts in a language other than the local language). Your contract (or statement) of employment may contain the following details:

- The names of the employer and employee;
- Your job title;
- Your salary details, including overtime pay and piece-rates, commission, bonuses and agreed salary increases or review dates;
- When the salary is to be paid, e.g. weekly or monthly;
- Your hours of work;
- Holiday and public holiday entitlements;
- Sickness and accident benefits;
- Pension scheme details;
- Probationary and notice periods (or the expiry date, if employment is for a fixed period);
- Disciplinary and grievance procedures (which may be contained in a separate document).

If there are no agreed terms under one or more of the above headings, this may be stated in the contract. Any special arrangements or conditions you've agreed with an employer should also be contained in the contract. If all or any of the above particulars are contained in a collective agreement or other documents, such as work rules or handbooks, wage regulation orders, or sick pay and pension scheme conditions, an employer may refer you to these. Before signing your contract of employment, you should obtain a copy of any documents referred to in the contract or general employment terms and ensure that you understand them.

Employment is usually subject to satisfactory references being received from your previous employer(s) and/or character references. In the case of a school-leaver or student, a reference may be required from the principal of your last school, college or university. For certain jobs, a pre-employment medical examination is required and periodical examinations may be a condition of employment, e.g. where good health is vital to the safe performance of your duties. If you require a work permit, your contract may contain a clause stating that 'the contract is subject to a work permit being granted by the authorities'. Employees must usually be notified in writing of any changes in their terms and conditions of employment, within a limited period of their introduction.

SPOUSES

If you're offered a position in the Far East and your spouse or partner also has a full-time job, there are three options: to turn down the offer, to go to the Far East and leave your spouse behind, or to take your spouse with you. In the last case, the spouse or partner must usually abandon or at least put on hold his or (almost always) her own career, which can cause resentment on her part and put immense strain on a relationship. A previously working spouse, used to the stimulation and reward of a career, often finds herself in the Far East with nothing to do; as a result, she may be bored, lack self-esteem and resent being financially dependent on her husband. In addition, she is in a foreign country where she may not speak the language or have any friends.

As an expatriate it may be difficult to find a full-time or even a part-time job, let alone one in your own field or profession. Labour laws vary considerably from country to country and may not allow spouses to work at all. Wages may be lower than you're used to and there will probably be intense competition among expatriates for any available positions.

If you're posted to the Far East, it isn't usually realistic to try to take your career with you but is more practical to put it on hold and consider alternative employment. In any case you should wait a few months after arriving in a country before accepting a job, as you will need time to organise your family, home and yourself, and to adapt to a new environment and situation.

However, before you go, there's a lot you can do to prepare the ground for finding a job, particularly regarding maintaining your self-esteem and motivation after you've left your job or given up your business. There are numerous general books on careers that you can study before you go, which can help you dispassionately assess your achievements and examine your preferences. Many contain self-assessment exercises, which help you to identify your strong points, what you enjoy doing most and your long-term goals. Once you have a better idea of what you like doing and have an objective view of your skills, you will be in a better position to use this knowledge to find a job opportunity in the Far East.

Before you go, find out as much as possible about local etiquette, particularly regarding business protocol. Customs vary considerably from country to country, but if you're well versed in the local etiquette, particularly how to greet someone and introduce yourself, the chances are that you will avoid unnecessary faux pas (a good website for business etiquette is 🖳 www.business culture.com). If you have time, it's wise to learn a few basic phrases of greeting and introduction in the language of the country you're moving to, or even take a course so that you can make simple conversation (not easy with Far Eastern languages!). Possible employers in the region rarely expect you to be fluent in their language but will certainly appreciate your attempts to speak it (however tortured).

Before you go, take time to study the many expatriate websites (see **Appendix C**), most of which provide useful contacts in the local expatriate network and allow you to post questions and queries that are answered by experienced expatriates. Take the opportunity to ask about job possibilities and the skills required, and to tap into other people's experiences so that you can use this knowledge later. There are websites specifically for expatriate wives and some women's groups have their own websites where you can contact them abroad by email or normal post.

Above all, you should try to view your career being put on hold for a period as a positive move and an opportunity to explore new and exciting horizons, rather than a problem or an obstacle in your life. Although your career may not be moving along the same direct path, you will undoubtedly learn new skills that may enhance your later promotion prospects.

Once you arrive in the country, you may be fortunate and be able to apply your skills to a ready-made local job, which is more likely if you speak the local language, but unlikely in Brunei or Indonesia, where women aren't an accepted part of the workforce. Options such as health care, teaching (particularly English as a Foreign Language), office management, and the hotel and travel industries are a good place to start. One of your first priorities should be to find out as much as you can about employment opportunities beforehand. Have plenty of copies of your CV to hand (plus copies of educational qualifications and employment references) and be prepared to make numerous 'cold' calls on schools, hotels, academies and offices. If they're interested in your application, they will contact you or put your CV on file for when a vacancy arises.

However, it's more likely that there isn't a suitable vacancy, particularly if you relocate to a developing country or region. Under these circumstances you will need to rethink your position and how your skills can be applied to the local job market. You will have to be imaginative and resourceful, and may need to invent a job based on local demand. Go out and meet people by joining expatriate groups, of which there are usually many in the form of women's groups, sports and special interest clubs, or the parents' association at your children's school. Have some business cards made and give them to anyone you think may be interested in your skills or who knows someone who could be. Listen to the expatriate grapevine and find out what they complain about or what they miss, which may provide an opportunity for you to fill.

Bear in mind that all societies have different needs; fulfilling one of these may provide you with a job. Try to stay motivated by setting yourself small, manageable tasks with achievable goals. Don't set yourself the goal of finding a job by the end of the first week, but instead give yourself the task of visiting say five contacts in one week. Flexibility is paramount and you may need to compromise, but the chances are that you will find yourself with a rewarding job that you'd never have dreamed of doing in your home country. It's also possible that your new employment may be far more satisfying and enriching than your previous career!

There are many good career publications written with the expatriate in mind, including *A Career in Your Suitcase* by Joanna Parfitt (Summertime Publishing) and *What Color is Your Parachute?* (updated annually) by Richard Nelson Bolles (Ten Speed Press).

Unemployment

If you aren't allowed to work or are unable to find a job, you may well find yourself alone in a new home with your husband away all day in a fulfilling job – one that provides him with lots of human contact with colleagues who speak his language – and your children settled into school (possibly in another country). This is a difficult situation, particularly when you may be suffering from culture shock (see page 414), including rejection of the new country and its people, and you find that your family members are experiencing an exciting new life while you sit at home wishing you had never come!

What can you do? You can sit at home and sink into disillusionment, unhappiness and possibly depression, or you can motivate yourself to participate fully in your new country and lifestyle. However, participation may be easier said than done and may be difficult, particularly if you're naturally shy or unused to taking the initiative. Relationships abroad are different from those at home, where everyone is on common ground in a familiar environment, and where you have many people you can relate to. Abroad foreigners are like 'fish out of water' and usually need to make the first move in unfamiliar circumstances. There may also be a limited number of English-speaking expatriates in your area and a relatively high turnover of foreigners. Relationships may be difficult to start, simply because everyone is experiencing the same adaptation difficulties and first impressions may be negative owing to the effects of culture shock and stress.

However, making friends is the first step to enjoying a new country and therefore it's necessary to go out of your way to be friendly to other expatriates, whether at your children's school, your husband's business functions or even in local supermarkets or cafés. Bear in mind also that expatriate wives who have been in the country longer than you have will know just how you feel and will be able to offer advice on how they coped as newcomers. You usually find that the expatriate community is close-knit and its members concerned about others; they will often go out of their way to help you.

The following list provides a number of ways to meet other expatriate wives and enjoy your time abroad:

- **Expatriate Clubs** – Most popular expatriate destinations have a network of clubs whose activities encompass a wide range of social, sporting and educational activities. These may include a number of women's clubs which organise specific activities for expatriates such as the Federation of American Women's Clubs Overseas (⌨ www.fawco.org), an organisation with clubs in some 37 countries, including China (Shanghai), Korea (Seoul), the Philippines (Manila) and Thailand (Bangkok). FAWCO was originally established by Americans but welcomes women of all nationalities. Contact your local embassy or consulate for a list of expatriate clubs in your area.

- **Schools & Nurseries** – School or childcare facilities provide a ready-made place for contact with other expatriate parents. If there's a parents' association, it's worthwhile becoming a member. There may also be a school café where you can drop in after ferrying your children to school and meet other mothers. Look on the school notice board for news about forthcoming events and meetings (you could also offer to help).

- **Language Classes** – Language lessons are a good place to meet expatriates, as well as offering help with integration into the local community and culture.

- **Sports Clubs** – Even if you aren't particularly sporty, the local sports club or gymnasium will probably offer tuition in various sports and the opportunity to play at different levels. Many clubs also operate leagues where you can take part in regular activities.

- **Volunteer Work** – If you cannot find a paid job or obtain a work permit, you may wish to consider volunteer work. Volunteering includes everything from listening to younger children read at your children's school to teaching English to the locals, from working alongside local people in the establishment of a health clinic to helping co-ordinate aid work. Opportunities are usually plentiful and volunteers are welcomed with open arms. You will probably also gain huge satisfaction from your endeavours. Contact your local embassy or consulate for information or international voluntary organisations before you enquire about opportunities locally. There are a number of publications that provide useful contacts and information, including *Work & Study in Developing Countries* by Toby Milner (Vacation Work) and *Work, Study, Travel Abroad* published by the Council on International Educational Exchanges (CIEE), 52 Poland Street, London W1V 4JQ, UK (☎ 020-7478 2007). See also **Voluntary Work** on page 60.

3.

ACCOMMODATION

In most Far Eastern countries, finding accommodation to rent isn't difficult, provided your requirements aren't too unusual, although rented accommodation in major cities is usually in high demand and short supply, and rents can be very high. Accommodation usually accounts for around 25 per cent of the average family's budget, but can be up to 50 per cent in major cities. In some of the 11 countries considered here, foreigners aren't permitted to buy property or may buy only apartments, as they aren't allowed to own land. Property prices and rents vary considerably according to the country, region and city, and have increased steadily in most major cities in recent years.

People in some Far Eastern countries aren't very mobile and move house much less frequently than the Americans and British, which is reflected in the fairly stable property market. It generally isn't worth buying a home in the region unless you plan to stay in the country for the medium to long term, say a minimum of five years and preferably 10 to 15. People in some Far Eastern countries don't buy domestic property as an investment, but as a home for life, and you shouldn't expect to make a quick profit when buying property in the region.

RELOCATION COMPANIES

If you're fortunate enough to have your move to the Far East paid for by your employers, it's likely that they will arrange for a relocation company to handle the details. There are relocation companies in most countries, particularly in the most popular major cities. In some countries there are different types of relocation companies, including corporate relocation companies (whose clients are usually large companies), commercial property companies and home-search companies, which act for individuals. The larger relocation companies may provide all three levels of service, while smaller companies may have just a few staff and offer only a home-search service.

The fees charged (and services provided) by relocation companies vary enormously, although most levy a registration (or administration) fee payable in advance, plus a daily fee for accompanied viewing of properties and other amenities. If finding a home is part of the service, a fee of 1 to 2 per cent of the purchase price is normal, with a minimum charge, e.g. US$1,000 to $2,000. An all-inclusive international relocation package which includes the rental or purchase of an employee's home and advice on mortgages (for house purchasers), schools, insurance and other matters, can easily run to between US$15,000 and $30,000.

Home-search companies are becoming more common and will undertake to find 'the home of your dreams'. This can save buyers considerable time, trouble and money, particularly if you have special or unusual requirements. Some specialise in finding exceptional residences only, costing upward of US$400,000 but can save you money by negotiating the price on your behalf.

Finding accommodation for single people or couples without children can usually be accomplished in a week or two, depending on the country and region, while family homes generally take a bit longer. You should allow at least two months between your initial visit and moving into a purchased property. Relocation companies may provide the following services:

House Hunting

This is usually the main service provided by relocation companies and includes both rented and purchased properties. Services usually include locating a number of properties matching your requirements and specifications, and arranging a visit (or visits) to view them.

Negotiations

Consultants usually help and advise with all aspects of house rental or purchase and may conduct negotiations on your behalf, organise finance (including bridging loans), arrange surveys and insurance, organise your removal abroad and even arrange quarantine for your pets (see page 276).

Schools

Consultants can usually provide a report on local schools (both state and private) for families with children. If required, the report can also include boarding schools.

Local Information

Most companies provide a comprehensive information package for a chosen area, including information about employment prospects, state and private health services, local schools (state and private), estate agents, shopping facilities, public transport, amenities and services, sports and social facilities, and communications.

Miscellaneous Services

Most companies provide advice and support (particularly for non-working spouses) both before and after a move, orientation visits for spouses, counselling services for domestic and personal problems, help in finding jobs for spouses and even marriage counselling services (moving abroad puts a lot of strain on relationships).

Although you may consider a relocation consultant's services expensive, particularly if you're footing the bill yourself, most companies and individuals consider it money well spent. You can find a relocation consultant in most countries through the yellow pages or via the Internet (using a search engine).

There's an 'association of relocation agents' in some western countries, such as the ARA in the UK (💻 www.relocationagents.com); Direct Moving (💻 www.directmoving.com) lists 8,000 relocation companies worldwide.

If you just wish to look at properties for rent or sale in a particular area, you can make appointments to view properties through estate agents in the area where you plan to live and arrange your own trip abroad. However, you must make certain that agents know exactly what you're looking for and obtain property lists in advance.

TEMPORARY ACCOMMODATION

On arrival in the Far East, it may be necessary to stay in temporary accommodation for a few weeks or months, e.g. before moving into permanent accommodation or while waiting for your furniture to arrive. Some employers provide rooms, self-contained apartments or hostels for employees and their families, although this is rare and is usually only for a limited period. Many hotels and bed and breakfast establishments cater for long-term guests and offer reduced weekly or monthly rates. In many areas, particularly in major cities, serviced and holiday apartments are available. These are fully self-contained, furnished apartments with their own bathrooms and kitchens, which are cheaper and more convenient than a hotel, particularly for families. Serviced apartments are usually rented on a weekly basis. Self-catering holiday accommodation is available in most countries, although it's prohibitively expensive during the main holiday season.

RENTED ACCOMMODATION

If you're planning to spend only a few years in the Far East – generally less than five – renting is usually the best decision. It's also the answer for those who don't want the trouble, expense and restrictions associated with buying a property, and obviously the only answer in areas where foreigners are prohibited from buying land or property (see **Property Market** on page 115). In fact, it's prudent for anyone looking for a permanent home abroad to rent for a period until you know exactly what you want, how much you wish to pay and where you want to live. This is particularly important for retirees who don't know a country well, as renting allows you to become familiar with an area, its weather, amenities and the local people, to meet other foreigners who have made their homes abroad and share their experiences, and, not least, to discover the cost of living at first hand.

Most Far Eastern countries have a strong rental market and it's possible to rent every kind of property, from a tiny studio apartment to a huge rambling pile. Rental properties are mostly privately owned, but include investment properties owned by companies and public housing owned by local councils. If you're looking for a home for less than a year, you're better off looking for a furnished apartment or house. Rental properties in most countries are let unfurnished, particularly for lets longer than a year, and long-term furnished properties are difficult to find. Bear in mind that in some countries, 'unfurnished' means that a property is completely empty, except perhaps for the bathroom porcelain and possibly a kitchen sink. There will be no kitchen cupboards, appliances, light fittings, curtains or carpets, although you may be able to buy these from a departing tenant. Semi-furnished apartments usually have kitchen cupboards and bathroom fixtures, and possibly a few pieces of furniture, while furnished properties tend to be fully equipped, including crockery, bedding and possibly towels (similar to renting a self-catering apartment).

Hotels

Hotel rates vary according to the time of year, the location and the individual establishment, although you may be able to haggle over rates outside the high season and for long stays. A single room in most of the region's countries (excluding major cities) costs from around US$30 and a double room from around US$50 per night. You should expect to pay at least double these rates (and often much more) in a major city, where cheap hotels are often used as permanent accommodation. Hotels aren't usually a cost-effective solution for anyone planning to stay in a country long term, although in some areas they're the only alternative and may have special low rates for long-term residents. Bed and breakfast accommodation is also available in many countries, although it isn't always budget accommodation, when you need to choose a hostel or pension, which may have self-catering apartments or studios.

Short-Term Furnished Rentals

Many countries have an abundance of self-catering accommodation and a wide choice. You can choose from cottages, apartments, villas, bungalows, mobile homes, chalets, and even castles and palaces, if your budget runs to them. Most property is available for short holiday lets only, particularly during the peak holiday season, and little furnished property is let long term. However, some owners let their homes long term, particularly outside the peak period. Note that, when the rental period includes the peak letting months, the rent may be prohibitive. If you rent for a short period from an agent, you should negotiate a lower commission than the usual one month's rent, e.g. 10 per cent of the total rent payable. You can make agreements by fax when renting from abroad.

Standards vary considerably throughout the Far East, from dilapidated, ill-equipped apartments to luxury properties with every modern convenience. A typical holiday rental is a small, self-contained apartment with one or two bedrooms (sleeping two to four and usually including a sofa bed in the living room), a large living room/kitchen with an open fire or stove, and a toilet and bathroom. Always check whether a property is fully equipped (which should mean whatever you want it to mean!) and whether it has central heating if you're planning to rent in the north of the region in winter or air-conditioning if you're living in one of the steamier regions (i.e. most of the Far East).

For short-term lets, the cost is calculated on a weekly basis (Saturday to Saturday) and depends on the standard, location, number of beds and the facilities provided. If you're looking for a rental property for say three to six months, it's best not to rent unseen, but to rent a holiday apartment for a week or two to allow you time to look around for a long-term rental or a property to buy. Properties for rent are advertised in local newspapers and magazines, including expatriate publications, and can also be found through property publications in many countries. Many estate agents offer short-term rentals and builders and developers may also rent properties to potential buyers. Short-term rentals can be found through local and state tourist offices abroad, travel agents, the Internet and many overseas newspapers.

Note that any rental laws providing protection for tenants don't usually extend to holiday lettings, furnished lettings or sub-lettings. For holiday letting, parties are free to agree such terms as they see fit concerning the period, rent, deposit and the number of occupants permitted, and there's no legal obligation for the landlord to provide a written agreement. However, you shouldn't rent a furnished property long-term without a written contract, which is important if you wish to have a deposit returned.

Long-Term Unfurnished Rentals

Unfurnished rental property is available in all 11 territories, although prices vary from modest to astronomical according to the country, area and district. Availability, rental rates and contractual arrangements are detailed under the country headings below.

Finding A Rental Property

Your success in finding a suitable rental property depends on many factors, not least the kind of accommodation you're seeking (a one-bedroom apartment is easier to find than a four-bedroom detached house), how much you want to pay and the area where you wish to live. There are a number of ways of finding a property to rent, including the following:

- If you have friends, relatives or acquaintances in the area, ask them to help spread the word. In many countries, the best properties are often found by word of mouth, particularly in major cities, where it's almost impossible to find somewhere with a reasonable rent unless you have connections.
- Check the small advertisements in local newspapers and magazines.
- Look for properties with a 'To Rent' sign in the window.

> - Visit accommodation and letting agents (listed in the yellow pages). Most cities and large towns have estate agents who also act as letting agents for owners. It's often better to deal with an agent than directly with owners, particularly regarding contracts and legal matters.
> - Look for advertisements in shop windows and on bulletin boards in shopping centres, supermarkets, universities and colleges, and company offices.
> - Check newsletters published by companies, colleges, churches, clubs and expatriate organisations, and their notice boards.

You must usually be quick off the mark to find accommodation through small ads in local newspapers. Buy newspapers as soon as they're published and start phoning straight away. You can also view rental advertisements on the internet, where all major newspapers have websites. Other sources include expatriate publications published in major cities and magazines published by estate agents. You must be available to inspect properties immediately or at any time. Even if you start phoning at the crack of dawn, you're likely to find a queue when you arrive to view a property in a major city.

The best days for advertisements are usually Fridays and Saturdays. Advertisers may be private owners, property managers or letting agencies (particularly in major cities). You can insert a 'rental wanted' advertisement in many newspapers and on notice boards, but don't count on success using this method. Finding a property to rent in the Far East's major cities is similar to the situation in London and New York, where the best properties are usually found through personal contacts.

Rents

Note that rents are very high in some countries, particularly in major cities, where rental property is in high demand and short supply. Rents may also be astronomical in relation to the local cost and standard of living, and foreigners may need to pay a high premium over what the locals pay. In many countries you must pay a year's rent in advance or for the whole period of your contract and landlords may demand a non-returnable deposit (called 'key' money), usually equal to a few months' rent, simply for the 'privilege' of being able to rent a property. For details of rental prices and conditions in the 11 territories, see below.

Brunei

Brunei is a tiny country, but there's no shortage of accommodation. Foreigners cannot own property in Brunei and there's a thriving rental market to serve expatriate workers, although renting can be expensive. Some short-stay expatriates live in hotels, where prices range from around B$40 to B$360 (US$25 to US$200) per night, although long-stay discounts can sometimes be negotiated, or serviced apartments, which are apartments maintained by the building's staff and leased on a month-to-month basis (but this can be expensive long-term).

Serviced apartment buildings often have facilities, including a clubhouse, indoor and outdoor swimming pools, a shop, a shuttle bus and optional extra maid service. Other expatriates choose to live in private apartments or houses. The standard of these is invariably high, with a full range of modern amenities, including air-conditioning, which is considered vital by many people in Brunei's humid climate.

Rates: Accommodation prices vary according to size, quality and location, with monthly rents for apartments in the range of BD$600 to BD$2,000 (US$1,000 to US$3,500) and for houses between BD$900 and BD$4,500 (US$1,500 and US$7,750).

Contracts: Contractual arrangements are generally straightforward.

China

China has an enormous choice of accommodation. Until the 1990s, most Chinese urban accommodation consisted of state-owned apartments in drab concrete blocks, usually with balconies, which were often glazed in the north of the country. Chinese citizens are now allowed to own their own apartments and many new buildings are being constructed to meet the demand. But there are still plenty of old blocks in most cities, the majority between three and five storeys high. Access is via stairs, only high-rise buildings (which are most common in Beijing, Guangzhou and Shanghai) having lifts (elevators).

Apartments usually have one or two bedrooms, a living room, a kitchen and a bathroom. Floors tend to be bare concrete, although some have carpet and/or linoleum, and increasing numbers of Chinese people are upgrading their homes and installing marble floors. Until recently, the kitchens in many apartments were at best spartan, with little more than a gas burner for a stove and a small sink, but today many have the usual white goods and facilities. Bathrooms and living rooms usually have basic furnishings.

Rates: Rental rates vary widely in China, with a vast difference, for example, between an apartment in an old block in an unfashionable suburb and one in a sleek, serviced block in the 'right' part of town. As a rough guide to current prices in Beijing and Shanghai (the most expensive cities), you pay between RMB2,000 (US$250) and RMB 4,000 (US$475) per month for a furnished two-bedroom apartment (around 100m²), and from RMB4,000 (US$475) to RMB 6,000 (US$725) for three bedrooms, but you can easily pay RMB6,500 (US$775) for a 75m², one bedroom apartment in a new block or RMB20,000 (US$2,400) for a large, serviced, luxury, two-bedroom apartment in a secure compound in the best part of town. Similarly, you can spend RMB40,000 (US$4,850) or more per month on a three-bedroom villa in an exclusive, executive development.

Compounds for foreigners are popular but expensive. An apartment in a compound costs between RMB16,000 and RMB64,000 (US$2,000 and $8,000) per month. If you work for the Chinese government you're likely to be provided with low-cost housing, although this is usually basic and sparse. Other options include renting a room from a Chinese family, which costs from RMB1,200 (US$150) per month, depending on the facilities and type of board.

Contracts: The landlord will be either a developer or a private individual. Rents are often lower if it's the latter, but be careful: it might be the first time he has rented an apartment, certainly to a foreigner, so ensure that the contract is clear regarding the landlord's obligations to carry out repairs, the standard of the appliances and fixtures, and the terms for ending the lease. Be sure to check that the landlord has an ownership certificate for the property and have a copy attached to your tenancy agreement. Many foreigners rent through agencies, which deal with these problems. Agency fees are usually paid by the landlord.

Rental contracts can be as short as three months, but the majority of leases are for a year. Avoid signing a lease for longer than two years; the price might be attractive but your circumstances might change, as might those around you: for example, with so much construction work in China, they might begin building an apartment block next to your building, making your life a nightmare of noise and dust for several months. Try to ensure that there's a cancellation clause in the contract so that you can break it if necessary and check that the penalty for cancellation isn't too punitive.

Ensure that a rental contract is specific as to what the rent includes: for example, does it include management charges, utilities and use of any building facilities? Also check that it specifies that your landlord must provide you with an official receipt for rental payment, known as *fa piao*. A standard deposit is two months' rent, with the first month paid in advance. The deposit is usually returned at the end of the contract, minus any charges for breakages or damage. If the contract is broken by you, it's standard for the landlord to retain the deposit as compensation.

It isn't unusual to negotiate the terms of a contract offered and you should be prepared to spend time doing this. Unless you speak fluent Chinese, ensure that there's an English as well as a Chinese version, and have somebody check that they correspond; if there's a dispute, the Chinese version is legally binding. When you've signed the contract, register it with the local housing bureau; this provides a back-up should any problems arise.

Hong Kong

Hong Kong offers a wide variety of accommodation for expatriates close to the major business districts. Single people and childless couples often choose to live near the Central District, within easy walking distance of work, shops, restaurants, bars and other nightlife. Families with small children favour beach-front areas, such as Repulse Bay on the south side of Hong Kong Island and Discovery Bay on Lantau Island. Those high up the corporate ladder gravitate towards Victoria Peak (usually just called 'the Peak'), a cool, green upland area (up to 550m/1,800ft above sea level) on Hong Kong Island, which also offers some of Hong Kong's leading private schools, a private hospital and up-market restaurants and leisure facilities. For further details of Hong Kong's residential districts see page 116.

The majority of Hong Kong's accommodation is in the form of apartments in high rise blocks, the best use of space in a location where it's at a premium. Many foreigners are disappointed by the small size of apartments. Town houses are uncommon and are seen as luxury accommodation in Hong Kong, with very high rents; villas even more so.

Many properties are rented through agents, who are paid by both you and the landlord. In theory, they should therefore balance the interests of the two. In practice, however, if the landlord is a large company, his interest might be more important; conversely, if you work for a large company that's an important customer of the agent, you might do better.

Property sizes in Hong Kong are often expressed as a floor area in square feet, and figures often include your share of the foyer, stairwell and perhaps even parking as well as the area of the actual accommodation.

Rates: There's a high demand for quality accommodation, which is in short supply and costs from HK$30,000 to HK$80,000 (US$3,850 to US$10,300) per month.

Contracts: Be prepared to negotiate over most aspects of the contract, and ask for more than you want or a lower rent than you're prepared to pay (around 20 per cent less is standard, the landlord usually meeting you half way). Check exactly what's included in the rent, and try to find out beforehand how much rent landlords of other apartments in the block are charging. Many expatriates look for accommodation in June, July and August, and prices rise by around 15 per cent at this time of year. Note also that 'gazumping' (where somebody betters your offer when you're on the point of signing a contract) isn't uncommon for apartments in popular buildings and locations.

Hong Kong is a society where saving face is important, so don't become annoyed or over-excited when negotiating a rental contract (or anything else). Don't appear too keen on a property (which will weaken your negotiating position), even if you love it and have been searching for accommodation for months.

Indonesia

The '90s building boom in Jakarta has generated plenty of property to rent, mainly apartments in modern, sleek blocks, many located near the 'Golden Triangle', which is the main business district. There are also plenty of apartments near the outer ring road, which offer easy access to the business district. Most apartments are new (less than ten years old, many less than five), but not all are in good condition: Jakarta's trying climate and a lack of maintenance mean that some have deteriorated quite badly. Watch out for wear and tear. Apartments vary enormously in size, from modest studios to rambling, five-bedroom properties.

It's relatively easy to find an apartment to rent in Indonesia without going through an agent. All apartment blocks have a management office, often staffed by English speakers, and you can deal directly with them. This restricts your choice, however, because they usually only show you management-owned apartments or those that they represent. If you deal through an agent, you also have access to privately-owned apartments, which tend to have lower rates, sometimes much lower. Another advantage of using an agent is that they invariably transport you around town to look at apartments, a distinct bonus in traffic-choked Indonesia. Many expatriates (most of whom live and work in Jakarta) choose to live near their place of work.

Many of the apartment blocks in Jakarta favoured by expatriates are of good quality, with facilities including a gym or fitness centre, children's play area and a modest shop. They're similar to apartments found in western cities, with one addition: quarters for household staff, often a small bedroom and bathroom located off the kitchen. This part of the apartment doesn't usually have air-conditioning (locals find it too cold) and it might have a separate entrance.

Rates: Rental rates for apartments in sought-after locations have until recently been high: Rp8.5 million to Rp25 million (US$1,000 to US$3,000) for a two-bedroom apartment and 12.5 million to 42.5 million (US$1,500 to $5,000) for a three-bedroom apartment, depending on the location and facilities. Note, however, that following the region's financial problems and Indonesia's recent instability, rents are falling and you're recommended to negotiate. It's usual to pay all the rent for the contract period in advance, as well as a security deposit.

Contracts: Since the economic downturn of 1997, Indonesia has been a renter's market and you can usually negotiate a contract in your favour. Whereas landlords used to be in the position to ask for all the rent for a contract period up-front, sometimes even for two or three-year contracts, they now have to accept shorter rental periods and a lower proportion of the rent up-front: a quarter is currently standard. Landlords also used to be able to insist on payment in US$, but it's now easier to secure agreement to payment in local currency if this is more convenient for you.

Japan

There's something of a Catch 22 with regard to renting accommodation in Japan unless you have a job contract before arrival in the country: it's difficult to find a job without a proper address (i.e. not a hotel) and it's difficult to find accommodation without a letter of guarantee from an employer. One way round the problem is to find a Japanese resident willing to act as guarantor; another is to offer a landlord a large deposit (e.g. US$3,000 to US$7,000).

Don't assume that all Japanese urban areas are similar, conforming to a model of the country portrayed on television or in films. There are vast differences between Japanese cities. Some are clean, organised and attractive, others are noisy, busy and ugly. Even within a city – Tokyo, for example – there may be almost rustic areas close to modern, mall-lined districts.

Apartments are generally made of wood, but some (known as *manshon*) are made of concrete. These are better insulated against sound and heat loss and are therefore slightly more expensive. Some apartments have European/North American-style rooms, but those described as *washitsu* have Japanese-style rooms, with *tatami* mat flooring (rather than wood or linoleum), *shoji* (paper screens) rather than curtains and *oshiire* (built-in cupboards with sliding doors).

Be prepared to work hard in your search for property. As well as looking in newspapers and asking friends and colleagues, make use of estate and rental agencies (*fudosan*), which are often situated close to railway stations. If possible, ask friends and colleagues and try to secure a personal introduction to an agent. Estate and rental agencies post details of available properties in their windows, often detailing the rent, deposit, size, amenities, nearest train station and other useful information. The size of Japanese apartments is often measured in *tatamis*, i.e. the number of *tatami* mats, which measure 2m x 1m, that fit in each room.

Properties for rent are sometimes described as 1K (one room and a kitchen), 1 or 2DK (one or two rooms, a dining room and a kitchen), or 1, 2 or 3DLK (one, two or three rooms, a dining room, living room and a kitchen). Space is at a premium in urban Japan and you should lower your expectations if you're used to living in a large property (unless you're prepared to pay a king's ransom in rent). The Japanese themselves refer to urban housing as *usagi no uchi* (rabbit warrens) and, if paying a low rent is your goal, be prepared to live in one room with few or no kitchen facilities, a 'squat' toilet and a shared bath in a rickety, old, wooden building, a fair distance from the nearest railway station.

Property in Japan is invariably let unfurnished and acquiring basic furnishings makes renting in the country even more expensive than it already is. But the Japanese tradition of replacing possessions regularly (this stems from the Shinto idea of cleansing) has come to the aid of many a cash-strapped foreigner: there's a monthly collection of outsize rubbish (*sodai gomi*) and on this day the Japanese dispose of their unwanted furnishings, many of them as good as new. The Japanese aversion to second-hand goods means that foreigners have their pick of these items before the refuse collectors arrive.

Gaijin Houses: The expense and uncertainty of renting in Japan mean that if you're single and aim to be in Japan for a year or less, it's often easier and cheaper to stay in a *gaijin* house, which simply require a month's rent in advance as deposit, around ¥60,000 to ¥80,000 (US$550 to US$725), which is returned when you leave. *Gaijin* houses provide inexpensive accommodation to a range of foreigners, including backpackers, short-term visitors and those who've come to work in Japan. A *gaijin* house is similar to a guesthouse and you receive a room simply furnished with a bed (or futon), wardrobe, cupboard and a heater (although some *gaijin* houses have shared rooms or sometimes dormitories). The kitchen and bathroom are communal and there might be a lounge, with a television, radio and small library. For those wanting a *gaijin* house in Tokyo, the weekly *Tokyo Journal* prints a list.

Public & Subsidised Housing: If you secure a job in a school, with an education authority or in local government, enquire about public housing. This consists of property owned or leased by your employer and rented to employees for considerably less than standard rents and without the need to pay key money. You also have colleagues as neighbours, which can be a great help with settling in.

Registered foreigners wanting to live in Osaka, you can apply for public housing even if you don't work for a school or local authority. Due to the high demand, properties are allocated by lottery twice a year, in February and July, exact dates being advertised in local newspapers. For further information, contact Osaka City Housing Corporation (☎ 06-243 0381).

Osaka also offers help to certain newlywed foreigners under the age of 40 who pay high private rents. Contact the Housing Corporation to see if you qualify. Foreigners (and natives) throughout Japan can also apply for subsidised accommodation from the Japan Housing and Urban Development Corporation (JHUD) if their income falls below a certain level. To check if you qualify, visit your local JHUD office and take your Alien Registration Card, passport, a completed application form (available from the offices) and a comprehensive statement of your income.

Rates: Rental rates in Japan vary widely according to the size, type, standard and location of accommodation. In Tokyo, for example, you can 'slum it' in a tiny, ancient, one-room home with a gas ring and no bathroom for ¥30,000 (US$275) per month, or live it up in a large, luxury penthouse in the town centre for ¥1 million (US$9,200) per month. If you want to rent a roomy, well-appointed house in one of Japan's cities, be prepared to pay tens of thousands of US$ every month for the privilege.

Between these extremes, standard monthly rents for reasonable accommodation in a reasonable area in the major cities are as follows (you pay between half and two-thirds of these rates in provincial towns):

- **Gaijin House** – ¥50,000 to ¥100,000 (US$460 to US$920);
- **One-Bedroom Apartment** – ¥200,000 to ¥300,000 (US$1,840 to US$2,750), depending on size;
- **Two-Bedroom Apartment** – ¥450,000 (US$4,125);
- **Three-Bedroom Apartment** – ¥600,000 (US$5,500).

Note that you may be required to pay up to six or seven months' rent in advance, not all of which you will receive back at the end of the contract. This advance payment is made up of the following (proportions vary slightly in different contracts):

- **Earnest Money (*tetsukekin*)** – An immediate payment of one month's rent to indicate your intention to sign a rental contract, even if the signing will be delayed. Earnest money is deducted from the amount of key money (see below) after the contract has been agreed. Earnest money is retained by the landlord if you don't sign a contract. When you do sign, the following are also due:

- **Deposit (*shikikin*)** – This is usually two months' rent and is lodged with the landlord as a guarantee against any damage to the property and its contents. It should be returned to you at the end of the contract – minus the cost of any repairs or damage – but getting it back can be a long, difficult process.

- **Key Money (*reikin*)** – This is also usually two months' rent and is effectively a gift/present to the landlord, a sort of advance 'thank you' for future help! As a gift, of course, this money is non-refundable. Many foreigners find this bewildering (i.e. a blatant rip-off), but it's unavoidable.

- **Agent's Fee (*chukai seenryo*)** – The law fixes this at no more than a month's rent.

- **Rent In Advance (*yachin*)** – This is one month's advance rent and you then pay at the beginning of each month.

As well as these up-front costs, you might be liable for the further expense of around ¥6,000 (US$55) per month for maintenance of the building, such as cleaning.

Contracts: In order to communicate with agents and landlords, you must almost always be able to speak adequate Japanese or co-opt a Japanese speaker who can spend part of at least several days translating for you.

For meetings and viewings with rental agents and landlords, always be well prepared: arrive exactly on time, be polite, bow deeply, greet people in Japanese (if you can) and have all the necessary paperwork (passport, bank account details, letters of recommendation and, if applicable, verification of employment). The more information you can provide, the better.

The letting agent will show you a floor plan of any apartments you're interested in and, although it's usual for Japanese customers to decide on the basis of these only (without seeing the actual property), it's wise to view the properties themselves before deciding.

When you find a property you like, fill out a rental application, which is shown to the landlord for his approval (or otherwise). Many landlords will not rent their properties to foreigners (*gaijin*), some of them simply because of xenophobia, others because they find that foreigners sometimes make too much noise, wear shoes indoors, put pictures on the walls, expect to receive their deposit back in full (see 'key money' below) and can only sign short leases, limited by the duration of their work contracts.

Check that the contract has a cancellation clause and what the terms are. Also note that most contracts prohibit the keeping of pets and that in properties with Japanese style rooms (*washitsu*) the contract might stipulate that you replace the *tatami* and *shoji* when you leave, which can be expensive.

Don't rush into a decision, as it can be difficult and expensive to break a rental contract in Japan. At best you will lose your deposit, at worst you will end up in court. Spend time examining a contract and check for any strings, for example 'No Visitors' or a requirement to give private English lessons to the landlord's children.

The advance payment or deposit you're expected to pay is usually around three to seven times the monthly rent, which can be a substantial amount of money, and it can be difficult to get it back at the end of the contract.

Help: If you encounter any problems with the complexities of renting property in Japan, there are two organisations that can offer help in English: the Foreign Residents' Advisory Centre (☎ 03-5320 7744) and The Shinagawa Tenant Leases Association. You need to join the latter, for a fee of around ¥5,000 (US$45) and then pay a monthly fee of around ¥1,500 (US$13.75).

Korea

As is the case in Japan, space is at a premium in Korea and accommodation is smaller than most westerners are used to. As a general rule, avoid basement apartments, as they often have poor ventilation, damp and insect problems.

Korea is well served by estate agents (*budeungsan*), which are found everywhere. Few of their staff, however, speak much English.

Rates & Contracts: Monthly rents start at SKW1.5 million (US$1,275) for a small apartment. Larger, western-style apartments (known as 'villas') with more amenities cost from SKW5 million (US$4,250). Houses are also sometimes available from SKW5 million.

Agents usually charge a fee of 3 per cent of the yearly rental, the cost of which is split between you and the landlord.

The traditional Korean system of rental is called *jeonsei*, under which the tenant pays a large deposit known as key money (this can be tens of thousands of US$) and then lives in the property rent-free for the length of the contract. The landlord collects interest off the key money instead of a monthly rent and returns the deposit at the end of the contract. You're recommended to avoid taking out a contract on this basis, as, with recent economic problems and falling stock markets, the money isn't always available at the end of the contract!

Fortunately, the 'western' way of renting is becoming much more common in Korea. Many landlords now accept a combination of key money and monthly rent. The usual arrangement and rate is SKW100,000 (US$85) per month for every SKW5 million (US$4,250) of key money. Instead of paying SKW40 million (US$33,750) in key money, a landlord might accept SKW10 million (US$8,500) for key money and SKW600,000 (US$500) per month rent. To ensure that you receive back the key money at the end of the contract, you should file a lien against the property with the local government agency. Estate agents do the requisite paperwork as a standard part of their fee.

Malaysia

There's plenty of choice for those wanting to rent property in Malaysia, with apartments, condominiums (apartments with extra facilities, often including a gym, swimming pool, 24-hour security guard and a small shop), bungalows and detached houses. Traffic in Kuala Lumpur is heavy and many expatriates choose to live near their place of work to minimise travelling time.

Rates: Current monthly rentals in Kuala Lumpur are as follows: a standard, two-bedroom condominium in the suburb of Bangsar costs RM3,000 (US$800); a large, three-bedroom condominium in Bangsar, RM7,500 (US$2,000); a semi-detached house in the central area, RM4,000 to RM6,000 (US$1,000 to US$1,600); and a large, detached house with a pool in the centre of the city, between RM9,000 and RM15,000 (US$2,400 and US$4,000).

Contracts: Leases are usually for a year, but it's sometimes possible to negotiate a six-month contract. The process is straightforward: when you find a property, you sign a letter of offer and pay one month's rent as an 'earnest deposit'. Within seven days, you pay two months' rent as a security deposit and around RM1,000 (US$260) as a utility deposit (the amount varies) and the tenancy agreement is stamped; you receive a copy and so does the landlord.

Philippines

Finding a property to rent in all price ranges is straightforward in the Philippines, where rented accommodation is really the only option for expatriates, due to property ownership restrictions. The majority of landlords prefer renting to foreigners than to Filipinos, as they feel more confident of receiving payment and also able to charge more (although prices are still modest by western standards). In view of the country's high crime rate and the risk of terrorism, many foreigners choose to live in apartment blocks with security guards or in houses in compounds, which are protected by security fences and patrolled by guards.

Apartment compounds rented exclusively by westerners, often with many amenities and sports facilities, are popular with expatriates.

Rates: Rents vary greatly, from a modest P8,250 to P11,000 (US$150 to US$200) per month for a large apartment or a small house in any city except the capital Manila to P55,000 (US$1,000) per month for a large, four-bedroom house in a security compound in the city of Cebu. In Metro Manila (i.e. including the city's outskirts), a fully furnished two-bedroom apartment costs between P20,000 to P180,000 (US$365 to US$3,270) per month and a house from P35,000 to P250,000 (US$635 to US$4,500), depending on the location and amenities.

Contracts: Rental agreements usually require an advance payment of at least two months' rent and a security deposit equal to two months' rent.

Singapore

Expatriates in Singapore have a wide range of properties to choose from, including a limited number of Housing and Development Board (HDB) flats (see below), as well as private apartments, bungalows and houses. HDB properties, which are built and maintained by the Housing and Development

Board, are sometimes referred to as 'public housing', although the term is confusing, as around 90 per cent of these properties are owned by those living in them. HDB properties are usually three, four or five-room flats, built and maintained to a reasonable standard, although they tend to be basic rather than luxurious. A three-room flat usually covers around 70m² (800ft²), a four-room around 90m² (1,000ft²), and a five-room flat around 110m² (1,200ft²); there are also 'executive' flats of around 150m² (1,600ft²).

HDB Properties: Around 85 per cent of native Singaporeans live in HDB properties and are around 6,000 are rented, although they rarely become available to foreigners. There are two ways to secure one: through the HDB itself or from owners of HDB properties who have permission from the HDB to rent them. The first method also includes a clumsily-named 'Scheme for Housing for Foreign Talents' (abbreviated to SHIFT!), which was launched in 1997 by the Jurong Town Corporation to attract foreigners to Singapore. It offers rents of around S$800 (US$465) per month for a three-room flat, S$1,000 (US$580) for a four-room, S$1,300 (US$750) for a five-room property and around S$1,500 (US$870) for an executive flat. In order to qualify, you must be a skilled worker, professional, student or graduate, have been working in Singapore for less than two years, and not own property. For further information, contact the JTC (☎ 6665-4670, 🖥 www.jtc.gov.sg). You pay one month's deposit and a month's rent in advance.

If you rent from an owner of an HDB property, it's more expensive; add around $350 (US$200) to each of the above figures.

Ask the landlord or agent who shows you the property to show you the necessary letter of approval from the Board; **there have been cases of owners renting their flats without official permission and, if this happens, the contract might be nullified and you could forfeit your deposit.**

As well as the attraction of low rents, living in HDB properties means that you're well served by transport links, shops and restaurants, since all the buildings are constructed near a wide range of services. The downside to living in HDB property is that some people find it soulless and basic and, while the larger flats tend to have most modern conveniences, the smaller ones don't always enjoy them; in fact, you might find yourself with a flat with bare walls and next to no furniture. A drawback to renting JTC properties is that you cannot view them: you tell the JTC what size of property you want and in which area, and you're then given the keys to one that fits the bill, if available.

Rates: Rental rates in Singapore vary widely according to the size, type, facilities and location of the property, but in general they range from around S$800 (US$465) per month for a basic, three-room HDB flat to S$1,500 (US$870) for an executive HDB flat (see below). For non-HDB properties, a monthly rent of around S$3,500 (US$2,000) will secure you a reasonable apartment of between 110m² (1,200ft²) and 275m² (3,000ft²), depending on location. A large, stylish apartment in a block with facilities (pool, tennis court and a gym) costs from S$8,500 to S$10,000 (US$5,000 to US$5,800) per month, while you need to spend between S$20,000 and S$30,000 (US$11,500 to US$17,500) for a luxury house with a spacious garden in a smart area.

Contracts: The initial lease on rented property in Singapore is usually for one or two years, and landlords invariably require three months' rent in advance as a deposit.

Taiwan

Rental accommodation is quite widely available in Taiwan. Many expatriates use estate agents when searching for accommodation to rent, but there are alternatives. The Bulletin Board at the Taipei American Club has notices about available properties, and the English-language newspapers *Taiwan News* and *China Post* have rental sections advertising properties.

If you use an agent, he receives commission from both the renter and the landlord, usually half a month's rent from each. A cause of disappointment to many foreigners is that it's unusual for Taiwanese estate agents to provide transport to and from property viewings. It's recommended to visit three or four agents and choose the friendliest and the one who, hopefully, can be persuaded to provide transport.

When viewing properties, avoid those that need repairs unless they're carried out before you sign the contract. If you sign and then expect the landlord to carry out the repairs, you could wait a long time. Be especially careful to check the plumbing and sanitation, even in new buildings; the standard of workmanship is sometimes poor and it isn't unknown for workers to flush excess cement down the toilet bowl when they've finished work, with predictably unpleasant consequences.

If you have a car, choose a property with a garage or you might find it all but impossible to park; triple parking on the street isn't uncommon in Taiwan.

Taipei's northern suburb of Tienmou is popular with Taiwan's English-speaking expatriate community. It's a fashionable area, with American, British and Japanese schools. Most of the accommodation is modern and of a reasonable standard, the majority of it apartments, with few houses. Slightly further out than Tienmou are the suburbs of Peitou and Tamshui, where prices are lower than in Tienmou. They've become more popular with expatriates since the opening of an MTR line. Above Tienmou and Peitou is Yangmingshan (Yang Ming Mountain), which is the most prestigious are in which to live, similar to the Peak in Hong Kong. It's the place for people who can afford to pay the earth for a house in extensive grounds and who have a chauffeur to drive them around; Yangmingshan enjoys cool mountain air but is inconvenient if you need quick access to the city. For people wanting to live in the heart of Taipei, the Hsinyi district is popular, although rents are around 50 per cent higher than in Tienmou.

Contracts: Most rental contracts are in Chinese and you should make sure that you understand all the conditions. Bear in mind that when you sign a contract you will be required to pay a damage deposit of between two and four months' rent. Check at the outset that the proposed rent includes everything. Be prepared to negotiate over the rent, and please note that this includes being prepared to give as well as take.

Rates: A two-bedroom apartment costs from NT$9,000 to NT$30,000 (US$265 to US$900) per month, a three-bedroom apartment from NT$12,000 to NT$35,000 (US$350 to US$1,000), depending on the location and amenities. Prices for apartments in Tienmou vary widely according to size, facilities and location, ranging from NT$25,000 (US$735) per month for a basic two or three-bedroom apartment to NT$200,000 (US$5,900) for a large, luxury property with extensive facilities.

Thailand

There's a wide choice of property to rent in Bangkok, including apartments, condominiums, serviced apartments, bungalows and houses, but competition for the better properties is stiff, with a limited supply and steady demand. Most accommodation is spacious with air-conditioning. Unaccompanied expatriates who work for large firms and receive reasonable housing allowances often choose upmarket serviced apartments in the city centre, which are similar to hotels, with daily cleaning and washing services included, and all furnishings, allowing you to move in with only a suitcase. Competition for these serviced apartments is quite intense. For corporate expatriates with families, large, centrally-located apartments and houses are popular, although expensive and in short supply.

Rates: At the bottom end of the market, a small studio apartment with basic furniture and air-conditioning costs around Bht6,000 (US$150) per month rent only, or around Bht9,500 (US$240) including electricity, telephone, water and laundry. A modest, two-bedroom townhouse starts at around Bht8,000 (US$200) per month, or around Bht12,000 (US$300) including electricity, water, laundry, telephone and cable TV. A serviced apartment on the city's edges costs from around Bht15,000 (US$375) per month, for which you receive a bedroom, bathroom and living room in a building offering amenities. Centrally-located apartments cost in the range of Bht60,000 to BHt90,000 (US$1,500 to US$2,250) per month, while two or three-bedroom houses cost up to Bht200,00 (US$5,000) per month.

Contracts: Rental contracts are usually for a minimum of a year and are generally written in English. Note that a standard one-year contract has no right of termination, unless one is specifically agreed. Longer contracts usually include a 'diplomatic clause', which becomes effective after the first year and allows for cancellation of the contract if 30 or 60 days' notice is given in writing by either party. If you're willing or able to pay six months' rent in advance, you can negotiate substantial rental reductions from many landlords. **It's recommended to rent through a reputable agent rather than independently.**

BUYING PROPERTY

Buying property in most countries is usually a sound long-term investment and is preferable to renting. However, if you're staying for only a relatively short term, say less than five years, as most foreigners are in the Far East, you may be better off renting. For those staying longer than this, buying is usually the better option, particularly as buying a house or apartment is generally no more expensive than renting in the long term and could yield a handsome profit. Provided you avoid the most expensive areas (i.e. major cities), property can be relatively inexpensive in many countries, although the fees associated with a purchase usually add between 5 and 15 per cent to the cost. You shouldn't expect to make a quick profit when buying property in the Far East. In most countries, property values increase in line with inflation, meaning that you must own a house for a few years simply to recover the fees associated with buying.

It isn't wise to be in too much of a hurry when buying a home. Have a good look around in your preferred area(s) and make sure that you have a clear picture of the relative prices and the kinds of properties available. Some people set themselves impossible deadlines in which to buy a property (e.g. a few days or a week) and often end up bitterly regretting their impulsive decision. It's a lucky person who gets his choice absolutely right first time, which is why most experts recommend that you rent before buying unless you're absolutely certain what you want, how much you wish to pay and where you want to live. To reduce the chances of making an expensive error when buying in an unfamiliar country or region, it's often prudent to rent for 6 to 12 months. This allows you to become familiar with the region and the weather, and gives you plenty of time to look around for a permanent home at your leisure.

To get an idea of property prices, check the prices of properties advertised in English-language property magazines and local newspapers, magazines and property journals (see **Appendix B**). In some countries, property price indexes for various regions are published by local property magazines, although these should be taken only as a rough guide. Before deciding on the price, make sure you know exactly what's included, as it isn't unusual for people to strip a house or apartment bare when selling and even remove the kitchen sink, toilets, light fittings and even the light switches! If applicable, have fixtures and fittings listed in the contract.

Avoiding Problems

The problems associated with buying property abroad have been highlighted in the last few decades or so, during which the property market in some countries has gone from boom to bust and back again. From a legal point of view, some countries are much safer than others, although buyers have a high degree of protection under the law in most countries. However, you should take the usual precautions regarding contracts, deposits and obtaining proper title. Many people have had their fingers burned by rushing into property deals without proper care and consideration. It's all too easy to fall in love with the beauty and allure of a home and sign a contract without giving it sufficient thought. If you're uncertain, don't allow yourself to be rushed into a decision, e.g. through fears of an imminent price rise or because someone else is interested in a property. It's vital to do your homework thoroughly and avoid the 'dream sellers' (often fellow countrymen) who will happily prey on your ignorance and tell you anything in order to sell you a home.

The vast majority of people who buy homes abroad don't obtain independent legal advice and most of those who experience problems take no precautions whatsoever. Of those who do take legal advice, many do so only after having paid a deposit and signed a contract or, more commonly, after they've run into problems. The most important point to bear in mind when buying property in the Far East is to obtain expert legal advice from someone who's familiar with local law. When buying property in any country, you should never pay any money or sign anything without first taking legal advice. You will find the relatively small cost (in comparison with the cost of a home) of obtaining legal advice to be excellent value, if only for the peace of mind it affords. Trying to cut corners to save a few pennies on legal costs is foolhardy in the extreme when a large sum is at stake.

There are professionals speaking English and other languages in all Far Eastern countries, and many expatriate professionals (e.g. architects, builders and surveyors) also practise abroad. However, don't assume that because you're dealing with a fellow countryman that he will offer you a better deal or do a better job than a local person (the contrary may be true). It's wise to check the credentials of professionals you employ, whatever their nationality. Note that it's never recommended to rely solely on advice proffered by those with a financial interest in selling you a property, such as a builder or estate agent, although their advice may be excellent and totally unbiased.

It's important to deal only with qualified and licensed agents, and to engage a local lawyer before signing anything or paying a deposit. A surveyor may also be necessary, particularly if you're buying an old property or a property with a large plot. Your lawyer will carry out the necessary searches regarding such matters as ownership, debts and rights of way. Enquiries must be made to ensure that the vendor has a registered title and that there are no debts against a property. It's also important to check that a property has the relevant building licences, conforms to local planning laws and that any changes (alterations, additions or renovations) have been approved by the local town hall. If a property is owned by several members of a family, which is common in some countries, all owners must give their consent before it can be sold. It's also important to ensure that a rural property has a reliable water supply.

Finally, if there's any chance that you will need to sell (and recoup your investment) in the foreseeable future, it's wise to buy a home that will be saleable. A property with broad appeal in a popular area will usually fit the bill, although it will need to be very special to sell quickly in some areas. A modest, reasonably priced property is usually likely to be much more saleable than a large expensive home, particularly one requiring restoration or modernisation.

Among the most common problems experienced by foreign buyers are buying in the wrong area (rent first!), buying a home that's unsaleable, buying too large a property and grossly underestimating restoration and modernisation costs, not having a survey done on an old property, not taking legal advice, not including the necessary conditional clauses in the contract, buying a property for business, e.g. to convert to self-catering accommodation, and being too optimistic about the income, overcharging by vendors and agents (a common practice when selling to foreigners), taking on too large a mortgage, and property management companies going bust or doing a moonlight flit with owners' rental receipts.

Other problems can be caused by properties without legal title, properties built or extended illegally without planning permission, properties sold that are subject to embargoes, properties that are part of the assets of a company, sold illegally by a bankrupt builder or company, undischarged mortgages from the previous owner, builders absconding with the buyer's money before completing a property, claims by relatives after a property has been purchased, properties sold to more than one buyer, and people selling properties they don't own. Always take care when a property is offered at a seemingly bargain price by a builder, developer or other businessman, and run a thorough credit check on the vendor and his business.

One law that property buyers should be aware of is the law of subrogation, whereby property debts, including mortgages, local taxes, utility bills and community charges, remain with a property and are inherited by the buyer in many countries. This is an open invitation to dishonest sellers to 'cut and run'. It is, of course, possible to check whether there are any outstanding debts on a property and your legal advisor must do this after you sign a contract and again a few days before completion.

It's wise to have your finance in place before you start looking for a property in the region and if you need a mortgage, to obtain a mortgage guarantee certificate from a bank that guarantees you a mortgage at a certain rate, which is usually subject to a valuation. Note, however, that in many countries, a buyer can withdraw from a contract and have his deposit returned if he is unable to obtain a mortgage. You will need to pay a deposit when signing a contract and must pay all fees and taxes on completion.

Choosing The Location

The most important consideration when buying a home is usually its location – or as the old adage goes, the three most important points are location, location and location! A property in a reasonable condition in a popular area is likely to be a better investment than an exceptional property in a less attractive location. There's no point in buying a dream property in a terrible location. The wrong decision regarding location is one of the main causes of disenchantment among foreigners who have bought homes in the Far East.

Where you buy a property will depend on a range of factors, including your personal preferences, your financial resources and, not least, whether you plan to work. If you already have a job, the location of your home will probably be determined by the proximity to your place of employment. However, if you intend to look for employment or start a business, you must live in an area that allows you the maximum scope. Unless you have reason to believe otherwise, it would be unwise to rely on finding employment in a particular area. If, on the other hand, you're looking for a holiday or retirement home, you can live virtually anywhere. When seeking a permanent home, don't be too influenced by where you've spent an enjoyable holiday or two. A town or area that was acceptable for a few weeks holiday may be far from suitable, for example, for a retirement home, particularly regarding the proximity to shops, medical facilities and other amenities.

If you have little idea about where you wish to buy, read as much as you can about the countries and regions on your shortlist and spend some time looking around your areas of interest. Note that the climate, lifestyle and cost of living can vary considerably according to the country, region and even within a particular region. Before looking at properties, it's important to have a good idea of the type of property you're looking for and the price you wish to pay, and to draw up a shortlist of the areas or towns of interest. If you don't do this, you're likely to be overwhelmed by the number of properties to be viewed. Real estate agents usually expect serious buyers to know where they want to buy within a 20 to 25mi (30 to 40km) radius and some even expect clients to narrow it down to specific towns and villages.

If possible, you should visit an area a number of times over a period of a few weeks, both on weekdays and at weekends, in order to get a feel for the neighbourhood (walk, don't just drive around!). A property seen on a sunny day after a delicious lunch and a few glasses of wine may not be nearly so attractive on a subsequent visit on a dull day or during the rainy season, without the warm inner glow. If possible, you should also visit an area at different times of the year, e.g. in both summer and winter, as somewhere that's wonderful in summer can be forbidding and inhospitable in winter. On the other hand, if you're planning to buy a winter holiday home in the north of the region, you should also view it in summer, as snow can hide a multitude of sins!

There are many points to consider regarding the location of a home, which include the following:

- For some people the climate is one of the most important factors when buying a home in the Far East, particularly a holiday or retirement home. Bear in mind both the winter and summer climate, the position of the sun, the average daily sunshine, plus the rainfall, humidity and wind conditions. You may also wish to check whether the area is noted for snow, ice or fog (large swathes of China, Korea and Japan are afflicted during the winter and spring), which can make for hazardous driving conditions. The orientation or aspect of a building is vital; if you want morning or afternoon sun (or both) you must ensure that balconies, terraces and gardens are facing the right direction.

- Check whether an area is particularly prone to natural disasters such as floods (which are common in some countries), storms (hurricanes, tornadoes, typhoons, etc.), forest fires, landslides or earthquakes. If a property is located near a coast or waterway, it may be expensive to insure against floods and tropical storms, which are a constant threat in some of the region's countries. In areas with little rainfall, there are often severe water restrictions and high water bills. See also **Climate** on page 242.

- Noise can be a problem in many cities and resort areas. Although you cannot choose your neighbours, you can at least ensure that a property isn't located next to a busy road, railway line, airport, industrial plant, commercial area, discotheque, night club, bar or restaurant (where revelries may continue into the early hours). Look out for objectionable properties that may be too close to the one you're considering and check whether nearby vacant land has been 'zoned' for commercial activities or tower blocks. In community developments (e.g. apartment blocks) many properties are second homes and are let short term, which means you may have to tolerate boisterous holidaymakers as neighbours throughout the year (or at least during the high season months).

- Bear in mind that if you live in a popular tourist area you will be inundated with tourists, and in much of the Far East, the tourist season is year-round. They won't only jam the roads and pack the public transport, but may also occupy your favourite table at your local café or restaurant (heaven forbid!). Although a 'front-line' property on a beach or in a marina development may sound attractive and be ideal for short holidays, it isn't always the best choice for permanent residents. Many beaches are hopelessly crowded in the high season, streets may be smelly from restaurants and fast food joints, parking impossible, services stretched to breaking point, and the incessant noise may drive you crazy. Some people prefer to move inland or to higher ground, where it's less humid, more peaceful and you can enjoy panoramic views. On the other hand, getting to and from hillside properties is often precarious and the often poorly maintained roads (usually narrow and unguarded) in many countries are for sober, confident drivers only. Note also that many country roads are suited only to four-wheel-drive vehicles.

- Do you wish to live in an area with many of your fellow countrymen and other expatriates or as far away from them as possible? If you wish to integrate with the local community, avoid foreign 'ghettos' and choose an area or development with mainly local inhabitants. However, unless you speak the local language fluently or intend to learn, you should think twice before buying a property in a village. The locals in some villages resent 'outsiders' buying up prime properties, particularly holiday homeowners, although those who take the time and trouble to integrate into the local community are usually warmly welcomed. If you're buying a permanent home, it's important to check your prospective neighbours, particularly when buying an apartment. For example, are they noisy, sociable or absent for long periods? Do you think you will get on with them? Good neighbours are invaluable, particularly when buying a second home.

● Do you wish to be in a town or do you prefer the country? Inland or on the coast? How about living on an island? Bear in mind that if you buy a property in the country, you will probably have to tolerate poor public transport (or none at all), long travelling distances to a town of any size, solitude and remoteness. You won't be able to pop along to the local bakers, drop into the local bar for a glass of your favourite tipple with the locals or have a choice of restaurants on your doorstep. In a town or large village, the market will be just around the corner, the doctor and pharmacy close at hand, and if you need help or have any problems, your neighbours will be close by.

● In the country you will be closer to nature, will have more freedom (e.g. to make as much noise as you wish) and possibly complete privacy, e.g. to sunbathe or swim au naturel. Living in a remote area in the country will suit nature lovers looking for solitude who don't want to involve themselves in the 'hustle and bustle' of town life (not that there's much of this in most rural towns). If you're after peace and quiet, make sure that there isn't a busy road or railway line nearby or a local temple, mosque or church within 'DONGING!' distance. Note, however, that many people who buy a remote country home find that the peace of the countryside palls after a time and they yearn for the more exciting city or coastal nightlife. If you've never lived in the country, it's wise to rent first before buying. Note also that while it's cheaper to buy in a remote or unpopular location, it's often much more difficult to sell.

● If you're planning to buy a large country property with an extensive garden or plot of land, bear in mind the high cost and amount of work involved in its upkeep, especially in the tropics with a year-round growing season. If it's to be a second home, who will look after the house and garden when you're away? Do you want to spend your holidays mowing the lawn, cutting back the undergrowth and shinning up the palm trees to clip the dead fronds? Do you want a home with a lot of outbuildings? What are you going to do with them? Can you afford to convert them into extra rooms or guest or self-catering accommodation?

● How secure is your job or business and are you likely to move to another country or area in the near future? Could you find other work in the same country or area, if necessary? If there's a possibility that you may need to move in a few years' time, you should rent or at least buy a property that will be relatively easy to sell and recoup the cost.

- What about your partner's and children's jobs or your children's present and future schooling? What is the quality of local schools? Even if your family has no need or plans to use local schools, the value of a home is often influenced by the their quality and location.

- What local health and social services are provided? How far is the nearest hospital with an emergency department?

- What shopping facilities are provided in the local neighbourhood? How far is it to the nearest sizeable town with good shopping facilities, e.g. a supermarket? How would you get there if your car is out of action? Note that many rural villages are dying and have few shops or facilities, and aren't necessarily a good choice for a retirement home.

- What is the range and quality of local leisure, sports, community and cultural facilities? What is the proximity to sports facilities such as a beach, golf course, ski resort or waterway? Bear in mind that properties in or close to ski and coastal resorts are usually considerably more expensive, although they also have the best letting potential. If you're interested in a winter holiday home, which area should you choose? While properties in ski resorts are relatively expensive, they tend to appreciate faster than properties in many other areas and generally maintain their value in bad times.

- Is the proximity to public transport, e.g. an international airport, port or railway station, or access to a motorway important? Don't, however, believe all you're told about the distance or travelling times to the nearest motorway, airport, railway station, port, beach or town, but check yourself. Being on a local bus route is also advantageous.

- If you're planning to buy in a town or city, is there adequate private or free on-street parking for your family and visitors? Is it safe to park in the street? In some areas it's important to have secure off-street parking if you value your car. Parking is a problem in many towns and most cities, where private garages or parking spaces are rare and can be expensive (although you may be able to rent a garage). Bear in mind that an apartment or townhouse in a town or community development may be some distance from the nearest road or car park. How do you feel about carrying heavy shopping hundreds of metres to your home and possibly up several flights of stairs? Traffic congestion is also a problem in many towns and tourist resorts, particularly during the high season.

- What's the local crime rate? In some areas, the incidence of housebreaking and burglary is high. Due to the higher than average crime rate (see page 247), home insurance is higher in major cities and some resort areas. Check the crime rate in the local area, e.g. burglaries, house breaking, stolen cars and crimes of violence. Is crime increasing or decreasing? Bear in mind that professional crooks like isolated houses, particularly those full of expensive furniture and other belongings that they can strip bare at their leisure. You're much less likely to be a victim of theft if you live in a village, where crime is usually virtually unknown – strangers stand out like sore thumbs in villages, where their every move is monitored by the local populace.

● Do houses sell well in the area? Generally, you should avoid neighbourhoods where desirable properties routinely remain on the market for three months or longer (unless the property market is in a severe slump and nothing is selling).

Buying Through An Offshore Company

This is (not surprisingly) popular among non-resident property buyers in many countries, as they can legally avoid paying wealth tax, inheritance tax and capital gains tax. Buyers can also avoid transfer tax or stamp duty when buying a property owned by an offshore company, which can be a good selling point. However, it isn't possible in many countries and in others the owners of properties purchased through offshore companies must register their ownership with the authorities or face punitive taxes. **Obtain expert advice from an experienced lawyer before buying through an offshore (or any other) company.**

Property Market

The following is a summary of the current state of the property market in the 11 territories covered by this book. For further information about mortgages see page 164.

Brunei

Foreigners aren't permitted to own property in Brunei.

China

The regulations and restrictions governing the ownership of property in China by foreigners re currently changing. Until recently, property ownership was restricted to 'foreign approved for sale' housing, which was often very expensive and also complicated to buy. Even then, you could hold and use a property for only 70 years before the title reverted to the state (there's no freehold in China). An exception was and remains the outward-looking city of Shanghai, where foreigners had more freedom and are currently free to buy property anywhere in the city. They've taken up this option with enthusiasm and in 2002 over 40 per cent of property transactions were made by foreigners. The situation in the rest of China looks set to be liberalised along Shanghai lines.

A complication is the difference between the right to own land and property. Land in China is subject either to government or collective ownership. You can, however, obtain the right to use the land to build on. But the right to do this is normally granted for a limited time and the question then arises of what happens to the right to a building after the land use right has expired. This problem hasn't yet been resolved, but China is looking to reform its property law over the coming years.

In most countries it's wise to hire a lawyer when buying property, but this is particularly so in China. The Chinese property market is new and many developers, estate agents and vendors are inexperienced, meaning that market practices and quality of service are either hazy or non-existent. The level, consistency and competence of government control is another grey area. If you decide to buy property in China, it's vital to check that the individual or company selling the property has the right to do so. The State-Owned Land Use Certificate and Pre-Sale Commodity Building Certificate need to be checked and this is best done by a lawyer. *Caveat emptor* (buyer beware) always applies to the purchase of property, but particularly in China!

Prices: In Shanghai prices vary greatly according to the location and age of a property; houses built before 1940 (known as 'old houses') are particularly expensive. Apartments in a desirable area with two to four bedrooms are available from RMB8,250 to RMB30,000 (US$1,000 to US$3,600) per m². Old houses, which are often large with gardens, cost from RMB10,000 to RMB40,000 (US$1,200 to US$5,000) per m².

Mortgages: Currently, foreigners cannot obtain mortgages except in Shangai, although this is also under review and it should soon be possible. Mortgages are available in Shanghai from Chinese state commercial banks for up to 80 per cent of a property's value, for up to 30 years if the loan is in RMB or up to 10 years for foreign currency loans.

Purchase Fees & Taxes: As property purchase is a recent phenomenon in China, fees and taxes have yet to be established in most areas.

Hong Kong

There are no restrictions on foreigners owning property in Hong Kong, but the last six years have been turbulent for the Hong Kong property market. This has been for a variety of reasons, including concern about the return to Chinese rule, the general malaise in many Far Eastern economies and the outbreak of the SARS virus. Houses are particularly expensive; but apartments are more reasonably priced, although most apartments are smaller than those in western countries. Many new apartments have pools, gymnasiums and other leisure facilities.

Despite being so small, Hong Kong has many different residential areas. Midlevels is above Central, overlooking the main business district. It's popular with expatriates for its views and convenient location. Happy Valley is near the famous racecourse, to the east of Central. There are building restrictions in this area, meaning that many of the buildings are low-rise. The area has a village atmosphere but many of its apartment blocks don't have as extensive range of facilities as in other areas.

The Peak is the highest part of Hong Kong, with fabulous views and a prestigious reputation. On the downside, despite cooler summer temperatures, it becomes very humid and isn't convenient for reaching town. On the west side of Hong Kong Island is Pokfulum, noted for its (relatively) clean air and cheaper property prices. Repulse Bay, despite the name, is one of the most expensive places to live, its proximity to a beach being a strong attraction. It's also quiet, yet close to the centre.

Shouson Hill in the centre of the Island is also popular with expatriates, although not as convenient as some areas for reaching Central. Clearwater Bay and Sai Kung have some of Hong Kong's lowest property prices, but journey times to work in Central are longer than from other residential areas. Discovery Bay is also inexpensive, but too quiet and off-the-beaten track for some. Cheapest of all is Lamma Island, but it's a 45-minute ferry trip to Central.

Prices: After a number of years of very high, rising prices, Hong Kong property values are down by up to two-thirds from their peak in 1997. Despite this – and an indication of how astronomical prices were – a well-located, one-bedroom apartment can cost around HK$7.8 million (US$1million), i.e. around the same as the better parts of Manhattan and twice as much as the best parts of Beijing and Shanghai! Prices, however, vary greatly in different parts of Hong Kong. A two or three-bedroom apartment covering between 40m^2 and 70m^2 costs from around HK$4.75 million (US$600,000) in the New Territories, but from HK$14 million (US$1.8 million) on Hong Kong Island. Luxury apartments are considerably more expensive.

Many observers believe that prices will fall by a minimum of 10 per cent and maybe as much as 20 per cent before starting to rise again. The low point is estimated to be some time in 2004 so it isn't recommended to buy before then.

Mortgages: Local banks provide mortgages for property purchase and usually lend up to 70 per cent of the purchase price.

Purchase Fees: A property purchase tax is levied on a sliding scale, with a maximum of 3.75 per cent of the purchase price on properties costing HK$6 million or over.

Property Taxes: Annual property tax is levied on land and buildings at a standard rate of 16 per cent (2004) of the ratable value, less a statutory deduction of 20 per cent for repairs and out-goings.

Indonesia

For many years, foreigners weren't allowed to buy property in Indonesia and many people believe that they still aren't, although in 1996 regulation No41/1996 was introduced allowing foreigners to buy apartments (and office space), provided the building isn't part of a government-subsidised housing development and has 'strata title status'. This means that a foreigner can own an apartment or office but not the land on which it stands . . . in theory!

Although the regulation is many years old, the legal situation is still unclear and very few, if any, foreigners have yet managed to obtain a strata title certificate of ownership to confirm their ownership of an apartment or office. The law states that foreigners are allowed to hold only 'land-use deeds', whereas most properties have 'right-to-build' deeds, thereby disqualifying foreigners from buying them. Confusion over different lengths of title for different buildings has further complicated the issue.

You can circumvent these problems by signing a Convertible Lease Agreement with an apartment's management office. This means that you purchase the apartment but the title remains in the name of the property management firm or developer. The Convertible Lease Agreement says that when (or if) the law changes and permits the lessee to become the legal owner, the lessor and lessee are legally required to sign a Deed of Sale and Purchase, transferring the title to the foreign owner. Needless to say, you should only consider such an arrangement if you've thoroughly investigated the management company or developer's reputation and financial standing. Even if you're satisfied with both, show all contracts to a lawyer before signing anything, to ensure that all your interests and every eventuality are covered (bearing in mind that Indonesia's instability means that there are few guarantees about anything in the country).

Another possibility is to buy a property in the name of an Indonesian citizen. Since this means that the person concerned is the legal owner, you obviously need to trust him absolutely. Indonesian law is clear on the point that foreigners cannot own land directly, but they can own it 'indirectly'. This is done by drawing up an agreement with an Indonesian, signed before a public notary. The agreement states that the Indonesian is the legal owner of the land, but the foreigner is the 'rightful owner' and thus the Indonesian must carry out the foreigner's wishes regarding the land, e.g. to sell it if he decides and pay the funds to the foreigner. Although this sounds like a way round the restriction, it's unclear whether it actually has any force under Indonesian law and the foreigner's entire investment could be at risk.

The rules concerning foreigners and property in the Barelang area (Batam, Rempang and Galang) are looser and foreigners can own a wider range, encompassing all residential and commercial property except low-cost housing.

Prices: A typical Indonesian house with two or three bedrooms costs between Rp650 million and Rp1.2 billion (US$75,000 to US$100,000), but they can be found for as little as Rp200 million (US$25,000) in outlying rural regions. Some of Indonesia's most sought-after and expensive property is on the holiday island of Bali, where a two-bedroom house costs around Rp2 billion (US$175,000) and a three-bedroom house with a swimming pool around Rp15 billion (US$1.35 million).

Japan

There are no legal restrictions on foreigners owning property in Japan (provided they have permanent residence), but there are practical ones. Renting is expensive enough, but buying even more so: Japan has the highest property prices in the world (see below). As a result of these prices, Japanese people can usually only afford to buy property if they take out multi-generational mortgages of between 75 and 100 years, the mortgage being inherited by children and grandchildren along with the property. Even with this facility, property ownership is low in Japan, at around 40 per cent. For the foreigner, the situation is even more difficult than it is for the Japanese, as it's hard to secure a home loan and a multi-generation mortgage isn't an option. Few foreigners are permanent residents and, even if you are, the process of securing a loan is torturous. Japanese banks lend only to those who have banked with them for years and they require substantial savings as collateral for the loan, references and possibly a local guarantor. Even if you manage to comply with this, the maximum loan will be no more than three times your salary, which means that you must be on a **very** high wage to be able to afford even a small apartment.

Even if you're in the fortunate position of being able to buy a property in Japan, recent economic woes, which have seen property prices fall (which highlights how incredibly high they were before), indicate that property purchase cannot be considered a good investment in the short to medium term.

If you decide to buy property in Japan despite all this, be prepared to take professional advice. The laws and procedures relating to buying in Japan are complex and confusing, to the extent that there's even a lack of consensus in legal circles as to what exactly is required to effect a transfer of possession! In fact, it's recommended that you seek help even before beginning to look for property, so different are the methods of negotiation in Japan.

Prices: A small, one-bedroom apartment in an outlying Tokyo suburb can cost ¥82.5 million (US$750,000), a two-bedroom apartment from ¥200 million (US$1.8 million) and a small house from ¥230 million (US$2 million), while a family house in popular areas of Toyo can sell for ¥1.65 billion (US$15 million).

Mortgages: Local mortgages are theoretically available for foreigners, but in practice are exceptionally difficult to obtain.

Purchase Fees: Fees total around 9 per cent of the purchase price and include a 4 per cent property acquisition tax and 5 per cent of the assessed value for registration of ownership. Note that this figure doesn't include legal fees.

Property Taxes: Property taxes are usually included in income tax payments and range from 5 to 12 per cent, depending on the locality and the amenities provided. The Tokyo district levies the highest rates.

Korea

The regulations regarding the ownership of property in Korea by foreigners are in a state of flux, with several laws currently under consideration to make things easier. However, it's currently difficult for foreigners to buy property (even though a law dating back to June 1998 should have eased the restrictions) and the vast majority of expatriates who own apartments or houses have a Korean spouse, with the title in the name of the spouse or a family member.

The majority of property in Korea is apartments, houses being particularly rare in crowded urban areas. Where houses do exist in urban areas, they're often on two or three storeys, the owner and his family living on one floor and the others rented out.

Prices: Property in Seoul is expensive and prices have risen sharply in recent months. Prices of new apartments and villas in some areas have increased by more than half and most prices have now regained their pre-1997 levels. If you're planning to spend five or more years in Korea, property may be a good investment.

Mortgages: In an attempt to control rising property prices, from the Korean government tightened the rules on mortgage lending in November 2003, limiting banks' lending to 40 per cent of the market value of a property.

Purchase Fees: Purchase fees include a 2 per cent acquisition tax and 3.6 per cent registration tax, plus legal expenses.

Property Taxes: Property taxes vary from 0.3 to 7 per cent of a property's value, depending on its location.

Malaysia

Regulations regarding property ownership by foreigners vary in each of Malaysia's 13 states and are subject to change. In Kuala Lumpur, which is home to the majority of the country's foreigners, foreigners can buy a maximum of two apartments, priced at RM250,000 (US$65,790) or more, although in some circumstances this is reduced to RM150,000 (US$39,475). Purchases require the approval of the Foreign Investment Committee (FIC) and foreigners aren't allowed to sell a property within three years of receiving FIC approval. Foreigners married to Malaysian citizens are allowed more leeway.

In view of the changing regulations regarding foreign property ownership, it's wise to consult a lawyer about all aspects of a potential transaction and also to contact the FIC about current rules and proposed changes (Unit Perancangan Ekonomi, Blok B5 and B6, Pusat Pentadbiran Kerajaan Persekutuan, 62502 Putrajaya, Malaysia, ☎ 8888-2935).

Prices: Prices in Malaysia are from RM250,000 to RM950,000 (US$65,000 to US$250,000) for apartments and bungalows, depending on size and location, but large villas (five to seven bedrooms) in the best locations, e.g. The Klang Valley near Kuala Lumpur, range from RM1 million RM5 million (US$375,000 to US$1.3 million).

Mortgages: Local mortgages of up to 60 per cent are available, but only for residential properties valued at over RM250,000 (US$65,790).

Purchase Fees: Fees include stamp duty of 1.5 to 1.75 per cent of the purchase price, a similar loan agreement fee and agents' fees (paid by the vendor) of around 3 per cent on a property value up to RM500,000 (US$130,000) and 2 per cent thereafter.

Philippines

Foreigners cannot own land in the Philippines and thus cannot buy houses. In apartment blocks, foreign ownership is limited to a maximum of 40 per cent of the properties. Practically, it's difficult for foreigners not married to Filipinos to buy property in the Philippines. And if the spouse dies, the property cannot pass to the foreign widow/widower or to any other foreigner, including the children (if they're non-Filipino). The property would pass to a Filipino named in the will or to the deceased spouse's nearest Filipino relative.

As is the case in several Far Eastern countries, the legal situation regarding foreigners and the ownership of property is rather vague and subject to interpretation and change. Therefore, consult a reputable lawyer before making any decisions.

Prices: Apartments in Manila cost between P4 million (US$72,750) and P25 million (US$450,500), depending on the area.

Mortgages: Local banks rarely give mortgages to foreigners, who must have a strong US$ deposit account in order to be considered for one. Loans are usually for a maximum of 50 per cent and, given the erratic Filipino lending rates, it's recommended to obtain a loan from a foreign bank.

Purchase Fees: Fees total at least 9 per cent of the purchase price and include 6 per cent transfer tax, 1.5 per cent stamp duty and 1.5 per cent legal fees. There are also registration and processing fees.

Property Taxes: Transfer taxes and costs (paid by the buyer) vary with the region between 5 and 7 per cent of a property's price. There are also agent's fees of around 5 per cent (paid by the vendor), although these are negotiable.

Singapore

There are restrictions for expatriates on the purchase of property in Singapore. In order to buy property, you must be a permanent resident, make an economic contribution to Singapore or have professional qualifications or experience useful to Singapore. If you qualify, you may buy property in residential premises in buildings which have six or more storeys, or in approved condominiums, irrespective of the number of storeys. In order to buy any other type of residential property, government approval must be sought, from the Controller of Residential Property Land Dealings (Approval Unit), Shenton Way, 27-02 Temasek Tower, Singapore 068811 (☎ 323-9853).

Prices: Property is expensive owing to the lack of building land: a two-bedroom apartment costs from S$500,000 (US$300,000), a small house from S$800,000 (US$475,000).

Mortgages: Mortgages are available from local banks for residents with an adequate income.

Property Taxes: Property taxes are generally 4 per cent of the ratable value of a property and are included in your utility bills from the Public Utilities Board.

Taxes include a small charge for water for sewage maintenance and S$8 to S$20 (US$4.75 to US$11.75) for refuse collection, depending on the type of property.

Taiwan

Generally, there are few restrictions on the foreign ownership of property in Taiwan's urban areas, but foreigners cannot buy any property in restricted areas such as forested land and certain coastal regions. Most accommodation is in the form of apartments rather than houses, and is very expensive (see details below).

Prices: Accommodation in Taiwan is generally very expensive: small apartments in Taipei start at around NT$9 million (US$270,000).

Mortgages: Taiwan's banks have been very keen to offer mortgages to property buyers in recent years and the resultant intense competition has meant that in 2003 some banks started to lose money on them! Mortgages are generally available for up to 80 per cent of the property price, for periods of up to 25 years.

Purchase Fees: Fees include deed tax at 6 per cent of the purchase price and stamp duty at 0.5 per cent.

Property Taxes: Property taxes are payable annually and range from 1.38 to 5 per cent of the assessed value of the property.

Thailand

As in some of the region's other countries, foreigners cannot own land in Thailand. In order to buy any property, you need approval from the Ministry of the Interior. Foreigners are allowed to own up to 49 per cent of apartments in a block (recently increased from 40 per cent). The purchase price must be paid in full with funds brought into Thailand for this purpose. You must ask your bank for a *Tor Tor Sam*, which is an official bank document issued by your bank upon receipt of the funds from abroad and specifying that the remittance is solely for the purpose of buying a property.

Some foreigners try to circumvent the law against owning land by using a Thai nominee to purchase the land, but the legal validity of such deals is uncertain, as are the foreigner's rights over his investment. It's essential to consult a knowledgeable lawyer before considering such a purchase.

A 1999 regulation allows Thais married to foreigners to buy land, but the Thai spouse has to prove that the money used for the purchase is legally solely theirs, with no foreign claim to it. This is usually achieved by the foreign spouse signing a declaration stating that the funds belonged to the Thai spouse before the marriage. This is obviously open to abuse, but the foreigner's legal claim to the land if the marriage breaks down is at best dubious.

Prices: In the aftermath of the Asian financial crisis of the late '90s, property prices in Thailand fell dramatically, although in recent years, prices have stabilised and property is a reasonable long-term investment. In Bangkok, two or three-bedroom apartments cost from Bht2 million (US$50,000) and houses from Bht2.5 million (US$62,500), depending on their location and age.

Mortgages: Local mortgages aren't available to foreigners and funds for the entire purchase price must be imported.

Purchase Fees: Stamp duty is charged at 0.5 per cent, a business tax at 0.11 per cent, income tax at 1 to 3 per cent and transfer fees at 0.01 per cent. The vendor pays the estate agent commission of between 3 and 5 per cent. Some agents try to charge a fee to the buyer and you should beware of this.

Property Taxes: Annual property tax rates vary according to the ratable value of land, although the average rate is 12.5 per cent. Note that owner-occupied residences are exempt.

REMOVALS

After finding a home in the Far East it usually takes around two weeks to have your belongings shipped from Australasia, around four weeks to have them shipped from Europe and the east coast of America, and around six weeks from the US west coast. You should enquire about customs formalities in advance. When moving to some countries you must present an inventory (usually in the local language) of the items that you're importing to your local consulate, which must be officially stamped. In any case, it's recommended to have an inventory to hand or give one to your shipper. If you fail to follow the correct procedure, you can encounter problems and delays, and may be charged duty or fined. The relevant forms to be completed may depend on whether your home in the region will be your principal residence or a second home. Removal companies usually take care of the paperwork and ensure that the correct documents are provided and properly completed (see **Customs** on page 400).

It's wise to use a major shipping company with a good reputation. For international moves it's best to use a company that's a member of the International Federation of Furniture Removers (FIDI) or the Overseas Moving Network International (OMNI), with experience in the country you're moving to. Members of FIDI and OMNI usually subscribe to an advance payment scheme providing a guarantee: if a member company fails to fulfil its commitments to a client, the removal is completed at the agreed cost by another company or your money is refunded. Some removal companies have subsidiaries or affiliates abroad, which may be more convenient if you encounter problems or need to make a claim.

You should obtain at least three written quotations before choosing a company, as costs vary considerably. Companies should send a representative to provide a detailed quotation. Most companies will pack your belongings and provide packing cases and special containers, although this is naturally more expensive than packing them yourself. Ask a company how they pack fragile and valuable items, and whether the cost of packing cases, materials and insurance (see below) are included in a quotation. If you're doing your own packing, most shipping companies will provide packing crates and boxes. Shipments are charged by volume, e.g. the square metre in Europe and the square foot in North America. If you're flexible about the delivery date, shipping companies will quote a lower fee based on a 'part load', where the cost is shared with other deliveries. This can result in savings of 50 per cent or more compared with an individual delivery. Whether you have an individual or shared delivery, obtain the maximum transit period in writing, or you may have to wait months for delivery!

Be sure to fully insure your belongings during removal with a well-established insurance company. Don't insure with a shipping company that carries its own insurance, as it may fight every penny of a claim. Insurance premiums are usually 1 to 2 per cent of the declared value of your goods, depending on the type of cover chosen. It's prudent to make a photographic or video record of valuables for insurance purposes. Most insurance policies cover for 'all risks' on a replacement value basis. Note that china, glass and other breakables can usually only be included in an all risks policy when they're packed by the shipping company. Insurance usually covers total loss or loss of a particular crate only, rather than individual items (unless they were packed by the shipping company). If there are any breakages or damaged items, they should be noted and listed before you sign the delivery bill (although it's obviously impractical to check everything on delivery). If you need to make a claim, be sure to read the small print, as some companies require clients to make a claim within a few days, although seven is usual. Send a claim by registered post. Some insurance companies apply an excess (deductible) of around 1 per cent of the total shipment value when assessing claims.

After considering the shipping costs to the Far East, many people decide to ship only selected items of furniture and personal effects, and buy new furniture locally.

If you're unable to ship your belongings directly to the region, most shipping companies will put them into storage and some allow a limited free storage period prior to shipment, e.g. 14 days. If you need to put your household effects into storage, it's imperative to have them fully insured, as warehouses have been known to burn down! Make a complete list of everything to be moved and give a copy to the shipping company. Don't include anything illegal (e.g. guns, bombs, drugs or pornographic videos) with your belongings, as customs checks can be rigorous and penalties severe.

Provide the shipping company with detailed instructions how to find your home from the nearest motorway or main road and a telephone number where you can be contacted. If your new home has poor or impossible access for a large truck, you should inform the shipping company (the ground must also be firm enough to support a heavy vehicle). Note also that if furniture needs to be taken in through an upstairs window, you may need to pay extra. Finally, bear in mind when moving home that everything that can go wrong often does, so you should allow plenty of time and try not to arrange your move from your old home on the same day as the new owner is moving in. That's just asking for fate to intervene! See also the **Checklists** on page 417.

INVENTORY

One of the most important tasks to perform after moving into a new home is to make an inventory of the fixtures and fittings and, if applicable, the furniture and furnishings. When you've purchased a property, you should check that the previous owner hasn't absconded with any fixtures and fittings that were included in the price or anything that you specifically paid for, e.g. carpets, light fittings, curtains, furniture, kitchen cupboards and appliances, garden ornaments, plants or doors. It's common to do a final check or inventory when buying a new property, which is usually done a few weeks before completion.

When moving into a long-term rental property, it's necessary to complete an inventory of its contents and a report on its condition. This includes the condition of fixtures and fittings, the state of furniture and furnishings, the cleanliness and state of the decoration, and anything that's damaged, missing or in need of repair. An inventory should be provided by your landlord or agent and may include every single item in a furnished property, down to the number of teaspoons. The inventory check should be carried out in your presence. If an inventory isn't provided, you should insist on one being prepared and annexed to the lease. If you find a serious fault after signing the inventory, send a registered letter to your landlord and ask for it to be attached to the inventory.

An inventory should be drawn up both when moving in and when vacating a rented property. If the two don't correspond, you must make good any damages or deficiencies or the landlord can do so and deduct the cost from your deposit. Although most landlords are honest, some will do almost anything to avoid repaying a deposit. (In some countries, you're unlikely to get your deposit back anyway, but that's another matter!) Note the reading on your utility meters (e.g. electricity, gas and water) and check that you aren't overcharged on your first bill. The meters should be read by utility companies before you move in, although you may need to organise it yourself.

It's recommended to obtain written instructions from the landlord or previous owner concerning the operation of appliances, heating and air-conditioning systems, maintenance of grounds, gardens and lawns, care of special surfaces such as wooden, marble or tiled floors, and the names of reliable local maintenance men who know a property and its quirks. Check with your town hall the local regulations regarding rubbish collection, recycling and on-road parking, etc..

HOME SECURITY

When moving into a new home it's often wise to replace the locks (or lock barrels) as soon as possible, as you have no idea how many keys are in circulation for the existing locks. This is true even for new homes, as builders often give keys to sub-contractors. If not already fitted, it's best to fit high security (double cylinder or dead bolt) locks. Modern properties may be fitted with high security locks that are individually numbered. Extra keys for these locks cannot be cut at a local hardware store and you need to obtain details from the previous owner or your landlord. Many modern developments have security gates and caretakers.

In areas with a high risk of theft (e.g. most major cities and coastal resorts), your insurance company may insist on extra security measures such as two locks on external doors, internal locking shutters, security bars on windows below a certain height from the ground, and grilles on patio doors. External doors should be of the armoured variety with a steel rod locking mechanism. An insurance policy may specify that all forms of protection must be employed when a property is unoccupied and if security precautions aren't adhered to a claim may be reduced by half. It's usually necessary to have a safe for any insured valuables, which must be approved by your insurance company.

You may wish to have a security alarm fitted, which is usually the best way to deter thieves and may also reduce your household insurance. It should include all external doors and windows, internal infra-red security beams, and may also include a coded entry keypad (which can be frequently changed and is useful for clients if you let a home) and 24-hour monitoring (with some systems it's possible to monitor properties remotely from another country via a computer). With a monitored system, a signal is sent automatically to a 24-hour monitoring station. The duty monitor will telephone to check whether it's a genuine alarm (a number or password must be given) and if he cannot contact you someone will be sent to investigate.

You can deter thieves by ensuring that your house is well lit and not conspicuously unoccupied. External security 'motion detector' lights (that switch on automatically when someone approaches), random timed switches for internal lights, radios and televisions, dummy security cameras, and tapes that play barking dogs (etc.) triggered by a light or heat detector may all help deter burglars. In remote areas it's common for owners to fit two or three locks on external doors, alarm systems, grilles on doors and windows, window locks, security shutters and a safe for valuables. The advantage of grilles is that they allow you to leave windows open without inviting criminals in (unless they're very slim).

You can fit UPVC (toughened clear plastic) security windows and doors, which can survive an attack with a sledgehammer without damage, and external steel security blinds (which can be electrically operated), although these are expensive. A dog can be useful to deter intruders, although he should be kept inside where he cannot be given poisoned food. Irrespective of whether you actually have a dog, a warning sign with a picture of a fierce dog may act as a deterrent. You should have the front door of an apartment fitted with a spy-hole and chain so that you can check the identity of a visitor before opening the door. Remember, prevention is better than cure as stolen property is rarely recovered.

Holiday homes are particularly vulnerable to thieves and in some areas they're regularly ransacked. No matter how secure your door and window locks, a thief can usually obtain entry if he is sufficiently determined, often by simply smashing a window or even breaking in through the roof or by knocking a hole in a wall! In isolated areas, thieves can strip a house bare at their leisure and an unmonitored alarm won't be a deterrent if there's nobody around to hear it. If you have a holiday home in the Far East, it isn't wise to leave anything of real value (monetary or sentimental) there. When closing a property for an extended period, you should ensure that everything is switched off and that it's secure.

If you vacate your home for an extended period, it may be obligatory to notify your caretaker, landlord or insurance company, and to leave a key with the caretaker or landlord in case of emergencies. If you have a robbery, you should report it immediately to your local police station, where you must make a statement. You will receive a copy, which is required by your insurance company if you make a claim.

Another important aspect of home security is ensuring that you have early warning of a fire, which is easily done by installing smoke detectors. Battery-operated smoke detectors can be purchased for around US$10, which should be tested periodically to ensure that the batteries aren't exhausted. You can also fit an electric-powered gas detector that activates an alarm when a gas leak is detected.

LETTING YOUR PRINCIPAL HOME

Many people planning to live in the Far East for a limited period let their home while they're away, which helps to pay the mortgage and running costs and ensures that your home isn't neglected and left empty. The costs incurred when letting a home are usually tax deductible and there may also be other tax advantages such as reduced capital gains tax and being able to offset mortgage interest against income tax. You can either let your home short term and use it yourself for holidays, or do as most people do when going abroad for a number of years, let it long-term. However, you need to be careful with contracts, as in some countries it can be difficult to evict a long-term tenant if they refuse to vacate your home, which is why some people stick to short-term lets. Short-term lets are more lucrative if your home is situated in a major city or resort, but it will need to stand up to a lot more wear and tear.

You will need a property management company that specialises in short or long-term letting. You can let a property yourself, although this is generally recommended only if you're letting it to a close friend or relative. The alternative is to ask a reliable friend or relative to handle the letting. Before letting an apartment you must check that letting is permitted. Short-term lets may be prohibited and you may also need to notify the building's administrator, your mortgage lender and your insurance company if a property is let. **Note that you (or your agent) should never finalise letting agreements via the Internet and should always interview tenants face to face, and obtain personal, professional and financial references.**

If you plan to engage a management company and wish to have a tenant as soon as possible after your departure, you will need to make arrangements two or three months in advance. A management company will charge commission based on a percentage of the gross rental income. This is usually around 10 to 15 per cent for letting and collection, and a further 5 to 10 per cent for management services. Take care when selecting a company and ensure that your income is kept in a separate bonded (escrow) account and paid regularly. It's essential to employ an efficient, reliable and honest company, preferably long-established. Ask for names of satisfied customers and check with them. The rent is usually set in consultation with the management company and based on existing rents in the area for similar properties. It's usually non-negotiable, although the terms of the lease are generally negotiable. The contract should be checked by your lawyer or solicitor.

A management company's services should include the collection and payment of rent, arranging routine maintenance and essential repairs to the building and garden, notifying insurance companies (where applicable) and obtaining approval for essential repairs, regular inspections, paying taxes (e.g. property tax) and insurance premiums (if not done by the owner), and forwarding post. Give the management company a telephone or fax number or an email address where you can be contacted abroad, so that you can approve major repairs or resolve other matters. If you have your own maintenance person or company, you should give their names to the management company, plus details of anything that's under warranty and the manufacturer's name and model numbers of major systems and appliances (e.g. heating and cooling systems, cooker, refrigerator and freezer).

The landlord is usually responsible for maintaining the structure, major installations and appliances such as the heating and cooling system, cooker, washing machine, refrigerator and freezer. Tenants are usually responsible for any damage other than normal wear and tear to fixtures and fittings, furniture and decoration, and for maintaining the garden. The landlord or agent should check the condition and state of repair of a property at regular intervals, and also make periodic checks when a property is empty (e.g. between lets) to ensure that it's secure and that everything is in order.

If you let a property, it's recommended to replace expensive furniture and furnishings and remove valuable belongings. Leave them with friends or relatives or put them into storage, and ensure they're insured for their full value with a reputable insurance company (preferably not with the storage company). When furnishing a property that you plan to let, you should choose dark, hard-wearing carpets that won't show stains, and buy durable furniture and furnishings. Simple, inexpensive furniture is best in a modest home, as it will need to stand up to hard wear. You must also decide whether you wish to let to families with young children (which may result in damage to expensive contents and decor) or pets, and whether you wish to allow sharers or smokers. Many people who are letting a luxury home insist on professional tenants or let only to companies. Note that letting to someone with diplomatic immunity can be risky, as they would be outside the jurisdiction of the local courts.

Other points to bear in mind are deposits (how much and who will hold them – usually a management company if you have one), and building and contents insurance. You will need a special contents insurance policy if you're letting (or leaving a property empty) and may need to obtain a policy from an insurance company that specialises in letting. Tenants should have insurance against damage caused to the building and its contents, and for their own belongings. Draw up an inventory of all contents and fixtures and fittings, and append it to the lease (a management company will usually arrange this for you). This must be checked and agreed by the tenants on moving in and when vacating the property.

Note that landlords must adhere to strict regulations in many countries, particularly regarding fire and safety matters, e.g. fire-resistant furniture, approved gas installations, fire and gas alarms and fire-fighting apparatus (e.g. fire extinguishers). It may be necessary to have a home inspected by an official inspector and to display a certificate confirming this in a prominent position in your home. If your principal home is in the UK, refer to the recently published *Buying, Selling & Letting Property* (Survival Books).

4.

HEALTH

One of the most important aspects of living in the Far East (or anywhere for that matter) is maintaining good health. The quality of health care and health care facilities vary considerably from country to country and there's a stark contrast between public and private health facilities in many countries. The provision of fully-equipped hospitals is rare in some Far Eastern countries (in some countries there's only one major general hospital, in the capital city), and nursing care and post-hospital assistance are often well below what most westerners take for granted. Health facilities in remote areas, even in developed countries, are often inadequate, and if you have a serious accident or need emergency hospital treatment in some countries, you will need to be evacuated to the nearest major city or possibly to another country.

The information in this chapter deals only with western-style hospitals and medical facilities in the Far East. But many of the countries also offer traditional treatments. Western science has often been sceptical or even dismissive of the effectiveness of non-western ways of treating illness. Yet Chinese medicine, for example, has been the main source of treatment for thousands of years in a country which now has a fifth of the world's population.

There have been recent controversies and scandals in some European countries about Chinese medicine, particularly the safety of certain treatments following the discovery that some contain dangerous substances like mercury and arsenic. For further information, see the website of the American Association of Oriental Medicine (💻 www.aaom.org), which has a list of products that have been found to be contaminated or to contain unsafe ingredients. For a useful introduction to Chinese medicine in general, see the website 💻 www.ahealthyme.com/article/primer/100026128, including a discussion about its safety, in the light of recent publicity.

Public Health Services

Some Far Eastern countries have a public health service providing free or low cost health care for those who contribute to social security, including their families. If you don't qualify for health care under a public health service, it's essential to have private health insurance (see page 143) – in fact it may be impossible to obtain a residence permit without it. Private health insurance is often recommended in any case, due to the shortcomings of public health services and long waiting lists in some countries. Visitors should have travel insurance (see page 178) if they aren't covered by a reciprocal health care agreement (see page 143). The World Health Organisation (💻 www.who.int) publishes regular surveys in which it rates countries according to their health care (of the territories considered here, only Japan and Singapore are among the current top ten).

Retirees

Health (and health insurance) is an important issue for those retiring abroad, many of whom are ill-prepared for old age and the possibility of health problems. There's a dearth of welfare and home-nursing services for the elderly in some Far Eastern countries, either state or private, and many foreigners who can no longer care for themselves are forced to return to their home countries. In most countries there are few state residential nursing homes and no hospices for the terminally ill, although many countries offer private sheltered homes and retirement developments for those who can afford them. Provision for disabled travellers and wheelchair access to buildings and public transport is also poor in some of the region's countries.

PRE-DEPARTURE CHECK

It's recommended to have a complete health check before going to live in the Far East, particularly if you have a record of poor health or are elderly. In many countries, children need to be immunised against a range of diseases in order to attend school. If you're already taking regular medication, you should note that brand names for drugs and medicines vary from country to country, and you should ask your doctor for the generic name. If you wish to match medication prescribed abroad, you will need a current prescription with the medication's trade name, the manufacturer's name, the chemical name and the dosage. Most medicines have an equivalent in other countries, although particular brands may be difficult or impossible to obtain.

It's possible to have medication sent from abroad and no import duty or tax is usually payable. If you will be living in the Far East for a limited period, you should take sufficient medicines to cover your stay or until you can find a source locally or have them sent from abroad. **Note, however, that it's illegal to import certain medicines into some countries, which may even include such things as Codeine!** In an emergency a local doctor will write a prescription that can be filled at a local pharmacy or a hospital may refill a prescription from its own pharmacy. It's also wise to take some of your favourite non-prescription medicines (e.g. aspirins, cold and flu remedies, lotions and creams), as they may be difficult or impossible to obtain in the region or may be much more expensive. If applicable, take a spare pair of spectacles, contact lenses, dentures or a hearing aid, plus a comprehensive first-aid kit. If you have any serious medical problems, you should make a note of the relevant details, including the treatment you were given with dates, and any medicines you're taking. You should also note your blood group and any medicines that you're allergic to.

Medic-Alert

If you have an existing medical problem that cannot easily be seen or recognised, e.g. a heart condition, diabetes, a severe allergy (e.g. penicillin) or epilepsy, or you have a rare blood group, you may wish to join Medic-Alert. Medic-Alert members wear an internationally recognised identification bracelet or necklace, on the back of which is engraved details of your medical condition, your membership number and a 24-hour emergency phone number. When you're unable to speak for yourself, doctors, police or paramedics can obtain immediate, vital medical information from anywhere in the world by telephoning this number. Medic-Alert is a non-profit registered charity and members pay for the cost of the bracelet or necklace (from around GB£30) plus an annual fee of GB£10. For more information contact the Medic-Alert Foundation, 1 Bridge Wharf, 156 Caledonian Road, London N1 9UU, UK (☎ 020-7833 3034, 🖳 www.medicalert. org.uk) or (🖳 www.medicalert.ca, Canada).

Further Information

There are many Internet sites where medical advice is available, such as the British sites Healthworks (🖳 www.healthworks.co.uk), Net Doctor (🖳 www. netdoctor.co.uk) and Patient (🖳 www.patient.co.uk) and the American Combined Health Information Database (🖳 http://chid.nih.gov), Healthfinder (🖳 www.health finder.gov) and Medline plus (🖳 www.medlineplus.gov). Bear in mind, however, that published information, although usually approved or written by medical experts, shouldn't be used as a substitute for consulting a doctor and that Internet 'doctors' and medical advice must be used with extreme caution (many are 'cyber quacks').

Among the many useful health guides are the British Medical Association's *Complete Family Health Guide* (Dorling Kindersley), the *Merck Manual of Medical Information: Home Edition* (Merck), *International Travel and Health 2003* (World Health Organization), the *Rough Guide to Travel Health* by Dr. Nick Jones, *Travel with Children* by Mike Wheeler (Lonely Planet), *The ABC of Healthy Travel* (British Medical Journal), *Traveller's Health* by Dr. R. Dawood (OUP) and the *First Aid Handbook* (National Safety Council).

COMMON HEALTH PROBLEMS

The prevalence and seriousness of health risks and conditions in individual countries in the Far East are constantly changing and any information and advice given here is necessarily provisional. The dangers of disease and infection are considerably greater in some countries and every precaution should be taken. Current health risks in individual countries are listed in the **Health By Country** section beginning on page 146. The following general remarks apply to the entire region.

Common health problems experienced by foreigners in the Far East include sunburn and sunstroke, stomach and bowel problems, which are usually due to the change of diet and, more often, water but can also be caused by poor hygiene, and various problems related to excessive alcohol consumption (there's a high incidence of alcoholism among expatriates in some countries). All food must be thoroughly washed and tap water boiled in some countries.

If you aren't used to the hot sun, you should limit your exposure and avoid it altogether during the hottest part of the day, wear protective clothing (including a hat) and use a sun block. Too much sun and too little protection will dry your skin and cause premature ageing, to say nothing of the dangers of skin cancer. Care should also be taken to replace the natural oils lost from too many hours in the sun, and the elderly should take particular care not to exert themselves during hot weather.

Health problems are also caused or exacerbated by the high level of air pollution in some countries (particularly in major cities in China), which will have a particularly detrimental effect on asthma sufferers and others with respiratory problems.

Dengue Fever & Schistosomiasis: Dengue fever epidemics are common in the region, especially in south China and Taiwan, and schistosomiasis (also known as bilharzia) is found in China, Indonesia and the Philippines, particularly the last.

Diarrhoea: Various forms of diarrhoea are common throughout the region, some of them dangerous. Dysentry, giardiasis, and typhoid are widespread in ten of the 11 territories covered in this book, and cholera is found in some regions; the risks are low in Japan.

Hepatitis: Hepatitis A and B are common throughout the region (vaccinations are recommended), as are a range of worm infections. Hepatitis C and E flare up from time to time.

Japanese Encephalitis: The risk from Japanese encephalitis (a virus spread by mosquitoes) is low but it's still found in every country covered in this book and if you plan to stay in a rural area, a vaccination is recommended.

Malaria: Malaria is found in parts of south China, Hong Kong, Indonesia, Korea, Malaysia, the Philippines and Thailand. Hong Kong and Korea are often portrayed as malaria-free, but a risk exists in small pockets of both. **Note also that you may be told that the risk of malaria exists only in rural areas; this isn't true and there's also a risk in urban areas.**

Rabies: Japan and Taiwan are currently rabies-free, but the disease is found throughout the rest of the Far East.

Other Diseases: In parts of the Far East there are also significant risks of illness or death from AIDS, tetanus, tuberculosis and yellow fever, which are widespread in some countries. Although the SARS virus appears to have disappeared, it's possible that there will be further outbreaks, and the avine (bird) flu 'epidemic' that broke out in several parts of the region in early 2004 could prove a significant danger. Check the current situation with a reliable source (see **Further Information** below and **Appendix C**).

Vaccinations: It's recommended that childhood vaccinations – particularly diphtheria, polio, tetanus and tuberculosis – are current. The following vaccinations are recommended for the territories specified **in addition to** any mentioned in the **Health By Country** section beginning on page 146 and should be arranged at least three months before travelling to the region:

- **Diphtheria** – for every country except Japan;
- **Hepatitis A** – for every country except Japan;
- **Hepatitis B** – for every country;
- **Japanese Encephalitis** – for every country except Hong Kong and Singapore;
- **Rabies** – for every country, except Hong Kong, Japan, Singapore and Taiwan;
- **Tuberculosis** – for every country except Japan;
- **Typhoid** – for every country except Japan.

For a worldwide vaccination guide, visit ▣ www.tmvc.com.au/info10.html.

General Advice

The following general health advice applies throughout the Far East:

- Wash your hands frequently with soap and water.
- Avoid tap water, water from drinking fountains and ice. Drink only boiled or bottled water.
- Eat only thoroughly cooked food and fruit and vegetables that you've peeled yourself.
- To lessen the risk of being bitten by insects, wear a long-sleeved shirt and trousers if possible when outside, particularly at night; use an insect repellent containing DEET (diethylmethyltoluamide), in 30 to 35 per cent strength for adults and 6 to 10 per cent for children; and use a mosquito net impregnated with permethrin (an insecticide) over your bed.
- To avoid fungal and parasitic infections, don't go barefoot and keep feet clean and dry.
- Don't eat street vendor food.
- Always use latex condoms when having sex with a new partner.

Further Information: Consult the World Health Organisation website (▣ www. who.int) in the months preceding your trip to the Far East to check the current situation in the country you're travelling to and which vaccinations and medicines are either recommended or compulsory in order to gain entry to the particular country. The site provides a wealth of information for travellers and those moving abroad, including health topics, communicable/infectious diseases, disease outbreak news, vaccines, environment and health statistics. Other useful websites include the Medical Advisory Service for Travellers Abroad (▣ www.masta.org), Medicine Planet (▣ www.travelhealth.com), and the British Government's Health Advice for Travellers (▣ www.doh. gov.uk/traveladvice/index.htm); a free booklet with the same name is available. Where applicable, specific health warnings are included in the **Health By Country** section starting on page 146.

EMERGENCIES

Keep a record of the telephone numbers of your doctor, local hospital and clinic, ambulance service, dentist and other emergency services (fire, police) next to your telephone. In many countries, emergency numbers are displayed at the front of telephone directories. If you're unsure who to call, dial the emergency number and you will be put in touch with the relevant service. The action to take in a medical emergency depends on the degree of urgency and may be one of the following:

- In a life-threatening emergency, such as a heart attack or serious accident, call the free emergency number and request an ambulance. State clearly where you're calling from and the nature of the emergency, and give your name and the number of the telephone you're calling from. Don't hang up until the operator tells you to. In many countries, ambulances are equipped with cardiac equipment and 'cardiomobiles' may be provided for emergency heart cases. There's also an emergency helicopter ambulance service in many countries, which may be privately operated with membership by subscription.

- If you're physically able, you can go to a hospital emergency or casualty department. All foreigners in some countries have the right to be treated free of charge in an emergency, irrespective of whether they have insurance.

- If you're unable to visit your doctor's surgery, your doctor may visit you at home provided you call him during surgery hours. If he is away, his office will usually give you the name and number of a substitute doctor on call. Local newspapers usually list duty chemists (pharmacies) – in major cities some may be open 24 hours per day.

- If you need urgent medical treatment outside surgery hours and cannot get to your nearest casualty department, there may be a local duty doctor service or emergency telephone helpline. Provided you call in response to a genuine emergency, you won't usually be charged for the use of the emergency services.

DOCTORS

The training proficiency and availability of doctors varies considerably according to the country and the city or region where you live. Those who live in a major city in a developed country have a far wider choice of practitioners (many English-speaking) than those living in rural areas in a developing country, where the nearest doctor may be hundreds of kilometres away. Even in developed countries, the quality and choice of doctors in remote areas is often poor, and you may be faced with a long journey to the nearest doctor's surgery or hospital. It's difficult to find English-speaking doctors in some Far Eastern countries, particularly some of the developing countries, and it's essential to have a working knowledge of the local language, which in an emergency could save your life. Embassies and consulates may keep lists of doctors and specialists in their area who speak English and other languages, and your employer, colleagues or neighbours may be able to recommend someone. General practitioners or family doctors are also listed in the yellow pages in most countries.

If you wish to take advantage of a free or subsidised public health service, one of the first things to do after arrival in a country is to register at the nearest office. When registering, you're required to choose a family doctor with a social security agreement and, if you have young children, possibly also a paediatrician. Local health authorities provide you with a list of doctors with whom you can register and you can choose anyone who's willing to accept you (although there may be a requirement to register with a doctor within a certain distance of your home). Each adult member of a family is usually issued with a membership number and card, which you must take with you when visiting a doctor or other health practitioner. School-age children are usually listed on their mother's card. If you want a doctor to visit you at home, you must telephone during surgery hours. House calls made by public health service doctors are usually free during normal working hours.

If you have private health insurance, you can usually see a private doctor, specialist or consultant at any time, although (depending on your level of insurance) you may need to pay for their services. Note that in many Far Eastern countries you're expected to settle the bill (usually in cash, although some doctors accept credit cards) immediately after treatment, even if you have health insurance, and you may need to prove that you can pay before any treatment is given. It's important to keep all medical receipts in some countries, which can be offset against your income tax bill.

There are certain health requirements for employees and schoolchildren in some countries. Employees who work in the food industry (bars, restaurants, food shops, factories producing food products, etc.) may need to obtain a health record book from the local public hygiene office and undergo an annual medical examination. Schoolchildren may need a health book in which compulsory immunisations are recorded and secondary school students may need to provide a medical certificate or undergo a medical examination before being allowed to participate in certain sports activities.

HOSPITALS & CLINICS

All cities and large towns have at least one clinic or hospital, usually indicated by the international sign of a red 'H' on a white background or the older white 'H' on a blue background. Public (state) hospitals may include community hospitals, district hospitals, teaching hospitals and university hospitals (or a combination of these). Major hospitals or general hospitals may be designated teaching hospitals, which combine treatment with medical training and research work, and are staffed and equipped to the highest standards.

Some hospitals and most clinics specialise in particular fields of medicine, such as obstetrics and surgery, rather than being full-service hospitals. In addition there may be specialist hospitals for children, the mentally ill and disabled, the elderly and infirm, and for the treatment of specific complaints or illnesses. There are also dental hospitals in many countries. Public hospitals may have a 24-hour accident, casualty or emergency department that provides treatment for medical emergencies and minor accidents, although this may apply only to major hospitals. In some countries there are also walk-in clinics (possibly 24-hour) where you can be treated on the spot for minor emergencies. Except in emergencies, you're normally admitted or referred to a hospital or clinic for treatment only after consultation with a doctor. Note that the best public hospitals often have long waiting lists.

In addition to public hospitals, there are usually private hospitals and clinics in major cities and resort areas in many countries, which may include American, British and international hospitals. There's a wide discrepancy between public and private hospital facilities (e.g. medical equipment, private rooms, catering, etc.) in many countries in the Far East, although in the more developed countries there's generally little difference between the quality of medical treatment (e.g. surgery). The best hospitals are invariably found in the wealthiest suburbs of major cities and large towns.

Your choice of hospital and specialist usually depends on whether you choose a public or private hospital and the treatment required. If you're treated in a public hospital under a state's public health service, you must usually be treated or operated on by the medical specialist on duty. If you request the services of a particular specialist or wish to avoid a long waiting list for an operation, you must usually pay the full cost of treatment. If you aren't covered by the public health service (if there is one), you may be required to pay before you receive treatment, irrespective of whether you have private health insurance. However, international health insurance companies usually have arrangements with certain hospitals and pay bills directly. Costs for private operations vary enormously according to the reputation of the specialists involved and the fees they command. Sometimes it's cheaper to have an operation abroad, e.g. in a neighbouring country. You should check the local hospital facilities in advance and, if necessary, ensure that your health insurance covers you for medical evacuation.

Basic accommodation in public hospitals normally consists of shared rooms, although single bedrooms are usually available with an en suite bathroom for a supplement or for private patients. In some countries, patients in public hospitals must bring everything they need with them, including towels, toiletries, pyjamas or night-dresses and dressing gowns, although meals are provided free of charge. Note, however, that the food may be inedible and you may need some outside assistance (food parcels) if you're to survive a stay! You may also need to get your family or friends to attend to your needs, as nursing services are sparse or non-existent in public hospitals in some countries.

In contrast, in private clinics and hospitals, accommodation is generally on a par with a luxury hotel, with air-conditioned single rooms, TV and telephone, gourmet food and an extra bed for a relative if required. Public hospitals usually have restricted visiting hours of around two or three hours per day, while private hospitals and clinics may have no restrictions.

CHILDREN'S HEALTH

If you qualify for treatment under a public health service, your children may be treated by your family doctor or you may be assigned a paediatrician, who generally treats children up to the age of around 14. If you're a private patient, you can generally see any doctor or specialist you wish. In many countries, children must have a vaccination record card and are required to have vaccinations against various diseases such as diphtheria and tetanus (DT), polio and hepatitis B. Vaccinations are usually provided free of charge and may be compulsory. Although they may not be mandatory, vaccinations against whooping cough, measles, mumps, German measles and HIB (which can cause serious illnesses such as meningitis) are also recommended. A whooping cough vaccination may be administered in combination with the diphtheria and tetanus vaccinations (called DTP). It's important to ensure that you keep all vaccinations up to date. When going to live abroad, you should take proof of immunisations with you, with official translations if necessary.

DENTISTS

The quality of dental treatment and its cost varies considerably from country to country. Many people are sceptical about the quality of foreign dentists and prefer to have treatment in their home country. In some Far Eastern countries, few dentists speak English, which can be an added problem. However, your country's local embassy or consulate may keep a list of English-speaking dentists in your area, or your employer, colleagues or neighbours may be able to recommend a local dentist. Dentists are also listed in local telephone directories and the yellow pages, although only names and addresses may be listed and information such as specialities and surgery hours may not be provided.

There are public health dental services in some countries, although the treatment provided is usually basic and may consist only of check-ups and emergency treatment. Note also that private dentists in some countries have a better reputation than those working for a public health service, although many dentists treat both public and private patients. You need to be wary of unnecessary treatment, which is a common practice in some countries ('drill for profit'!). If you have regular check-ups and usually have little or no treatment, you should be suspicious if a new dentist suggests you need a lot of fillings or extractions. In this case you should obtain a second opinion before going ahead (note, however, that two dentists rarely agree on exactly the same treatment).

Always try to obtain an accurate (preferably) written quotation before beginning a course of treatment, although few dentists will quote an exact fee for work, and often a 'rough estimate' is only a fraction of the final bill. For extensive work, such as root canal treatment, or cosmetic treatment bills can be astronomical. As with private doctors, it's usual to pay a dentist before a course of treatment begins in most countries. If your family requires expensive dental treatment, e.g. crowns, bridges, braces or false teeth, it's worthwhile checking whether treatment is cheaper abroad, e.g. in your home country.

OPTICIANS

As with other medical practitioners abroad, it isn't necessary to register with an optician or optometrist. You simply make an appointment with the practitioner of your choice, although it's wise to ask your friends, colleagues or neighbours if they can recommend someone. Opticians are listed in the yellow pages. The eye care business is competitive in most Far Eastern countries and prices for spectacles and contact lenses aren't controlled, so it's wise to shop around and compare costs. There are large optical chains in some countries, where spectacles can be made on the spot or within 24 hours, although if you have your prescription you can sometimes buy ready-made reading spectacles from pharmacies. Always obtain an estimate for contact lenses and ask about extra charges for fittings, adjustments, lens-care kits and follow-up visits.

To be treated under a public health service, it may be necessary to have your eyes examined by an eye specialist or oculist, for which you generally need to obtain a referral from your family doctor. An oculist can make a more thorough test of your eyesight than an optician and is able to test for certain diseases that can be diagnosed from eye abnormalities, e.g. diabetes and some types of cancer. If glasses are necessary, he will write a prescription that you can take to an optician or spectacle maker.

It's wise to have your eyes tested before going to the Far East and to take a spare pair of spectacles and/or contact lenses with you. You should also bring a copy of your prescription in case you need to obtain replacement spectacles or contact lenses urgently.

SEXUALLY-TRANSMITTED DISEASES

The spread of sexually-transmitted diseases, particularly AIDS, has caused a lot of anxiety throughout the Far East, particularly in regions where sex tourism thrives. However, AIDS isn't as widespread as in Africa, where up to half the population is infected in some countries. It's necessary to be extremely careful when choosing medical practitioners (such as doctors and dentists) in countries with high rates of infection and to use only clinics and hospitals approved by your local embassy or consulate. Condoms can be purchased from pharmacies, family planning clinics and vending machines in most countries.

Free (or low-cost) and anonymous testing for HIV, which is usually conducted at least one month after patients have been at risk, is available in most Far Eastern countries at special clinics or departments of infectious diseases in public hospitals and other public health centres. A doctor's referral isn't usually required. In most countries there are free telephone help lines where you can obtain confidential advice, although if you test positive your name may be reported to the local health authorities. Note that some countries require testing for HIV/AIDS for certain immigrants and residents (see **Health Risks** in the **Health By Country** section starting on page 146). For the testing and treatment of other contagious diseases (e.g. hepatitis B and C, syphilis and gonorrhoea), it may be necessary to be referred by your family doctor, although there are free and confidential clinics in many countries.

BIRTHS & DEATHS

Births and deaths in the Far East must be registered within a certain time, e.g. seven days, at the local births and deaths registry office of the town where they take place. Registration applies to everyone irrespective of their nationality and whether they're residents or visitors. In the case of births, registration is usually carried out by the hospital or clinic where a child is born. However, if you give birth at home, you need to complete the registration yourself. A local birth certificate is usually issued automatically. Undertakers normally register deaths.

In the event of a death, all interested parties must be notified. If a death takes place in a hospital, the attending doctor will complete a certificate stating the cause of death; you should make several copies of this, as they will be required by banks and other institutions. If death occurs at home, you should call your family doctor or the local police. If a death occurs in suspicious circumstances, a post mortem (autopsy) must usually be performed.

Dying abroad can be very expensive and is best avoided if at all possible. Burial grounds are extremely limited in some countries, where it may be necessary to be buried in a tomb in a wall or in a communal burial ground, which is recycled after five or ten years and used for new burials. Cremation is possible in many countries, although you may be unable to keep the ashes at home or dispose of them as you wish, e.g. by scattering them at sea or on the pitch of the deceased's favourite football club. The body of a deceased person can usually be shipped to another country for burial. You will need to provide the funeral agent with the documents relating to the death and the identity of the deceased, so that he can obtain the necessary permits. Your local embassy may be able to help arrange this.

HEALTH INSURANCE

One of the most important aspects of living in the Far East is having adequate health insurance, as the cost of being uninsured or under-insured can be astronomical and could even prove fatal! **The cost of private health insurance can be prohibitively expensive in some countries and if you have a poor health record you may be unable to obtain insurance for an affordable premium.** Long-stay visitors (e.g. six months or more) and residents should have travel or long-stay health insurance or an international health policy. If your stay in the region will be limited, you may be covered by a reciprocal agreement between your home country and the country where you will be living (see page 143).

The majority of residents in some Far Eastern countries are covered for health treatment under a public health service or compulsory private health insurance schemes. Many countries provide emergency treatment for visitors, sometimes under reciprocal agreements, although these don't apply to citizens of some countries, e.g. the US. Visitors spending short periods in the region should have travel health insurance (see page 178) if they aren't covered by a reciprocal agreement or an international health policy.

If you will be living in the Far East permanently and don't qualify for medical treatment under a public health service, it's usually imperative that you have private health insurance (unless you have a very large bank balance), which is compulsory in many countries. In countries with a public health service, those who can afford it often take out complementary private health insurance, which provides a wider choice of medical practitioners and hospitals and frees you from inadequate public health services, waiting lists and other restrictions. Private insurance may also allow you to choose an English-speaking doctor or a hospital where staff speak English or other languages.

A health insurance policy should, if possible, cover you for all essential health care whatever the reason, including accidents (e.g. sports accidents) and injuries, whether they occur at your home, place of work or while travelling. Policies offered in different countries vary considerably in the extent of cover, limitations and restrictions, premiums, and the free choice of doctors, specialists and hospitals. Don't take anything for granted, but check in advance.

Note that insurance companies in some countries can (and will) cancel a policy at the end of the insurance period if you have a serious illness with constant high expenses, and some companies automatically cancel a policy when you reach a certain age, e.g. 65 or 70. You should avoid such a policy like the plague, as to take out a new policy at the age of 65 or older for a reasonable premium is difficult or impossible in some countries.

Reciprocal Health Agreements

Some people are covered by reciprocal health agreements when visiting or living in the Far East, although this may apply in emergencies only and there are currently no reciprocal agreements with Australia or the US and the only UK agreement is with the Philippines. (British visitors planning to travel abroad can obtain information about reciprocal health treatment from the Department of Social Security, Overseas Branch, Newcastle-upon-Tyne, NE98 1YX, UK.)

Even where a reciprocal agreement exists, full payment (possibly in cash) must usually be made in advance for treatment received abroad, although you will be reimbursed on your return home. **Note, however, that you can still receive a large bill, as your local health authority usually assumes only a percentage of the cost.** Reimbursement is based on the cost of comparable treatment in your home country.

International Policies

If you do a lot of travelling, it's recommended to have an international health policy. These generally offer wider cover than local policies. Most international health policies include repatriation or evacuation (although it may be optional), which may be an important consideration if you need treatment that's unavailable locally but is available in your home or another country. Repatriation may also include shipment (by air) of the body of someone who dies abroad to his home country for burial. Some companies offer policies for different areas, e.g. South-east Asia, worldwide excluding North America, and worldwide including North America. A policy may offer full cover anywhere within South-east Asia and limited cover in North America and certain other countries. Note that an international policy also allows you to choose to have non-urgent medical treatment in another country. Most companies offer different levels of cover, e.g. basic, standard, comprehensive and 'prestige'.

There's always a limit on the total annual medical costs, which should be at least US$500,000 (most go up to US$1.5 million or higher), and some companies limit costs for specific treatment or costs such as specialist's fees, surgery and hospital accommodation. Some policies include permanent disability cover, e.g. US$150,000, for those in full-time employment.

Claims are usually settled in all major currencies and large claims are usually settled directly by insurance companies (although your choice of hospitals may be limited). Always check whether an insurance company will settle large medical bills directly. If you're required to pay bills and claim reimbursement from an insurance company, it may take you several months to receive your money (some companies are slow to pay). It isn't always necessary to have bills translated into English or another language, although you should check a company's policy. Most international health insurance companies provide 24-hour emergency telephone assistance.

A medical isn't usually required for health policies, although 'pre-existing' health problems are excluded for a period, e.g. one or two years. However, with most international insurance policies, you must enrol before you reach a certain age, e.g. between 60 and 80, to be guaranteed continuous cover in your old age. Companies may also have restrictions on where you live permanently and your nationality.

The cost of international heath insurance varies considerably according to your age, the extent of cover, the insurer, and, not least, your home country or the country where you're resident. In some countries, premium increases are limited by law, although this may apply only to residents in the country where a company is registered and not to overseas policyholders. Although there may be significant differences in premiums, generally you get what you pay for and can tailor your premiums to your requirements. The most important questions to ask are whether a policy provides the cover you need and is good value. If you're in good health and are able to pay for your own out-patient treatment, such as visits to your family doctor and prescriptions, then the best value for money policy is usually one covering only specialist visits and in-hospital treatment. Premiums can sometimes be paid monthly or quarterly, although some companies insist on payment annually in advance.

When comparing policies, carefully check the extent of cover and exactly what's included and excluded (which may be noted only in the very small print), in addition to premiums and excess charges (see Checklist below).

Among the many companies offering international private medical insurance are Axa PPP Healthcare (💻 www.ppphealthcare.com), BUPA International (💻 www.bupa-intl.com), Expacare (💻 www.expacare.net), Goodhealth (💻 www.goodhealth.co.uk), InterGlobal Insurance Services (💻 www.interglobalpmi.com), International Private Healthcare (💻 www.iph.uk.net), Medicare International (💻 www.medicare.co.uk), Morgan Price International Healthcare (💻 www.morgan-price.com) and William Russell (💻 www.william-russell.co.uk).

Health Warning: Make sure you're fully covered abroad before you receive a large bill. It's foolhardy for anyone living in the Far East (or even visiting) not to have comprehensive health insurance. If you or your family is inadequately insured, you could be faced with some very high medical bills. When changing employers or moving to the region, you should ensure that you have uninterrupted health insurance and if you're planning to change your health insurance company ensure that important benefits aren't lost.

Checklist

When comparing the level of cover provided by different health insurance schemes, the following points should be considered:

- Does the scheme have a wide range of premium levels and are discounts or special premium rates available for families or children?
- Is private, semi-private (e.g. a two-bed room) and standard hospital cover available? What are the costs? Is there a limit on the time you can spend in hospital?

- Is dental cover offered? What exactly does it include? Can it be extended to include extra treatment? (Dental insurance usually contains numerous limitations and doesn't cover cosmetic treatment.)

- Are accidents covered, e.g. sports injuries, wherever and however they occur? (As a general rule, health insurance includes cover for accidents, but may exclude car accidents and accidents incurred when participating in certain 'dangerous' sports, such as skiing and hang-gliding. Check the definition of 'dangerous' sports because it varies among different insurers.)

- What are the restrictions regarding hospitalisation in a region or country other than the one where you have your permanent home? What level of cover is provided in other countries? What are the limitations?

- What emergency ambulance or other transportation fees are covered?

- Is there a qualification period for specific benefits or services?

- What is the cover regarding pregnancy, hospital births and associated costs? What is the position if conception occurred before joining an insurance scheme?

- Are all medicines covered or are there restrictions?

- Are convalescent homes or spa treatments covered when prescribed by a doctor?

- What are the restrictions on complementary medicine, e.g. chiropractic, osteopathy, naturopathy, massage and acupuncture? Are they covered? Must a doctor make a referral?

- Are extra premiums or charges likely and, if so, what for?

- Are spectacles or contact lenses covered and, if so, how much can be claimed and how frequently? Some insurance policies allow you to claim for a new pair of spectacles every two or three years.

- Is the provision and repair of artificial limbs and other essential health aids covered?

- Is evacuation and the cost of medical treatment abroad covered in full?

- Will the insurer provide a cash deposit or guarantee payment in advance if a hospital requires it?

HEALTH BY COUNTRY

Brunei

Health Risks: Brunei is one of the region's safest countries from a health point of view (and also because of its low crime rate). A cholera vaccination certificate hasn't been a requirement for entry into Brunei since 1973, but there was an outbreak of the disease in the Maura District in 1999 and you're recommended to check with your doctor regarding a vaccination; medical opinion is divided as to its effectiveness. Brunei is sometimes said to be malaria-free; this isn't quite true, although it's very uncommon – there's a slight risk in border areas. A yellow fever vaccination is required for travellers aged one year and over who have visited an endemic or infected area in the week prior to entering Brunei. Take precautions against insect bites.

Facilities & Services: Despite Brunei's wealth, high per capita income and image as a luxurious destination, the country's health facilities are adequate for basic medical conditions but a lack of materials and some types of medical staff mean that many people travel to Malaysia or Singapore for complicated care or surgery. Therefore it's strongly recommended that your medical insurance specifically includes cover for such an eventuality and emergency medical evacuation. Note also that doctors and hospitals in Brunei usually require immediate cash payment for treatment (and all medical care, whether in the public or private sector, has to be paid for by foreigners).

Brunei has six hospitals, four of them government hospitals, two private. Of the latter, the 110-bed Jerudong Park Medical Centre is open to all, the other is only for employees of Brunei Shell Petroleum. Of the government hospitals, Raja Isteri Pengiran Anak Saleha Hospital (RIPAS) in the capital Bandar is Brunei's largest and most comprehensive medical facility. It has 880 beds and provides a wide range of specialist services, including dermatology, renal dialysis, obstetrics, psychiatry and radiology.

Suri Seri Begawan Hospital in Kuala Belait is Brunei's oldest hospital (opened in 1972) and the second-largest. It was renovated in 2000 and also provides a wide range of specialist services, including radiology and cardiac endoscopy. Tutong boasts the hospital with the longest name, Pengiran Muda Mahkota Pengiran Muda Haji Al-Muhtadee Billah Hospital. It has 139 beds and offers a range of care, from out-patients and accident and emergency to dentistry and physiotherapy. Pengiran Isteri Hajah Mariam Hospital in Temburong has a modest 50 beds, but provides extensive care, including accident and emergency, obstetrics, dentistry, physiotherapy, paediatrics and a chest clinic. In addition to the hospitals, there's a wide range of health clinics throughout Brunei, both public and private.

China

Health Risks: Tropical and equatorial countries are most closely associated with malaria, but much of China also has a problem with this endemic disease, although only a small southern fringe of the country reaches south of the Tropic of Cancer. The most common forms of malaria in China are falciparum and vivax, but the disease is rare in major cities and at altitude (above around 1,500m). Malaria transmission is seasonal: between July and November in northern China, between May and December in central China, and all year in the south. Falciparum and vivax are found in different regions and are prevented with different medicines, so check with your doctor about what is suitable for the region(s) you're travelling to.

Hepatitis B is common throughout China and hepatitis E is common in the north. Japanese encephalitis is found in the rural north of China between May and September, and in the rural south between April and October. Schistosomiasis is common in many of China's rivers and lakes, and tuberculosis is common throughout the country. Bengal cholera has been found in western China and rabies from dogs is a risk everywhere; man's best friend or not, dogs are best avoided in China.

China's cities and industrial regions have some of the highest levels of air pollution in the world and those with respiratory and/or skin conditions might be adversely affected; dust in some regions (notably Tibet, where you're also at risk of altitude sickness) exacerbates the problem.

The only mandatory vaccination for entry to China is yellow fever, applicable to travellers coming from infected areas. If you intend to stay in China for longer than six months, you need to pass an HIV test.

Facilities & Services: The country's major cities have plenty of doctors and hospitals and, since foreign doctors have been allowed to practise in China, there are increasing numbers of international health clinics staffed by highly trained doctors in the larger cities, many of whom speak at least some English. However, Chinese state hospitals are sometimes very basic and their lack of facilities (and hygiene) comes as a shock to many foreigners. Modern procedures may not be available, medicines are sometimes in short supply and English-speaking doctors rare, as are ambulances. Injured or ill people, rather than waiting to see if an ambulance turns up, often go to hospital by taxi. Even if an ambulance does arrive, they rarely have much equipment and the personnel often have little if any medical training.

The vast majority of expatriates (if they have any sense) have extensive medical insurance, including emergency evacuation to specialist hospitals in Hong Kong. Some health insurance companies have clinics in major Chinese cities. For example, International SOS have four clinics in China (in Beijing, Guangzhou, Nanjing and Tianjin) and two alarm centres, in Beijing and Shanghai.

Beijing United Family Hospital and Clinics (☎ 6433-2345, 🖳 www. bjunited.com) remains the only foreign-funded, full-service, international standard hospital in Beijing. It offers a range of services, including family practice, physiotherapy, obstetrics, gynaecology, dentistry, surgery and psychiatry, as well as a 24-hour emergency service, staffed by foreign doctors. Staff speak fluent English, and some also speak French, German, Japanese, Spanish and Swedish, among others.

Hong Kong

Health Risks: Hong Kong has fewer health threats than most of the Far East. Malaria occurs occasionally in border regions, and Japanese encephalitis is a low risk in the New Territories between April and October. There are no vaccination requirements for international travellers.

Facilities & Services: Hong Kong enjoys a wide range of excellent health facilities, catering for most eventualities, the equal of the best in most western cities. Many of Hong Kong's doctors and dentists undergo postgraduate training in western countries. While Hong Kong residents receive subsidised medical treatment (they pay a modest charge), non-residents must pay for all treatment, often up-front. This can be very expensive and it's essential to have extensive private medical insurance.

Details of the location of public health centres and clinics are available from the Department of Health (☎ 2961-8989). Attendance at out-patient clinics is on a first-come-first-served basis and the fee is HK$45 (US$5.80) for Hong Kong ID Card Holders, HK$215 (US$27.70) for other patients. Fees include the consultation cost, prescriptions, X-rays and laboratory tests. Fees for admission to public hospitals are HK$50 (US$6.45) for Hong Kong ID card holders. If you don't have a local ID card, you must pay a massive HK$3,300 (US$425) for admission to a general hospital or HK$1,200 (US$155) for a psychiatric hospital. Fees for admission to private hospitals vary greatly, but are much higher. There are also plenty of private doctors.

Better-known public hospitals include Queen Elizabeth Hospital, Kowloon (☎ 2958-8888), Queen Mary Hospital, Hong Kong (☎ 2855-3111) and Prince of Wales Hospital, New Territories (☎ 2632-2415). Private hospitals include Hong Kong Adventist Hospital, Hong Kong (☎ 2574-6211), Hong Kong Baptist Hospital, Kowloon (☎ 2339-8888), Shatin International Medical Centre, New Territories (☎ 2890-6008) and St Paul's Hospital, Hong Kong (☎ 2608-3388). For further information call the Hong Kong Medical Association (☎ 2527-8285).

Indonesia

Health Risks: Malaria is found year-round in Indonesia, but mainly in rural areas. A combination of chloroquine and proguanil is the standard prophylaxis (preventive treatment), but in higher risk Irian Jaya, mefloquine is usually prescribed because there's chloroquine resistance. Japanese encephalitis is also found in rural areas. A yellow fever vaccination is required for entry into the country for travellers coming from infected areas.

Facilities & Services: Levels of health care and sanitation in Indonesia are much lower than in western countries. General medical care is available in most Indonesian cities, but for anything serious or specialised, most expatriates elect to travel abroad for treatment, usually to Singapore or Australia. Until recently, only Indonesian-trained doctors who held Indonesian citizenship were allowed to practise in the country and, although recent legislation has allowed foreigners to practise, this is only on a limited basis. Indonesia currently has 1,145 hospitals, providing 124,800 beds. This sounds a lot, but it's estimated that another 600 hospitals are needed to provide adequate health coverage.

Healthcare funding in Indonesia is a major concern, and many Indonesians are unable to pay for medical insurance or medical treatment. Hospitals are increasingly wary of bad debts and therefore unwilling to admit patients who might not be able to pay. It's a criminal offence for them to demand deposits in the case of emergency treatment, but some do so nevertheless. Immediate cash payment is invariably required by doctors and hospitals, and **it's therefore vital for foreigners to have extensive medical insurance, including coverage for transportation and medical care abroad if necessary, and emergency repatriation coverage**.

As a result of the crisis in funding, the Ministry of Health (DEPKES) is drafting regulations to introduce a compulsory National Health Insurance Scheme (JPKM) – in effect an additional tax – likely to be around 6 per cent of salary, to be paid by employers, irrespective of whether they already have a medical scheme for their staff.

Japan

Health Risks: Health risks in Japan are among the region's lowest. Japanese encephalitis is a low risk in rural areas between April and October, and eating the much-loved raw fish carries the risk of paragonamiasis. Otherwise, the main health risk is from pollution in Japan's large cities and industrial areas. There are no vaccination requirements for international travellers.

Facilities & Services: Medical care and facilities in Japan are excellent, and everybody is required by law to contribute to a health insurance policy, meaning that subsidised medical treatment is available, people usually paying between 10 and 30 per cent of their medical costs, making treatment relatively inexpensive. The elderly pay around 8 per cent. This system covers medical treatment, prescription medicines, long-term care, prosthetics, accident and emergency care, home nursing for the old and hospital food. Some dental treatment, spectacles, check-ups and cosmetic surgery aren't covered.

There are two main schemes, 'Social Insurance' (*Kenko-Hoken*) and 'National Health Insurance' (*Kokumin-Kenko-Hoken*), the former usually for company employees, the latter for students and the self-employed. Premiums are based on your taxable income and calculated using your previous year's tax return. During the first year, you pay the minimum amount. You're given a medical card to show you're in a scheme and ask about details when you apply for your Alien Registration Card.

Japan has an abundance of excellent hospitals, but treatment can be very expensive and hospitals often insist on payment in full at the time of treatment or proof of your ability to pay after the treatment. Non-Japanese speakers at Tokyo hospitals are well-served by a telephone translation service (☎ 3 5285 8185), and there's a general medical information service available in English, Chinese, Korean, Spanish and Thai (☎ 3 5285 8181).

The All Japan Medical Facility Network has a website (🖳 www. hospital.ne.jp) with information about Japan's medical facilities, including those where staff speak English. Among the general hospitals in Tokyo with English-speaking doctors and 24-hour emergency care are the International Catholic Hospital (☎ 3 3951 1111), Japan Red Cross Medical Center (☎ 3 3400 1311), St. Luke's International Hospital (☎ 3 3541 5151) and the Tokyo Adventist Hospital (☎ 3 3392 6151).

Hospitals in Osaka include the Japan Red Cross Hospital (☎ 06 6771 5131), Osaka Central Hospital (☎ 06 6313 3461), Osaka University Hospital (☎ 06 6879 5111) and Sogo Kano Hospital (☎ 06 6351 5381). Hospitals in Fukuoka include Fukuoka Red Cross Hospital (☎ 092 521 1211), Fukuoka University Hospital (☎ 092 801 1011) and Kyushu University Hospital (☎ 092 641 1151).

English-speaking doctors, however, are difficult to find in Japan and their services are invariably expensive.

Korea

Health Risks: Like Japan, Korea is a relatively safe destination from a health point of view. There's a risk of malaria (vivax) in some northern regions, but because most of the affected zone is militarised the risk to visitors is negligible. Japanese encephalitis is sometimes a risk in rural areas between July and October. Long-stay visitors to Korea must take an HIV test. There are no vaccination requirements for international travellers.

Facilities & Services: Korean medical facilities are reasonable but inferior to those in most western countries. People who've been resident in the country for at least a year and who have a job that's registered with the Korean Labour Union have access to state-funded medical facilities (otherwise, you need private medical cover). Workers contribute around 2.5 per cent of their salary to the scheme (or their employer does, or it's split between them), which offers basic medical cover, although you must pay part of the cost of treatment – usually around 20 per cent. You must also pay extra to include 'specialist' treatment, including that for car crash injuries and cancer.

Between 2000 and 2002, Korea's medical system went through a period of upheaval. Doctors had traditionally dispensed their own prescriptions and this had generated much of their income; over-prescription was therefore rife. In an attempt to correct this, the government proposed that dispensing be transferred to pharmacies, as in the UK and US. Korean doctors went on strike to protest and further strikes are a possibility, but the government seems to have placated doctors by allowing them to increase their fees.

You might have trouble finding doctors who speak fluent English in Korea and are recommended to take a Korean-speaker with you.

The quality of hospitals in Korea is reasonable and improving. Many, however, are less than spotless and it's normal to see dusty medical equipment and spider's webs adorning the corners of consulting rooms. A peculiarity of the health service is that people seeking treatment in Korea's hospitals are, more often than not, given an injection, whatever their complaint. Many Korean doctors and some nurses speak at least some English. A comprehensive list of Korean hospitals and medical facilities with staff that speak good English is available at the US Embassy website (💻 http://us embassy.state.gov/seoul/wwwh3470.html).

Malaysia

Health Risks: Malaria (mainly falciparum) is present in Sabah, where because of chloroquine resistance mefloquine is the usual prophylaxis, and in Peninsular Malaysia and Sarawak, where the risk is lower, as the disease is mainly present in remote, forested areas. Cholera has been a problem in some regions, and there's a low risk of Japanese encephalitis.

The only mandatory vaccination is yellow fever, for travellers over the age of one coming from infected areas.

Facilities & Services: Western-trained doctors and facilities can be found in most of Malaysia's cities and offer good-quality treatment. Payment is usually expected immediately, often in cash, although credit cards are becoming more accepted. Free medical treatment is often provided in expatriate employment packages in Malaysia and to government employees. If it isn't, extensive private medical insurance is essential, as treatment can be expensive. Prices, however, are under review, as Malaysia is looking to lure Bruneians and other foreigners who normally seek medical care in Singapore. The plan is part of a thrust to attract more foreign business to the country in 2004.

Malaysia has plenty of hospitals, many with a good reputation, and the quaintly named HospitalSoup.com website has a comprehensive listing of hospitals and medical facilities throughout Malaysia (💻 www.hospital soup.com/rn/asp/CountryID.98/pt/HospitalListings.asp). A list of doctors and hospitals in Malaysia is also available on the website of the Malaysian Medical Association (💻 www.mma.org.my).

Philippines

Health Risks: Malaria (primarily falciparum) is found in lower lying (below around 600m) rural areas, but there's little risk in Manila. The highest risk is in the Palawan, Luzon and Mindanao. Japanese encephalitis is a risk in some regions, and chikungunya fever is common in some cities, including Manila. A stubborn, penicillin-resistant strain of gonorrhoea is a problem in the Philippines, particularly in the large cities.

A yellow fever vaccination certificate is required by travellers aged one and over coming from infected areas. Permanent residence applicants must pass an HIV test.

Facilities & Services: Standards of health care are good in Manila and some of the large cities, but elsewhere levels of care and supplies are inadequate. Foreigners must pay for all medical treatment (often immediately and in cash) and private medical insurance is therefore essential. Medical treatment in the

Philippines can be very expensive. For a list of clinics and hospitals, consult the website of the Department of Health (💻 www.doh.gov.ph).

For an extensive list of the Philippines' many hospitals and medical facilities, see the government website (💻 www.doh.gov.ph/hosp/hospitalist.htm).

Singapore

Health Risks: Singapore is a very low risk destination health-wise. It's almost as if germs and viruses don't dare to stalk its scrubbed streets and pristine gardens. A yellow fever vaccination is required for travellers aged one and over coming from infected areas. All workers who earn less than S$1,250 (US$725) per month and applicants for permanent residence are required to pass an HIV test.

Facilities & Services: Singapore has state-funded medical facilities (paid for by employee contributions from their salaries) which foreign workers can use if they contribute; charges are low. Standards of care are high, including those of specialist treatment, but not as high as in the private sector, which is state-of-the-art, although expensive. Medical insurance is often included in expatriate employee packages; many foreigners who aren't offered insurance by their employers choose to buy it.

The better-known public hospitals in Singapore include Changi General Hospital (☎ 6788-8833), National University Hospital (☎ 6772-5555), Singapore General Hospital (☎ 6222-3322) and Tan Tock Seng Hospital (☎ 6256-6011). All provide multi-disciplinary in-patient and specialist out-patient services, and 24-hour accident and emergency services. The last two also provide specialised treatment, including coronary bypass surgery, in-vitro fertilisation and micro-vascular surgery. The government also runs 13 dental clinics, including one at the National University Hospital, providing basic treatment.

Private hospitals include East Shore Hospital (☎ 6340-8666), Gleneagles Hospital (☎ 6470-5688), Mount Alvernia Hospital (☎ 6347-6688), Mount Elizabeth Hospital (☎ 6731-2218) and Thomson Medical Centre (☎ 6256-9494). Singapore has over 420 private dentists.

Taiwan

Health Risks: Japanese encephalitis and filariasis are low risks in rural areas and even lower in urban areas; the odd case of the former has been reported in Taipei. Taiwan is more stringent in its health requirements than other countries in the region: a cholera vaccination certificate is required of travellers arriving from infected areas, a yellow fever vaccination is necessary for travellers coming from affected areas, and anybody staying in the country for longer than 90 days must pass an HIV test.

Facilities & Services: Taiwan has a National Health Insurance Scheme, mainly subsidised by the government, to which employers pay a contribution of around 4.5 per cent of a worker's salary and employees around 1.3 per cent on monthly salaries of up to NT$60,800 (US$1,785). This makes medical costs in Taiwan among the cheapest in the region. As a result, the Taiwanese have a reputation for visiting their doctor more frequently than is necessary.

To receive National Health Insurance, you must either be a citizen of Taiwan or hold an Alien Residence Certificate (see page 36). You're given a Health Insurance Card, on the back of which are six sections, stamped each time you visit a hospital or clinic. If you forget to bring your card or it has expired, you must pay in advance for treatment and bring the card to the hospital within a week for reimbursement. Even without National Health Insurance, medical bills for 'standard' illnesses are reasonable in Taiwan. Nevertheless, private health insurance is recommended.

Most doctors in Taiwan speak some English (but might be nervous about using it), although nurses and other medical staff tend not to. When visiting hospitals in Taiwan, foreigners are sometimes struck by the lack of privacy and personal attention. You're treated as a number more than a person, and doctors sometimes seem to want to 'process' you as quickly as possible, although medical staff often make a special effort to help foreigners. As a result, the first time you visit a clinic or hospital, it's wise to take with you a Taiwanese-speaker to help you.

As well as plenty of public hospitals and health clinics, Taiwan has a number of private ones, often run by staff who also work for the public system. In view of the number of patients at public health facilities, the government encourages people to use private clinics for less serious conditions. Indeed, private clinics sometimes accept National Health Insurance patients and are given government incentives to ensure that their fees are competitive; in fact, they can be lower than public hospital fees. Private clinics and hospitals are usually smaller and less well-equipped than public facilities, but they're more convenient, being more widespread and having longer opening hours. You also receive more personal attention. Dental care in Taiwan is almost always at private clinics, which are well-equipped.

Thailand

Health Risks: The risk of malaria in Bangkok, Chiang Mai and the tourist areas of Ko Samui, Pattaya, Phuket and Songhkla is very low, but it's higher in areas bordering Cambodia and Myanmar (Burma). The risk of Japanese encephalitis is generally quite low, but there are occasional outbreaks in the Chiang Mai region and there have been cases in Bangkok. Sexually transmitted diseases are rife in Thailand, particularly HIV among the prostitutes of the cities and tourist resorts (see below). A yellow fever vaccination certificate is required by travellers over the age of one arriving from infected areas.

Facilities & Services: Thailand has some public health provision and it's of a reasonable standard (fees are charged according to a patient's income), but private sector treatment is much better, although expensive, and private health insurance is essential.

There are plenty of hospitals in Thailand, those in the main cities and tourist centres offering a high level of treatment. For a list of the country's government and private hospitals, see ⌨ http://eng.moph.go.th/RelatedSite/index.asp). Medical facilities in Bangkok are of a particularly high standard, the equal of those in many western cities for most types of healthcare. Outside the capital, however, standards are lower and in some places barely adequate, especially on the islands.

Medical fees aren't regulated in Thailand and doctors and hospitals set their own charges, which vary very widely. Fees in Bangkok can be as much as four times as high as those in the provinces, although standards are often much higher. Many Thai doctors speak English.

5.

FINANCE & INSURANCE

One of the most important aspects of living in the Far East (even for brief periods) is finance, which includes everything from transferring and changing money to banking, obtaining mortgages (where applicable) and paying taxes. If you're planning to invest in a property or business in the region financed with funds imported from another country, it's important to consider both the present and possible future exchange rates (don't be too optimistic!). On the other hand, if you live and work in the Far East and earn your income in the local currency, this may affect your financial commitments abroad (particularly if the local currency is devalued). **Bear in mind that your income can be exposed to risks beyond your control when you live abroad, particularly regarding inflation and exchange rate fluctuations.**

Apart from possible currency fluctuations, if you plan to live in the Far East you must ensure that your income is (and will remain) sufficient to live on, bearing in mind rises in the cost of living (see page 173) and unforeseen expenses such as medical bills or anything else that may reduce your income, such as stock market crashes and recessions! **Foreigners, particularly retirees, often under-estimate the cost of living abroad and some are forced to return to their home countries after a few years.** It's important to obtain expert financial advice before going to live in the Far East from an independent and impartial source, i.e. **not** someone who's trying to sell you something!

If you're a non-resident and own a home in the Far East, it's wise to employ a local professional, e.g. an accountant or tax adviser, as your representative to look after your local financial affairs and declare and pay your taxes. You can also have your representative receive your bank statements, ensure that your bank is paying your standing orders (e.g. for electricity, gas, water and telephone bills), and that you have sufficient funds to pay them. If you let a home in the region through a local company, they may perform the above tasks as part of their services.

Although many people prefer to pay cash (which cannot be traced by the taxman!) rather than use credit or charge cards (see page 163), it's wise to have at least one international credit card when visiting or living in the Far East. Note, however, that not all businesses accept credit cards (businesses in developing countries rarely accept them), and you should check in advance.

This chapter includes information about importing and exporting money, banking, credit, debit and charge cards, mortgages, pensions, taxes (income, property, capital gains, wealth, inheritance and gift tax), wills, the cost of living, and insurance.

CURRENCY

Each of the 11 territories discussed in this book uses a different currency. These are listed below, with exchange rates (against the US$) current in late 2003; where a currency is divided into smaller units, these are shown in brackets. Note that exchange rates can change rapidly and substantially and you should always check the current rate before converting money from one currency to another. For conversion calculations, you can use the universal currency converter (🖳 www.xe.com/ucc). For further information about each currency, see **Currency** sections in Country Profiles (**Chapter 9**).

Territory	Currency	Abbr./Symbol	US$1 =
Brunei	Brunei Dollar (100 cents)	BD$	1.6
China	Renminbi, Yuan or Renmibi Yuan (10 chiao/jiao or 100 fen)	RMB/Y/RMBY	8.25
Hong Kong	Hong Kong Dollar (100 cents)	HK$	7.8
Indonesia	Rupiah	Rp	8,500
Japan	Japanese Yen	¥	110
Korea	South Korean Won	SKW	1,175
Malaysia	Ringgit or Malaysian dollar (100 sen)	RM	3.8
Philippines	Philippine Peso (known as the piso) (100 centavos)	P	5.5
Singapore	Singapore Dollar (100 cents)	S$	1.7
Taiwan	New Taiwan dollar (100 cents)	NT$	34
Thailand	Baht (100 satang)	Bht	40

IMPORTING & EXPORTING MONEY

Exchange controls have been abolished in the last few decades in most countries. However, many countries require foreigners to declare imports or exports of funds above a certain amount and have restrictions on the amount that can be imported or exported in cash, notes and bearer-cheques in any currency, plus gold coins and bars. Where necessary, it's particularly important to declare large sums, e.g. for the purchase of a business or home in the Far East, as it may be impossible legally to export funds from some countries if they weren't declared when imported. These regulations are usually designed to curb criminal activities (e.g. money laundering) and tax evasion, and may also apply to travellers simply passing through a country. In some countries, foreigners must declare the origin of funds used for the purchase of a business or property – if you don't, they may be confiscated.

International Money Transfers

Making international money transfers between different countries can be a nightmare and can take anything from a few minutes to many weeks (or months if the money gets 'lost'), depending on the banks and countries involved. A bank to bank transfer can usually be made by a 'normal' postal transfer or via an electronic transfer (such as SWIFT).

Most international transfers are slow and costly, even between banks and countries with sophisticated, state-of-the-art banking systems. A normal transfer within the Far East is supposed to take three to seven days, but in reality it often takes much longer and some transfers take many weeks or even get lost completely, whereas a SWIFT telex transfer should be completed in a few hours, funds being available within 24 hours. Banks in some countries are notoriously slow and have been accused of deliberately delaying transfers in order to earn interest on money 'stuck in the pipeline'. The cost of transfers varies considerably – not only the commission and exchange rates, but also transfer charges (such as the telex charge for a SWIFT transfer).

Shop around banks and financial institutions for the best deal and don't be afraid to change your bank if the service provided doesn't meet your requirements. Many banks subscribe to an international electronic network to (hopefully) facilitate fast and inexpensive transfers between members. Telegraphic transfers can be made via specialist companies such as Western Union between some 200 countries, which is the quickest (around ten minutes!) and safest method, but also one of the most expensive.

In many countries, there isn't a lot of difference in cost between buying foreign currency or travellers' cheques or using a credit card to obtain cash. Many foreigners living in the Far East keep the bulk of their money in a foreign account (perhaps in an offshore bank) and draw on it using a cash or credit card when abroad, which is a convenient solution for short trips abroad. However, many people simply take cash when travelling abroad, which is asking for trouble, particularly if you have no way of obtaining more cash, e.g. with a credit or debit card. **One thing to bear in mind when travelling anywhere isn't to rely only on one source of funds!**

Bank Drafts: If you aren't in a hurry, you can send a bank draft, which should be sent by registered post. Note, however, that in the unlikely event that it's lost or stolen, it's impossible to stop payment and you must wait six months before a new draft can be issued. In some countries, bank drafts aren't treated as cash and must be cleared like personal cheques.

If you intend sending a large amount of money to the Far East for a business transaction such as buying a business or property, you should ensure that you receive the commercial rate of exchange rather than the tourist rate (shop around for the best rate).

Personal Cheques: It's also possible to pay a cheque drawn on a bank in your home country into a bank account in the Far East, although these take a long time to clear (usually a number of weeks) and fees are high. A personal cheque drawn on a European or American bank can take three or four weeks to clear, as it must be cleared with the paying bank. However, some banks allow clients to draw on cheques issued on foreign banks from the day they're paid into a client's account. Note that most American banks don't accept cheques drawn on foreign bank accounts written in a foreign currency. When transferring small amounts it's better to use a money order.

Travellers' Cheques: Travellers' cheques are widely accepted in countries with a well-developed tourist industry (most of the Far East) but may be restricted only to major currencies (if in doubt, buy them in US$) and may only be cashed by banks in major cities. The commission for cashing travellers' cheques is usually 1 per cent, depending on the issuer and where you cash them. Lost or stolen travellers' cheques can be replaced in most countries (the easiest to replace are American Express), but you must keep a separate record of the cheque numbers.

BANKS

Although it's possible to live in the Far East without having a local bank account – by using credit and debit cards and travellers' cheques – this isn't recommended and is an expensive option. In any case, residents and homeowners usually need a local bank account to pay their utility and tax bills, which are best paid by direct debit. If you have a holiday home in the region, you can usually have all documentation (e.g. statements) sent to your permanent home address. Many foreign banks have branches in major cities in the Far East, although few have extensive networks. Note also that foreign banks in the region usually operate in exactly the same way as domestic banks, so you shouldn't expect, for example, a branch of Barclays or Deutsche Bank in your Far Eastern country of residence to operate like a branch in the UK or Germany.

Non-residents can open a bank account in most countries by correspondence, although it's best done in person in the country concerned. Ask your friends, neighbours or colleagues for their recommendations and visit the bank of your choice and introduce yourself. You must provide proof of identity (e.g. a passport or identity card) and your address in the region. If you open an account while in your home country, you must obtain an application form from an overseas branch of your chosen bank or from a bank in the region. If you open an account by correspondence, you also need to provide a reference from your current bank.

Note that banks in most countries make few or no concessions for foreign customers, e.g. the provision of general information and documentation such as statements in foreign languages and staff who speak foreign languages. However, some banks offer a multilingual service and go out of their way to attract foreign customers. In some countries there are restrictions regarding the types of account a non-resident foreigner may open, although residents can usually open any type of account.

Note that overdrawing a bank account (bouncing cheques) in many countries is a criminal offence, and offenders can be barred from maintaining a bank account for a period (it will also severely damage your credit rating).

Offshore Banking

If you have a sum of money to invest or wish to protect your inheritance from the tax man, it may be worthwhile investigating the accounts and services (such as pensions and trusts) provided by offshore banking centres in tax havens such as the Caribbean Islands, Channel Islands (Guernsey and Jersey), Gibraltar and the Isle of Man – some 50 locations worldwide are officially classified as tax havens. Offshore banking has had a good deal of media attention in recent years, during which it has also been under investigation by the EU and the OECD, who have imposed restrictions on banks and a system of accountability allowing investors to be identified by the relevant tax authorities.

The major attractions of offshore banking are that money can be deposited in a wide range of currencies, customers are usually guaranteed complete anonymity, there are no double-taxation agreements, no withholding tax is payable and interest is paid tax-free. Many offshore banks also provide telephone (usually 24 hours per day, seven days per week) and Internet banking.

A large number of American, British and other European banks and financial institutions provide offshore banking facilities in one or more locations. Most institutions offer high-interest, instant-access accounts, deposit accounts for long-term savings and investment portfolios, in which funds can be deposited in most major currencies. It's also possible to invest in a range of bonds, funds, trusts, pensions, equities and other investment vehicles, which are usually intended for long-term investments. Many people living in the Far East keep a local account for everyday business and maintain an offshore account for international transactions and investment purposes. However, most financial experts advise expatriates not to deposit their life savings in an offshore financial centre until they know what their long-term plans are.

Most accounts have minimum deposits levels, which usually range from the equivalent of around US$750 to US$15,000, with some as high as US$150,000. In addition to large minimum balances, accounts may have strict terms and conditions, such as restrictions on withdrawals or high early withdrawal penalties. You can deposit funds on call (instant access) or for a fixed period, e.g. from 90 days to one year (usually for larger sums). Interest is usually paid monthly or annually; monthly interest payments are slightly lower than annual payments but have the advantage of providing a regular income. There are usually no charges, provided a specified minimum balance is maintained. Many accounts offer a cash or credit card (e.g. MasterCard or Visa) that can be used to obtain cash from cash machines (ATMs) throughout the world.

When selecting a financial institution and offshore banking centre, your first priority should be for the safety of your money. In many offshore banking centres, bank deposits are guaranteed under a deposit protection scheme, whereby a maximum sum is safeguarded should the financial institution go to the wall (the Isle of Man, Guernsey and Jersey all have such schemes). Unless you're planning to bank with a major international bank, you should check the credit rating of a financial institution before depositing any money, particularly if it doesn't provide deposit insurance. All banks have a credit rating (the highest is 'AAA') and a bank with a high rating will happily tell you what it is (but get it in writing). You can also check the rating of an international bank or financial organisation with Moodys Investors Service (🖳 www.moodys.com). **You should be wary of institutions offering higher than average interest rates; if it looks too good to be true it probably will be!**

When choosing an offshore bank, you may also wish to consider its communications network (24-hour telephone banking, fax, email, internet banking), your personal contact (will you have one?) and its geographical location – it's best to choose a bank in a similar time zone if possible, or you may be calling your advisor in the middle of the night!

Useful websites for further information about offshore banking include Investors Offshore (🖳 www.investorsoffshore.com) and Tax News (🖳 www. tax-news.com).

DEBIT, CREDIT & CHARGE CARDS

'Plastic money' in the form of cash, debit, credit and charge cards is widely used in towns and cities in all Far Eastern countries (but rarely in rural areas), where banks are busy trying to create a cashless society.

All cards allow holders to withdraw cash, e.g. US$150 to $750 (or the foreign currency equivalent) per day from automated teller machines (ATMs) and obtain account balances and mini-statements. Cash can also be obtained from the ATMs of other networks (other than the one your card belongs to), although there's usually a fee. Most ATMs accept a bewildering number of cards, which may be illustrated on machines, including credit (Euro card, MasterCard, Visa) and charge (Amex, Diners Club) cards. Note that, although debit cards such as those belonging to the Visa network can be used to obtain cash abroad, they may be treated as credit cards and a charge levied.

Cash & Debit Cards

Cash and debit cards are issued by most banks and many can be used worldwide via the American Express, MasterCard and Visa networks. With a cash/debit card (they're usually the same card), cash withdrawals and purchases are automatically debited from a cheque or savings account. All withdrawals or purchases are shown on your monthly statement and you cannot usually run up an overdraft or obtain credit (unless arranged beforehand).

Credit & Charge Cards

Credit and charge cards are usually referred to collectively as credit cards, although not all cards are real credit cards, where the balance can be repaid over a period. Visa and MasterCard are the most widely accepted credit cards in most

Far Eastern countries and are issued by most banks. Charge cards, such as American Express and Diners Club, aren't widely accepted in some countries, particularly by small businesses (who wisely prefer cash). Never assume that a business (such as a restaurant) accepts a particular credit or charge card but ask **before** running up a bill!

Note that, when using a credit card in some countries, you usually need to enter a PIN number into a machine, without which you may be unable to use your credit card. You also need a PIN number to withdraw cash abroad from an ATM with a credit card (there's a limit to the amount that can be withdrawn). Note that using a foreign credit card to obtain cash abroad is expensive, as there's a standard charge (e.g. 1.5 per cent), a high interest rate, which is usually charged from the day of the withdrawal, plus possibly a poor exchange rate.

Even if you don't like credit cards and shun any form of credit, they do have their uses: for example, no-deposit car rentals, no pre-paying hotel bills (plus guaranteed bookings), obtaining cash 24-hours per day, simple telephone and mail-order payments, greater safety and security than cash, and above all, convenience. They're particularly useful when travelling abroad and you also need some form of credit card if you wish to make purchases by phone or via the Internet.

MORTGAGES

Mortgages or home loans for those buying a home in the Far East may be available in your home country, the country where the property is situated, and possibly also from financial institutions in offshore banking centres. The amount that can be borrowed varies according to the country where the property is situated, the country where the loan is to be raised, the lender, and, not least, your financial standing. Local mortgages aren't available in all 11 territories (see **Property Market** on page 115).

In the last decade, lenders have tightened their lending criteria in many countries due to the repayment problems experienced by recession-hit borrowers in the early '90s, and some lenders apply strict rules regarding income, employment and the type of property on which they will lend. Foreign lenders, such as banks in offshore financial centres, also have strict rules regarding the nationality and domicile of borrowers, and the percentage they will lend.

In some countries the law doesn't permit banks to offer mortgages or other loans where repayments are more than one-third of net income (which includes existing mortgage or rental payments). Joint incomes and liabilities are included when assessing a couple's borrowing limit (usually a bank will lend to up to three joint borrowers). Most banks require proof of your monthly income and all outgoings such as mortgage payments, rent and other loans and commitments. Proof of income includes three months' pay slips for employees, confirmation of income from your employer and tax returns. If you're self-employed, you usually require an audited copy of your balance sheets and trading accounts for the past three years, plus your last tax return. However, 'no-income qualifier' loans of up to around 60 per cent of a property's value are available in many countries. If you want a mortgage to buy a property for commercial purposes you must usually provide a detailed business plan.

In many countries it's customary for a property to be held as security for a loan, i.e. the lender takes a first charge on the property which is recorded at the property registry.

Mortgages are granted on a percentage of a property's valuation, which itself may be below the actual market value. The maximum mortgage granted in most countries is 70 to 80 per cent of the purchase price, although it can be as low as 50 to 60 per cent for non-residents and buyers of second homes. Loans may be repaid over 5 to 30 years (or 75 to 100 years in Japan, where multi-generation mortgages exist), depending on the lender and country, although the usual term in most countries is 10 to 20 years for residents and possibly less for non-residents. Repayment mortgages are the most common type in most countries, although endowment and pension-linked mortgages may also be offered. Repayments are usually made monthly or quarterly, but bi-weekly payments (which reduce the interest considerably) are also possible in some countries.

There are various fees associated with mortgages, e.g. all lenders charge an 'arrangement' fee and, although it's unusual to have a survey in most countries, lenders usually insist on a 'valuation' before they grant a loan. Always shop around for the best interest rate and ask the effective rate, including all commissions and fees.

Foreign Currency Loans

It's generally recognised that you should take out a mortgage in the currency in which your income is paid. The advantage is that, if the currency is devalued against the currency of the country where you own a property, you will have the consolation that the value of your home will (theoretically) have increased by the same percentage when converted back into your 'income' currency.

However, it's also possible to obtain a foreign currency mortgage in major currencies such as GB£, US$ or euros. **You should be extremely wary of taking out a foreign currency mortgage, as interest rate gains can be wiped out overnight by currency swings and devaluations.**

When choosing between various currencies, you should take into account the costs, fees, interest rates and possible currency fluctuations. Irrespective of how you finance the purchase of a home in the region, you should always obtain professional advice. **If you have a foreign currency mortgage, you must usually pay commission charges each time you transfer currency to pay your mortgage or remit money abroad.** If you let a home in the Far East, you may be able to offset the interest on your mortgage against rental income, but pro rata only. If you raise a mortgage abroad or in a foreign currency, you should be aware of any impact this may have on your tax allowances or liabilities.

Mortgages For Second Homes

If you have equity in an existing home, it may be cheaper to re-mortgage (or take out a second mortgage) on that property than to take out a new mortgage for a home in the Far East. It entails less paperwork and therefore lower legal fees. Depending on the equity in your existing property and the cost of a home in the Far East, it may also enable you to pay cash for a second home. The disadvantage of re-mortgaging or taking out a second mortgage is that you reduce the amount of equity available in a property, which is useful if you need to raise cash in an emergency.

Payment Problems

If you're unable to meet your mortgage payments, some lenders will renegotiate mortgages so that payments are made over a longer period, thus allowing you to reduce your payments. Although interest rates have fallen dramatically in recent years, many lenders are slow to reduce their interest rates for existing borrowers and some try to prevent existing mortgage holders transferring to another lender offering a lower rate by imposing prohibitive fees. However, some countries have introduced legislation to enable borrowers with fixed rate mortgages to change their mortgage lender or re-negotiate a mortgage with their existing lender at a greatly reduced cost. A mortgage can usually be taken over (assumed) by the new owner when a property is sold, which can be advantageous for a buyer. Note that, if you stop paying your mortgage, your lender can embargo your property and could eventually force its sale at auction to recover his loan.

PENSIONS

Before deciding whether to or where to work in the Far East, it's important to consider how this will affect your state and/or private pensions. In some countries you can continue to contribute to social security when working abroad in order to qualify for a full state pension, although if the pension is insignificant you may be better off not doing so. Company pensions in many countries are transportable between employers in the same country, but are rarely transportable to another country (unless you remain with the same employer). You may, however, be able to continue paying into a private pension when you work abroad, although you will lose any tax benefits in your home country (most pension contributions are tax-free up to certain limits). This also applies in reverse: i.e. if you contribute to a company pension abroad, you won't be able to transfer it back home unless you remain with the same employer (and penalties may apply).

It's compulsory to contribute to the local social security system in most countries, which usually includes a state pension, although it may take 10 or 15 years of contributions to qualify for a part pension and the amount may be insignificant. However, when you leave the country you may be able to reclaim your pension payments or claim a reduced pension when you reach the local retirement age, e.g. 65. When you have a company or private pension abroad (which may be mandatory) which isn't transportable to another country, you will be able to reclaim the sum accrued in your pension fund (possibly including your employer's contributions) when you leave.

One option worth investigating if a job in the Far East doesn't come with a company pension or a mandatory state pension (particularly for anyone who does contract work in different countries) is to contribute to an offshore pension fund or other investment. You can then continue to contribute to it irrespective of the country where you work, although you may not receive any tax benefits on your contributions.

Before making any decisions about pensions, it's important to consult an independent pensions' advisor.

TAX

Before planning to live or work in the region, it's wise to investigate the taxes that will be payable, particularly income tax, social security contributions and other taxes incurred by residents. If you plan to buy a home, you may also need to take into account property taxes (rates), capital gains tax, wealth tax and inheritance tax. For many people, moving to the Far East is an opportunity to reduce their overall taxes, particularly when moving from a high to a low-tax country, when the timing of a move can be decisive. Some countries encourage foreigners (e.g. retirees) to take up residence by offering tax incentives and many countries provide tax incentives for foreigners employed for a limited period by a foreign company. None of the 11 territories considered here levies a wealth tax. For details of taxes in each territory, see the **Taxation** sections in the Country Profiles chapter (**Chapter 9**).

Income Tax

Income tax is of particular interest (or concern!) to those planning to become residents abroad, although most countries also levy income tax on income earned by non-residents, such as the income from letting a home. If you're planning to live or work in the Far East permanently you should also take into account social security contributions, which are high in some countries, particularly for the self-employed. If you're planning to work or start a business abroad, you should seek expert tax advice, both in your present country of residence (regarding your tax liability there) and the country where you plan to work. Note that the combined burden of income tax, social security contributions and other taxes can make a considerable hole in your income in some countries.

Liability

Under the law of most countries you become liable to income tax (a 'fiscal resident') if you spend 183 days during a calendar year there or your main centre of economic interest, e.g. investments or business, is there. Temporary absences are usually included in the calculation of the period spent abroad, unless residence is shown to have been in another country for 183 days in a calendar year. If your spouse (and any dependent minor children) normally resides in a country where you have a home, has a residence permit, and isn't legally separated from you, you may also be considered to be a tax resident in that country (unless you can prove otherwise). Some countries restrict the visits of non-residents over a certain period, e.g. the UK limits visits by non-residents to 182 days in any tax year or an average of 91 days per year over four consecutive tax years.

Dual Residence: It's possible for some people to have 'dual residence' and be tax resident in two countries simultaneously, in which case your 'tax home' may be resolved under the rules of international treaties. Under such treaties you're considered to be resident in the country where you have a permanent home. If you have a permanent home in both countries, you're deemed to be resident in the country where you have the closest personal and economic ties. If your residence cannot be determined under the above rules, you're deemed to be resident in the country where you have a habitual abode. If you have a habitual abode in both or in neither country, you're deemed to be resident in the country of which you're a citizen. Finally, if you're a citizen of both or neither country, the authorities of the countries concerned will decide your tax residence between them and let you know!

Double-Taxation Treaties: Residents in most countries are taxed on their worldwide income, subject to certain treaty exceptions. Non-residents are usually taxed only on income arising in a particular country. Citizens of most countries are exempt from paying taxes in their home country when they spend a minimum period abroad, e.g. one year, although this doesn't apply to US citizens. Many countries have double-taxation treaties with other countries, which are designed to ensure that income that has been taxed in one treaty country isn't taxed again in another. The treaty establishes a tax credit or exemption on certain kinds of income, either in the country of residence or the country where the income is earned.

Double-taxation treaties vary according to the country and, where applicable, have priority over domestic law. In the absence of a double-taxation treaty between your home country and the country where you're planning to live or work, check how this will affect you. In many cases, even when there's no double-taxation agreement between two countries, you can still usually obtain relief from double taxation. In this case, tax relief is usually provided through direct deduction of any foreign tax paid or through a 'foreign compensation' formula. Note that if your tax liability in one country is less than in another, you may be required to pay the tax authorities the difference in the country where you're resident. If you're in any doubt about your tax liability in your home country or a country where you're living in the Far East, contact your nearest embassy or consulate for information. The US is one of the few countries that taxes its non-resident citizens on income earned abroad – Americans can obtain a copy of a brochure, *Tax Guide for Americans Abroad*, from American consulates.

Moving Abroad: Before leaving a country for good, you usually need to pay any tax due for the previous year and the year of departure, and you may also need to apply for a tax clearance. A tax return must usually be filed prior to departure and must include your income and deductions for the current tax year up to the date of departure. The local tax office will calculate the taxes due and provide a written statement. In some countries, a tax clearance certificate is necessary to obtain a 'sailing or departure permit' or an exit visa. A shipping or moving company may also need official authorisation from the tax authorities before they can ship your personal effects abroad.

Planning: If you're planning to move to the Far East permanently, you should plan well in advance, as the timing of a move can make a big difference to your tax liabilities, both in your present and your new country of residence. Find out what you must do to become an official non-resident in your current country of residence and how long you will need to be resident in your new home to qualify as a resident for tax purposes. In most countries you automatically become liable for income tax if you spend longer than six months (183 days) there during a calendar year.

If you intend to live in the Far East permanently, you should notify the tax and social security authorities in your previous country of residence well in advance. You may be entitled to a tax refund if you leave during the tax year, which usually requires the completion of a tax return. The authorities may require evidence that you're leaving the country, e.g. evidence of a job in the region or of having purchased or rented a property. If you move to the Far East to take up a job or start a business, you must register with the local tax authorities soon after your arrival.

Property Taxes

Property taxes (also called real estate taxes or rates) are levied by local authorities in most countries and are payable by all property owners, irrespective of whether they're residents or non-residents, and may also be payable by tenants. In some countries an additional 'residential' or local income tax is also paid by residents. For details of property taxes payable in each of the 11 territories, see the **Property Taxes** sections under **Property Market** on page 115. Before buying a property, check the tax rate with the local town hall, as rates usually vary from community to community.

Property taxes pay for local services which may include rubbish collection, street lighting, sanitary services (e.g. street and beach cleaning), local schools and other community services, local council administration, social assistance, community substructure, cultural and sports amenities, and possibly water rates.

Property tax is usually payable irrespective of whether a property is inhabited, provided it's furnished and habitable. It may be split into two amounts, one for the building and another for the land, with tax on land payable irrespective of whether it's built on or not. Before buying a property you should check that there are no outstanding property taxes for the current or previous years, as in many countries the new owner assumes all unpaid property related taxes and debts, although you may be able to reclaim the tax from the previous owner – if you can find him!

Property taxes are normally based on the fiscal or notional letting value of a property, which is usually lower than the actual purchase price or a property's market value. If the fiscal value increases greatly, check that it has been correctly calculated. You can appeal against the valuation of your property if you believe it's too high, particularly if it's higher than that of similar properties in the same area. **However, an appeal must be lodged within a limited period** (check with the local town hall). It's important that the fiscal value of your property is correct, as in some countries a number of taxes are linked to this value, such as property letting tax, wealth tax, transfer tax on property sales and inheritance tax.

Capital Gains Tax

Capital gains tax (CGT) is payable on the profit from sales of certain assets in some countries. See the **Capital Gains Tax** sections in the Country Profiles (**Chapter 9**), which may include property (real estate) and also antiques, art and jewellery, stocks, bonds and shares, household furnishings, vehicles, coin and stamp collections and other 'collectibles', gold, silver and gems, and the sale of a business. International tax treaties usually decree that capital gains on property are taxable in the country where it's situated.

If you move to the Far East permanently and retain a home in another country, this may affect your position regarding capital gains there. If you sell your foreign home before moving to the region, you're usually exempt from CGT as it would have been your principal residence. However, if you establish your principal residence in the Far East, your property in your home country becomes a second home and thus you may be liable to pay CGT when it's sold. In some countries you're exempt from CGT on a second home if you don't own your main residence, i.e. if you're a tenant or leaseholder, although this may apply only to the first sale of a second home. **Capital gains tax can be a complicated subject and you should always obtain legal advice before disposing of property or buying property abroad.** Note that the tax authorities in many countries co-operate to track down those who attempt to avoid capital gains tax. Where applicable, a sum may be withheld by the official handling the sale in lieu of capital gains tax or the buyer must retain a percentage when the seller is a non-resident.

Most countries provide an exemption if gains don't exceed a certain amount. Certain types of gain are also exempt and may include those resulting from the death of a taxpayer, gifts to government entities, donations of certain assets in lieu of tax payments, and the contribution of assets in exchange for a life annuity for those aged over 65. Capital losses can usually be offset against capital gains (but not against ordinary income), and it's usually possible to carry forward capital losses (or a percentage) in excess of gains and offset them against future gains for a limited period (this may also be possible with business losses). In most countries, capital gains are treated as ordinary income for residents.

A property capital gain is based on the difference between the purchase price and the sale price. However, in most countries there are exemptions, which usually depend on the number of years a property has been owned. If an asset has been owned for less than a certain period, capital gains are taxed in full. Most countries allow a tax exemption (called indexation relief) on the sale of your principal residence, although some allow an exemption only if you buy another home within a limited period, and levy tax on any profits that aren't re-invested. In some countries, capital gains made by non-residents are taxed at a flat rate and there may be no reduction for the length of time you've owned a property. However, in most countries the amount of CGT payable is reduced the longer you've owned a property until it's no longer applicable. In some countries you can protect yourself and your survivors from capital gains tax by bequeathing appreciated property, rather than giving it away while you're alive.

You should keep all bills for the fees associated with buying a property (e.g. lawyer, estate agent and surveyor), plus any bills for renovation, restoration, modernisation or improvement of a second home, as these can usually be offset against CGT and may be index-linked. If you work on a house yourself, you should keep a copy of all bills for materials and tools, as these can also be offset against CGT. Losses on rentals may also be able to be carried forward and offset against a capital gain when a property is sold. Costs relating to a sale can also usually be offset against any gain, as can interest paid on a loan taken out to purchase or restore a property.

Inheritance & Gift Tax

Dying doesn't free you (or more correctly, your beneficiaries) from the clutches of the tax man. Some countries impose an inheritance (also called estate tax or death duty) and gift tax on the estate of a deceased person. See the **Inheritance & Gift Tax** sections in the Country Profiles (**Chapter 9**). Where inheritance tax applies, both residents and non-residents are usually liable if they own property abroad. The country where you pay inheritance and gift tax is usually decided by your domicile. If you're living permanently in the Far East at the time of your death, you will be deemed to be domiciled there by the local tax authorities. If you're domiciled in the region, then inheritance and gift tax payable there will apply to your worldwide estate (excluding property); otherwise it applies only to assets held in the Far East, such as a second home. It's important to make your domicile clear so that there's no misunderstanding on your death. See also **Liability** on page 167.

Inheritance Tax

In many countries, inheritance tax is paid by the beneficiaries and not by the deceased's estate. This may mean that, if you inherit a home in the Far East, you may need to sell it to pay tax. The rate of inheritance tax payable usually depends upon the relationship between the donor and the recipient, the amount inherited, and (in some countries) the current wealth of the recipient. Direct descendants and close relatives of the deceased usually receive an allowance before they're liable for inheritance tax. Some countries have strict succession laws (they don't always apply to foreigners) regarding who you can leave your assets to. To take advantage of lower tax rates, it's recommended to leave property to your spouse, children or parents, rather than to someone unrelated. Most countries don't recognise the rights to inheritance of a non-married partner, although there are a number of solutions to this problem, e.g. a life insurance policy.

There are a number of ways to avoid, reduce or delay inheritance tax depending on the country, including buying property through an offshore company or trust, or inserting a clause in a property purchase contract allowing a property to be left in its entirety to a surviving spouse without being shared among the children. A surviving spouse can also be given a life interest in an estate in preference to children or parents, through a 'gift between spouses'. Some bequests are exempt from inheritance tax, including certain types of properties and legacies to charities and government bodies. **It's important for both residents and non-residents owning a business or property in the Far East to decide in advance how they wish to dispose of it.** If possible, this should be done before buying a home or other property in the region, as it can be complicated and expensive to change later.

Inheritance law is a complicated subject and professional advice should be sought from an experienced lawyer who's familiar with the inheritance laws of the country where you plan to buy a business or home and any other countries involved. Your will (see below) is a vital component in keeping inheritance and gift tax to the minimum or delaying its payment.

Gift Tax

Gift tax is calculated in the same way as inheritance tax, according to the relationship between the donor and the recipient and the size of the gift. A reduction is usually granted according to the age of the donor (generally the younger the donor the larger the reduction).

WILLS

It's an unfortunate fact of life that you're unable to take your hard-earned assets with you when you take your final bow. All adults should make a will, irrespective of how large or small their assets. The disposal of your estate depends on your country of domicile (see **Liability** on page 167). Most countries permit foreigners who aren't domiciled in the Far East to make a will in any language and under the law of any country, provided it's valid under the law of that country. However, if there's a conflict of law, the law that generally applies is the law of the country where the testator was a citizen at the time of his death. A will must usually be in writing but not necessarily in the hand of the testator.

Note that 'immovable' property, i.e. land and buildings, must usually be disposed of (on death) in accordance with local law. All other property in the Far East or elsewhere (defined as 'movables') may be disposed of in accordance with the law of your home country or domicile. Therefore, it's important to establish where you're domiciled. One solution for a non-resident wishing to avoid foreign inheritance laws may be to buy a business or property through a company, in which case the shares of the company are 'movable' assets and are therefore governed by the succession laws of the owner's country of domicile.

In many countries, the law gives the immediate family (i.e. spouse, children and parents) an absolute right to inherit a share of an estate, and therefore it isn't possible to disinherit them as can be done in some other countries (e.g. the UK). However, a foreigner who wishes to dispose of his estate according to the laws of his home country can usually state this in his will. **In many countries, marriage doesn't automatically revoke a will, as it does, for example, in the UK.**

If you have a large estate in the Far East, it's wise to consult a lawyer when drawing up a will. It's possible to make two wills, one relating to property in your home country and another for any foreign property. Experts differ on whether you should have separate wills for property in different countries, written under local law, or have one will in your home country with a codicil (appendix) dealing with any foreign property. However, most lawyers believe that it's better to have a local will in any country where you own immovable property, which will speed up and reduce the cost of probate. **If you have more than one will, you must make sure that they don't contradict each other.**

You will also need someone to act as the executor of your estate, which can be particularly costly for modest estates. In some countries, many people appoint their bank, lawyer or other professional to act as the executor, although this should be avoided if possible as the fees can be astronomical. It's recommended to make your beneficiaries the executors; they can instruct a lawyer after your death if they require legal assistance. Note that probate (the proving of a will) can take a long time in some countries.

Keep a copy of your will(s) in a safe place and another copy with your lawyer or the executor of your estate. Don't leave it in a safe deposit box, which in the event of your death may be sealed for a period under local law. You should keep information regarding bank accounts and insurance policies with your will(s), but don't forget to tell someone where they are!

Note that inheritance law is a complicated subject and it's important to obtain professional legal advice when writing or altering your will(s).

COST OF LIVING

No doubt you'd like to estimate how far your money will stretch in the Far East and how much you will have left after paying your bills. The cost of living has risen considerably in most countries in the last decade or so, and some countries that previously enjoyed a relatively low cost of living are no longer quite so attractive, particularly for retirees. On the other hand, foreigners whose income is paid in 'hard' currencies, such as those of most northern European countries, the US and Canada, have seen their incomes (when converted to local currency) in many countries rise in recent years. If anything, the difference in the cost of living in the Far East and that of 'rich' North American and northern European countries has remained the same or has widened in favour of the richer countries.

If you spend only a limited time in the Far East each year, you won't be too concerned about the local cost of living. However, **if you plan to live in the region permanently you should ensure that your income is, and will remain, sufficient to live on bearing in mind currency devaluations (if your income isn't paid in local currency), inflation, and extraordinary expenses such as medical bills or anything else that may drastically reduce your income (such as stock market crashes and recessions)**. Note that if your pension is paid in a currency that's devalued, this could have a catastrophic affect on your standard of living. Note also that some countries (e.g. the UK) freeze state pensions at the current rate for those going to live permanently in certain countries.

It's difficult to calculate an average cost of living for any country, as it depends very much on an individual's circumstances and lifestyle as well as where he lives. It's generally cheaper to live in a rural area than in a large city or a popular resort area (homes are also much cheaper). Prices in each country's cities are similar (e.g. Beijing, Shanghai and Guangzhou in China), and city prices are around double those of modest towns, but three to ten times those of backward, isolated rural areas, although these are disappearing fast in all 11 countries, including China.

Food in most warm countries is cheaper than in most northern European countries, although North Americans will find it costs around the same or more as at home. The equivalent of around US$250 should feed two adults for a month in most countries, including inexpensive local beer or spirits, but excluding fillet steak, caviar and expensive imported foods. In fact many northern Europeans (particularly Scandinavians) and North Americans find that if they live modestly without overdoing the luxuries, their cost of living in the Far East (excluding Hong Kong, Japan, Singapore and some of the region's cities) is around half that in their home countries.

A couple owning their home (with no mortgage) in potential 'retirement' areas (e.g. parts of Thailand) can 'survive' on a net income of as little as US$450 per month (some pensioners live on less) and most can live quite comfortably on an income of US$750 per month – this applies mainly to basic needs and doesn't include 'luxuries'.

Comparing prices and where feasible shopping abroad (possibly by post or via the internet – see page 283) for expensive items can yield huge savings. It may also be possible to make savings by buying clothes, general household items, furniture and furnishings, and even your car abroad. Where possible, foreign newspapers and magazines should be purchased on subscription. If you have a tight budget, you should avoid shopping in fashionable towns or shopping centres and 'tourist' shops, which may include supermarkets in areas inhabited mainly by foreigners. Ask the locals where to shop for the lowest prices and best value.

There are many websites providing cost of living comparisons between countries and major cities, including the Economic Research Institute (🖥 www. salariesreview.com and 🖥 www.erieri.com/sources), ECA (🖥 www.wind hamint.com/html/cd-biz. html), Money Manager (🖥 www.moneymanager. com.au/personal_finance/calcs/ costliving.html), Runzheimer International (🖥 www.runzheimer.com), Expat Forum (🖥 www.expatforum.com), the University of Michigan (🖥 www.lib.umich.edu/libhome/documents.center/ steccpi.html) and Career Perfect (🖥 www.careerperfect. com/careerperfect/ salaryinfo.htm).

Mercer Human Resources Consulting publishes an annual cost of living survey, which ranks world cities. The 40 most expensive cities for 2003 are shown in the table below (with cities in countries covered by this book highlighted); the Index figure shows the cost of living as a percentage of that in New York, which is taken arbitrarily as the 'standard'. Note that these figures include the cost of accommodation, which varies enormously from country to country and from city to city – see **Accommodation** in the Country Profiles (**Chapter 9**).

Rank	City	Index
1	**Tokyo, Japan**	**126.1**
2	Moscow, Russia	114.5
3	**Osaka, Japan**	**112.2**
4	**Hong Kong**	**111.6**
5	**Beijing, China**	**105.1**
6	Geneva, Switzerland	101.8
7	London, England	101.3
8	**Seoul, Korea**	**101.0**
9	Zurich, Switzerland	100.3
10	New York, US	100
11	**Shanghai, China**	**98.4**
12	St Petersburg, Russia	97.3
13	Oslo, Norway	92.7
14	Hanoi, Vietnam	89.5
15	Copenhagen, Denmark	89.4
16	Ho Chi Minh City, Vietnam	88.5
17	Milan, Italy	87.2
18	**Shenzhen, China**	**86.7**
18	**Guangzhou, China**	**86.7**
20	White Plains, NY, US	86.2
21	Dublin, Ireland	86.0

22	Los Angeles, US	85.6
23	Paris, France	84.3
24	Kiev, Ukraine	84.2
25	Beirut, Lebanon	83.9
25	Chicago, US	83.9
27	Miami, US	83.7
27	Riga, Latvia	83.7
29	**Taipei, Taiwan**	**83.5**
30	San Francisco, US	83.0
31	Douala, Cameroon	82.9
32	**Singapore**	**82.8**
33	Honolulu, US	82.8
34	Vienna, Austria	82.4
35	Abidjan, Ivory Coast	81.3
36	Helsinki, Finland	80.9
37	Budapest, Hungary	80.2
38	**Jakarta, Indonesia**	**80.0**
39	Abu Dhabi, UAE	79.5
40	Tel Aviv, Israel	79.1

The table below shows Mercer's world ranking of the 25 most expensive Asian cities (with those in countries covered by this book highlighted):

Rank	City	Index
1	**Tokyo, Japan**	**126.1**
3	**Osaka, Japan**	**112.2**
4	**Hong Kong**	**111.6**
5	**Beijing, China**	**105.1**
8	**Seoul, Korea**	**101.0**
11	**Shanghai, China**	**98.4**
14	Hanoi, Vietnam	89.5
16	Ho Chi Minh, Vietnam	88.5
18	**Shenzhen, China**	**86.7**
18	**Guangzhou, China**	**86.7**
29	**Taipei, Taiwan**	**83.5**
32	**Singapore**	**82.8**

38	Jakarta, Indonesia	80.0
94	Dacca, Bangladesh	67.6
97	Kuala Lumpur, Malaysia	67.3
101	Tianjin, China	66.4
103	Bandar Seri Begawan, Brunei	66.0
109	New Delhi, India	63.3
114	Mumbai, India	62.5
118	Colombo, Sri Lanka	60.0
125	Bangkok, Thailand	58.3
130	Karachi, Pakistan	56.5
132	Madras, India	51.1
135	Manila, Philippines	49.5
138	Bangalore, India	47.8

INSURANCE

An important aspect of living in the Far East is insurance, including health insurance (see page 143), travel insurance (see below), home insurance, third party liability insurance and car insurance (see page 228). In many countries, the government and local law provide for various obligatory state and employer insurance schemes. These may include sickness and maternity, accidents at work and occupational diseases, invalidity, old-age and survivor's pensions, unemployment insurance, and family allowances. It's unnecessary to spend half your income insuring yourself against every eventuality from the common cold to being sued for your last penny, but it's important to insure against any event that could precipitate a major financial disaster, such as a serious accident or your house falling down. Social security benefits in many countries may be non-existent or less than you're used to, and in most countries you'd be unwise to rely solely on state benefits to meet your needs.

As with anything concerning finance, it's important to shop around when buying insurance. Just collecting a few brochures from insurance agents or making a few phone calls could save you a lot of money. Note, however, that not all insurance companies are equally reliable or have the same financial stability, and it may be better to insure with a large international insurance company with a good reputation than with a small local company, even if this means paying higher premiums. Major international insurance companies have offices and representatives throughout the Far East.

Read all insurance contracts before signing them. If a policy is written in a language that you don't understand, get someone to check it and don't sign it unless you clearly understand the terms and the cover provided. Policies often contain traps and legal loopholes in the small print, and it's therefore essential to obtain professional advice and have contracts checked before signing them. Some insurance companies will do almost anything to avoid paying out in the event of a claim and will use any available legal loophole. Therefore it pays to deal only with reputable companies – not that they won't necessarily do likewise!

In all matters regarding insurance, you're responsible for ensuring that you and your family are legally insured abroad. Regrettably you cannot insure yourself against being uninsured or sue your insurance agent for giving you bad advice!

Bear in mind that if you wish to make a claim on an insurance policy, you may be required to report an incident to the police within 24 hours (this may also be a legal requirement). You should obtain legal advice for anything other than a minor claim, as the law in your Far Eastern country of domicile may differ considerably from that in your home country or your previous country of residence, so never assume that it's the same.

Travel Insurance

Travel Insurance is recommended for all who don't wish to risk having their journey spoiled by financial problems or to arrive broke. As you probably know, anything can and often does go wrong when travelling, sometimes before you even reach the airport or port (particularly when you don't have insurance). Travel insurance is available from many sources, including travel and insurance agents, motoring organisations, transport companies and direct from insurance companies. When you pay for your travel costs with some credit cards, your family (including children under the age of 25) are provided with free travel accident insurance up to a specified amount. However, you shouldn't rely on this insurance, as it usually covers death or serious injury only.

Level Of Cover

Before taking out travel insurance, carefully consider the level of cover you require and compare policies. Most policies include cover for loss of deposit or travel cancellation, missed flights, departure delay at both the start and end of a journey (a common occurrence), delayed and lost baggage and money, medical expenses and accidents (including repatriation if necessary), personal liability, legal expenses, and protection against a travel company or operator going bust. You should also insure against missing your flight due to an accident or transport breakdown. Note that some policies limit the amount you can claim for belongings to around US$300 per item.

Medical Expenses

Medical expenses are an important aspect of travel insurance and it isn't recommended to rely on reciprocal health arrangements (particularly in the Far

East – see page 143). You also shouldn't rely on travel insurance provided by charge and credit card companies, house contents policies or private medical insurance, none of which usually provide adequate cover (although you should take advantage of what they offer).

Most travel and holiday insurance policies don't provide the level of cover that most people need. The minimum medical insurance recommended by most experts is around US$400,000 in most Far Eastern countries and US$750,000 to $1.5 million in others, e.g. Japan. If applicable, check whether pregnancy-related claims are covered and whether there are any restrictions for those over a certain age, e.g. 65 or 70. Third party liability cover should be between US$750,000 and $1.5 million in most countries or US$1.5 to $3 million in the more litigious ones (principally Ireland and the US). Always check any exclusion clauses in contracts by obtaining a copy of the full policy document, as all relevant information isn't included in insurance leaflets.

Annual Policies

For people who travel abroad frequently or spend long periods abroad, an annual travel policy usually provides the best value, but always carefully check exactly what it includes. Many insurance companies offer annual travel policies for a premium of around US$150 to $250 for an individual (the equivalent of around three-months insurance with a standard travel insurance policy), which are excellent value for frequent travellers. The cost of an annual policy may depend on the area covered, e.g. South-east Asia, worldwide excluding North America and worldwide including North America, although it doesn't usually cover travel within your country of residence. There's also a limit on the number of trips per year and the duration of each trip, e.g. 90 or 120 days. An annual policy is usually a good choice for owners of a home in the Far East who travel there frequently for relatively short periods. However, carefully check exactly what's covered or omitted, as an annual policy may not provide adequate cover. A policy recommended by the Medical Advisory Service for Travellers Abroad is the Worldwide Travel Protector policy (☎ UK 0870-120 0112).

Claims

Although travel insurance companies gladly take your money, they aren't so keen to pay claims and you may have to persevere before they pay up. Fraudulent claims against travel insurance are common, so unless you can produce evidence to support your claim the insurers may think you're trying to cheat them. Always be persistent and make a claim irrespective of any small print, as this may be unreasonable and therefore invalid in law. All insurance companies require you to report any loss (or any incident for which you intend to make a claim) to the local police or carriers within 24 hours and to obtain a report. Failure to do this means that your claim usually won't be considered.

6.

EDUCATION

The quality and variety of schools in the Far East is an important consideration for families with school-age children. The quality of schools, their teaching staff and the education they provide vary considerably according to the country, region, city and even the neighbourhood of a city, as well as from school to school. There are good private and international (usually English-language) schools in most of the region's major cities, although the standard of state-funded education may leave a lot to be desired, particularly in run-down neighbourhoods. Education is compulsory in many countries between the ages of around 5 and 16, although students are increasingly encouraged to remain at school until the age of 18 and go on to university. For details of educational requirements and facilities in each territory, see the **Education** sections in the Country Profiles (**Chapter 9**).

Owing to language difficulties and the fact that most foreigners spend a relatively short time in the Far East, the vast majority of expatriate parents in the region send their children either to a local private school (often following the curriculum of their home country) or to a school in their home country.

Your choice of school should be made only after consideration of all the options and obtaining independent expert advice. You should think long-term and consider your children's interests, particularly regarding their education when your period in the region ends and you return home. If your children have any special education needs (see page 186), and especially if they have learning difficulties, you should seriously consider whether relocation is in the family's best interests, as it's unlikely that you will find the right sort of help and support in the Far East.

If you're able to choose the country where your child is educated the following checklist will help you decide:

- How long are you planning to remain in the Far East? If you're uncertain, it's probably better to assume a long stay. Due to language and other integration problems, enrolling a child in a foreign school with a foreign syllabus (state or private) is recommended only for a minimum of five years, particularly for teenage children (see **Language** on page 185).

- If you will be living in the Far East for a limited period, do you know where you're going to live afterwards? This may be an important consideration with regard to your children's schooling. How old are your children and what age will they be when you plan to leave the region? What plans do you have for their education and in which country?

- Should you send your children to a boarding school? If so, in which country?

- What are the secondary and further education prospects for your children abroad or in another country? Are foreign educational qualifications recognised in your home country or the country where you plan to live next?

- Does a school have a good academic record? Most schools must provide exam pass rate statistics and a prospectus, which they may post (mail) to you.

- What are the facilities for art and science subjects, for example arts and crafts, music, computer studies (how many computers?), science, hobbies, drama, cookery and photography? Does the school have an extensive library of up-to-date books (a good library is usually an excellent sign)? These should be listed in a school's prospectus.
- How large are the classes? What is the teacher:pupil ratio?

Obtain the opinions and advice of others who have been faced with the same decisions and problems as you, and collect as much information from as many different sources as possible before making a decision. Speak to teachers and the parents of children attending schools on your shortlist. If possible, interview the head teacher before making a decision. Most parents find that it's desirable to discuss the alternatives with their children before making a decision.

If you're able to choose between state and private education, the following checklist will help you decide:

- Bear in mind that the area in which you choose to live may affect your choice of local school(s). Although it may be unnecessary to send your children to the state school nearest your home, you may have difficulty obtaining admission to a state school if you don't live within its catchment area. If you choose a private day school, it must obviously be within a reasonable travelling distance of your home.
- What age are your children and how will they fit into a private school or the state school system in the Far East? The younger they are, the easier it will be to place them in a suitable school.
- If your children are English-speaking, how do they view the possibility of studying in a foreign language? Will they be able to communicate with their teachers? Is teaching available in English in a state school? (It invariably isn't).
- What are the school hours? What are the school holiday periods? How will the school hours and holidays influence your (and your spouse's) work and leisure activities? Note that state schools in some countries have classes on Saturday mornings.
- Will your children require your help with their studies? Will you be able to help them, particularly with a foreign language? See **Language** on page 185.
- Is religion an important consideration in your choice of school? In state schools in some countries, religion is a compulsory subject. Parents can, however, usually have their children excused religious instruction, although some schools are maintained by religious organisations and may make stipulations as to religious observance. Religion is an issue in every area of life in some countries (e.g. Brunei and parts of Indonesia and Malaysia), where education is strictly divided along religious lines.

- Do you want your children to attend a co-educational (mixed) school? State schools in most countries are co-educational.

- In many countries there are separate state schools for children with special educational needs (see page 186), including those with emotional and behavioural difficulties, moderate and severe learning difficulties, communication problems, hearing or sight impairment, or physical handicaps. There may also be special schools or facilities for gifted children.

See also **State Schools** below and **Choosing A Private School** on page 189.

Further Information

In many countries, both state and private schools publish prospectuses and there are also independent (state and private) school guides published by local councils, newspapers and publishers. You can obtain information from embassies and consulates, many of which have an education section or officer, and there are other official organisations in many countries. For example, the British Council (which has offices in around 80 countries) provides foreign students with information concerning all aspects of education in the UK, while the Fulbright Commission provides an 'Educational Advisory Service' in many countries for students planning to study at an American college or university. United States Information Services' (USIS) offices located in all American embassies also provide information.

In many countries, the Ministry of Education has a website (possibly with an English-language version) and individual education authorities or even schools (particularly private schools) often have their own websites. Other useful sources of information include the following:

- The European Council of International Schools (⌨ www.ecis.org), which publishes an *International Schools Directory*;

- International Schools Services (⌨ www.iss.edu), which serves international schools around the world and produces *The Directory of Overseas Schools for Americans*;

- The US State Department (⌨ www.state.gov/www/about_state/schools), whose site contains information about American-sponsored elementary and secondary schools overseas;

- The International Baccalaureate Organisation (⌨ www.ibo.org), which has offices in 13 countries;

- Schools Worldwide (⌨ www.schoolsworldwide.com), whose site contains a database of hundreds of international English-speaking schools;

- Ibiblio – the Public's Library (⌨ www.ibiblio.org/cisco/schools/international), whose site contains a list of American international school;

- The Guide to Study Abroad (⌨ www.studyabroad.nu, where you can search for vocational schools, universities and language schools worldwide);

- International Schools and Bilingual Education (⌨ www.nanana.com/inter schoollinks.html), whose site has links to useful educational websites;

- International School.Com (⌨ www.internationalschool.com), whose site contains a list of countries with international schools and a free employment service for schools and teachers seeking a position abroad.

LANGUAGE

There are many considerations to take into account when choosing an appropriate school in the Far East, not least the language of study. In countries where English isn't one of the local languages, the only schools that use English as the teaching language may be foreign (e.g. American and British) and international private schools. In some countries there are also multilingual schools, which teach students in both English and the local language (but not simultaneously!). If your children attend any other school, they must study all subjects in the local language. Many state schools also teach regional languages, although these may be optional or taught outside normal school hours. However, in some countries, state schools in certain autonomous regions may teach most or all lessons in a local language or dialect, which may leave you no option but to pay for a private school (or move to another region).

For most children, studying in a major foreign language isn't such a handicap as it may at first appear, particularly for those aged under ten. The majority of children adapt quickly and most become reasonably fluent within three to six months (if only it were so easy for adults!), although you shouldn't underestimate the difficulties they will initially face. All children don't adapt equally well to a change of language and culture, particularly teenagers (at around 10 to 12 years of age children begin to learn languages more slowly), many of whom encounter great difficulties during their first year or so.

State school systems in all 11 territories make little or no concession to children who don't speak the local language fluently, for example by providing intensive language lessons. This can make the first few months quite an ordeal for foreign children. It's worthwhile inquiring about the availability of extra classes before choosing where to live.

While undergoing extra language study, children may fall behind in other subjects. In many countries, children who don't make the grade must repeat a year (or even two) and there's usually a fairly wide age range in the higher school classes. There's often no stigma attached to the repetition of classes (except among some children), as children learn at different speeds and many school systems simply recognise this fact. However, if a child fails to maintain the required standard in a higher grade secondary school, e.g. a high school, he may be required to join another school with a less demanding curriculum.

If your local state school doesn't provide extra language classes, your only choice will be to pay for private lessons or send your child to another (possibly private) school, where extra tuition is provided. Some parents send a child to an English-speaking school for a year, followed by a move to a bilingual or local language school. Other parents believe that it's better to throw their children in at the deep end. Given the choice (and with hindsight!), many children prefer to attend a local school which allows them to become fully integrated into the local community, language and culture. It depends on the character, ability and wishes of the child.

Whatever you decide, it will help if your child has some intensive language lessons before you move to the Far East. It may also be possible to organise an educational or cultural exchange with a school or family in the region before you make the move, which is a considerable help in integrating a child into the local language and culture. Parents should also learn some of the local language!

If you speak English, you should ensure that your children learn English as well as the local language and speak it daily at home, as they may not start learning English in state schools until they reach secondary level, and even then it may be voluntary (although in many countries children now start learning English in primary school). English may become compulsory only when a child is studying modern languages, for example in a high school, or when a specialist subject is studied requiring English-language proficiency. In some countries, English-speaking parents organise private English classes for their children or teach them themselves.

SPECIAL EDUCATION

The provision of special education for children with particular education needs – with moderate or severe learning difficulties (e.g. a hearing, speech, or sight impediment, a physical handicap, dyslexia or autism) or a behavioural problem, which either prevents or hinders them from attending a mainstream school for their age group – varies considerably from country to country and is poor or non-existent in many countries.

Some countries provide dedicated schools, while others prefer (whenever possible) to educate children with special needs in mainstream schools, in order to give them the same education as other children. Unfortunately, there's often a shortage of places at special schools and too many children whose special needs aren't best suited to 'normal' education are taught in mainstream schools.

Some special schools are run privately by voluntary bodies, which may receive a grant from central government for capital expenditure and equipment, and some private schools provide education wholly or mainly for children with special education needs. Most education systems provide an educational psychological service for children with behavioural problems.

In some countries, the state education system also provides special teaching and facilities for exceptionally gifted children, but in most the only avenue open to most parents is to pay for private tuition or apply for a private school scholarship. Some organisations, such as Mensa (🖳 www.mensa.org), provide help to develop the potential of gifted children through special schools and individual counselling. There are Mensa groups in 6 of the 11 territories: Hong Kong (🖳 http://hkmensa.org); Indonesia (🖳 62-21 4600847); Japan (🖳www.japanmensa.org); Korea (🖳 www.mensakorea.org); Malaysia (🖳 www. malaysianmensa.org); Philippines (🖳 www.ph.mensa.org); Singapore (🖳 www. mensa.org.sg). It's as important to choose the best possible school for a talented or gifted child as it's for a child with learning difficulties.

STATE SCHOOLS

You may have the right to express a preference for a particular state school, but priority is often given to children living in a school's catchment area, families with a child already at a particular school and children with special family or medical circumstances. **It's therefore vital to research the best schools in a given area and to ensure that your child will be accepted at your chosen school before buying or renting a home.** Not surprisingly, homes near the best state schools are at a premium and prices in some areas are driven up by the high demand. Note also that schools are sometimes forced to reduce their catchment area, thus excluding many children whose parents may have moved home specifically so their offspring could attend a particular school. **In some areas, children can be denied the right to attend a particular school simply because they live on the wrong side of a street.**

Enrolment

To enrol your children in a state school, you should enquire at the local town hall or the local schools information service. You may also be able to obtain information by post or via the internet. When enrolling, you need to provide details of a child's age, previous schooling and knowledge of the local language. You must also provide certain documents which may include a child's birth certificate or passport, with an official translation (if necessary), proof of residence and possibly proof of immunisation (see **Children's Health** on page 140). In many countries, immunisations are recorded in a child's health book, which is issued to parents when a child is born.

PRIVATE SCHOOLS

Fee-paying schools – all or part of whose funding comes from private sources rather than the state – are usually termed private schools, although they may be called independent or 'public' schools. Private schools may be owned by an individual, an institution or a company and, although traditionally the preserve of the wealthy, in many countries they attract an increasing number of pupils from less privileged backgrounds.

Private schools range from nursery (kindergarten) to day and boarding schools, and include both experimental schools and traditional institutions. In many countries, private schools take pupils from the ages of 2 to 19 and include boarding and day schools (some are both), single-sex and mixed (co-educational) schools. In some countries, most private schools are single-sex, although there are also usually mixed schools. Some schools cater for special education needs (see page 186) and there are also private schools for gifted children in art, music, theatre or dance in some countries. Some private schools follow special or unorthodox methods of teaching, for example Montessori nursery schools and Rudolf Steiner schools, although all schools must usually meet certain criteria and be registered with the local Ministry of Education. There are also private schools for religious and ethnic minorities, for example schools for Muslims in non-Muslim countries, where there's a strict code regarding the segregation of boys and girls.

In many countries, private schools include international schools, and American, British and other foreign-nationality schools (which may include Canadian, Chinese, Dutch, French, German, Greek, Japanese, Norwegian, Spanish and Swedish schools), usually located in or near the capital city. There are also commercial tutorial colleges or 'crammers' in many countries, providing a one-term or one-year 'resit' course for students who have failed their university entrance exams.

Students at American schools are prepared for entry to an American college or university through Advanced Placement (AP) courses or follow the International Baccalaureate pre-university curriculum (see below). American and British schools usually accept students of all nationalities and religious backgrounds, although they may give priority to American or British citizens. Non-English-speaking students receive intensive tuition in English, where necessary. Many international schools have a comprehensive English-Second Language (ESL) programme and attract students from many countries. Note that the fees at American schools may be considerably higher than those at other private schools, particularly for boarders.

In most countries, private schools follow a similar curriculum to state schools, although foreign schools may follow the curriculum (and examinations) of their mother country and may also offer the two-year International Baccalaureate (IB) pre-university course, which provides an international university-entry qualification. International schools usually prepare students for the local university entrance examination plus the IB exam. Many North American universities grant students with an IB diploma up to one year's credit. Some international schools offer an American curriculum in addition to the IB curriculum. For information contact the International Baccalaureate Organisation (🖳 www.ibo.org), which has offices in around 13 countries. International schools generally provide a better standard of education than state schools, although the regime may be tougher and children should be prepared for this.

A complete list of international schools in 75 countries worldwide is contained in the International Schools Directory, published annually by the

European Council of International Schools (ECIS), 21 Lavant Street, Petersfield, Hants. GU32 3EL, UK (☎ 01730-268244, 🖳 www.ecis.org). Information about foreign and international schools is also available from the appropriate embassy.

Private school fees vary considerably according to a variety of factors, including the country, the age of pupils, the reputation and quality of the school, and its location (schools in major cities are generally much more expensive than those situated in rural areas). Day school fees vary from as little as a few thousand US$ per year or term for primary schools up to tens of thousands of US$ per year or term for a senior boarding school. Fees aren't usually all-inclusive and additional obligatory charges are made in addition to optional extra services. Private schools aren't always run for profit and surplus income is often reinvested in the running of schools (many private schools are run by charitable foundations). Many schools provide scholarships for bright or talented pupils, usually awarded as a result of competitive examination, which vary in value from full fees to a proportion only.

Don't assume that all private schools are excellent or that they offer a better education than state schools. In many countries, the vast majority of parents choose to send their children to a state school, even when the cost of private education isn't an important consideration. However, private schools may provide a more broad-based education and offer a more varied approach to sport, music, drama, art and a wider choice of academic subjects than a state school. Their aim is usually the development of children as individuals and the encouragement of their unique talents, which is made possible by small classes that allow teachers to provide pupils with individually-tailored lessons and tuition. Some private schools cater for special needs, including gifted children and slow learners or those who suffer from dyslexia.

Make applications to private schools as far in advance as possible (before conception for the best schools). Obviously, if you're coming from abroad, you won't usually be able to apply one or two years in advance, which is usually considered to be the best time to book a place. Although many nursery and junior schools accept pupils on a first-come, first-served basis, the best and most exclusive schools have waiting lists or a demanding selection procedure. Entrance to private schools is by examination, report or assessment, interview or a combination of these. Most popular schools, particularly day schools in major cities, have long waiting lists. Don't rely on enrolling your child in a particular school and neglect other alternatives, particularly if your chosen school has a rigorous entrance examination. When applying, you're usually requested to send previous school reports, exam results and records. Before enrolling your child in a private school, ensure that you understand the withdrawal conditions.

Choosing A Private School

The following checklist is designed to help you choose an appropriate and reputable private school in the Far East:

- Does the school have a good reputation? Does it belong to a recognised national body for private schools? How long has it been established? Is it financially stable?

- Does the school have a good academic record? For example, what percentage of pupils receive good examination passes or go on to good universities? What subjects do the pupils do best in? All schools provide exam pass-rate statistics. On the other hand, if your child isn't exceptionally bright, you may prefer to send him to a school with less academic pressure.

- What does the curriculum include (a broad and well-balanced curriculum is best)? Ask to see a typical pupil timetable to check the ratio of academic to non-academic subjects. Check the number of free study periods and whether they're supervised.

- Do you wish to send your children to a single-sex or a co-educational school? Many children, particularly girls, make better progress without the distractions of the opposite sex (although their social education may be neglected).

- If you're considering a day school, what are the school hours? Does the school provide transport for pupils to and from home? Some schools offer weekly boarding, which allows pupils to return home at weekends.

- If you've decided on a boarding school, what standard and type of accommodation is provided? What is the quality and variety of food provided? What is the dining room like? Does the school have a dietician?

- Do you intend to send your children to a junior or senior private school only or both?

- How many children attend the school and what's the average class size?

- What's the ratio of teachers to pupils? Are pupil numbers increasing or decreasing? Has the number of pupils increased dramatically in the last few years (which could be a good or a bad sign)? Check that class sizes are in fact what the prospectus says they are.

- What are the qualification requirements for teachers? What is the mother tongue of the majority of teachers? What is the teacher turnover? A high turnover is a bad sign and usually suggests under-paid teachers and poor working conditions.

- What extras will you have to pay? For example, you may have to pay for optional lessons (e.g. music, dancing and sports), lunches, art supplies, sports equipment, school trips, phone calls, clothing (most private schools have obligatory uniforms, which can be expensive), insurance, textbooks and stationery. Most schools charge parents for every little thing.

- Which countries do most students come from?

- Is religion an important consideration in your choice of school? What is the religious bias of the school, if any?

- Are special English classes provided for children whose English doesn't meet the required standard? Usually if a child is under ten it doesn't matter if his English is weak. However, children over this age may not be accepted unless they can read English fluently (as printed in textbooks for their age). Some schools provide intensive language tuition for foreign students.

- What languages does the school teach as obligatory or optional subjects?

- What is the student turnover?

- What are the school terms and holiday periods? Private school holidays are much longer than state schools in some countries, e.g. four weeks at Easter and Christmas and ten weeks in the summer, and they often don't coincide with state school holiday periods.

- What are the withdrawal conditions, should you wish to remove your child? A term's notice is usual.

- What examinations are set? In which subjects? How do they fit in with your child's education plans?

- What sports instruction and facilities are provided?

- What are the facilities for art and science subjects, e.g. arts and crafts, music, computer studies (how many computers?), science, hobbies, drama, cookery and photography?

- What sort of outings and holidays does the school organise?

- What medical facilities does the school provide, e.g. infirmary, resident doctor or nurse? Is health and accident insurance included in the fees?

- What sort of discipline and punishments are imposed and are restrictions relaxed as children get older?

- What reports are provided for parents and how often? How much contact does the school have with parents?

- Last, but not least, unless someone else is paying, what are the fees?

Draw up a shortlist of possible schools and obtain a prospectus (some schools provide a video prospectus). If applicable, also obtain a copy of the school magazine. Before making a final choice, it's important to visit the schools on your shortlist during term time and talk to teachers and students. Where possible, check the answers to the above questions in person and don't rely on a school's prospectus to provide the information. If you're unhappy with the answers, look elsewhere. Having made your choice, maintain a check on your child's progress, listen to his complaints and compare notes with other parents. If something doesn't seem right, try to establish whether a complaint is founded or not and, if it is, take action to have the problem resolved.

HIGHER & FURTHER EDUCATION

Post-school education is generally divided into higher and further education, although the distinction is often blurred. Higher education is usually defined as advanced courses of a standard higher than a secondary school-leaving certificate (such as the International Baccalaureate) and usually refers only to first degree courses. Further education generally embraces everything except first degree courses. Courses may be full-time, part-time or sandwich courses (courses that combine periods of full-time study with full-time training and paid work in industry and commerce).

As at all levels of education, the quality and value of higher and further education varies considerably according to the country and, more importantly, the educational establishment. Each year hundreds of thousands of English-speaking students, including those whose families are based in the Far East, study in countries such as Australia, Canada, the United Kingdom and the US, where teaching foreign students is a lucrative business.

The minimum age of admission to university in most countries is 18, although some universities admit exceptional students at a younger age, and first degree courses usually last for a minimum of three years, including those in the countries mentioned above. In contrast, in many continental European countries, courses have no set length and many students take as long as seven to nine years to attain their degree.

Foreign students may need a student visa or residence permit (see page 19). A foreign national over 18 years of age who wishes to study full-time in the Far East on a course lasting longer than three or six months (depending on the country) and which will lead to a professional or educational qualification must provide evidence of his educational qualifications and his financial means. Evidence must be provided to both the educational establishment and the immigration authorities.

Entrance Qualifications

The minimum qualification for entrance to a university in most countries is the examinations that students take before leaving high school at the age of 17 or 18, e.g. the International Baccalaureate. Generally the better the university (or the better the reputation) and the more popular the course, the higher the entrance qualifications. Minimum entrance requirements are set by individual universities and colleges and may vary considerably. However, universities and other institutions may be flexible in their entrance requirements, particularly regarding 'mature' students (e.g. those aged 21 or over) and those with qualifications other than standard school-leaving diplomas.

Generally, overseas students' qualifications which would admit them to a university in their home country are taken into consideration, although passes in certain subjects may be mandatory, depending on the course. Whatever your qualifications, all applications are considered on their merits. All foreign students require a thorough knowledge of English or the language of study, which will usually be tested unless a certificate is provided. Most universities accept the International Baccalaureate certificate as an entrance qualification, but an American high school diploma isn't usually accepted. Contact individual universities for detailed information.

Applications

To apply for a place at university you should begin by writing to the Admissions Officer of selected universities, giving your personal details and asking for information. If you're encouraged by the reply, you must then apply formally. Applicants can apply for a number of courses (which may be at different universities), for which there may be a nominal fee. Note that the number of applicants per university place varies considerably from university to university. You'd be wise not to make all your applications at universities where competition for places is at its fiercest (unless you're a genius). The university year begins in October in many countries and you must usually make an application in the autumn of the year before you plan to start your course, i.e. a year in advance.

Accommodation

Following acceptance by a college or university, students are recommended to apply for a place in a hall of residence ('in hall') or other college accommodation, such as self-catering houses and apartments. Such accommodation is usually limited, although many universities accommodate all first year students and may give priority to foreign students, particularly those paying full fees! You should write as soon as possible after acceptance to accommodation or welfare officers, whose job is to help students find suitable accommodation (both college and private). In some countries, many students rent privately-owned apartments or houses, which are shared with other students, although this kind of accommodation may be difficult to find and expensive. Another alternative is to find lodgings where you rent a room in a private house with meals included.

Fees & Costs

Most countries set different fee levels for local students (e.g. those from local schools or the local county or state), students from other counties or states within the same country (who may be termed 'home' students), and foreign students. There are no fees for local students in many countries or nominal fees only, and these may also apply to foreign students who have lived in a country for a number of years, e.g. those who have attended a local secondary school.

Students whose parents are resident in the same country may also pay the same fees as local students.

The cost of living (excluding course fees) varies considerably with the country, region and particular city or town. In many countries, students are forced to choose their university according to where they can more easily survive or where they can get a part-time job rather than according to where they can follow their preferred course. The cost of accommodation is a major factor for many students when deciding which university to attend, and in many countries the majority of students live at home and study locally to reduce costs. The cost of living, particularly accommodation, is generally much lower in a provincial town than in a major or capital city (see page 173).

Many universities have 'job clubs' or agencies to help students supplement their income and in some countries students work their way through university. Overseas students studying in an EU country for longer than six months are entitled to free health care from the public health service. However, in countries without a public health service (or when students aren't eligible), it's usually mandatory to have private health insurance. **Note that financial hardship is a major cause of student drop-outs in many countries.**

Grants & Scholarships

In most countries there are grants (e.g. from governments, professional bodies, educational trusts, universities and colleges), public and private scholarships and award schemes available to overseas students, particularly at postgraduate level, which are awarded to the most needy students. Many universities offer sports scholarships. It's wise to apply as early as possible for a grant or scholarship. In many countries, companies and professional organisations (plus the military) also sponsor higher education, in return for a number of years' service. Note, however, that even with a grant you must be able to support yourself during your studies.

Student Bodies

In most countries, universities have a huge variety of societies and clubs, many of which are organised by a students' union or council, which is the centre of social activities. Note that universities in some countries ban alcohol on campus and there are no student bars, such as are common in other countries (e.g. the UK). Most universities have excellent sports facilities. Wherever you're studying, take at least a dozen passport-size photographs for student identity cards, travel cards, etc..

Further Information

There are a number of books for anyone planning to continue higher or further education abroad, these include the *ECIS Higher Education Directory* (⌨ www.

ecis.org), *Making the Most of Higher Education*, *Which Subject?* (Which?, UK), *The Student Book* by Klaus Boehm and Jenny Lees-Spalding (Macmillan, UK), which contains everything you need to know about how to get into and survive university, *The Times Good University Guide* (UK) and *Barron's Profiles of American Colleges*.

LEARNING THE LANGUAGE

If you don't speak the local language fluently, you may wish to take a language course. Obtaining a working knowledge of the local language in many countries is relatively easy, as you will be constantly immersed in the language and will have the maximum opportunity to practise. However, if you wish to speak or write it fluently, you will probably need to attend a language school or find a private tutor. It's usually necessary to have a recognised qualification in the local language in order to be accepted at a college or university.

It's sometimes thought that the official languages of the 11 countries in this book (Cantonese, Filipino, Indonesian, Japanese, Korean, Malay, Mandarin and Thai) are all-but impossible for foreigners to learn, even sufficiently to read a menu or road sign. This isn't true, although Chinese languages and Japanese don't have alphabets, which makes learning them more difficult than the others, certainly at the beginning. Korean, on the other hand, has an easy-to-learn alphabet, as does Thai. Even more western-friendly, Indonesian has the same alphabet as English, the Latin script has been adopted to write the Malay alphabet (it used to be in Arabic) and the Filipino alphabet of 31 letters includes the 26 of the English alphabet.

Although it isn't essential for retirees and residents who live and work in many Far Eastern countries to learn the local language, it certainly makes life easier and less frustrating, and gives you an advantage in the job market. In some countries, many foreign residents make little effort to learn the local language beyond the few words necessary to buy the weekly groceries and order a cup of coffee, and many live as if they were on a short holiday. However, for anyone living in the region permanently, learning the local language should be seen as a necessity, not an option. It's vital to start studying as soon as possible after you arrive and to avoid foreign 'ghettos' and live among the local people if you really want to learn the language.

You will need to learn enough to understand your bills, use the phone, deal with shop assistants and service people, and communicate with your local town hall, for example. If you don't, you will be continually frustrated in your communications and will be constantly calling on friends and acquaintances to assist you, or even paying people to do jobs you could easily do yourself. However, the most important and serious purpose of learning the local language is that in an emergency it could save your life or that of a loved one! Learning the language also helps you appreciate the local way of life and make the most of your time in the Far East, and opens many doors that remain firmly closed to resident 'tourists'.

A big handicap for English speakers is that in most Far Eastern countries there's usually someone around who speaks English, particularly when you want to speak the local language. Although you can travel the world speaking only English, it can be a distinct disadvantage when you need to learn a foreign language. Don't get caught in the trap of seeking refuge in the English language or allowing others to practise their English at your expense. You must persist in speaking the local language; give in too easily and you will never learn. One of the penalties of being a native English speaker is that you may receive little or no encouragement to learn the local language, but will be condemned as a lazy foreigner if you don't learn it. **Note that most foreigners living abroad find that their business and social enjoyment and success is directly related to the degree to which they master the local language.**

Further information about language courses in most countries can be obtained from embassies and consulates, Chambers of Commerce, trade organisations, universities and colleges, via the internet, and direct from language schools (see the local yellow pages).

Methods

Most people can teach themselves a great deal through the use of books, tapes, videos and computer software courses. However, even the best students require some help. Classes are offered in most countries by language schools (see below), local and foreign colleges and universities, private and international schools, foreign and international organisations, local associations and clubs, Chambers of Commerce and town halls, and private teachers (see below). In some countries, there's an ethnic minority language service providing information and counselling in a variety of languages. These may organise classes, including home tuition, at beginner and intermediate levels.

Free language courses are available for foreigners in some countries, while in others immigrants who don't speak the local language must learn at their own expense. Classes range from language courses for complete beginners, through specialised business and cultural courses, to university-level seminars leading to recognised diplomas. Most universities offer language courses all year round, including summer courses, which are generally cheaper than language schools, although classes may be much larger. If you already speak the local language but need conversational practice, you may wish to enrol in an art or craft course at a local institute or club.

Language Schools

There are language schools in most large towns and cities in the Far East, offering a wide range of classes. Most schools run various classes according to language ability, how many hours you wish to study per week, how much money you want to invest, and how quickly you wish to learn. Some employers pay an employee's course fees or provide free in-house language classes. For those to whom money is no object (hopefully your employer), there are total immersion courses, where you study for at least eight hours per day (including lunch and sometimes dinner), five days per week, for two to six weeks. Language classes generally fall into the following categories: extensive (4 hours per week), intensive (15 hours) and total immersion (20 to 40 hours).

Don't expect to become fluent in a short period unless you have a particular flair for languages or already have a good command of a language. Unless you need to learn a language quickly, it's probably better to arrange your lessons over a long period. However, don't commit yourself to a long course of study (particularly an expensive one) before ensuring that it's the right course. Most schools offer free tests to help you find your level, a free introductory lesson and small classes or private lessons. It's important to choose the right course, particularly if you're studying a language in order to continue with full-time education (or get a job) and need to reach a minimum standard or gain a particular qualification.

Some schools offer combined courses where language study is linked with optional subjects, including business language, art and culture, reading and commenting on a daily newspaper, conversation, local history, and traditions and folklore. Some schools also combine language courses with a range of social and sports activities such as horse riding, tennis, windsurfing, golf, skiing, hang-gliding and scuba-diving.

Private Lessons

You may prefer to have private lessons, which are a quicker but more expensive way of learning. The main advantage of private lessons is that you learn at your own speed and aren't
 back by slow learners or left floundering in the wake of the class genius. A cheaper way to improve your language ability is to find a person wishing to learn English (or your mother tongue) and make a 'language exchange', spending half the time speaking the local language and half speaking your language. You can advertise for a private teacher or exchange partner in local newspapers, on bulletin and notice boards (in shopping centres, supermarkets, universities, clubs, etc.), and through your or your spouse's employer. Don't forget to ask your friends, neighbours and colleagues if they can recommend a private teacher. Private teachers often advertise in local English-language publications. See also **English Teachers & Translators** on page 61.

7.

TRANSPORT

For many people an important aspect of living in the Far East is being able to get around easily, cheaply and safely. Public transport services in the region's countries vary considerably, from excellent to terrible or even non-existent, according to where you live. In some countries, public transport is generally poor and there's no rail service and only an infrequent and unreliable local bus service. Public transport tends to be excellent or adequate in major cities, however, where there may be an integrated system encompassing buses, trains, trams and possibly a metro or ferry system. Outside the main towns and cities, public transport can be sparse and most people who live in rural areas find it necessary to own a car.

PUBLIC TRANSPORT

If you don't drive or aren't planning to own a car in the Far East, you should investigate the frequency and cost of local public transport such as buses, trains, ferries and taxis; if you need to rely on public transport, you usually need to live in a city or large town. Even in a city, you may need to use taxis to carry your shopping home or have it delivered – unless you can afford to eat out all the time!

Bear in mind that in some of the region's countries, public transport is dangerous, with old unserviceable 'equipment' (aircraft, buses, ferries, taxis, trains, etc.), a lack of safety equipment and procedures (life-belts, life-rafts, seat-belts, etc.), overloading, or poorly trained or incompetent drivers and operators. **Poorly maintained public transport is a bigger danger than that posed by private vehicle users, and is responsible for between 60 and 70 per cent of transport accidents in developing countries.**

Taxis are common and plentiful in most countries, although they can be prohibitively expensive or dangerous in some. In some countries there are inexpensive shared taxis or mini-buses, which will pick up and drop off passengers at any point along their route. In some countries foreigners are warned not to use public transport except for official taxis. Details of public transport by country are given below.

Brunei

Most people in Brunei own a car (or cars) and public transport is thin on the ground (whether this is a cause or an effect of high car ownership is debatable). Brunei has a ratio of around one car to every 1.7 people, the world's third-highest rate, 30 per cent higher than the US, 50 per cent higher than the UK and around four times higher than Malaysia.

Buses

Brunei's bus system is modern, inexpensive (fares start at BD$1/US$1.73) and reliable, its main drawback being that it shuts down at 6pm. There are five bus routes operating daily between 6am and 6pm in the capital and only main town, Bandar Seri Begawan, as follows:

- **Central Line** – Buses run every 15 minutes and stop at the International Airport, post office, government offices, government schools, Terrace Hotel, Sheraton Utama Hotel, the Youth Centre, the main bus terminal in Bandar, the Arts and Handicraft Museum, the Brunei Museum and the Malay Technology Museum.

- **Circle Line** – Buses run every 20 minutes and stop at the main bus terminal in Bandar, the Ripas Hospital, Jame' Asr Hassani Mosque, Gadong fish and vegetable market, Centrepoint in Gadong, government offices, the Immigration and Labour Department, the Sultan Haji Hassanal Bolkiah National Stadium, the Pusat Dakwah Islamiah, Supa Save Mabohai, Sheraton Utama Hotel, Terrace Hotel and the Youth Centre.

- **Northern Line 1 and 2** – Buses run between Berakas Camp, Brunei International Airport and the bus terminal in Bandar.

- **Northern Line 3** – Buses run between Berakas Camp, the bus terminal and the Malay Technology Museum in Kota Batu.

Buses also operate from Bandar Seri Bagawan to Seria (57mi/91km from Bandar), Kuala Belait (10mi/16km from Bandar), Tutong (30mi/48km from Bandar) and Muara (17mi/27km from Bandar), but services are much less frequent than within the capital and, for travel outside Bandar Seri Begawan, the car is used by most people.

Taxis

Taxis are available in Bandar Seri Begawan, usually metered, with fares starting at BD$4 (US$6.90), with a 50 per cent surcharge between 9pm and 6am, and a BD$5 (US$8.65) surcharge for trips to the airport, plus BD$1 (US$1.73) for each piece of luggage loaded into the boot. The average fare from the city centre to the Brunei Museum is BD$5 to 7 (US$8.65 to 12.10) and from the airport to the centre (7mi/11km) BD$15 to 20 (US$26 to 35). Tipping isn't expected.

Ferries

There are 'water taxis' from Bandar to Kampong Ayer (Brunei's famous water village), with stops at Jalan Kianggeh and Jalan McArthur. The fare is around BD$2 (US$3.45) for a short trip. Services also operate from Bandar to Bangar, Limbang (on Sarawak) and some towns in Malaysian Sabah.

China

Buses

China's city and town buses are frequent and inexpensive (usually between RMB1 and RMB 2 (12¢ and 24¢) for most journeys within town, RMB2 to RMB

10 (24¢ to US$1.20) for suburban journeys and RMB2 to RMB 8 (24¢ to 96¢) for air-conditioned bus journeys within town), but are often crowded (you must become used to pushing in order to get on) and popular with pickpockets. You buy your ticket from a ticket seller on the bus who sits near the door in the middle of the bus. You must be able to say the name of the destination or have it written in Chinese, as the seller almost certainly won't speak or understand English.

Long distance buses are frequent and inexpensive in China, but they're also crowded and stuffy and trains or aeroplanes are generally preferred for long distances (see below).

Beijing: Beijing's buses serve around 140 routes and run frequently from 5.30am to 11pm, with a limited night service between 11pm and 5.30am. Buses can become very crowded, particularly during rush hours (6.30 to 8.30am and 5 to 7pm), when it can be difficult to see out of the windows and know when to get off! You therefore need to ask other people, meaning that some knowledge of Mandarin Chinese is needed to be able to use the city's buses.

Shanghai: In Shanghai, the huge volume of traffic and one-way system mean that buses are slow, and you also need a knowledge of Mandarin Chinese to be able to navigate the system. City buses run from 5am to 11pm but become unbearably crowded during rush hours (6.30 to 8.30am and 5 to 7pm). A flat fare of RMB1 (12¢) is paid to the conductor, or up to RMB3 (36¢) on air-conditioned buses. Many city-centre buses are helpfully numbered, but suburban buses usually display their destination in letters. There's also a limited minibus service, the flat fee of RMB2 (24¢) guaranteeing a seat.

Underground

Foreigners in Beijing and Shanghai invariably ignore the buses in favour of the underground (subway).

Beijing: Beijing's underground is clean, rapid and smooth-running, and operates from 5.30am to 11pm. Trains can become packed during rush hours but otherwise you can usually travel comfortably. The underground has two lines: the East to West line runs from Pingguoyuan to Sihui, while the Ring line follows the second ring road. Each journey costs around RMB3 (36¢), and you must buy ticket cards in advance, which are inserted into machines. Station entrances are marked by a square inside a C. Signs and announcements are in English as well as Chinese. Beijing's underground is beginning to show its age and is due to be renovated before the 2008 Olympics.

Shanghai: Shanghai's underground operates from 5am to 11pm and, like Beijing's, is clean, fast and efficient. Three lines run as follows: Number 1 runs north-south from Shanghai Railway Station to Xinzhuang; Number 2 runs west-east from Zhongshan Park to Longyang Lu; and the Pearl Line runs north-south from Jiangwan Zhen to Shanghai south station. Tickets are RMB3 (36¢) for journeys up to 13 stops, RMB4 (48¢) for longer ones. As yet, there are no 'travel cards'. Stations are marked by a red sign resembling an M. As in Beijing, signs and announcements are in English as well as Chinese, and there are plans to expand the system.

Taxis

China's two major cities are also well-served by taxis.

Beijing: Beijing's are metered, inexpensive and easy to find: they wait at hotels, railway stations and near department stores, and can also be hailed in the street. The city's taxis are often red hatchbacks or saloons; the smaller and older the car, the lower the fare tends to be. All taxis have a back window sticker showing its rates, generally RMB10 (US$1.20) for the first 4 or 5km, thereafter RMB1.2 (14¢) to 1.75 (21¢) per km. A 20 per cent surcharge operates after 11pm. Most Beijing taxi drivers don't speak English so you should write your destination in Chinese or point to it on a map. Tipping isn't expected.

Shanghai: Shanghai's taxis are also plentiful, reliable and inexpensive. Don't let the metal cages around the drivers put you off; taxis are also safe. Journeys are metered and many of the city's taxis are Volkswagens (usually Passats or Santanas), run by a variety of fleet companies. Fares are around RMB10 (US$1.20) for the first 2km, thereafter RMB2 (24¢) per km. Between 11pm and 5am, fares rise to RMB13 (US$1.57) for the first 2km, thereafter RMB2.6 (31¢) per km. As in Beijing, very few drivers understand English and you must write your destination in Chinese or point to it on a map.

Bicycles

Another option for short-distance travelling in China (and an iconic image of the country) is the bicycle, China having the highest number of bicycles in the world and plenty of bicycle hire (rental) outlets, including hotels. Hotel hire prices are between RMB10 and RMB20 (US$1.20 and US$2.40) per hour or around RMB40 (US$4.80) per half-day, and a deposit is required.

Rates at hire shops are usually lower. Although China's roads are extremely dangerous, Beijing has dedicated cycle lanes, which make cycling relatively safe and are used by several hundred thousand cyclists during rush hours. You must park your bicycle in bike parking areas, which have guards and cost next to nothing to use. Bring your own lock.

Bicycles are also popular in Shanghai, but you need strong nerves and a fondness for inhaling pollution to brave the city's roads on two wheels. You also need to be officially registered, for which you must visit your nearest main police station. Bicycles can be hired for around RMB20 (US$2.40) per day, with a deposit of around RMB100 (US$12). Park your bicycle in bike parks and note that bicycle theft is common.

Trains

The Chinese rail network extends for almost 58,000km (36,250mi) and train services reach every province except Tibet (although a service is expected by 2007). Trains are cheap, relatively fast and less accident-prone than buses, with four classes of ticket: hard seat, soft seat, hard bed and soft bed. 'Soft' means padded or cusioned; 'hard' means hard! Frequent luggage theft and the appalling state of the toilets are the major drawbacks of the Chinese train system.

Trains can become very crowded and it's recommended to reserve seats, especially if you're intending to travel during a holiday period. Tickets can be booked at railway stations, travel agencies and some hotels. There's no on-line China rail timetable in English, but the Thomas Cook *Overseas Timetable* is an excellent source of information, published every two months and available for around US$16. To travel by rail from Beijing to Kunming in the far south of the country (on roughly the same latitude as Taipei – around 150mi/240km north of the border with Vietnam) takes around 17 hours and a hard bed costs RMB580 (US$70), a soft bed RMB890 (US$107).

Airline Services

In a country as large as China, internal travel by air is popular. The Civil Aviation Administration of China (CAAC) controls 14 regional airlines with routes linking Beijing to around 80 other cities, and several private carriers. Flights are often full during popular travelling times (May, September and October) so book well in advance. Note that many Chinese airlines have a poor safety record and in-flight conditions tend to be inferior to what most westerners are used to. It's recommended to fly on airlines which use European or American-manufactured aircraft (check the airline's website), which have a much better safety record than. A one-way, coach class airfare from Beijing to Kunming, for example, costs around RMB1,673 (US$200).

Hong Kong

Public transport is vital in Hong Kong – a small, crowded place where driving is stressful and time-consuming, even for experienced locals. Fortunately, the public transport system is one of the world's best and is invariably efficient, inexpensive and quick. The disadvantages are that it's heavily used and, because of the diversity of operators, isn't fully integrated: you need separate tickets for each part of a journey unless you have an Octopus Card (see below). There are, however, plans to increase integration.

Octopus Cards: An Octopus Card can be used on the MTR, the KCR, most buses and some minibuses and ferries, and there are plans to expand its applicability. A card costs around HK$150 (US$19.32, which includes a HK$50/US$6.44 refundable deposit) and functions like a debit card: when you insert it into a sensor at the start of a journey, the cost is automatically deducted from the remaining credit. If there's credit remaining when you return the card, it's refunded. You can buy Octopus Cards (and MTR Tourist Tickets) from any MTR station (see **Trains** below).

Buses

The bus system is extensive and is the best way to travel around the south of Hong Kong Island and the New Territories, but it can be confusing for the newcomer. Buses become very crowded and if you don't have an Octopus Card (see above) you must pay with the exact money. Several companies operate Hong Kong's buses and their main services run from around 6am to 12.30am, with an infrequent service during the night. An average Hong Kong bus fare is around HK$5 (64¢).

Minibuses operate like taxis (you must flag them down) but on fixed routes. Drivers often wait until they have a reasonable load of passengers before setting off and they're known for their aggressive driving. Fares vary according to the distance travelled and can be difficult to understand; the average fare is around HK$7 (90¢). Some minibuses accept the Octopus Card (see above). Minibuses run between 6am and 12.30am, with some night services on major routes.

Trams

Trams are an efficient, air-conditioned way to travel in the New Territories and in the north of Hong Kong Island. A standard fare on Hong Kong Island is HK$2 (25¢).

Bicycles

Bicycle riders have a hard time of it in Hong Kong. They're prohibited in Central, and in the rest of Hong Kong the choking traffic and pollution make cycling unhealthy, dangerous and stressful. If you're determined (or mad), you can hire a bicycle for around HK$50 (US$6.44) per day. You're recommended to go to the quieter New Territories.

Trains

Kowloon and the north of Hong Kong Island are admirably served by Hong Kong's sleek Mass Transit Railway (MTR). The MTR runs between 5.55am and 12.35am every day and has five lines, including two cross-harbour lines (☎ 2881-8888, 🖥 www.mtrcorp.com for further details). You can buy an MTR Tourist Ticket for HK$50 (US$6.44) that entitles you to unlimited travel for one day as well as a map and souvenir ticket. Other passes are available for longer periods, and for a small surcharge (around HK$20/US$2.57) can be extended to include most other public transport services.

The Kowloon-Guangzhou (Canton) Railway (KCR) is Hong Kong's other railway system; it has 13 stations and runs from Kowloon to the Chinese border at Lo Wu, stopping in the New Territories. Fares start at HK$4 (51¢) for up to two stations.

Ferries

Hong Kong's ferries have a deservedly high reputation and can be faster and cheaper than other means of transport, to say nothing of providing marvellous views. Some are 'hover ferries', which are faster than ordinary ferries. The Star Ferry (☎ 2367-7065, 🖥 www.starferry.com.hk) is the cheapest way to cross the harbour and provides an unforgettable experience, particularly at night. The crossing costs HK$1.70 or HK$2.20 (22¢ or 28¢) on the upper deck, and the service operates from 6.30am to 11.30pm from the terminals in Central and Tsim Sha Tsui.

Taxis

Taxis are a popular means of transport in Hong Kong and are plentiful and inexpensive. The minimum fare in central Hong Kong is HK$15 (US$1.93), but most journeys cost less than HK$25 (US$3.22) – sometimes more if you have luggage. There are taxi ranks at popular locations and you can flag down taxis in the street. Taxis are red on Hong Kong Island and in Kowloon, green in the New Territories and blue on Lantau Island. Taxi journeys through the cross-harbour tunnel attract a surcharge of around HK$20 (US$2.57). Tipping isn't expected, although fares are often rounded up to the nearest dollar. Many Hong Kong taxi drivers speak some English, although it's still recommended to have your destination written in Chinese.

Indonesia

Buses

Buses are the main form of transport in Indonesia, which has three types of bus:

- **'Ekonomi' buses**, as their name suggests, are cheap and basic, and you must often share the bus with livestock as well as plenty of other people;
- **Express buses** are a step up in quality and speed, but you still have the opportunity to acquaint yourself with chickens and other fowl;
- **Luxury, air-conditioned buses** are as good as the world's best buses and operate locally and between towns and cities, at night as well as during the day.

Whatever type of bus you take in Indonesia, you're likely to be driven by somebody who adds a new dimension to the meaning of the word 'reckless'. Accidents involving buses are common and often catastrophic.

Trains

There are around 7,000km (4,350mi) of railway track on Java, Madura and Sumatra, train services ranging from cheap, slow and uncomfortable to sleek and expensive. Children under three travel free, those aged three to seven pay half fare. Buy tickets at least a day in advance in order to guarantee a seat. At Ketapang in east Java, the rail service connects with the ferry to Bali, while at Merak in the west it connects with the ferry to Sumatra. The main lines run between Jakarta and Surabaya, one via Yogya and Solo, the other via Semarang. The rest of Indonesia's network is very limited and buses are usually the only means of inter-city travel.

Ferries

Ferries are a popular way of travelling between Indonesia's islands. Pelini, the state-owned shipping company, has six ferries connecting the main ports, and several foreign cruise liners also ply Indonesia's waters.

Taxis

Taxis are widely available in Indonesia's cities and larger towns (and have yellow number plates, in common with all public transport vehicles), but many aren't metered, so you should agree a fare beforehand; you might also have to give the driver directions to where you want to go. Jakarta's traffic is nothing short of nightmarish, meaning that all road travel around the city is slow.

Other Local Transport

'Alternative' means of local public transport in Indonesia include *bajaj* (motorised rickshaws), *becaks* (bicycle rickshaws), *dokars* (horse-drawn carts), *opelets* (minibuses) and *bemo* (pick-up trucks). These are all relatively cheap but vary greatly in comfort and safety as well as in the extent to which you need to haggle over fares.

Airline Services

Indonesia – a large country consisting of several islands – is well served by domestic flights, which link the capital Jakarta with most of the country's other cities and large towns. The major operators are Bouraq Indonesia Airlines (BO),

Garuda Indonesia (GA) and Merpati Nusantara Airlines (MZ). **Note that Indonesia's airlines have some of the worst safety records in Asia.**

Frequent fliers are recommended to buy an Asean (sic) Air Pass, which offers cheap fares on domestic flights. The pass cannot be bought in Indonesia, but is available at Garuda Indonesia offices in Australasia, Europe, Japan and the US. Current prices and further information are available from Garuda International (UK ☎ 020-7467 8600, ✉ enquiries@garuda-indonesia). Indonesia has a departure tax of between Rp8,000 and Rp20,000 (US$175 and US$436), depending on the airport used.

Japan

Within Japanese cities, if there's a metro, it's usually the quickest way to travel. Intercity bus services in Japan are invariably slower than trains, but they can be much cheaper. If you're travelling overnight and aren't prepared or able to pay for a bed, it's easier to sleep in a reclining bus seat than in a fixed train seat. Tokyo enjoys one of the world's most efficient and safest public transport systems, encompassing a train network, underground, monorails and buses. It doesn't operate around the clock, however, and late-night revellers either have to wait for the trains to begin running early in the morning or rob a bank to pay Tokyo's wallet-shattering late-night taxi fares.

Buses & Trams

All towns and cities have bus services, but these have a (mainly undeserved) reputation for being difficult for foreigners to use, especially if they don't speak the language. Fares within cities are usually around ¥200 (US$1.88) and bus services usually stop at around 10pm (night buses are rare). Trams operate in some cities and tend to be more user-friendly than the buses. Tokyo's bus service is much less popular than the trains because the city's traffic is very slow and the buses finish early in the evening. The city has only one remaining tram service.

Trains & Underground

Trains are the most commonly used public transport in Japan (although the railways' share of passengers is declining), the rail system rightly being a source of national pride. Japanese trains are sleek, comfortable, quick (sometimes dizzyingly so) and frequent, but they can be expensive. There's a range of services, from local lines up to super expresses (*shinkansen*) – the famous 'bullet trains', which travel at up to 270kph (167mph) and are one of the ultimate symbols of Japanese technical excellence. If you intend to travel by train in Japan, you're recommended to buy a Rail Pass, which must be pre-purchased abroad, and which is valid for most rail services in the country.

Examples of single rail fares are: Tokyo to Hiroshima ¥19,680 (US$180); Tokyo to Sapporo ¥22,530 (US$205); Tokyo to Nagasaki ¥26,020 (US$240).

Tokyo: Tokyo's rail system can be confusing for the newcomer because the city is served by a combination of Japanese Railways (JR), private inner-city subway lines and private suburban lines, which can mean changing between different systems. The underground lines are operated by two different companies and there are easy connections between them, although they operate on separate tickets. Travellers in Tokyo who wish to JR trains, the underground and buses can buy a Tokyo combination ticket for ¥1,580 (US$14.48), which is a day pass that allows unlimited use of all three. If you only wish to use the underground, you can buy an SF Metro Card. Tokyo's trains run from around 5am to midnight or 1am and become very crowded during rush hours (7.30 to 9am and 5 to 7pm). The average city journey costs around ¥200 (US$1.85).

Taxis

Taxis in Tokyo can be found at ranks or hailed in the street. Fares vary between different companies, but all are high: around ¥650 (US$6) for the first 2km, thereafter ¥80 (73¢) for every 275m. After 11pm, fares rise by around 30 per cent and it can be difficult to find a taxi after 1am, when the trains finish and taxis are in demand. Taxi drivers rarely speak English, so you must have your destination written in Japanese or be able to point to it on a map. The rear doors of Japanese taxis are operated automatically by the driver; don't try to open or close them yourself. **Tips aren't given and doing so can cause offence.**

Airline Services

Flying between Japan's cities and islands is common and sometimes cheaper than going by train, particularly if you qualify for discounts; always ask the airlines about any discounts and offers they're running.

Examples of single airfares are: Tokyo to Hiroshima ¥13,300 to ¥26,300 (US$120 to US$240), depending on the grade of ticket; Tokyo to Sapporo ¥14,300 to ¥28,300 (US$130 to US$260); Tokyo to Nagasaki ¥16,800 to ¥33,300 (US$155 to US$305).

Korea

Korea is well-served by public transport and city services are integrated.

Buses

Buses operating in Korean cities can be difficult for foreigners to negotiate because the names of the stops aren't given in English. In Seoul, buses operate from around 5.30am until midnight, but become very crowded during rush hours. There are also private minibuses, operated illegally, which travel to outlying areas, not reached by other services; despite being illegal, they're tolerated by the authorities because of this. Korea has a fast, reliable long-distance bus service. There are two types of long-distance bus: express (non-stop) and inter-city (stopping). Seats must be reserved on express buses but cannot be unreserved on inter-city services.

Trains

Korea has an extensive rail network and frequent services. A high-speed service runs the length of the country and there are also local services. There are four classes of train: *bidulgi* and *kkachi* are very slow; *tongil* trains are cheap but basic; *mugunghwa* are fast and efficient; and *saemaeul* are the fastest. KR Rail Passes allow three, five, seven or ten days of unlimited travel on Korean trains. A KR Pass voucher can be purchased at overseas travel agents and exchanged for a Pass at Korean railway offices. Vouchers are currently available in the following countries: Australia, Brazil, Canada, China, France, Germany, Italy, Japan, Mexico, Russia, Singapore, Taiwan, the UK and the US. They can also be purchased via the internet (🖳 www.korail.go.kr – press the icon top right for the English version). Prices (in US$) are currently as follows:

| Validity | Normal Pass | | Youth Pass | Saver Pass* |
	Adult	Child		
3 Days	47	24	38	43
5 Days	70	35	56	63
7 Days	89	45	71	80
10 Days	102	51	82	92

* A Saver Pass can be used by two to five people travelling together, each of whom pays the above prices.

KR Passes entitle holders to discounts on various attractions in Korea. For those planning to travel to Japan and China as well as Korea, the above website also has details of combined Korea/Japan and Korea/China tickets.

Underground

Korean cities' underground systems are much easier to use than the buses (signs are in Korean and English), cheap and quick. Seoul's underground has eight lines, which are colour-coded, and announcements are multi-lingual. The adult fare for bus journeys in Seoul is SKW600 (50¢), irrespective of distance. Tickets for the underground cost SKW600 (50¢) for Area 1 and SKW700 (58¢) for Area 2.

Taxis

Taxis are plentiful and inexpensive in Korea. The minimum fare for a regular taxi is around SKW1,175 (US$1), or SKW1,765 (US$1.50) for the superior (*mobom*) taxis, which are black with a yellow sign on the top.

Malaysia

Public transport in Malaysia is generally of a high standard. The capital, Kuala Lumpur, is particularly well-served by public transport.

Buses

Peninsular Malaysia has an extensive, rapid and inexpensive bus system. Inter-state services feature modern, air-conditioned express buses operated by a range of companies (with similar prices). Long-distance buses often leave very early in the morning, whereas those on shorter routes operate throughout the day. Booking is rarely necessary, except on the most popular routes, e.g. Kuala Lumpur to Penang, a journey of around eight hours (costing around RM25/US$6.50).

Kuala Lumpur: Kuala Lumpur's bus system is comprehensive but complicated, being operated by different companies with different fares. Buses generally run from around 5am to midnight, tickets are bought on board (you need the exact money) and fares are rarely more than RM1 (26¢).

Trains

Peninsular Malaysia has a railway network, which is operated by Malayan Railway (Keretapi Tanah Melayu Berhad or KTM, 🖥 www.ktmb.com.my), consists of just two lines: one links Singapore with Thailand via Kuala Lumpur and Butterworth; the other branches off it at Gemas and runs to Kota Bahru. Some people find the trains comfortable and civilised, others slow and expensive. Children under four travel free, children aged four to 11 pay half fare. Ten and 30-day Railway Passes are available, allowing unlimited travel on Malaysian and Singaporean trains.

Kuala Lumpur: The capital is well-served by public transport. KTM operates two electric train lines (called 'Kommuter' lines), which run between Sentul and Port Klang and between Rawand and Seremban, from 5am to midnight. A single journey costs between RM1.50 (39¢) and RM5.50 (US$1.44); return fares and 12-trip tickets are also available. You can buy two-day passes for unlimited travel on weekdays or weekends from station vending machines. These offer good value, costing between RMB5 and RMB10 (US$1.31 and US$2.62).

Kuala Lumpur also has two Light Railway Transit (LTR) lines, from Sentul Timur to Sri Petaling and Ampang, and from the Putra Terminal to the Lembah

Subang Depot. Trains run from 6am to midnight on weekdays and from 7.30am to 11pm at weekends. Fares vary from around RM1 to RM5 (26¢ to US$1.31).

An elevated monorail opened on 31 August 2003 (it was due to have opened in 1999 and eventually cost of RMB1.18 billion/US$310 million). It's 8.6km (5.34mi) long and runs from the Pekeliling Bus Terminal through the business district to KL Sentral in Brickfields. There are 11 stations, between 600 and 1,000 metres apart, and the complete journey takes 18 minutes. During peak hours, trains operate every two to five minutes, off-peak every five to ten minutes. See 💻 www.monorail.com.my for further information.

Ferries

Ferries sail to the islands off the Peninsula's coasts but the service in the east is severely curtailed during the monsoon season (November to February). There are no ferries from the Peninsular to East Malaysia (see **Airline Services** below).

Taxis

Many of Peninsular Malaysia's towns have a long-distance taxi rank. Taxis offer a reliable service and are much quicker than buses. Fares are fixed and are up to double the bus fare. The trip from Kuala Lumpur to Butterworth costs around RM30 (US$7.89) per person; Kuala Lumpur to Kota Bharu is around RM35 (US$9.21). Taxis have four seats and you must wait until they're full before leaving, but this rarely takes long.

Kuala Lumpur: In Kuala Lumpur, taxis can be found at taxi ranks (there are long queues during rush hours) or hailed in the street. Most are metered and the rate is usually RM2 (52¢) for the first 2km (1.25mi), thereafter RM0.10 (2.6¢) for each 200m. Between midnight and 6am, there's a 50 per cent surcharge. You pay an extra RM1 (26¢) per piece of luggage and RM0.20 (5¢) for more than two passengers. Tips aren't expected.

Airline Services

Flying is a popular form of transport in East Malaysia and is often the only quick, reliable way to travel long distances. Flights are therefore often busy or fully booked (particularly during school holidays); they're also sometimes delayed by bad weather. The Malaysian national airline, MAS, operates a wide range of domestic flights, the most popular routes being those between Peninsular Malaysia and East Malaysia. For example, the flight from Kuala Lumpur to Langkawi costs around RM210 (US$55) and takes just under an hour. The same journey by bus and ferry would take 12 hours (11 of them on the bus). If you fly at night, you can save money. For example, the night flight from Kuala Lumpur to Alor Setar is around RM115 (US$30) rather than RM175 (US$46).

On return flights between Peninsular Malaysia and East Malaysia and between Sabah and Sarawak, three or more people travelling together get a 50 per cent discount. Blind or disabled passengers can get up to 50 per cent flight discounts. Be sure to ask MAS about current offers and discounts before booking a flight. For example, in late 2003 you could buy a Discover Malaysia Pass entitling you to five flights within the Peninsular for US$99 or five flights throughout Malaysia for US$199. Passes are valid for 28 days.

Philippines

Buses

Buses are a cheap option for journeys of between two and ten hours and are available with or without air-conditioning. Outside the conurbation of Manila (officially known as Metro Manila), the Philippine Transport Company (Philtranco) is the largest bus company, providing country-wide services. On islands other than Luzon, jeepneys are the most popular form of public transport (see **Taxis** below).

Manila: Metro Manila has an extensive bus network, but it suffers from the common Far Eastern problem of delays caused by heavy traffic. Several bus companies operate in the city, so there are no city-wide bus passes. Buses ply the city's major roads but aren't allowed into much of Manila (i.e. the city centre). Fares vary between around P5 and P15 (9¢ and 27¢), according to distance travelled and whether the bus is air-conditioned or not. Buses generally run between 5am and 11.30pm.

Trains

The Philippines has only one long-distance railway line, on which there are three trains daily in each way direction between Manila and Naga in southern Luzon. However, this service isn't recommended, being slow and subject to occasional criminal and terrorist activity, and buses are the main form of inter-city travel.

Manila: Manila's trains are much quicker than its buses, but it can take newcomers a little time to get used to the range of services. The elevated Metrorail or Mass Rail Transit (MRT) has two lines, with more planned, and is quick although it becomes very congested at peak times. The Light Rail Transit (LRT) has been in operation since 1985 and has 16 stations, with services between 4.30am and 10.45pm. The Metrostar runs from EDSA/Taft Avenue in the south to North station, between 6am and 9.30pm. City train fares average P12 (22¢), but you can buy a range of (ever-changing) passes and saver tickets from railway stations; ask about current offers and discounts.

Ferries

There are plenty of ferries operating between the islands, although the quality and safety of these varies enormously, and ferry accidents are common. A reliable inter-island operator is WG&A Super Ferry (🖳 www.wgasu superferry.com), ranked as the best service by the Philippine Maritime Authority. Overnight boat fares (tourist class) cost between P370 (US$6.75) and P430 (US$7.75).

Taxis

Taxis and FX taxis (which are larger and carry up to ten people) are normally hailed in the street; the only rank is at the airport. Different taxi operators have cars with different liveries, often striped. The average minimum fare is P25 (45¢) and then P2 (4¢) per km. Tipping is usually by rounding up the fare to the nearest P5 or P10 (9¢ or 18¢). **Insist that the driver uses the meter or you might be overcharged.**

Manila is also served by 'Jeepneys', which are brightly coloured jeeps, often trailing streamers and decked with mirrors. They operate 24 hours per day and are certainly an experience, albeit a sometimes frightening one. Jeepneys display their destination on a sign in the window and it's estimated that they carry around a third of Manila's commuter traffic (there are around 30,000 Jeepneys in Manila). Fares are inexpensive, between P5 and P10 (9¢ and 18¢).

Airline Services

There are four major airlines serving internal routes in the Philippines: Philippine Airlines (PAL), which is the official flag carrier, Cebu Pacific, which has a reputation for punctuality, Asian Spirit, a newcomer, and Air Philippines. PAL has the best safety record, but a (not entirely deserved) nickname of 'Plane Always Late'. Fares for domestic flights are usually in the range of P3,200 (US$60) to P4,000 (US$75). There's a departure tax of P100 (US$1.80) for internal flights from Manila.

Singapore

Singapore is admirably served by clean, efficient public transport services and, with typical Singaporean efficiency, the major transport operators have set up a service called TransitLink Hotline (☎ 1800-767 4222 or 6767-4333) providing information about public transport. You can buy electronic passes called Ez-link cards (🖳 www.ezlink.com.sg) from MTR stations (see **Trains** below); these cover travel on MRT, LRT and buses. They cost S$10 (US$5.80) plus a deposit of S$5 (US$2.90). When the S$10 (US$5.80) has been used up, the card can be topped up at a machine in a station.

As well as the services described below, rickshaws operate in Chinatown; negotiate a fare before the journey. Ferries run regularly from the World Trade Centre to Sentosa and other islands.

Buses

Singapore's buses are run by the Singapore Bus Service (☎ 1800-287 2727, 🖥 www.sbstransit.com.sg) and Trans Island Bus Service (☎ 6482-3888, 🖥 www.tibs.com.sg). Buses generally run from 6am to midnight, with fares around S$0.70 to S$1.50 (41¢ to 87¢) for non-air-conditioned buses, and S$0.80 to S$1.80 (46¢ to US$1.04) for air-conditioned buses. Night buses operate between midnight and around 4am, with fares of S$3 (US$1.74).

Trains

Trains are operated by Singapore Mass Rapid Transit/MTR (☎ 6336-8900, 🖥 www.smrtcorp.com.sg), the two main lines running from north to south and east to west. Trains run every three to six minutes, from 5.30am to 12.30am, and fares are modest: between S$0.80 and S$1.80 (46¢ and US$1.04). MTR also operates a Light Rapid Transit System/LRT (☎ 6893-6455/6, 🖥 www.sirt. com.sg), with 14 stations from Bukit Panjang New Town to Choa Chu Kang. Trains run every three to five minutes and fares are between S$0.80 and S$1.80 (46¢ and US$1.04).

Taxis

Singapore has nearly 20,000 taxis, most of them metered, air-conditioned and inexpensive. As in many cities, however, taxis can be difficult to find during rush hours and also when it rains (which is often in Singapore, although rarely for long). You can hail taxis in the street and they also wait at stands outside shopping centres and hotels. Fares vary slightly between companies. Fares are rarely more than S$2.40 (US$1.40) for a single journey within Singapore. Surcharges of around S$1 (60¢) apply for rush hour fares and pick-ups in the Central Business District (CBD). A 50 per cent surcharge operates between midnight and 6am and a S$5 (US$2.90) surcharge between 5pm and midnight on Fridays, Saturdays and Sundays. Tips aren't expected.

Taiwan

Taiwan has plenty of choice in public transport, which is currently not well integrated, although integration is set to be achieved by 2008.

Buses

Taiwan's bus network is extensive, but this makes it confusing for the newcomer, as does the fact that six private bus companies operate inter-city buses throughout the country. Taiwan's cities have government-run and private bus services, the latter cheaper and faster but more accident-prone. Traffic congestion slows bus services in all the island's cities, particularly Taipei. The major problem for the foreign bus passenger in Taiwan is that timetables and signs on the buses themselves are invariably in Chinese only.

Taipei: Taipei's traffic congestion makes the city's buses slow.

Trains

Rail is one of the most efficient ways to travel in Taiwan and rail services, operated by the Taiwan Railway Administration (🖳 www.railway.gov.tw), cover much of the island. Trains are reliable, clean and air-conditioned, and there are four classes of service: three are more expensive than the island's buses, the fourth is cheaper but snail-slow. Children under three travel free, children aged 3 to 13 pay half fare. Train tickets can be bought at some hotels in Taipei as well as at stations. The main station in Taipei is foreigner-friendly, with an English-language information booth at the eastern counter, as well as English-language information boards.

Taipei: Preferable to the city's buses is the inexpensive, efficient Metropolitan Rapid Transit (MRT) system, which operates six lines from around 6am to midnight, with a train every four to seven minutes. Single journeys cost from NT$20 (85¢) to NT$65 (US$1.90), depending on distance. You can buy a one-day pass at MRT stations for NT$150 (US$4.40), allowing unlimited MRT travel for a day.

Taxis

Major cities have an abundance of taxis, which are metered and inexpensive. Charges are around NT$70 (US$2.05) for the first 1.5km and NT$5 (15¢) for each additional 300m. A 20 per cent surcharge applies between 11pm and 6am, and luggage accommodated in the boot (trunk) costs an extra NT$10 (30¢). Fares vary in different cities, being set by local governments, but differences are modest. Most Taiwanese taxi drivers don't speak much English and you need to be able to write your destination in Chinese or be able to point it out on a map.

Airline Services

Taiwan's domestic airlines industry is active (Taiwan is almost as large as Switzerland), flying being nearly as common as taking long-distance buses, and services are offered by around nine carriers, including Far Eastern Air Transport, Mandarin Airlines, Tranasia Airways and Uni Air. Taipei has a separate airport for domestic flights – Sung Shan Domestic Airport.

Thailand

Local transport in most towns and cities consists of buses, taxis, *tuk-tuks* (motorised rickshaws), *samlors* (bicycle rickshaws) and *songthaews* (converted 'pick-up' trucks), the last three being inexpensive but often rickety and almost always hair-raisingly fast. Agree the fare beforehand. Bangkok's public transport system is extensive and cheap. Chiang Mai hasn't had any bus services since 1997 and *songthaews* are the most common public transport in the city.

Buses & Boats

Inter-city buses are a popular means of transport in Thailand. They're well-equipped and usually air-conditioned, but also notoriously fast. Thailand also has women-only buses, introduced in June 2000 to protect women passengers from crime and sexual harassment.

Bangkok: Bangkok's complex bus system is run by the Bangkok Mass Transit authority (☎ 246-0973, 💻 www.bmta.motc.go.th). Different types of bus have different liveries and you need a bus route map (obtainable from hotels and book shops) to make sense of the range of bus types, routes and prices. Buses operate between 5am and 11pm, with fares between Bht3.50 and Bht5 (9¢ and 13¢) on standard buses and between Bht5 and Bht15 (13¢ and 38¢) on air-conditioned buses. A limited service operates between 11pm and 5am. Bangkok's bus system is at the mercy of the city's horrendous traffic and also prey to bag-snatchers and 'razors' (thieves who quietly and dextrously cut your bag with a razor and remove the valuables).

The most relaxed, often coolest (in terms of both temperature and stress level) way to travel in Bangkok is by boat on the rivers and canals, in what are effectively water buses. Sadly, this isn't as practical as it once was, because many of the city's waterways have been replaced by roads. Boats on the Chao Phraya River operate between 6am and 6.40pm, with fares from Bht5 to Bht15 (13¢ to 38¢). Stops are marked by coloured flags.

Trains & Underground

For those of a nervous disposition (and with a desire for a long life), Thailand's trains are the preferred means of transport, the service being efficient, comfortable and reasonably priced, albeit slow (or 'leisurely' depending on your point of view). The network covers 4,600km (2,860mi) and links all the major towns except Phuket. The service is run by State Railways of Thailand (💻 www.srt.or.th).

Bangkok: The Bangkok Transit System (BTS) is an elevated railway network covering the city that beats Bangkok's notorious road traffic problems (☎ 617-7300, 💻 www.bts.co.th). It's sometimes called the 'Skytrain' and operates on two lines: the Silom Line runs from Saphan Taksin to the National Stadium, and the Sukhumvit Line from On Nut to Mo Chit. Extensions have been approved across the river and to the south. Trains run from 6am to midnight, every three or four minutes during rush hours and every five or six minutes at other times. Individual tickets cost between Bht10 and Bht40 (25¢ and US$1), and 10, 15 and 30-journey passes can be bought for Bht250, Bht300 and Bht540 (US$6.26, US$7.50 and US$13.53). Three-day visitor passes cost around Bht280 (US$7).

Bangkok is building a 20km (12mi) underground system, due to open in 2004, a further attempt to reduce or circumvent the city's chronic road traffic congestion and pollution.

Taxis

Bangkok's taxis can be hailed on the street. If a taxi is metered, check that the meter is turned on. The rate is Bht35 (88¢) for the first 2km, thereafter Bht5 (13¢) per km. In unmetered taxis, agree the fare before the journey. Tipping isn't expected. Bangkok also has rickety and unstable motorcycle taxis, which are a good way to beat the traffic jams provided you're prepared to put your life in the driver's hands. You're provided with a helmet, which you must wear by law. Fares range from Bht15 to Bht100 (38¢ to US$2.50) according to distance, and include a free adrenaline rush!

Airline Services

Thai Airways International (⌨ www.thaiair.com) flies to 22 airports within Thailand, while Bangkok Airways (⌨ www.bkk.air.co.th) covers seven routes. Discounts and offers are common. There's a departure tax of Bht50 (US$1.25) for domestic flights, Bht400 (US$10) from Samui Airport; children under two are exempt.

MOTORING

If you're wedded to your car (or at least to having your own transport), you probably wouldn't consider living anywhere you cannot get around independently. Having your own transport also allows you a much wider choice of where you can live. However, it isn't always necessary or desirable to own a car in the Far East and many people use taxis for local trips and rent a car for longer journeys. It might come as a surprise to learn that the majority of foreigners in the region – even long-term residents – rarely if ever drive, preferring public transport or employing a chauffeur.

Bear in mind that driving is a nerve-wracking and dangerous experience in many of the region's countries, and most people are more accident-prone when driving abroad. Driving in Far Eastern cities is often totally chaotic at the best of times, particularly when traffic drives on a different side of the road from that in your home country. A car can be a liability in towns if you don't have private parking, and you will save a lot of money if you can manage without one (which is why many people on a limited budget live in towns). Singapore is probably the safest, sanest place to drive of the 11 territories considered here, but it's also expensive and the fact that Singapore is so small often makes it unnecessary.

When buying or renting a car in the Far East, it's worth choosing one with air-conditioning, which is a blessing in hot, humid climates. If you're planning to import a car (new or second-hand) into most countries, it must have local type-approval and meet certain technical standards. You must usually also have owned and operated a vehicle abroad for six months to qualify for tax-free importation. You must be resident in some countries in order to own a car with local registration plates.

Importing A Car

Car importation is a popular topic of conversation among expatriates in some countries in the Far East, where importing a car often entails a prolonged battle with local authorities. Cars are usually imported from one of the region's countries to another, as the distance from their home country for most western expatriates makes importing a car to the Far East unfeasible. Most countries allow residents to import a car that has been owned for a limited period, e.g. six months. In most countries a permanent resident isn't permitted to operate a car on foreign registration plates and must import it and operate it on local plates. Note also that a vehicle must be de-registered in its original country after it has been re-registered abroad. A vehicle that's imported tax and duty-free mustn't usually be sold, rented or transferred within one year of its registration. The registration of a right-hand drive vehicle in a country where traffic drives on the right (and vice versa) may be prohibited. In many countries, you can buy a tax-free car and operate it for six months before exporting it, which may help reduce your tax liability.

An imported vehicle must comply with certain safety and other requirements (called homologation) before it can be registered. Homologation can be prohibitively expensive in some countries. Local taxes must usually be paid when importing a car, depending on its year of manufacture, where it was manufactured and its current registration. These may include value added tax, sales tax, registration or car tax, and import duty. The amount payable is usually based on the vehicle's original price with a reduction for its age.

The procedure for the importation of a boat, caravan or motorcycle (with an engine capacity of 50cc or more) is usually the same as for a car. Mopeds with engines below 50cc can be freely imported into many countries and require no special paperwork.

Non-Residents: Non-residents can operate a foreign-registered vehicle in most countries for up to six months in a calendar year without paying local taxes and may be permitted to keep a foreign-registered vehicle permanently at a holiday home in the Far East. The vehicle must be road-legal in its home country, meaning that it must be inspected (for roadworthiness) and taxed each year in its country of registration (which may entail taking it home each year to have it tested!), and must be insured for local use. Non-residents can operate a car on tax-free (or 'tourist') plates in some countries. Note that anyone who illegally operates a vehicle on foreign or tax-free plates can be fined and the vehicle confiscated.

Car Hire

The major multinational hire (rental) companies, including Alamo, Avis, Budget, Hertz and Thrifty, have offices in most Far Eastern countries, particularly at major airports and in major cities. There are also cheaper local hire companies. Car hire companies are listed in yellow pages and local companies are listed by town. You may be approached at airports by representatives of local hire companies, who may not be reputable (check their credentials). It's wise to reserve a hire car before arriving in the region, particularly during peak periods. When booking, remember to specify an automatic model if you aren't used to a manual (stick-shift) gearbox, as most hire cars are manual. Fly-drive deals are available from most airlines and travel agents.

Car hire rates vary considerably in different countries in the region, and they also vary according to the location and season. Many companies have lower rates for weekend hire, e.g. from 4pm on Fridays to noon on Mondays, and for hire periods of 14 days or longer. The rates charged by major international companies vary little, although you may get a better deal by booking in advance. One of the advantages of using a national company is that you can hire a car in one town and drop it off in another, although you should check the cost of this service. Although cheaper, small local companies require you to return a car to the office you hired it from or to the local airport. Note also that some of the cheaper hire companies cut corners on maintenance and repairs, and cars can sometimes be unsafe to drive.

When comparing rates, check that prices include all necessary insurance and taxes, that insurance cover (including personal accident) is adequate, and that there are no hidden costs. When comparing prices, check whether any 'extras' are included in the basic price, such as collision damage waiver (CDW), theft cover, personal accident insurance (PAI), airport tax, roof rack, baby seat, air-conditioning, additional drivers and local taxes (e.g. sales, purchase or value added tax). If required, check that you're permitted to take a car out of the country where you rent it, as you may need extra insurance. Some companies don't offer unlimited kilometres/miles, which usually works out more expensive unless you plan to cover relatively little distance. Always check the contract and car (e.g. for body damage and to ensure that everything works) carefully before setting out.

To hire a car in most countries you must be at least 21, which is increased to 25 for certain categories of car. Note that some companies also have an upper age limit, e.g. 70. Drivers must produce a valid licence (a copy isn't acceptable) with photographic identification and some drivers require an international driving permit (IDP). If more than one person will be driving a vehicle, all the drivers' names must be entered on the hire agreement. If a credit card isn't used, there's usually a high cash deposit and possibly the whole hire period must be paid for in advance. When paying by credit card, carefully check your bill and statement, as unauthorised charges aren't unknown. It may be possible to sign a credit card authorisation slip and then pay by cash when you return a car. However, if you do this, you must make sure that you obtain (and destroy) the credit card payment slip.

Hiring a car is prohibitively expensive in some countries, particularly during the high season or for long periods. One way to reduce the cost is to rent a car through the American office of an international car rental company such as Alamo (☎ 1-9633), Avis (☎ 1-331-1212), Budget (☎ 1-0700) or Hertz (☎ 1-3131) and pay by credit card. The US freephone (800) numbers of other international rental companies can be obtained from international directory enquiries. Note that when dialling freephone numbers from abroad, you're charged at international rates.

Driving Licence

Ensuring that you're licensed to drive in some countries can be simple or infuriatingly complicated. This depends not on your nationality, but on the country that issued your licence. In some countries you can drive with a foreign licence (possibly with a translation) for a limited period, although many countries require foreigners to have an international driving permit (IDP), also called an international licence. Usually residents have a limited period (e.g. six months or a year) in which to exchange a foreign licence for a local one, after which it becomes invalid and you need to take a driving test.

If your current licence isn't recognised in the country where you're planning to live, it may be possible to obtain a licence from a country whose licences are recognised, although you must do this before taking up residence abroad. Recognition of your licence will depend on whether your home country (or the country or state that issued your licence) has a reciprocal agreement (known as 'reciprocity') with the country where you're planning to live. If it doesn't, make sure that you start the process for obtaining a local licence as soon as possible after your arrival, as it can take some months to obtain. If you don't obtain a local licence by the deadline, you may be prohibited from driving or may need to take a driving test, even if one wasn't originally required. You may need to do any or all of the following (detailed requirements for each of the 11 territories are given below):

- Undertake a first-aid course.
- Take a number of 'lessons' with a local driving school.
- Pass written and practical driving tests.
- Undergo a medical and eye examination.
- Provide a copy and official translation of your driving licence.
- Supply a number of photographs.

- Obtain a residence permit.
- Complete various forms.
- Produce your passport.
- Pay a hefty fee.

If you wish to drive a car with a manual gearbox and passed your test in a car with an automatic gearbox, you must usually take a driving test.

Your existing licence may be stamped and returned to you, retained until you leave the country, or returned to the country of issue. If you will need it to drive in your home or another country, be sure to obtain a copy before going abroad.

Brunei

You can use your home country driving licence or international driving licence for three months in Brunei. After that, you need a Brunei licence issued by the Land Transport Department (🖥 www.land-transport.gov.bn). In order to secure one, you need a completed application form (available from the same office), a copy of your passport, two copies of your current (foreign) driving licence and a fee of BD$10 (US$5.80) for a one-year licence, BD$20 (US$11.60) for a two-year licence or BD$30 (US$17.40) for a three-year licence. These licences can subsequently be renewed at Land Transport Branch Offices or at most post offices.

China

An international driving licence isn't recognised in China and foreigners cannot drive in the country without a Chinese driving licence. In order to get one, visit the local Police Licensing Department (at the Public Security Bureau) taking your home country driving licence, a translation into Chinese and a photocopy. Your photograph is taken for your licence (at a cost of around RMB70/US$8.45) and you must have 12 medical/optical tests (at a cost of around RMB100/US$12.08), which take some time because you must visit 12 different rooms to have them done!

You must return two days later to complete the application process. There's a multiple-choice test (in English), which is actually a memory test because you're given in advance a book with 120 questions and another book with the answers. The test consists of 20 of the questions, taken at random. To pass, you must get at least 16 correct. When you pass, you're (sometimes) asked to drive a car, to test your competence. The licence is ready around a week later.

Hong Kong

You can drive in Hong Kong using your foreign licence or an IDP provided that you don't plan to stay for more than 12 months. If you do, you must apply for a local licence. If you hold an overseas licence issued by an approved country, which is current or expired not more than three years previously and was obtained by passing a driving test in the country of issue, you may apply for a full driving licence without needing to take a test. You may only apply for a licence equivalent to the class(es) covered in your existing licence and you must satisfy **one** of the following three conditions:

- Have resided in the issuing overseas country for not less than six months;
- Have held the licence for five years or more;
- Hold a passport of the country where the licence was issued.

You apply by completing application form TD63A and returning it to the Hong Kong Licensing Office, along with your foreign licence and a photocopy, plus an officially certified translation if it's in a language other than English or Chinese, your Hong Kong identity card (see page 24), the fee (around HK$900/US$115), and a medical certificate (for applicants aged 70 or over).

If you hold an overseas licence issued by a country not approved in Hong Kong, you must apply for a temporary driving licence. To obtain a temporary licence, you must satisfy one of the above three conditions and you must apply for a driving test within three months of arriving in Hong Kong. A temporary licence, valid for three months, is issued immediately but, if you subsequently fail any part of the driving test, your temporary driving licence is cancelled immediately. You're usually given a test date within the three month period; if you aren't, you can renew your temporary licence. A temporary licence costs HK$698 (US$90); a renewal costs HK$349 (US$45). The fee for the driving test is around HK$510 (US$65).

You apply for a temporary licence by completing application form TD181 and returning it to the Hong Kong Licensing Office, along with your passport, foreign driving licence (and an officially certified translation if it's in a language other than English or Chinese), Hong Kong identity card (see page 24), the fee (see below), and a medical certificate (for applicants aged 70 or over).

Indonesia

If you're an Indonesian resident, you can drive in the country using an IDP for as long as the licence is valid under the regulations of the country that issued it. Many expatriates in Indonesia, however, obtain an Indonesian licence (if they have a valid licence from their home country), known as a *SIM* (*Surat Izin Mengemudi*). The process takes a couple of hours (strangely and worryingly, you're rarely required to take a test, either written or driven), and there are agents who will do the job for you, for a fee of around Rp200,000 (US$23); you must meet them at the Department of Motor Vehicles for photographs, fingerprints and your signature. Foreigners are issued with licences that are valid for one year. They're allowed to obtain only Class A licences (for private cars) or Class C licences (for motorcycles).

If you wish to apply for the licence yourself, the procedure is relatively straightforward, provided that you have the correct documents. You must do the following:

- Visit the Department of Motor Vehicles, JL Daan Mogot Km 11, Jakarta Barat, which is responsible for issuing licences for residents of Jakarta, Bekasi, Depok and Tangerang, or the local Department of Motor Vehicles (listed in the phone book). The main office is open between 8am and 4pm, Monday to Friday, and between 8am and midday on Saturday. If your application is received before midday, it's completed that day. Applications submitted between midday and 1pm must be collected the following day. No applications are accepted after 1pm, but applications submitted earlier that day are processed until closing at 4pm. It's recommended to apply as early in the morning as possible (from 8am onwards), from Monday to Thursday. The worst time to go is Friday just before noon, when employees take a long lunch break to go to Friday prayers. The office is busier at the beginning of each month.

  You must take your passport and a photocopy, your KITAS (temporary stay permit – see page 25) and a photocopy, your foreign licence or IDP and a photocopy, and photocopies of the photograph and visa pages of your passport.

- Go to one of the two bank offices on the premises (Bank International Indonesia and Bank Rakyat Indonesia) and buy a payment slip (*Tanda Pembayaran Permohonan Pembuatan Surat Ijin Mengemudi*) for Rp52,500 (US$6.15).

- Present this slip at the adjoining booth, where you're given an application form (*Surat Permohonan SIM*). Complete it and go to the foreigners' window, number 17 (*Loket Orang Asing*) where you must present your passport, KITAS card and current driving licence and copies of these (the official will keep only the photocopies), the payment slip, the completed application form and additional payment as follows:
  - Rp80,000 (US$9.37) if you have a licence from your home country;
  - Rp70,000 (US$8.19) if you have an IDP;
  - Rp100,000 (US$11.71) if you don't have a valid licence of any kind.
  - Rp20,000 (US$2.34) if you're extending a valid Indonesian licence (this must be done annually).
  - Rp40,000 (US$4.68) if you're extending an expired Indonesian licence.

- Go to windows 23 to 26, where your picture is taken and your fingerprints scanned, you sign a piece of paper and the signature is scanned. There's a 'donation' box near the camera into which you're expected to put around Rp3,000 (35¢). If you don't, the attendant will encourage you to do so!

● Go to the waiting area, and after around 30 to 45 minutes, your name is called and you pick up your licence from windows 26 to 28, depending on the class of licence you're collecting. You're expected to make another 'donation' of Rp3,000 (35¢).

Japan

To drive in Japan, you require either an IDP (note that IDPs issued in Brazil, China, Germany and Mexico aren't valid in Japan) or a Japanese licence. The IDP must be obtained before you arrive in Japan and is valid for a year after you arrive, after which it must be exchanged for a Japanese licence. To apply for a Japanese licence, you need your original licence (which you must have held for at least three months before your arrival in Japan), an authorised translation of the licence into Japanese (ask at the nearest embassy about translators), your passport, your Alien Registration Card (see page 29) and two photographs measuring 3cm by 2.4cm.

All applicants must have their eyesight and their knowledge of the traffic code tested. Whether you need to take a driving test depends on which country your licence was issued in.

● Applicants from the following countries aren't required to take a written or road test: Australia, Belgium, Canada, Denmark, Finland, France, Germany, Greece, Holland, Iceland, Ireland, Italy, Luxembourg, New Zealand, Norway, Portugal, Spain, Sweden, Switzerland and UK.

● Applicants from the following countries and regions are required to take both a written and a road test: Africa, Asia, Eastern Europe and the US.

Your first Japanese driving licence is valid until your third birthday after the date of issue. The current licence processing fee is around ¥4,150 (US$38), the test fee ¥2,400 (US$22), which is payable each time you sit it, and it costs around ¥3,000 (US$27.50) for a certified translation of your licence.

Korea

You can drive in Korea for a year with an IDP, after which you must obtain a Korean licence, which is valid for seven years (and can be renewed in the three months before expiry). You can obtain a licence at one of the country's 24 Driver's Licence Examination Offices. You require a notarised translation of your foreign licence, your passport or a certificate of immigration and four passport-size photographs. A physical examination is required but no theory or practical tests and the fees for the examination and the application are SKW5,000 (US$4.20) each. Processing takes between seven and ten days.

Malaysia

The situation regarding driving licences for foreigners in Malaysia isn't as clear-cut as in the region's other countries (except Thailand). You can drive in Malaysia on a licence from another Association of South-east Asian Nations (ASEAN) country (Brunei, Cambodia, Indonesia, Laos, Malaysia, Myanmar, the Philippines, Singapore, Thailand and Vietnam) and in theory on a licence from many other countries (particularly western countries, especially if the licence is endorsed by the Registrar of Motor Vehicles in Malaysia). In practice, however, it isn't uncommon for foreigners to be 'scrutinised' by the Malaysian police if unable to produce a local licence. As a result of this, it's recommended that foreigners staying in Malaysia for over a year obtain a Malaysian driving licence or at least an annually renewed IDP.

To apply for a local licence, visit the Road Transport Department office, taking your foreign licence, your passport and a photocopy, two passport-size photos and a local identity card, e.g. a work permit. The licence is issued after around two weeks and you're informed by post when it's ready for collection. The fee is around RM50 (US$13.15). Holders of British and American licences aren't required to take a local driving test, but one is sometimes required for drivers holding licences from other countries (although rarely western ones).

Philippines

You can drive in the Philippines on your foreign licence for up to 90 days, but after that must obtain a Philippine licence. The Land Transportation Office (LTO) issues licences and there are offices throughout the country. You must take your foreign licence and a photocopy (plus a translation from the embassy of the issuing country if the licence isn't in English) and a completed application form. If your foreign licence has expired or if you require a professional licence, you must take written and road tests. The LTO gives you a receipt which acts as a temporary licence for 60 days, pending the issue of the licence. A non-professional licence costs around P250 (US$4.50) and is valid for three years.

Singapore

You can drive on a foreign licence in Singapore for up to six months (not 12 months, as is sometimes supposed). After that, you must obtain a Singapore licence, from 10 Ubi Avenue 3, Singapore 408865 (☎ 547-0000). You must have held your foreign licence for at least six months before your arrival in Singapore and must pass the Basic Theory Test, conducted in Singapore by the Singapore Traffic Police. The test fee is around S$6 (US$3.48) and the instruction course preceding the test (lasting an hour and three-quarters) costs around S$65 (US$37.75).

To apply for a licence, you need your passport, confirmation of having passed the Basic Theory Test, your employment/dependant/student pass, your foreign licence (plus an extract of your driving licence record from the relevant licensing authority if your licence doesn't show the date of first issue), and a translation of your licence if it isn't in English.

Taiwan

If you don't have an IDP, you cannot drive in Taiwan until you've obtained a permanent driving licence. With an IDP, you can drive for up to 30 days but must then apply to the Commission of Motor Vehicles for a temporary or permanent driving licence.

To obtain a temporary driving licence, you must present an IDP, your passport or Alien Residence Certificate (see page 36), an application form and one passport-size photograph. There's no fee and the period of the licence varies between 6 and 12 months.

For a permanent driving licence, you must present your passport and Alien Residence Certificate and a photocopy of each, your foreign licence or IDP and a photocopy, plus a translation into Chinese by a registered translation company, a health certificate issued by a public hospital, an application form, two passport-size photos and the fee of NT$200 (US$5.87).

If your home country licence isn't accepted in Taiwan (and licences from many US states aren't – in retaliation for the fact that Taiwan licences aren't accepted there!), you must also take written and road tests. The written test is very easy but most drivers fail the road test (which is taken on a closed course and therefore totally unrepresentative of real driving conditions) the first time and must retake it.

Thailand

Thai regulations regarding foreign driving licences aren't clear and, as with many aspects of life in Thailand, are subject to change. You can drive in Thailand if you hold a licence issued in Laos, Malaysia or Singapore or have an IDP. What's unclear is how long you can drive in Thailand on an IDP before needing to obtain a Thai licence. Some authorities say three months, others six. It's therefore wise to apply for a Thai licence within three months if you have an IDP. If you don't, you must apply for a local licence before driving in Thailand.

You must apply at the local Transport Office and take your passport and valid non-immigrant visa (a tourist visa isn't sufficient), evidence of residence address certified by your embassy or the Immigration Bureau, a medical certificate confirming that you're in reasonable general health, two passport-size photographs and your foreign driving licence. You can only apply for a licence to drive a motorcycle or a car. The fee for the former is Bht55 (US$1.38), for the latter Bht105 (US$2.63).

You must complete an application form and then take a two-hour class on driving in Thailand, which takes place at the local Transport Office. It's in Thai and foreigners who don't speak the language must take a Thai-speaking friend or interpreter with them. You must then take a test for colour-blindness and a written driving test, also in Thai, before a test of your driving skill. A Thai licence lasts for a year and must be renewed annually, which is a straightforward process.

Car Insurance

When driving in the Far East, ensure that you have valid car insurance. The rules and requirements concerning car insurance are being changed in many of the region's countries, as the authorities try to improve road safety and increase driver responsibility. This is a complicated subject and the types of insurance, what's included and the cost vary considerably from country to country. In some countries, it isn't mandatory to have liability insurance and, even when it is, the minimum liability limits are usually woefully inadequate (car insurance that provides added protection is available from some travel agents). **Never take it for granted that your car insurance is sufficient for you and your passengers, but check in advance and obtain it in writing – this is particularly important when hiring a car.**

Breakdown Insurance

When driving in the Far East, it's important to have motor breakdown insurance (which may include holiday and travel insurance), including transport home for your family and your car in the event of an accident or breakdown. If you're a member of a motoring organisation, you may be covered when travelling abroad by a reciprocal agreement with national breakdown services, although cover is usually fairly basic.

Car Crime

Most countries in the region have high rates of car theft and theft from cars, particularly in major cities and resort areas. If you drive anything other than a worthless wreck you should have theft insurance that includes your car stereo and belongings (although this may be prohibitively expensive). If you drive a new or valuable car, it's wise to have it fitted with an alarm, an engine immobiliser (the best system) or other anti-theft device, and also to use a visible deterrent such as a steering or gear stick lock. It's particularly important to protect your car if you own a model that's desirable to professional car thieves, e.g. most new sports and executive models, which are often stolen by crooks to order.

The best security system (available in many countries) for a valuable car is a tracking device that's triggered by concealed motion detectors. The vehicle's movements are tracked by radio or satellite and the police are automatically notified and recover over 90 per cent of vehicles. Some systems can immobilise a vehicle while it's on the move (which may not be a good idea!). The main drawback is that tracking systems are expensive, although many insurance companies offer a discount on comprehensive insurance when you have a tracking system fitted.

Few cars are fitted with deadlocks and most can be broken into in seconds by a competent thief. A good security system won't usually prevent someone from breaking into your car or even stop it from being stolen, but it makes it more difficult and may persuade a thief to look for an easier target. Nevertheless, when leaving your car unattended, store any valuables, including clothes, in the glove box or boot (trunk). Note, however, that storing valuables in the boot doesn't necessarily prevent them from being stolen, particularly if the boot can be opened from inside the car. If a car is empty a thief may be tempted to force open the boot with a crowbar. Some people leave their car doors and boot unlocked (and empty!) to avoid having their windows smashed or the boot broken open. It's never recommended to leave your original car papers in your car (which may help a thief dispose of it). When parking overnight or when it's dark, it's wise to park in a secure overnight car park or garage, or at least in a well-lit area.

If your car is stolen or anything is stolen from it, report it to the police in the area where it was stolen. You can usually report it by telephone, but must go to the station to complete a report. Don't, however, expect the police to find it or even take any interest in your loss. Report a theft to your insurance company as soon as possible.

Driving In The Far East

According to the Road Traffic Injury Research Network, a UN-sponsored body, traffic accidents are set to become one of the world's largest killers, with pedestrians most at risk; and accident rates in South Asia (along with sub-Saharan Africa) are among the world's highest. Studies by the Asian Development Bank in the late 1990s came up with the sobering statistic that the Asia and Pacific region suffers the greatest death toll from road accidents, with 44 per cent of the world's road deaths but only 16 per cent of its motor vehicles. These findings are based on official statistics, and the situation in the region is almost certainly even worse, as under-reporting of road fatalities is common in many Asian countries. For example, the Beijing Traffic Engineering Research Institute estimates that actual road death figures are over 40 per cent higher than official figures.

China has the region's largest number of road fatalities per year (over 100,000), which is to be expected in the country with the world's largest population, but other countries in the region have far higher fatality risks, as shown by the table below:

Country	Annual Road Deaths Per 100,000 Population
Malaysia	30.7
Thailand	28.0
Korea	27.8
Brunei	22.4
Taiwan	13.9
Japan	8.2
Singapore	7.4
China	5.9
Indonesia	5.6
Hong Kong	3.9
Philippines	0.9

Note that some of the above figures are to be taken with a pinch of salt in view of the under-reporting previously mentioned. In particular, the figures for Indonesia and the Philippines look suspiciously low in view of driving standards in those countries.

A contributing factor to the number of traffic accidents in South Asia has been the rapid motorisation of the region (much of this has been an increase in the number of motorcycles), with a recent surge in the number of new and inexperienced road users. The number of vehicles in China has trebled over the last decade and more than doubled in many other Asian countries.

Driving in many of the region's countries is totally chaotic – a bit like a fun-fair dodgem car track without the fun, and nerve-racking at the best of times. If you're in doubt about your ability to cope with the stress or the risks involved, you'd be wiser to use public transport – not that that's always safe (see page 200). The following tips are designed to help you survive driving in the region. Detailed information about each territory is provided below.

● In 7 of the 11 territories considered here, motorists drive on the left, in the other four on the right (when not driving in the middle!). It saves confusion if you drive on the same side as the majority. If you aren't used to driving on the left or right, take it easy until you're accustomed to it. Be particularly alert when leaving lay-bys, T-junctions, one-way streets, petrol stations and car parks, as it's easy to lapse into driving on the wrong side. It's helpful to display a reminder (e.g. 'Think Left!' or 'Think Right!') on your car's dashboard.

- Note that the procedure following an accident isn't the same in all countries, although many countries use a standard accident report form provided by insurance companies. As a general rule it's recommended to call the police to the scene for anything other than a minor accident.

- Drivers of foreign-registered cars must have the appropriate nationality plate or sticker affixed to the rear of their car when motoring in the region. In many countries you can be fined on the spot for not displaying it, although the law isn't often enforced judging by the number of cars without them. Cars must show the correct nationality plate only and not an assortment.

- Ensure that your car complies with local laws and that you have the necessary equipment: for example, spare tyre, bulbs and fuses, warning triangle (in some countries you need two), first-aid kit, fire extinguisher, petrol can (note that carrying a can of petrol or petrol in plastic cans is forbidden in some countries) and headlight beam deflectors. Check the latest regulations with a motoring organisation in your home country.

- If you're planning a long journey, a mechanical check-up for your car is recommended, particularly if it's a while since its last service.

- Make sure that you have sufficient spares, particularly if you're driving a rare car (i.e. any car that isn't sold locally). A good map will come in handy, particularly when you're lost. If your car runs on leaded petrol or LPG, make sure that this is available locally and in all the countries you intend to visit or pass through.

- Seat belts must be worn at all times in many countries.

- In some countries dipped headlights (low beam) must be used at all times.

- The legal blood alcohol level when driving varies according to the country and is zero in some. Note that the strength of alcoholic beverages (and the size of drinks) varies considerably from country to country. The best policy is not to drink alcohol at all when you're driving.

- Emergency (ambulance, fire, police) and public utility (electricity, gas, telephone, water) vehicles attending an emergency have priority on all roads in most countries.

- At roundabouts (traffic circles),vehicles on the roundabout have priority and not those entering it, usually indicated by a give way sign.

- Never carry anything across an international border unless you're absolutely sure what it is, as it could contain drugs or other illegal substances. The same applies to any passengers (and their baggage) that you pick up on your journey. Note that it's illegal to transport produce, plants, alcohol and minors (apart from your own children) across international or state borders in some countries.

- When driving anywhere NEVER assume that you know what another motorist is going to do next. Just because a motorist is indicating left doesn't mean he is actually going to turn left – in some countries he is just as likely to be turning right, stopping or about to reverse – and in many countries motorists make turns without any indication at all! Don't be misled by any semblance of road discipline and clearly marked lanes. Try to be courteous, if only in self-defence, but don't expect others to reciprocate.

● Take extra care in winter in parts of China, Korea and Japan, when ice and snow can make driving particularly hazardous.

Brunei

Side: Driving is on the left and overtaking is allowed only to the right.

Signs: The country uses internationally-approved road signs and, although words on signs are in Malay and English in most places, in certain areas they're only in Malay, which can be challenging for foreigners. Always stop at junctions with stop signs; even if the road is clear, stop for at least two seconds.

Speed Limits: Speed limits (which are displayed on signs on many roads) are 24kph (15mph) in school zones, 48kph (30mph) in business or residential areas and 88kph (55mph) on highways. Speed traps are common, with on-the-spot fines of BD$50 to BD$250 (US$86.50 to US$432) – sometimes more.

Parking: Cars must be parked in the direction of the traffic flow. Parking fines in Brunei are between BD$50 and BD$200 (US$86.50 and US$346). Never leave your car with the engine running.

Safety: Seatbelts must be worn at all times by everybody in a car, and children under three must be fastened securely in a government-approved car seat. Always use your indicator when turning or changing lanes, and your hazard warning lights when approaching an accident or if your vehicle is disabled.

Other Requirements: Wherever you're driving in Brunei (especially in and around the capital), police motorbikes might direct you to pull off the road to allow a royal motorcade to pass. Failure to do so can land you in jail.

China

If you decide to drive in China, you will be sharing the roads with increasing numbers of new, inexperienced drivers, because China's burgeoning middle class is taking to car ownership in a big way. There are around 700,000 privately owned cars in Beijing, and 3 million Beijing residents hold a driving licence. New roads are being built in the city, but road space is already limited and lengthy traffic jams are a fact of life. And matters are set to become much worse. The Chinese Academy of Social Sciences estimates that China will become the world's largest car market by 2019, buying 30 million per year.

Driving etiquette is conspicuous by its absence, so prepare to toughen up if you intend to drive in China. Drivers rarely give an inch and try to create space for themselves. As a result, cars entering traffic from side roads often do so aggressively because nobody will let them join if they don't push. Sudden lane changing is common and horns are in constant use as drivers warn others of their presence. The huge volume of bicycles on the roads is another obstacle for car drivers.

Side: Driving is supposed to be on the right, although it isn't always, especially on minor roads, and it isn't uncommon to find traffic going the wrong way on roads or roundabouts.

Signs: Few road signs are in English, and finding an English-speaker to give you directions when you're lost can be very difficult.

Speed Limits: Unless indicated otherwise, speed limits are 70kph (43mph) in towns and cities, 110kph (68mph) on highways and between 60 and 80kph (37 and 50mph) on other roads.

Safety: Seatbelts are mandatory for all the occupants of a car, although many Chinese parents carry small children in their arms when travelling and drivers in cities (especially Beijing) often drive without belting up.

Other Requirements: You're required always to have in your car the purchase papers and certificates from when you bought or imported your car and certificates proving that you've paid car tax and insurance.

If you have an accident, wait for the police and don't move your car. The police will take the driving licences of those involved and the next day you're required to visit the nearest Police Bureau for Foreigners to fill out paperwork and then report the accident to your insurance company. **In the event of an accident, a foreigner is invariably assumed to be in the wrong.**

Hong Kong

Few foreigners, even long-term residents, drive in Hong Kong. The excellent public transport system and the expense of driving (100 per cent vehicle import tax, petrol tax and high insurance and vehicle registration fees) make it unnecessary to brave the traffic: in fact, it's estimated that at least 90 per cent of people in Hong Kong use public transport.

For those who do get behind the wheel, you will spend a lot of time in traffic jams in this small, crowded part of south China. Hong Kong is, however, one of the safest places in the region for drivers and is proud of its relatively safe roads. The lack of serious accidents is probably due largely to the difficulty of driving quickly in such a crowded place rather than to exemplary driving skill.

Side: Driving is on the left.

Speed Limits: The speed limit is 50kmph (31mph) in urban areas and 80kmph (50mph) on highways, unless otherwise indicated.

Safety: The use of front and rear seat belts (in vehicles which have them) is mandatory in Hong Kong, and the authorities are trying to stamp out the use of hand-held mobile (cellular) phones while driving: fines for doing so are up to HK$2,000 (US$257).

Alcohol: The legal limit is 50mg per 100ml of blood.

Indonesia

The vast country of Indonesia has over 378,000km (234,360mi) of roads, but only around 28,500km (17,670mi) of them are main or national roads, and a tiny 200km (125mi) are motorways. Roads on Java are generally good, roads on Bali and Sumatra are reasonable, but the standard on the other islands is often poor (although it's improving).

Driving in Indonesia isn't a relaxing experience, and traffic is often congested and undisciplined. Ironically, the congestion in the cities has a beneficial side-effect: it reduces driving speeds to such an extent that accident rates are low, especially for serious accidents.

Many of Indonesia's roads outside the cities are only one lane in each direction, meaning that overtaking is dangerous. Drivers rarely leave much of a gap between their car and the one in front, and overtaking on the hard shoulder (if there is one) is common. The prevalence of 'developing world' vehicles on Indonesia's roads presents an additional hazard, and you often come across horse and ox carts, pushcarts and variations on the bicycle, driven or ridden with varying levels of competence and awareness. Driving at night outside of urban areas is particularly dangerous in Indonesia. Many rural roads are unlit and many drivers refuse to use their lights!

As a result of the driving conditions in Indonesia, the majority of foreigners (and wealthy Indonesians) employ professional drivers. Take advice from other expatriates and ask for recommendations of drivers. Salaries paid to drivers vary, with the average around Rp900,000 (US$105) per month.

Side: Traffic drives on the left, sometimes more in theory than practice.

Safety: Indonesian law requires the use of seatbelts in the front seats (most Indonesian cars don't have seatbelts in the rear seats). The use of infant and child car seats is uncommon and you need to hunt around to buy or hire one. The law requires motorcyclists to wear helmets but, as in countries all over the world, the rule is widely ignored (particularly by passengers) and inconsistently enforced. **Note that accidents on rented motorcycles are the principal cause of death and serious accidents among foreign visitors to Bali.**

Other Requirements: In the event of an accident, both drivers are required by law to wait for the police to arrive in order to report the accident. Although Indonesian law requires third party insurance, the majority of Indonesian drivers aren't insured and, if even if they are, insurance companies often try to wriggle out of paying claims (even more so than in other countries). If a pedestrian is injured in an accident, the driver of the vehicle responsible is often expected to drive the injured person to hospital; ambulances in Indonesia are sometimes unreliable. In the case of fatal traffic accidents, particularly in rural areas, it isn't unknown for locals to attack the driver who's seen as being responsible. This is more likely to happen to Indonesian drivers, but has also happened to some foreigners.

Car drivers in Indonesia are recommended to pay particular attention to buses and trucks, which are often dangerously overloaded and therefore unstable, and which drive at excessive speed.

Japan

Many expatriates don't drive in Tokyo because the public transport system is excellent and driving is 'challenging' on account of the heavy traffic, a lack of parking space and street names (see **Signs** below). If you decide to drive in Japan, you will find that Japanese drivers are usually polite and sensible, a radical difference from drivers in most of the rest of the Far East. The exception is taxi drivers, who drive aggressively (as in many countries). Despite being courteous, Japanese drivers tend to speed.

Side: Driving is on the left.

Signs: Usually only main thoroughfares are named, although signs are often written in English as well as Japanese; other roads have unrelated numbers that only local postmen can work out. The best way to navigate is to identify local landmarks rather than street signs.

Speed Limits: The speed limit is usually 50kph (31mph) in built-up areas, 60kph (37mph) on ordinary inter-city roads, 60 to 80kph (37 to 50mph) on expressways and 80 to 100kph (50 to 62mph) on motorways.

Alcohol: The legal blood alcohol limit is zero, and insurance is invalidated if you're involved in an accident and are found to have any alcohol in your blood.

Other Requirements: Registration and insurance documents must be carried in the car at all times. In the event of an accident, the police should be told immediately, by dialling ☎ 110. Your insurance company should also be told as soon as possible and will require copies of the police report and any medical reports, if applicable.

Korea

Driving in Korea isn't for the faint-hearted, and the country has some of the highest accident rates in the world. There are too few roads and too many cars, despite the large amount of road building and maintenance being undertaken. The Korean love of speed adds to the confusion and carnage, as does a sometimes total lack of road discipline and awareness, and a drinking culture. Koreans change lane at the drop of a hat, rarely slow down when traffic lights change colour, use mobile phones all the time, tailgate, mount the pavement when doing a U-turn, park anywhere, don't wear seatbelts and ignore the presence of motorcyclists and pedestrians. **You have been warned!**

Side: Driving is on the right.

Speed Limits: Speed limits range from 30 to 70kph (18 to 43mph) on most roads, sometimes according to road and weather conditions, although they're rarely observed.

Alcohol: The legal limit is 50mg of alcohol per 100ml of blood.

Other Requirements: Minor collisions are usually settled between drivers but if you're involved in a more serious accident, as a foreigner you should be prepared to be discriminated against. Carry with you the phone numbers of a Korean friend, a lawyer and your embassy. Keep a camera in the car and photograph the scene of the crime for evidence. Telephone ☎ 112 and report the accident to the police. Cars should then be pulled over to the side of the road and you should inform your insurance company.

Malaysia

Malaysia's traffic accident statistics are among the world's worst and driving is best avoided, although the heavy traffic in Kuala Lumpur makes it one of the safer parts of the country in which to drive a car (accident rates for bicycles and motorcycles are high) because speeds are severely restricted by the congestion. The city's roads are generally in a reasonable condition, but the various one-way systems and the congestion don't make for enjoyable driving. A map is essential.

The condition of roads in Peninsular Malaysia is generally good or very good, but this isn't the case in Sabah and Sarawak, where roads are also liable to flash flooding.

Side: Malaysians drive on the left (theoretically).

Speed Limits: Speed limits are 50kph (31mph) in built-up areas, 90kph (56mph) on trunk roads and 110kph (68mph) on motorways. Limits are often flouted, despite speed traps being common, with fines of up to RM300 (US$80).

Safety: Wearing seat belts in the front seats is compulsory.

Other Requirements: The North-South Highway is a toll road and costs around RM1 (26¢) per 7km (4.34mi) covered.

Philippines

As in much of the Far East, driving in the Philippines isn't recommended and should be undertaken only if absolutely necessary. Let a professional drive you instead. If, however, you have a rush of blood to the head and decide to take the wheel, note that drivers in the Philippines are noted for their aggression, disregard for traffic regulations and addiction to sounding their horns. Lane discipline is non-existent, traffic lights and one-way streets are ignored, and don't expect anybody to give way for you. Manila has the added joys of heavy congestion and smog, and throughout the country the poor state of many pavements (sidewalks) means that pedestrians sometimes walk in the road.

Side: Driving is on the right.

Signs: A plus point for the foreign driver is that many road signs are in English.

Safety: Front-seat occupants are required by law to wear seat belts.

Other Requirements: Always carry your car registration certificate, official receipt for the purchase of the car (if bought), a photocopy of your licence and insurance documents in the car. In the event of an accident (which is likely), you're required to report to the local police station to give a statement. Give the photocopy of your licence to the police; don't leave the original, as it's likely to be lost. Don't admit fault or liability.

Singapore

Compared with the driving chaos found in much of the region, Singapore's roads are a haven of tranquillity. Partly as a result of the toll system (see below), traffic runs fairly smoothly – helped by the fact that Singapore's drivers are generally law abiding, although their lane discipline is sometimes lax.

Side: Driving is on the left.

Speed Limits: The speed limit is 50kph (31mph) on all roads except highways, on which it's 70 to 80kph (43 to 50mph).

Parking: Parking is easy to find and inexpensive, around 50 cents per half hour. The country is hard on traffic offenders, with hefty fines and prison sentences.

Safety: Wearing seat belts is compulsory in the front seats and child seats are mandatory. Headlights must be used between 7pm and 7am.

Alcohol: The legal limit is 80mg of alcohol per 100ml of blood.

Other Requirements: As with everything in the country, driving is heavily regulated. To ease congestion in the Central Business District (CBD), vehicles entering between 7.30am and 7pm pay a toll, which varies according to the time. Singapore's highways also levy tolls during peak morning and evening hours, using the Electronic Road Pricing Scheme (ERP), which automatically deducts tolls from an 'In-Vehicle Unit' (IU), a device that must be fitted in all vehicles in Singapore (you can buy or rent one). You must buy a rechargeable card and insert it in the IU.

In the event of minor accidents, with no injuries and minor vehicle damage, it's usual for both parties to settle matters without recourse to the police. If, however, you want to claim from your insurance company, you must submit a police report within 24 hours.

Taiwan

Driving in Taiwan is stressful, road courtesy is in short supply and local driving skills vary between bad and awful. Roads are usually very busy (in a country with around 23 million people, there are over 10 million registered vehicles), especially during rush hours. The unpleasant conditions make drivers impatient and aggressive, with traffic rules often ignored. Illegal lane changes, turns and the shooting (running) of red lights are common. The many scooters on Taiwan's roads and the cavalier way in which they're often driven, weaving in and out of traffic at high speed, are an additional hazard. As if these dangers weren't enough, foreigners also have to contend with the fact that important road information is often only in Chinese.

Side: Driving is on the right.

Speed Limits: Limits are 50kph (31mph) in urban areas and 90kph (56mph) on highways, unless otherwise indicated. Speed traps are common; in fact the speeding laws seem to be the only traffic rules regularly enforced in Taiwan!

Safety: Car theft is common, as is the 'keying' of parked cars by bored or jealous locals. Don't be tempted to antagonise, provoke or shout at other drivers (however awful) because road rage is common.

Other Requirements: In the event of a minor accident, the Taiwan government encourage drivers to sort matters out between themselves. This is an arbitrary procedure and can be difficult to negotiate if you don't speak much Chinese and are being harangued by an aggressive driver. Carry a mobile phone and seek help from a Chinese-speaking friend. If the accident is serious or cannot be resolved between the drivers, call ☎ 110 to inform the police. The Taiwan police are usually fair and helpful when dealing with foreigners, but don't sign any statements unless you're sure you know and agree with exactly what they say.

Thailand

The death rate on Thailand's roads is anything but amusing, and so is the standard of driving. Right of way in Thailand is effectively decided by size: the larger vehicle wins (this also applies to elephants and water buffalo, which you sometimes come across on the country's roads). Buses have a habit of overtaking at the most inopportune moments, for example on bends, when going uphill and when there's traffic coming in the opposite direction. If you decide to overtake another vehicle, don't be surprised if the driver behind takes this as a cue to overtake you – at the same time!

Driving at night carries its own hazards, in addition to those already mentioned, and is best avoided if possible. A lot of vehicles in Thailand don't have rear lights, notably vulnerable motorcycles, bicycles and carts. And plenty of vehicles only have one front light, so don't assume that an oncoming vehicle showing one light is a motorcycle or bicycle; it might well be a juggernaut. Driving is particularly dangerous on the outskirts of major cities at dusk, when commuters are returning to outlying villages.

There might, however, be signs of hope for Thailand's road users. The country's National Road Safety Centre has been lobbying (in summer 2003) for government funds to buy breathalysers and speed cameras, and to build dedicated motorbike lanes in the country's main cities (around 75 per cent of accidents in Thailand involve motorcycles). It's also proposing a special traffic court to deal with the growing number of traffic offenders, the renovation of 1,200 bottle-neck traffic junctions and improvements to the uneven surface on 31,000mi (50,000km) of roads (a mammoth task).

Side: Thais drive on the left . . . most of the time.

Speed Limits: Speed limits vary between 60kph (37mph) in towns and 90kph (56mph) on highways.

Safety: Although you might not notice the fact, it's compulsory for drivers to wear seatbelts.

Alcohol: The legal limit is 80mg of alcohol per 100ml of blood.

Other Requirements: If you're involved in an accident, leave the vehicles where they stopped, so that police can apportion blame. Contact them immediately (☎ 191, a freephone number). Note that, as a foreigner, in the event of any ambiguity about whose fault an accident was, you're likely to be blamed.

8.

MISCELLANEOUS MATTERS

This chapter contains various important considerations and information for those planning to live or work in the Far East, including climate, crime and safety, leisure, pets, religion, shopping abroad, social customs, television and radio, and time difference.

CLIMATE

For most people the climate is a significant factor when deciding where (or whether) to live in the Far East, particularly if you have a choice of countries or are planning to retire in the region. When choosing where to live you should bear in mind both the winter and summer climate, the average daily sunshine, plus the rainfall, humidity and wind conditions. You may also wish to check whether an area is noted for snow, ice and fog (which are common during winter in the north of the region).

The best climate in which to live is generally considered to be one without extremes of cold and heat, either from day to night or from season to season. Coastal regions of the southern Far East enjoy year-round temperatures in the low to upper eighties Fahrenheit (upper twenties to low thirties Celsius), the heat tempered by sea breezes and acceptable levels of humidity. Many cities throughout the region, however, are very hot, humid and stifling for much of the year (as are the summer months in the north of the region), many people spending their time scuttling between air-conditioned environments.

You may also wish to avoid the Far East's coldest regions – the northern parts of China, Japan and Korea – where winters can be severe and last up to six months, and driving conditions can be hazardous. Temperatures are often reduced considerably by the wind speed, which creates what's known as a 'wind chill factor', where a temperature of 10°F (-12°C) combined with a wind speed of 40kph (25mph) results in a wind chill factor of -29°F (-34°C). If you're a keen skier, you will welcome some snow in a region not generally noted for it but won't perhaps be so enthusiastic when snowdrifts make roads impassable, engulf your home and cut you off from the outside world for days on end!

It's important to check whether an area is susceptible to natural disasters such as floods (which are common in China, for example, where 500,000 people were evacuated from their homes in the north of the country in autumn 2003), storms (hurricanes, tornadoes, typhoons, whirlwinds, etc.), forest fires, landslides or earthquakes. Earthquakes, for example, are a constant threat in Indonesia, Japan and the Philippines.

Flash floods are a danger in many countries in the region, particularly in mountainous areas, and if you live near a coast or waterway it can be expensive to insure against floods. The good news is that your chance of experiencing a severe cyclone, hurricane, tornado, flood, earthquake or forest fire is small in most areas, although when they do strike, the results can be devastating.

Many expatriates in the region use powerful air-conditioning to counteract the heat and humidity, but this can lead to uncomfortably dry air (which can cause or aggravate respiratory problems), and some people use humidifiers to inject some moisture back into the air. Humidifiers vary in price between around US$50 and US$200 (making it expensive to have one of the better units in each room of a large property) and some models require regular cleaning and the filter pads replacing; they can also be noisy (see also **Chapter 4**).

Details of climatic conditions in each territory are given below. Further information and regional and local weather forecasts are given in daily newspapers, are broadcast on radio and television, and are available via numerous websites, including ⌨ www. worldclimate.com, www.world weather.com, www.cnn.com/weather, http://weather. yahoo.com and www. bbc.co.uk/weather.

Brunei

Brunei's equatorial climate is fairly constant, with little seasonal variation. There are no marked wet and dry seasons, with rainfall throughout the year, although this is at its heaviest between September and January. Humidity averages a sticky 79 per cent and temperatures are high throughout the year, ranging from 26°C (79°F) to 31°C (88°F). Brunei is located away from the typhoon and earthquake 'belts'.

China

As the world's third-largest country, with topographies ranging from hot deserts to high mountains, China has a variety of climates, although not as many as its size might suggest. The north and inland regions of the country experience a climate of extremes, with long, bitter winters lasting from November to March, when temperatures fall as low as -40°C (-40°F), and hot, sometimes humid summers between May and September, with temperatures often reaching 38°C (100°F). Central China and the north-east coast are milder in winter but still hot and humid in summer. The far south also has hot, humid summers with temperatures regularly over 32°C (90°F) and mild, dry winters, with temperatures in the upper teens Celsius (upper fifties and lower sixties Fahrenheit). The far north-west of China has hot, dry summers and freezing winters.

The rainy season in much of the country is April to September, coinciding with the hottest time of the year and making for stifling conditions, and typhoons affect south-east China between July and September.

Beijing & Shanghai: As for the climate of the country's two major cities, Beijing is stifling in summer and freezing in winter, while spring can be distinctly chilly, with plenty of wind and dust to add to the discomfort. The autumn months of September to November are the most pleasant, often warm and dry.

Shanghai is a steaming city in the summer, with temperatures reaching an uncomfortable 40°C (104°F), while winter can be cold (around freezing, or below, although not as marrow-piercing as in the north of the country) with frequent drizzle. April, May, October and November, on the other hand, can be very pleasant, with warm temperatures and moderate humidity and rainfall.

Hong Kong

Hong Kong has much to recommend it, but the climate is rarely mentioned as one of its assets. The weather is hot, humid and sometimes wet between April and October, and also frequently either hazy or cloudy. The winter months (January and February) can be surprisingly cool for a territory that lies just south of the Tropic of Cancer: temperatures average in the mid-teens Celsius (upper fifties to low sixties Fahrenheit), although they can drop below 10°C (50°F), which is hardly typical of the tropics. November, December and March enjoy the best weather, with sunshine, breezes and temperatures in the low to mid-twenties Celsius (upper sixties to mid-seventies Fahrenheit). Typhoons can strike in late summer and September.

Indonesia

The climate of this sprawling country is surprisingly uniform, all parts of Indonesia being on or close to the equator. It's hot and wet from October to April, and hot and dry from May to September. Coastal temperatures are between 29°C (84°F) and 32°C (90°F) throughout the year, hilly and mountainous regions inland being somewhat cooler.

Bali and Lombok are at their best between April and October, the weather being hotter, wetter, cloudier and more humid during the rest of the year. Jakarta and the rest of Java are hot and wet throughout the year, although it's drier and less humid between May and September. Sumatra is also hot and wet much of the time, although less so between April and October, with May and October the most pleasant months.

Japan

Japan's latitudinal spread, from a sub-arctic north to a sub-tropical south gives it a range of climates. Winters are bitter in the north and parts of the centre of the country, with temperatures well below freezing for much of the time between November and March. Southern and central coastal Japan enjoy milder winters, with temperatures often reaching the mid-teens Celsius (upper fifties Fahrenheit), but cold snaps are quite common. Summer throughout most of Japan is unpleasantly hot (warm in Hokkaido), wet and humid, with temperatures often reaching 32°C (90°F) and sometimes higher. March, April and May are pleasant months, dry and sunny, still cold in the north but mild or warm in the centre and south. September to November are usually regarded as the most pleasant months, similar to spring but warmer.

Rainfall is spread throughout the year in most of Japan, and is generally high: Tokyo, for example, receives two and a half times as much rainfall as London. June and early July is the wettest time in much of Japan, and central and southern regions sometimes have a second rainfall peak in late summer and early autumn. Hokkaido is much drier than the Tokyo area during the summer.

Winter precipitation is heavy on the west coasts of Hokkaido and Honshu (sometimes as snow), while elsewhere in Japan, winter is relatively dry. Japan is vulnerable to typhoons: five or six usually strike between August and September, and they can be very destructive.

Korea

Unlike much of the Far East, Korea has four distinct seasons. Winter lasts from November to March and can be very cold, with temperatures below freezing for long periods, but it's often dry, with clear, sunny skies. Spring (April and May) can be a beautiful time of year: cool or warm, dry and sunny. Summer (June to August) is often unpleasantly hot, wet, humid and typhoon-prone, with temperatures reaching 32°C (90°F) or more. Autumn (September and October, and into November in the milder south) is the most residents' favourite season: warm, sunny and dry, although also typhoon-prone (over 100 people were killed when a particularly destructive typhoon struck in September 2003).

Malaysia

All of Malaysia is hot and humid throughout the year, with coastal and lowland temperatures of 30 to 32°C (86 to 90°F), although it's somewhat cooler in the mountains, and humidity up to a suffocating 90 per cent. Rain falls throughout the year, and the wettest times vary across the country. On the west coast of Peninsular Malaysia, September to December is the wettest season, on the east coast and in Sabah and Sarawak, it's between October and February. It doesn't often rain all day, the rain being concentrated in short, torrential downpours.

Philippines

The geographical spread of the innumerable Philippine islands means that there's some climatic variation, but the climate generally conforms to the South-east Asian norm: hot and humid throughout the year, although there are wider seasonal temperature variations than in many parts of the region. The average is 30°C (86°F) but temperatures can range between 25°C (77°F) and 40°C (104°F), May often being the hottest month. Rainfall patterns vary between the islands and within them, but the dry season generally runs from January to June, the wet season from July to December. Typhoons can strike between June and November, and February to April is generally regarded as the most pleasant period.

Singapore

Singapore has been described as a 'giant sauna', on account of the year-round heat and humidity. Temperature variations are minimal, most days reaching 30 or 31°C (86 or 88°F). Even at night, temperatures average 24°C (75°F) and rarely drop below 21°C (70°F). Humidity is around 75 per cent throughout the year, and rainfall is spread fairly evenly, with November to January the wettest months, May to July the driest.

Taiwan

Taiwan straddles the Tropic of Cancer and its climate is between the equatorial conditions of the southern Far East and the seasonal climates of the north, although closer to the former. There's rainfall and high humidity throughout the year, and typhoons can strike between June and October. Summer is hot and sticky in all the lowland regions of the island, with temperatures averaging 30°C (86°F) and frequent short rain showers. Mountainous areas can be cool or cold in summer and receive lots of snow between December and January. Winter in the northern coastal region (including Taipei) is particularly wet, with average temperatures a pleasant 20°C (68°F), although it can turn chilly at times between November and April, when it's also often cloudy. The south-west has warmer, drier winters. October and November are the most pleasant months in most of Taiwan, with moderate rainfall and moderate temperatures.

Thailand

Thailand has more climatic variations than is sometimes supposed and isn't simply a country of unrelenting heat, humidity and rain. Thailand's climate is governed by monsoons, which produce three seasons throughout the country except in the extreme south, which has the same conditions as Peninsular Malaysia. The three seasons are as follows:

- **November To March** – The 'cool' season, with temperatures in the upper twenties Celsius (mid-eighties Fahrenheit) in Bangkok and humidity levels at their lowest (around 75 to 80 per cent). In the northern city of Chiang Mai, temperatures are around 21°C (70°F) and humidity decreasing from 79 per cent in November to a modest 58 per cent in March.
- **March To May** – The hot season sees temperatures of 30 to 32°C (86 and 90°F) in Bangkok, sometimes higher, and humidity between 75 and 80 per cent. Chiang Mai is usually around 26°C (79°F) with humidity of 65 to 70 per cent.
- **June To October** – The rainy season, with Bangkok temperatures in the upper twenties Celsius (mid-eighties Fahrenheit), high humidity (80 per cent plus) and plenty of rain: over 30cm (12in) in September. Chiang Mai has temperatures around 25°C (77°F), humidity in the low eighties and a lot of rain: almost as much as Bangkok in September.

The cool season is generally regarded as the best time to visit Thailand, as nights are pleasantly cool even without air-conditioning. Some people, however, prefer Bangkok in the rainy season because the downpours clear some of the pollution from the air.

CRIME

The crime rate (and what constitutes a crime) varies considerably from country to country, so it's important to investigate the level in a particular country, region or city before deciding where to live. Many Far Eastern countries are very safe places to live, On the other hand, western governments currently advise against staying in much of Indonesia and parts of the Philippines. Not surprisingly, major cities have the highest crime rates, and some districts are best avoided at any time. Many cities are notorious for 'petty' crime such as handbag snatching, pick-pocketing and theft of (and from) vehicles. In contrast, crime in villages and rural areas (away from tourist areas) is virtually unknown in most countries, and windows and doors are often left unlocked.

Theft is most common, which takes a multitude of forms. One of the most common criminals is the bag snatcher, possibly on a motorcycle, who grabs hand or shoulder bags (or cameras) and rides off with them, sometimes with the owner still attached (occasionally causing serious injuries). It's wise to carry handbags on the side away from the street and to wear shoulder bags diagonally across your chest, although it's better not to carry a bag at all (straps can be cut) but to wear a wrist pouch or money belt. You should also be wary of bag-snatchers in airport and other car parks, and never wear valuable items of jewellery in high-risk areas. Motorcycle thieves may smash car windows at traffic lights to steal articles left on seats, so bags should be stowed on the floor or behind seats.

Tourists, travellers and naive expatriates are the targets of many of the world's most enterprising criminals, including highwaymen, who pose as accident or breakdown victims and rob motorists who stop to help them. Beware also of gangs of child thieves in cities, pick-pockets and over-friendly strangers. Always remain vigilant in tourist areas, queues and anywhere there are large crowds, and never tempt fate with an exposed wallet or purse or by flashing money around. One of the most effective ways of protecting your passport, money, travellers' cheques and credit cards is with a money belt.

Foreigners (particularly holiday homeowners) are often victims of burglary. Always ensure that your home is secure (see page 125) and that your belongings are well insured, and never leave valuables lying around. It's recommended to install a safe if you keep valuables (e.g. jewellery) or cash in your home. In some countries, housing developments may be patrolled by security guards, although they often have little influence on crime rates. It's wise to arrange for someone periodically to check a property when it's left unoccupied.

Fortunately, violent crime is relatively rare in most Far Eastern countries, although muggings, murders, rapes and armed robbery have increased considerably in the last decade or so in many. Hitch-hiking isn't recommended anywhere. Women travelling alone are particularly at risk, and sexual harassment is prevalent in some countries, particularly towards blondes. It's recommended for lone women to use taxis rather than public transport late at night.

Drug addiction is the main impetus for crime in many countries. Drug addiction is a growing problem throughout the region and drug addicts (and prostitutes) are a common sight in many towns and cities. It's an offence to possess soft drugs such as hashish in many countries, while in some it's legal for personal use or the law tends to turn a blind eye to its use. However, the possession and use of hard drugs such as heroin and cocaine is strictly prohibited in most countries and the penalty for trafficking can be death! Many countries are particularly harsh in their treatment of foreign drug dealers, who may be held on remand for years without trial. **When travelling to and from any country in a vehicle, you should take particular care, as vehicles are frequently found to contain hidden drugs planted by drug dealers.** You should also be wary of giving strangers lifts and never transport anyone across an international border.

The age of consent for male/female sexual activity in the 11 territories is as follows: Brunei 14 (but 13 within marriage); China 14; Hong Kong 18 for males, 16 for females; Indonesia 17; Japan 13; Korea 13; Malaysia 16 and you must be married, although the law is unclear; Philippines 12 to 18 (the law is unclear, and the age varies according to circumstances and interpretation!); Singapore 16; Taiwan 16; Thailand 15.

Some Far Eastern countries have strict laws regarding matters such as alcohol (both its sale and its consumption), pornography (which has different definitions in different countries), displays of homosexuality, adultery, dress for women and dress in holy places. Often these have religious connotations, particularly in Muslim countries (Brunei, Indonesia and Malaysia), and it's important to be aware of them. It's easy to unwittingly offend your hosts and in certain cases even to be arrested for what may appear to be innocuous behaviour. In some countries 'petty' laws (such as illegal parking and jaywalking) may be widely ignored, while in others they're strictly enforced, so it's important to know the local 'ropes' (see country-by-country details below and **Social Customs & Rules** on page 285).

One of the biggest financial threats to foreigners in the Far East is their own countrymen and other foreigners. It's common for expatriate 'businessmen' in some countries to run up huge debts, through dishonesty or incompetence, and to cut and run owing clients and suppliers a fortune. In many resort areas, fraudsters lie in wait around every corner and newcomers must constantly be on their guard (particularly when buying a business). Fraud of every conceivable kind is a fine art in many countries and is commonly perpetrated by foreigners on their fellow countrymen. **Always be wary of someone who offers to do you a favour or show you the ropes, or anyone claiming to know how to 'beat the system'.** If anything sounds too good to be true, you can safely bet that it is! It's a sad fact of life, but you should generally be more wary of doing business with your fellow countrymen in the Far East than with the local populace.

Crime Prevention & Safety

Despite the foregoing catalogue of dangers, in most Far Eastern countries you can usually safely walk almost anywhere at any time of the day or night, and there's no need for anxiety or paranoia about crime. However, you should be 'street-wise' and take certain elementary precautions, which includes learning the local 'ground rules' (see below). If you follow the rules, your chance of being a victim of crime is usually low; break the rules and it rises dramatically. Basic precautions include avoiding high-risk areas, particularly those frequented by drug addicts, prostitutes and pick-pockets. As with most things in life, prevention is better than cure. This is particularly true when it comes to crime prevention, as only a relatively small percentage of crimes are solved and the legal process in many countries is agonisingly slow. It's also important to have adequate insurance for your possessions.

Staying safe in a large city is largely a matter of common sense (plus a little luck), although you need to develop survival skills in some cities. Most areas are safe most of the time, particularly when there are a lot of people about. At night, stick to brightly lit main streets and avoid secluded areas (best of all, take a cab). Walk in the opposite direction to the traffic so no-one can kerb-crawl (drive alongside) you and walk on the outside of the pavement (sidewalk), so you're less likely to be mugged from a doorway, but with your bag facing away from the street. Avoid parks at night and keep to a park's main paths or where there are other people during the day.

If you find yourself in a deserted area late at night, remain calm and look as though you know where you're going by walking briskly. If you need to wait for a train or bus at night, do so in the main waiting room, a well lit area, or where there's a guard or policeman. If possible, avoid using subways in the late evening or at night. Most major cities have 'no-go' areas at night and some have areas that are to be avoided at any time. When you're in an unfamiliar city, ask a tourist office official, policeman, taxi driver or other local person whether there are any unsafe neighbourhoods – and avoid them! Women should take particular care and should never hitch-hike alone; rape statistics are high in some countries and most go unreported.

Some experts advise you to keep your cash in at least two places and to split cash and credit cards. Don't keep your ID card or passport, driving licence or other important documents in your wallet or purse where they can be stolen. It's recommended always to carry a certain amount of cash, say US$20 to 50 – referred to as 'mugger's money' in the US – in case you're mugged; this is usually sufficient to satisfy a mugger and prevent him from becoming violent (or searching further). In some countries, parents give their children mugger's money as a matter of course whenever they leave home.

Never resist a mugger. It's far better to lose your wallet and jewellery than your life! Many muggers are desperate and irrational people under the influence of drugs, and they may turn violent if resisted. Anaesthetic sprays sold in drugstores or ordinary hair or insect sprays are carried by some people to deter assailants (as are pepper sprays and mace, although they're usually illegal). These are, however, of little use against an armed assailant and may increase the likelihood of violence.

You should warn your children about the dangers of 'street life', particularly if you've been living in a country where it's taken for granted that you can safely go anywhere at any time of the day or night. It may be necessary totally to re-educate your family regarding all aspects of public life. Wherever you live and whatever the age of your children, you should warn them against taking unnecessary risks and discourage them from frequenting remote or high risk areas, talking to strangers or attracting unwanted attention.

Don't leave cash, cheques, credit cards, passports, jewellery and other 'valuables' lying around or even hidden in your home (crooks know all the hiding places). Good quality door and window locks and an alarm will help but may not deter a determined thief. In many cities, triple door locks, metal bars and steel bars on windows are standard fittings. If you live in a city, you should be wary of anyone hanging around outside your home or apartment block. Have your keys ready and enter your home as fast as possible. Most city dwellers always lock their doors and windows, even when going out for only a few minutes.

Often apartments are fitted with a security system, so that you can speak to visitors before allowing them access to your building. Luxury apartment buildings may have (armed) guards in the lobby with closed-circuit TV and voice identification security systems. In addition, most apartment doors have a peephole and/or a security chain, so you can check a caller's identity before opening the door. Be careful who you allow into your home and check the identity of anyone claiming to be an official inspector or an employee of a utility company. Ask for identification and confirm it with his office before opening the door. Also beware of bogus policemen (who may flash an imitation badge) that stop you in the street and ask to see your money and passport – and then run off with them!

Store anything of value in a home safe or a bank safety deposit box and ensure that you have adequate insurance. Never make it obvious that no one is at home by leaving tell-tale signs such as a pile of newspapers or post. Many people leave lights, a radio or a TV on (activated by random timers) when they aren't at home. Ask your neighbours to keep an eye on your home when you're on holiday. Many towns have 'crime watch' areas, where residents keep an eye open for suspicious characters and report them to the local police.

If you're driving, keep to the main highways and avoid high-risk areas. Never drive in cities with your windows or doors open or valuables (such as handbags or wallets) on the seats. Take extra care at night in car parks and when returning to your car, and never sleep in your car. If you have an accident in a dangerous area (e.g. any inner-city area), police often recommend you not to stop, but to drive to the nearest police station to report it. In remote areas, accidents are sometimes staged to rob unsuspecting drivers ('highway hold-ups') and cars are deliberately bumped to get drivers to stop (again, find the nearest police station). If you stop at an accident in a remote area or are flagged down, keep the engine running and in gear and your doors locked, and only open your window a fraction of an inch to speak to someone. **Note that in some countries hire cars are targeted by muggers and you should be wary of collecting a hire car from an airport at night.**

Following the Bali nightclub bombing in October 2002, when over 200 people were killed, the British and American governments are warning westerners throughout South-east Asia to be extra vigilant and wary. It's important to be aware of anything that's happening in a country where you're planning to live or work that could affect your safety, such as wars, riots, military coups, terrorism, kidnappings and general civil unrest, to name but a few. If you have any problems concerning safety while in the Far East, you should contact your local consulate or embassy for advice. If you register with your local embassy (see page 406) they will contact you in times of serious civil unrest or wars and may assist you in returning home (if necessary).

Most governments post warning on official websites for their nationals, which, in many cases, apply to all travellers and can (of course) be referred to by anyone. The US Department of State website has two general warning sections (🖳 http://travel.state.gov/travel_warnings.html and http://travel.state.gov/warnings_list.html) as well pages providing warnings about drugs (🖳 http://travel.state.gov/drug_warning.html) and a list of useful travel publications (🖳 http://travel.state.gov/travel_pubs.html). Other useful websites include the British Foreign and Commonwealth Office (🖳 www.fco.gov.uk/travel), Gov Spot (🖳 www.govspot.com/ask/travel.htm), Travelfinder (🖳 www. travel finder.com/twarn/travel_warnings.html), SaveWealth Travel (🖳 www.save wealth.com/travel/warnings), and the Australian Department of Foreign Affairs and Trade (🖳 www.dfat.gov.au/consular/advice/advices_mnu.html).

There are a number of books about safety for travellers, including *World Wise - Your Passport to Safer Travel* by Suzy Lamplugh (Thomas Cook), *Safety and Security for Women Who Travel* by Sheila Swan (Travelers' Tales), *Business Smarts – Business Travel Safety Guide* by Aura Lee O'Banion (Safety First) and *Travel Can be Murder: A Business Traveler's Guide to Personal Safety* by Terry Riley (Applied Psychology Press). Further information can be found in **How To Avoid Holiday And Travel Disasters** by this author (Survival Books – see page 444). Safety information may also be available via your local television teletext service, e.g. BBC2 Ceefax page 470+ in the UK. In many countries, police forces, governments, local communities and security companies publish information and advice regarding crime prevention, and your local police station may carry out a free home security check. Details of dangers and safety measures specific to each territory are given below. See also **Car Crime** on page 228, **Home Security** on page 125 and Health (**Chapter 3**).

Brunei

Brunei experiences very little civil disobedience or crime. The country is a monarchy subject to Islamic rules and values, with a culture of quiet agreement with the edicts of the Sultan. There's little impetus for crime in this tax-free, subsidised society, whose population has one of the world's highest per capita incomes. Levels of all crimes are very low, particularly crimes of violence, and the highest risk you face is that of petty, opportunist theft (which is rare). **Avoid becoming involved with drugs of any kind because penalties are severe – often death.**

China

Serious crime against foreigners is rare in China, but the view that China, as a totalitarian state, has little or no dissension or disorder is inaccurate. Crime does occur, in cities and rural regions. Pick-pockets and muggers are a problem in larger towns and cities, and often target markets, tourist sites and bars frequented by tourists and expatriates. Never resist a robbery, as thieves often carry knives and you might be seriously injured. Petty thefts are common on overnight buses and trains.

There's a low risk of terrorism directed at westerners or western interests in China, but 'protest bombings' occasionally occur, for example at Qinghua and Beijing Universities in Beijing in February 2003.

Some parts of the country are poorly or sparsely policed and extra care should be taken in the regions bordering Burma, Laos, Pakistan, Siberia and Vietnam. Drug smuggling and related crimes of violence are on the increase in Yunnan, and armed bandits are a threat in certain remote areas, particularly on the Gansu-Sichuan border. There have been attacks on single foreign travellers trekking in isolated areas of China, particularly along stretches of the Great Wall, and trekking alone isn't recommended (for anyone). There has also been an increase in piracy in the South China Sea.

Hong Kong

Hong Kong is a (relatively) safe city, with a very low incidence of violent crime. Pick-pocketing and other street crime are a risk, particularly in crowded markets, and thieves often steal luggage from people checking out of hotels.

Indonesia

Indonesia is the most dangerous country in the Far East for the traveller and expatriates, with a significant risk of terrorism and violence from religious fundamentalists and regional separatists, particularly against US and UK nationals and their 'allies' – actual or perceived. At the end of 2003, the British and US governments were advising against all non-essential travel to Indonesia, and against **all** travel to Aceh, where the Indonesian government has declared martial law and violence is increasing.

The extensive list of recent terrorist attacks in Indonesia includes a bombing close to the US Embassy in central Jakarta in September 2002, the bombing of a nightclub on Bali in October 2002, an attack on a McDonald's restaurant in Makassar in December 2002, an explosion near Jakarta Police Headquarters in February 2003, attacks near UN offices and at Jakarta International Airport in April 2003, an explosion in Jakarta's Parliament Complex in July 2003 and another at the Marriott Hotel in central Jakarta in August 2003. Latest intelligence information points to the likelihood of further attacks, particularly against western and Indonesian government targets.

Foreigners in Indonesia are recommended to exercise great caution in public places, including hotels, bars, restaurants, nightclubs, shopping malls, recreation areas, public and commercial buildings, transport offices and terminals, and places of worship. It's also recommended to avoid large, boisterous street crowds, which isn't always easy in Indonesia, where demonstrations are a common mode of political expression.

Foreign institutions and businesses – particularly US and British – are prime targets and have been advised to review or improve their security arrangements. British, American and International schools have also received threats. Foreigners are recommended to avoid travelling alone at night and, when taking taxis, to use only known, reputable firms, preferably booking by telephone. For longer road journeys, where possible you're recommended to travel in a 'convoy'; there have been incidents of lone cars being stopped and the passengers robbed.

Another prevalent (albeit less dangerous) crime throughout Indonesia is credit card fraud and you're recommended never to let your credit card out of your sight during transactions (except when using an ATM!). Pirate attacks against ships in Indonesian waters are also a risk. Unsurprisingly, in a country as large as Indonesia (over 13,500 islands spread over 3,000 miles), crime and other risks vary in different regions, as follows:

Aceh: The Indonesian government declared martial law in Aceh on 19 May 2003, since when violence has increased. Two Germans were shot in June 2003. British, American and other western nationals are recommended to avoid travelling to Aceh and those already there are recommended to leave. The Indonesian government has declared that the waters inside a 12 nautical mile limit around Aceh are closed to all foreign ships.

Bali: Since the terrorist nightclub bombing in October 2002, the situation in Bali has stabilised, but the risk of further attacks is high, on an island that attracts (or rather, used to attract) large numbers of western visitors. Another risk on the island for foreigners is of becoming involved with illegal gambling and being held to ransom by the gangs running the gambling establishments.

East Kalimantan (Borneo) & North Sulawesi: The Philippine terrorist group calling itself Abu Sayyaf ('sword bearer') has extended its activities into Malaysia and is rumoured to be planning also to kidnap tourists from neighbouring areas of coastal Indonesia.

Kalimantan (Borneo): Since an outbreak of ethnic violence between Dayaks and Madurese in 2001 led to several hundred deaths, the situation has calmed down, but there's still a risk of violence resurfacing and travellers are recommended to avoid mixed Dayak/Madurese areas.

Lombok: There haven't been any incidents of terrorism on Bali's neighbouring island of Lombok and crime levels are generally very low. Visitors, however, are recommended not to use freelance guides, who offer cheap rates but can be unreliable and aren't vetted. Instead, seek an official guide through a local hotel.

Maluku & North Maluku Province: Maluku Province is under emergency rule and is closed to foreigners, following sectarian violence between Christian and Muslim groups. A peace agreement seems to be holding (with a few exceptions) and, under certain circumstances, foreigners in transit can travel through the province (apply to the Provincial Government in Ambon). A similar emergency rule in North Maluku Province was lifted in May 2003, but caution is still recommended.

Sulawesi: Christian/Muslim violence in Poso and surrounding areas of Central Sulawesi has decreased, but there are still incidents and it's recommended to avoid the Poso District and check the advisability of visiting other areas. In Southern Sulawesi, a bomb exploded in a McDonald's restaurant in December 2002 and extreme caution is recommended; take particular care not to offend Muslims.

West Timor: UN staff haven't returned to West Timor since three were killed at Atambua in September 2000 and foreigners are recommended to avoid travelling there.

Japan

Japan has some of the lowest crime levels in the industrialised world, particularly for violent crime. This stems mainly from the traditional belief that the individual is obliged not to bring shame on any group to which he belongs. There is, however, an increasing incidence of juvenile crime, including violence, and commentators wonder if the old order is beginning to crumble. Some think that recent economic problems will exacerbate this.

Organised crime, however, is a fact of life in Japan. It's run by the *Yakuza* (underworld), a mafia-like group which operates throughout the country, specialising in extortion and violence. Expatriates and foreigners rarely come across 'ordinary' crime in Japan and there have been no terrorist attacks since 1995, when a religious cult released poison gas on the Tokyo subway.

Korea

Korea is a very safe country for the traveller and expatriate. The level of crime against foreigners is low and there are no specific risks in the country. In fact, levels of some crimes are notably low: for example, in the late 1990s there were a mere nine robberies per 100,000 people reported in Korea compared with 86 in Germany and 258 in the US. Even levels of car theft are low, and some people leave the keys permanently in their car ignition, although this isn't recommended. As in Japan, levels of petty crime among schoolchildren are increasing, which is a warning sign for the future. A common crime in this alcohol-loving society is drunk driving, a constant hazard on Korea's already dangerous roads.

The threat from terrorism in Korea is considered to be low, although developments in the country's volatile relationship with North Korea could lead to terrorist attacks.

Malaysia

Malaysia is generally a pleasant, law-abiding country with low levels of crime. Violent crime against foreigners is very rare and the main risks you face are pick-pocketing, car break-ins, and bag, mobile phone and wallet theft, often by youths on motorcycles, and credit card fraud which, as in Indonesia, is on the increase; don't let your credit card out of your sight during transactions. Robberies at supermarkets and in underground car parks have also been reported, and the theft of passports is on the increase, particularly on aircraft and in airport buildings. You should also be wary if approached by strangers and invited to take part in gambling and/or offered drinks. There have been incidents of drinks being spiked and subsequent robberies and assaults, even in 'respectable' bars and restaurants in Kuala Lumpur. Those travelling by ship are at (low) risk from piracy attacks in and around Malaysian waters.

Following the terrorist attack in Bali, the Malaysian government has made a creditable effort to tighten security against terrorism, but there is a risk that Islamic fundamentalists will find support among Malaysia's Muslim community and carry out similar acts in Malaysia. Foreign businesses, institutions and schools are seen to be particularly at risk. There's also a continuing risk from the Philippines-based terrorist group Abu Sayyaf, which in 2000 extended its activities into Malaysia by kidnapping tourists from Sabah. In 2001 it also took hostages from a Philippines island close to the Philippines/Malaysia border. The Malaysian government has increased security in the region and the Philippines government has had some success in reducing the terrorist group's numbers, but the risk remains, particularly in the islands and coastal areas of Sabah.

Philippines

Crime is a serious problem in parts of the Philippines, particularly Manila. Poverty is a major 'cause' of street crime, which includes pick-pocketing and bag snatching, so it's recommended to avoid carrying too much cash and to leave valuable jewellery and cameras at home. Credit card fraud is common, so never let your card out of your sight during transactions. As in Malaysia, beware of taking drinks from strangers, which may be spiked, and avoid gambling with 'new friends'; the games are often confidence tricks.

Piracy against the many ships that ply the waters between the Philippines islands is another risk, with kidnappings from boats a speciality. Boat safety is also an issue: there are around 100 ferry accidents per year in the Philippines, many leading to massive loss of life. Apart from bad weather, one of the main reasons for the number of accidents is that many of the ferries are criminally under-maintained and overcrowded. There have been recent calls to introduce the death penalty for negligent operators whose vessels sink. **It's strongly recommended that you avoid ferries that look overcrowded or poorly maintained.**

Another specialist crime in the Philippines, a country with laws that take a particularly dim view of paedophilia, is 'entrapment', where single male foreigners are befriended by strangers with children; a charge of abuse is then made, in order to try to extort money. **Please note that the death penalty is often passed in child abuse and rape cases, and that under Filipino law, a child is anybody under the age of 18.**

Terrorism and kidnapping, carried out by criminal gangs and religious and other extremists, are also serious risks in the Philippines. The threat against westerners and western interests is particularly high. In 2002, there were numerous terrorist bombings in the Philippines, particularly in Manila and Mindanao, including attacks on transport services, public places and the communications and utilities infrastructures. There were also around 100 kidnapping incidents in 2002, some involving foreigners. Extreme violence and execution are sometimes used by the kidnapping gangs, and botched rescue attempts have also resulted in hostage deaths.

Bombings and kidnappings in the Philippines are carried out by a variety of individuals and groups, some of them criminals looking for financial gain, others looking to settle grievances or disputes, and a range of extremists, including the communist New People's Army, and Abu Sayyaf and splinter groups from Islamic separatist organisations, some linked to international groups, including Al Qaeda. The New People's Army operates throughout the Philippines, Abu Sayyaf and other Islamic groups are concentrated in the south, but also target Manila.

In late 2003, the British, American, Australian and Canadian Governments were strongly advising against travel to central, southern and western Mindanao, Basilan and the Sulu archipelago. Non-essential travel to the rest of Mindanao should be avoided, and care is recommended in Manila, Palawan and in all tourist areas and coastal resorts.

Singapore

Singapore's reputation as an ordered, crime-free society is generally accurate. Violent crime is rare, but petty crime is increasing, particularly bag-snatching, and it's recommended not to carry valuables or much cash. As in most of the region, piracy is also a risk in the waters off Singapore.

The general risk of terrorist attack in South-east Asia also applies to Singapore. The country's authorities are very vigilant and security-conscious and there have been no terrorist attacks in recent years. However, in late 2001 and mid-2002, the authorities arrested over 30 people who had been planning attacks against the US Embassy and British High Commission, and intelligence reports indicate that further attacks against western interests are planned.

Taiwan

Crime levels are low in Taiwan and the main threats are from low-level, street crime and pick-pocketing on the Mass Transit Railway system. House burglaries are also increasing, particularly in the mountainous suburbs of Taipei. As for terrorism, Taiwan is seen as low to very low risk. In fact the main dangers in Taiwan come not from other people, but from earthquakes and typhoons.

Thailand

Crime isn't a major problem in much of Thailand, although recent years have seen an increase in the incidence of pick-pocketing, purse-snatching and burglary, occasionally involving violence. Violent crime, however, is still rare, particularly against foreigners. Much more common is drugging, often by bar workers or prostitutes, followed by robbery.

Foreigners are recommended to avoid the Cambodian and Myanmar border areas, which contain a variety of hazards, including bandits, land mines, rebels and smugglers. Camping in undesignated areas in national parks is dangerous; in 2000 an Australian tourist was murdered in the Doi Ang Khan National Park in Chiang Mai.

Thailand has experienced several internationally publicised incidents of (unbelievably naive) foreigners being caught for smuggling drugs after having accepted free air tickets and new luggage from recently acquired 'friends'. Needless to say, you should resist any such offer – tempting as it may be. **Penalties for involvement in drugs are severe in Thailand: at best a long prison sentence (of between 10 and 50 years), at worst death.**

Be careful when buying gems in Thailand, as there are many conmen. Only use reputable dealers and avoid strangers who approach you offering to sell you items at silly prices. As with most things, if something appears too good to be true, it invariably is. The fake gems and metals they sell you will be virtually worthless.

LEISURE

Brunei

Brunei's only large settlement is the capital, Bandar Seri Begawan, which has a population of around 70,000. It's a clean, modern, spacious city, with several attractions. Outside the capital city, Brunei has several other sites worth visiting. Sport, eating out and shopping are popular and well catered for but nightlife is virtually non-existent.

Culture

Bandar Seri Begawan: The Omar Ali Saifuddin Mosque stands in a lagoon close to the Brunei river and is one of the region's most impressive modern mosques, with a huge golden dome. Bandar also has two worthy museums, the general-interest Brunei Museum and the Malay Technology Museum. The Sultan's palace, Istana Nurul Iman, is a magnificent building but is open to visitors only at the end of the month of Ramadan. Kampung Ayer is another local attraction, a collection of water villages built on stilts in the Brunei River.

Other Sites: Around 12km (7mi) south-west of Bandar lies Wasai Kandal, a forest with waterfalls, pools and a picnic area. Near the town of Tutong (which has a market every morning) is Pantai Seri Kenangan (also called Pantai Tuton), probably the best beach in Brunei, with white sand and a rustic restaurant. Around 40km (25mi) south-east of Bandar is Batang Duri, a 'longhouse' which gives an insight into the life and culture of Brunei's indigenous inhabitants, the Iban. Nearby is the Kuala Belalong Field Studies Centre, which undertakes research into tropical rainforest fauna. There's also a zoo in the vicinity, Taman Batang Duri. The surrounding jungle is rich in flora and fauna, but it's easy to become lost (one of the few dangers in Brunei) and you should only venture off marked paths with an experienced guide.

Sport

Sport is popular in Brunei and the Hassanal Bolkiah National Stadium is an impressive facility, including a running track, tennis centre, squash courts and a swimming pool. Golfers have an international-standard, 18-hole, par 72 course at the Mentiri Golf Club and there's a driving range near the airport. Watersports are popular in Brunei, where swimming, sailing, jet skiing, scuba-diving and fishing are practised, particularly around Brunei Bay. You can also play polo, hockey and the ubiquitous football (soccer) – even in Brunei you cannot escape football shirts with 'Beckham' on the back!

Restaurants

Eating out is popular, with European, Malaysian, Chinese and Indian food served in hotel restaurants. Local restaurants often serve local cuisine, which is similar to Malaysian food, with plenty of spicy dishes featuring fresh fish and rice.

Nightlife

Nightlife in the form of bars, pubs, discos and nightclubs in teetotal Brunei is conspicuous by its absence and the streets of Bandar are usually deserted by 9pm. But there are other types of club with a thriving social scene, including the Royal Brunei Yacht Club, The Mabohai Sports Centre and The Panaga Club. Those who want an alcoholic drink can visit Labuan, a duty-free Malaysian island around an hour away by ferry, or you can drive to the Sarawak border crossing, only 20km (12.5mi) from the capital.

Shopping

Shopping is another local leisure pursuit, with shopping centres in Bandar Seri Begawan, Kuala Belait and Seria, and a night market in Bandar, which sells food and antiques. Shopping hours in Brunei are usually from 8am to 9pm.

China

Whereas Brunei is tiny, with a limited amount of attractions and leisure facilities, China is vast and has innumerable sites of interest. Facilities for sport and nightlife, however, are generally limited.

Culture

Beijing: A major attraction is the capital, Beijing, a huge city with long straight roads crisscrossed by lanes and alleys. Sites located on the main thoroughfares are easy to find, but if you need to venture into the lanes and alleys, you can become hopelessly lost. The city's famous Forbidden City is the largest and best preserved set of old buildings in China, a collection of palaces, courtyards, pavilions and gardens that were once home to China's emperors, their eunuchs and concubines. It covers 720,000m² and has 800 buildings and 9,000 rooms.

The infamous Tiananmen Square sits in the middle of Beijing, its name still tainted after the 1989 crushing of pro-democracy demonstrations by troops and tanks. It's a vast space where people go to walk, meet and fly kites. Surrounding it are many of Beijing's attractions, including the Museum of Chinese History, the Museum of the Revolution, the Mao Mausoleum and the Great Hall of the People.

Tiantan Park is home to classic Ming architecture, including the Round Altar, Hall of Prayer for Good Harvests and Imperial Vault of Heaven, which are monuments to the ancient gods. Many people visit the Great Wall of China at the city's Badaling section, but it's crowded with tourists and the wall is better seen at Simatai, a mere day trip out of Beijing, where there's a 19km (12mi) section.

Shanghai: China's second city, Shanghai, enjoys a variety of nicknames, ranging from 'The Pearl (or Queen) of the Orient' and 'the Paris of China' to 'the Whore of the East'. One of its major draws is the Bund, a grand, waterfront strip of shops, hotels and nightclubs, evocative of old and new Shanghai. West of it lies the nightly Yunnan Road Night Market, Shanghai's major eating area, where anything with a pulse is likely to be on the menu. Frenchtown is a Mecca for shoppers and diners, while Nanjing Lu is also a shopper's paradise. The Shanghai Museum is a new building, impressive both as architecture and for its collections of Chinese art. The Huzhou Pagoda, which dates from 1079, lies 20km (12mi) south-west of Shanghai and is China's answer to the Leaning Tower of Pisa.

Xi'an: The city of Xi'an lies in north central China and is one of the country's major attractions. It once rivalled Rome and later Constantinople for the accolade of the world's greatest city, lying on the main crossroads of the lucrative trading routes from China to central Asia. Its major draw today is the site of the Terracotta Army, where some 10,000 figures have been unearthed since 1974.

Other Sites: The old colonial posts of Hong Kong and Macau are among China's premier attractions. Hong Kong is an intriguing blend of China and the west, one of the world's leading shopping and eating destinations (see below). Macau is a fascinating blend of China and Portugal, and a major draw for gamblers. The city of Nanjing lies north-west of Shanghai and is one of China's most attractive cities. It has broad streets and around 20km of impressive city wall dating from the Ming dynasty. Guizhou province in south China boasts the Longgong Caves, one of the world's natural wonders, a network stretching through 20 mountains.

Sport

Sports facilities are found throughout the country, but they're usually basic outside the major cities. Badminton, table tennis, swimming, martial arts and athletics are popular, and China has enthusiastically joined most of the rest of the world in its devotion to football (soccer). Golf courses are springing up near the big cities, but it's still a sport for the wealthy. China's most popular 'sporting' activity is cycling, and short and long-term bicycle trips are common holidays. Hiking is also popular, but the need to obtain expensive permits means that climbing, rafting and hang-gliding are rarely engaged in, which is a pity given China's extensive facilities for all three. Caving is excellent in the south, and camel riding is popular in desert regions. Tai Chi, a sort of slow-motion aerobics, is seen in most of China's parks every morning.

Nightlife & Restaurants

Although they're great smokers of cigarettes, many Chinese drink alcohol only with formal meals, so bars and nightclubs are uncommon outside the major cities. Eating is a popular leisure activity but isn't for the squeamish. The Chinese themselves say that they will eat anything with four legs, except a table. Karaoke is a popular form of evening entertainment. The Chinese don't just pop into a karaoke bar for a couple of drunken songs, but stay for hours and take the singing seriously. If you're invited to a karaoke evening, be warned that these can be interminable and include endless renditions of long, anguished, melodramatic Chinese 'classics'. Other leisure activities in the major cities include trips to the Chinese ballet, opera, theatre and circus.

Hong Kong

Hong Kong Island is a crowded, bustling centre of world capitalism, with a dynamism rarely matched elsewhere in the world. But it isn't all high-rise offices and apartment blocks, and there are several expatriate sports clubs.

Culture

At Aberdeen in the south of the island, over 6,000 people live and work on junks bobbing in the harbour, while nearby Repulse Bay is a popular beach. Victoria

Peak (552m/1810ft above sea level) affords beautiful views of Hong Kong, especially over the world's busiest deepwater port. The views are well worth taking in at night as well as in daylight.

Tsim Sha Tsui on Kowloon is packed with shops, restaurants, bars and strip clubs, and nearby are the more highbrow attractions of the Museum of History, the Space Museum and the Hong Kong Cultural Centre. By way of contrast, the New Territories offer places to escape the bustle of the rest of Hong Kong and Kowloon and are a draw for walkers, cyclists and campers. Bird watchers can visit the Mai Po Marsh, while the 62mi (100km) MacLehose Trail runs across the New Teritories, an attraction for hikers.

Hong Kong has 234 outlying islands, but most are little more than bits of rock protruding from the sea. Some, however, make a good excursion to escape the bustle of the main island and Kowloon. Lantau is the largest and offers greenery, a walking trail and some attractive monasteries, particularly Po Lin, which has a huge bronze Buddha.

Hong Kong is also one of Asia's major cultural centres, home to the Hong Kong Ballet, Hong Kong Philharmonic, Hong Kong Chinese Orchestra and the Hong Kong Repertory Theatre. Hong Kong's city halls, Cultural Centre and Academy for Performing Arts offer year-round programmes, with details posted in the local press. Hong Kong also has important art galleries and museums, with a range of Asian and some western art.

The Hong Kong Tourism Board website (🖳 www.discoverhongkong.com) is a useful source of information about events in Hong Kong. *HK Magazine* and *bc magazine*, which are free and distributed by shops, bars and restaurants, carry weekly listings of current events, exhibitions and openings.

Restaurants & Shopping

Eating and shopping are probably Hong Kong's major leisure pursuits and facilities for both are among the best in the world, although certainly not the cheapest. Shopping hours vary, but are usually from 10am to between 7 and 9pm, and many shops are open every day.

Sport

As well as the above-mentioned hiking and cycling, fishing is popular off Hong Kong's shores and in its reservoirs. There are five courses for golfers, tennis is popular and so are windsurfing and sailing, the latter attractive for the socialising as much as for anything to do with powering boats through salt water. For such a small place, Hong Kong hosts a surprising amount of internationally renowned sporting events, including the Hong Kong Sprint (the world's richest horse race over 1km), the Rugby Sevens Tournament, and the Hong Kong International Dragon Boat Races – one of the world's great boating spectaculars.

Hong Kong has a number of private clubs which are popular with expatriates, including the following:

- **The Aberdeen Marina Club** (☎ 2555-8321, 🖥 www.amchk.com.hk) – Offers a choice of restaurants and facilities for badminton, basketball, bowling, gymnastics, ice hockey, ice-skating, martial arts, squash, swimming and tennis.

- **The American Club** (🖥 www.americanclubhk.org) – Split into two: The Town Club in Exchange Square, which has restaurants, a reading room, a business centre and a fitness centre, and The Country Club on the south of Hong Kong Island, which offers a wide range of sports.

- **Hong Kong Cricket Club** (🖥 www.hkcc.org) – Offers many sports in addition to cricket, as well as restaurants, a dance studio and a busy social programme.

- **Hong Kong Football Club** (☎ 2830-9500) – Offers soccer and rugby facilities in a 2,300-seat stadium, bowling greens, squash and tennis courts and swimming pools. It hosts such international events as the Carlsberg 10s Rugby Tournament.

- **The Hong Kong Jockey Club** (🖥 www.hongkongjockeyclub.com) – One of Hong Kong's most prestigious clubs, with three clubhouses, two racecourses and a wide range of sporting and social activities.

- **The Pacific Club** (🖥 www.pacificclub.com.hk) – Sits on its own pier and offers a wide range of sports and social facilities.

Indonesia

Indonesia is a huge, sprawling country and has a wide range of scenery, culture and leisure attractions.

Culture

Jakarta: Although the capital Jakarta is most renowned for its heat, pollution and outbreaks of instability, it does have a few sites of interest. The old town of Batavia retains colonial Dutch influences and is home to the Jakarta History Museum, many of the exhibits dating from the Dutch period. The Indonesian National Museum is one of the country's best, with a huge collection of objects from Indonesia's many ethnic and cultural groups. The city's modern monuments (many built by ex-President Soekarno) are also a draw, tending to be in a 'so ugly they're beautiful' style. The best example is the 132m (433ft) National Monument, which is a sort of phallic symbol in gold and marble – not to be missed! More attractive are the numerous brightly painted boats that fill Jakarta's old port of Sunda Kelapa and make it a spectacular sight.

Java: The rest of the island of Java offers the impressive architecture of Borobudur and Prambanan, while Bandung lies at 750m (2,460ft) above sea level, with a refreshingly cool climate and superb surrounding countryside. The city of Yogyakarta in the middle of the south coast is Indonesia's cultural and intellectual heart, with universities, museums and arts centres. It's also a good place to eat and has an attractive beach. The Baluran National Park in north-east Java is one of the most accessible of Indonesia's wild areas, a blend of grassland and mangrove swamps, full of wildlife.

Sumatra: Sumatra has stunning, unspoilt forests, mangrove swamps, rivers and wildlife, including tigers and two-horned rhinos. The capital of north Sumatra, Medan, has some stunning architecture, especially the Maimoun Palace and Mesjid Raya, and some interesting museums. The hill town of Berastagi has a cool climate and is close to excellent trekking country. One of Sumatra's most impressive sights is Lake Toba, the largest lake in south-east Asia, set in a volcanic crater. The island of Borneo boasts jungles, exotic wildlife and headhunters, while Irian Jaya's main attraction is as one of the world's least exploited wildernesses, with spectacular scenery and Stone Age tribes.

Bali & Other Islands: The mainly Hindu island of Bali is one of the world's most beautiful, with tropical beaches, lush forests, cloud-bathed volcanoes and hills of paddy fields, making it a favourite destination for holiday brochure photographers. The hill town of Ubud is Bali's cultural heart, with lots of galleries and centres displaying the island's arts and crafts. It's also the best place to listen to Balinese music and watch Balinese dancing, and one of the best places to eat. Surrounding Ubud are some of Bali's most important ancient monuments, including cave shrines and rock carvings. The nearby island of Lombok, which is mainly Muslim, has a similar feel to Bali but is less commercialised – for the time being.

The small islands of Komodo and Rinca are home to the world's largest lizard, the Komodo dragon, the closest thing the modern world has to a dinosaur. Dragon-spotting treks are a unique attraction. The north coast of the island of Sulawesi has beautiful coral reefs, while the villages, burial grounds and elaborate ceremonies of the hill region of Tanatoraja in the centre are a major attraction.

Sport

Watersports are popular in Indonesia, particularly snorkelling, scuba diving and windsurfing. Surfing is also practised in many areas. Trekking and climbing are emerging attractions in Indonesia's many jungle and mountain regions.

Restaurants

Restaurants are plentiful and usually inexpensive in Indonesia, the majority of them serving Indonesian cuisine. This a blend of many influences, mainly Chinese, Indian, Portuguese and Dutch. Most Indonesian dishes are only moderately spicy, using ginger, garlic and fresh turmeric rather than cayenne pepper and chilis. But people who don't enjoy hot food should avoid the spicy, chili relish sambal, served on Java, and be aware that the Padang food enjoyed in parts of Sumatra can be very spicy. Balinese dishes differ slightly from those in much of the rest of Indonesia, as Bali is a Hindu rather than Muslim island, with different restrictions regarding what can be eaten.

Nightlife

Bali, the most tourist-oriented part of Indonesia, has the most bars and clubs, although the capital Jakarta is also well served. Elsewhere, although the Indonesian population is mainly Muslim (and hence teetotal), many hotels have bars and nightclubs. In rural areas, however, entertainment spots are few and far between, with 'nightlife' conducted at home or by visiting friends.

Shopping

The best shopping bargains in Indonesia include batiks, silver, cloth, porcelain, tin art objects, canvas, wood and leather goods. Bali is particularly attractive to shoppers, with a wide range of goods, although you should avoid using guides, who steer visitors to the establishments which pay them the highest commission rather than to those with the most interesting, best priced goods. Throughout Indonesia, be prepared to bargain, and aim to pay around half the seller's initial offer price.

Japan

Japan is an intriguing blend of the very modern and the traditional and boasts leisure attractions and facilities to suit almost every taste, including a variety of western and Asian sports.

Culture

As well as the attractions listed below, Japan boasts innumerable cinemas, theatres and concert halls. Traditional Japanese entertainment includes *bunraku*, a type of puppet theatre, and *kabuki* and *noh* drama, traditional Japanese theatre. Some of Japan's cultural highlights are its religious festivals, the most colourful of which are held in Kyoto.

Tokyo: Even in business districts, there are small shops and restaurants between the skyscrapers, which humanise the city. It's short of old buildings, however, much of the city having been flattened during the second world war, so don't expect a plethora of architectural wonders.

Ginza is the capital's premier shopping district and also has lots of small private galleries. Ueno-Koen, a park, has some of Tokyo's best museums and art galleries, including the Tokyo National Museum, which houses the world's largest collection of Japanese art, the huge National Science Museum and the Shitamachi History Museum. The Asakusa region of Tokyo is home to Senso-ji Temple, a centre of Buddhism.

Kyoto: Kyoto – the country's capital between 794 and 1868 – is the place for those seeking the traditional Japan, with its temples, gardens with raked pebbles and geishas. The Sanjusangen-do and Kinkaku-ji Temples are particularly impressive, while Himeji-jo Castle near Kyoto is Japan's most impressive castle.

Kyoto is also renowned for the number of its festivals and is one of the best places in Japan to eat well and affordably.

Other Sites: Around 100km (60mi) from Tokyo lies Japan's most famous natural attraction and the country's highest mountain, Mount Fuji, a 3,776m (12,385ft) volcano. Unfortunately for the sightseer, it's frequently shrouded in cloud. Winter and spring are the best times to view it, when the weather is at its clearest and the snow cap completes the postcard scene.

Lovers of the great outdoors will also enjoy the Daisetsuzan National Park on the island of Hokkaido, Japan's largest national park, covering 2,309km² (1,432mi2). It encompasses volcanoes, lakes, forest and mountains and is spectacular hiking and skiing country. The Kirishima National Park on the island of Kyushu also has wonderful mountain scenery, as well as volcanoes and hot springs, offering some of Japan's best hiking country.

By way of contrast with traditional Kyoto, one of Japan's most arresting modern sites is the Seagaia Ocean Dome, a 140m (460ft) white beach with ocean, sitting under a 'blue sky' in south Kyushu: an artificial beach next to the real beach.

Sport

Sport is very popular in Japan. Sumo wrestling and judo are the national sports and attract huge crowds. Sumo has six tournaments per year, each lasting 15 days. Three are held in Tokyo, the others in Fukuoka, Nagoya and Osaka. The best place to watch judo is the Kodokan Judo Hall in Tokyo (☎ 3818-4172); for further information about the sport, visit the All Japan Judo Federation's website (🖳 www.judo.or.jp). Also practised are *karate* (self defence), *kendo* (Japanese fencing) and *kyudo* (Japanese archery).

Football (soccer) has taken off over the last decade or so and the country has its own league, the J-League. Co-hosting the World Cup with Korea in 2002 gave Japan even more impetus in the sport. Golf is popular with people who can afford it, and those wanting to play should contact the Japan Golf Association (☎ 3215-0003, 🖳 www.jpa.or.jp).

Winter sports are also popular in Japan and there are over 50 ski resorts, most in the Japanese Alps and on the island of Hokkaido. Equipment is easy to hire, although westerners sometimes have trouble finding equipment large enough to fit them. Diving and snorkelling aficionados should head for the small southern Kerama Islands, near Okinawa, which boast some of the world's clearest waters. They're also good for fishing and, between January and March, whale watching. Hiking is also popular in parts of Japan, particularly in April and May, the cherry blossom season.

Restaurants

Japan is full of restaurants, bars and nightclubs and many people's social lives revolve around these (if their pockets are deep enough). As in western countries, restaurants serving Japanese food tend to be expensive, and some of the dishes in specialist fish restaurants have jaw-dropping prices. Nevertheless, the budget diner can eat well and inexpensively at the many noodle shops, which are the country's primary 'fast food' outlets. Japanese restaurants serve much more than the raw fish and rice of popular imagination and the country boasts many fine Chinese restaurants, as well as plenty of western fast food outlets. Many Japanese restaurants have a window display of the food that they serve, which may take the place of a menu and is a great help to non-Japanese speakers, who can simply point at what they want.

Nightlife

Japan has plenty of nightlife, both modern and traditional. Clubs, discos and bars proliferate, and you can also visit traditional opera, ballet, drama and musicals.

Shopping

Shopping is a popular leisure pursuit, the Japanese being ardent, even ravenous, consumers. Best buys include pearls (black pearls from Okinawa are a speciality), lacquerware, silks, pottery, furniture, cotton robes (yukatas), cameras, green tea and kites. Be careful when buying lacquerware: the best is lacquer over wood, although much that's sold is over plastic. Japanese department stores are well worth visiting and sell a massive range of goods.

Korea

One of Korea's major attractions is its natural beauty and Koreans are renowned for being almost obsessed with nature, especially mountains, and outdoor pursuits.

Culture

For those in search of traditional Korean culture, *Seokcheonje* is a Confucian event held in March and September, when people visit shrines to watch costumed rituals and listen to traditional orchestras (an acquired taste). Buddha's birthday (late April or early May) is celebrated by lantern parades, and in September the National Folk Arts Festival is a celebration of traditional culture.

Seoul: Korea's capital city Seoul is an engaging mix of the old and the new. There's more of the latter because much of the city was destroyed during the Korean War, but Seoul still has ancient pagodas, palaces, temples and gardens. Parts of central and northern Seoul offer enjoyable walks through traditional residential areas (except in summer, when it's too hot and sticky to venture out of an air-conditioned environment). There are also attractive palaces to explore, many dating from the Joseon dynasty, which lasted from the 14th to the 19th centuries. Gyeongbokgung Palace is the city's best known palace. Partially rebuilt several times, following various invasions and wars, it consists of several buildings, including a beautiful pagoda. Changgyeonggung Palace dates from 1104 and is another of the city's landmarks, as is the Namdaemun Gate, an island of elegance in a maelstrom of traffic.

National Parks: An hour's drive north of Seoul lies Bukhansan National Park, with magnificent views and hiking, although it becomes crowded with city dwellers getting a rural 'fix', especially in autumn. Seoraksan National Parkon the east coast is regarded as Korea's most spectacular, although it too can become very crowded. The Songnisan National Park also attracts plenty of hikers and is best known for Beopjusa, one of Korea's most impressive temples, originally dating from 553 but rebuilt in 1624; its 33m (108ft) Buddha is the largest standing figure in East Asia.

Sport

Many of Korea's leisure activities revolve around outdoor exercise, which might come as an unpleasant surprise to those whose main exertion is walking to the kitchen to grab another bottle. Hiking and mountain biking are very popular in the country's rugged terrain, and skiing is possible between December and March, especially near Yongpyong and in the Seoraksan National Park.

For lovers of other sports, Korea has a wide range of modern facilities. The country played host to the 1986 Asian Games, the 1988 Olympic Games and the 2002 Asian Games and co-hosted the 2002 World (football) Cup with Japan, and the legacy is plenty of high quality sporting venues. Golf is popular and the country has around 80 courses, many in the area around Seoul. The most popular traditional sports are *T'aekwondo* (a martial art), *Ssirum* (Korean wrestling), kite-flying and archery.

As might be expected in a peninsular, watersports are popular in Korea, especially on the south coast and some of the outlying islands. The water is at its warmest between June and November, and facilities are widespread for most watersports, especially scuba-diving, deep-sea fishing, waterskiing and windsurfing.

Restaurants

Korea's cuisine is more robust than that in much of the rest of Asia. It's usually spicy and salty, and meat is more common. Koreans are among the world's most frequent restaurant-goers, but this is a recent development; between 1990 and 2000, the number of restaurants increased nearly two and a half times. Now, around 40 per cent of Korean adults go to a restaurant every day. Most of the country's restaurants are either Korean, Chinese, 'western' (particularly American fast food outlets) or Japanese. Few have menus in English.

Nightlife

Korea has an extensive range of bars, clubs, music venues and traditional Korean arts and theatre outlets. Bars are particularly plentiful, as alcohol plays a prominent role in Korean leisure.

Shopping

Shopping is popular and, although Korea isn't particularly cheap, there are bargains, including brassware, furs, lacquerware, silks, leather, bamboo goods, toys, masks and china. Followers of fashion are recommended to visit the factory outlets, which sell designer clothes and sports shoes at competitive prices (they're often made in local factories). Prices are fixed in Korean supermarkets, but rarely elsewhere, so try to bargain.

Malaysia

Malaysia boasts a rich cultural heritage and excellent sporting facilities, as well as plenty of restaurants, bars and nightlife.

Culture

Kuala Lumpur: The capital city is a blend of modern architecture and attractive colonial buildings. Malaysians obviously think size is important because Kuala Lumpur was until recently (see **Taiwan** on page 272) the proud home of the world's tallest building, the twin Petronas Towers (a mind-boggling 452m/1,483ft high), and the Merdeka Square flagpole rises to 95m (312ft), reputedly the world's tallest.

Medeka Square in Kuala Lumpur is surrounded by other interesting buildings, including the Sultan Abdul Samad building, the Royal Selangor Club, the National History Museum and the Dayabumi Complex. Another city attraction is Jelan Petaling, a spectacular market which is best seen at night, when it's a riot of sights, sounds and smells.

Other Sites: One of Kuala Lumpur's premier attractions lies 13km (8mi) north of the city, the Batu Caves – a series of massive caves which are a focus for Hindu celebrations. The nearby town (11km/7mi away) of Petaling Jaya is home to the Sunway Lagoon, a theme park featuring waterslides and the world's largest surf-wave pool (another example of Malaysia's apparent obsession with size).

Melaka lies along the coast to the south-east of Kuala Lumpur and is Malaysia's most historic city, an engaging blend of British, Chinese, Dutch and Portuguese influences. Highlights include the Ethnographic Museum and the Cheng Hoon Teng Temple. The holiday island of Penang lies off Peninsula Malaysia's north-west coast. As well as the beaches, its main attraction is the capital city, Georgetown, with its pronounced Chinese flavour.

Another of Malaysia's attractions is the Cameron Highlands, a hilly region in the middle of Peninsula Malaysia. Tours of the tea plantations and jungle walks in the cool, upland weather are its main draws. Sarawak in East Malaysia has unspoilt jungle (although this is under threat from loggers and 'developers') and the chance to experience local Dayak culture. Sabah is renowned for its glorious scenery and wildlife.

Sport

Outdoor types have ample opportunity to indulge themselves in Malaysia. Diving and snorkelling are particularly well catered for, with water visibility often 30m (100ft) and many excellent sites. Trekking and caving are also well served, with nearly 75 per cent of Malaysia still covered by forest (although not for much longer if the loggers have anything to do with it). There are seven national parks and many wildlife reserves, and Malaysia is popular with bird watchers.

The country's sports facilities were upgraded before Malaysia hosted the 1998 Commonwealth Games and further development in anticipation of an Olympic bid. Golf is popular, with around 250 courses, as is karate, with over 150 karate training centres. Malaysia's traditional sports include *sepak takraw*, which is similar to volleyball, although players cannot use their hands, and *main gassing* (top-spinning), using wooden tops that can spin for up to an hour, the artists who make them competing to see who has the longest-running top (sounds like a strong contender for Olympic status!).

Restaurants

Increasing numbers of visitors are travelling to Malaysia primarily for the food. The country's restaurants offer a wide variety of cuisines, mainly Chinese, Indian and Malay, but Malaysia's cities also offer restaurants serving everything from Mexican to North African food. Malaysian cuisine itself involves the liberal use of chicken, fish, noodles and coconut milk.

Nightlife

Malaysian nightlife includes a wide range of bars, clubs, discos and karaoke lounges, and 'supper clubs' are also popular, which offer fine cuisine and live entertainment.

Shopping

Shoppers are well catered for, the best buys including batiks, silverwork, brocade, carvings and handicrafts (especially in Kota Bharu). Don't buy anything made from the skin of the endangered pangolin (a scaly anteater), as it will be confiscated at customs when you return to most western countries.

Philippines

There are many beautiful places scattered around the Philippines' 7,000 islands, although Manila is less of a draw than the capitals of most of the region's countries - except for its nightlife. As well as its bars, dens of iniquity and natural wonders, the Philippines has other leisure options.

Culture

Manila: There's little history because the city was all but destroyed during the second world war, although some colonial ruins remain, particularly in Intramuros, the old walled Spanish town.

Other Sites: One of the Philippines' most impressive sites is the rice terraces around Banaue in north Luzon. They were carved by Ifugao tribesmen between 2,000 and 3,000 years ago and are said to resemble stepping stones to the sky, rising to 1,500m (4,920ft). The island of Boracay claims to have some of the best beaches in the world, although their popularity has led to pollution and contamination, and Puerto Galera on Mindoro and Puraran off Luzon are currently competing for the title of 'sand heaven'. Other spectacular sites include the volcanic crater Lake Taal, south of Manila, the Chocolate Hills of Bohol, the Sagada burial caves and Lake Sebu, a stunning inland sea on Mindanao.

The Philippines government is looking to exploit the country's undoubted natural beauty by encouraging 'ecotourism'. For example, you can 'canopy walk' (you're lifted by pulleys to the tree canopy and negotiate walkways slung between trees) in the rainforest near Cagayan de Oro, while whale and dolphin watching have become popular in the Tanon Strait near Bohol Island.

Sport

Luzon's east coast offers superb trekking country, while the many islands have plenty of opportunities for water sports, particularly snorkelling and diving. The islands of Batangas, Bohol, Mindoro and Palawan have some of the best diving sites and the Philippines Department of Tourism is busy promoting the country as a destination for divers.

Fishing is also popular in the Philippines (the country ranks 12th in worldwide fish production, with $2,000,000km^2/772,200mi^2$ of fishing grounds), its waters boasting around 2,400 species of fish, including game fish: barracuda, marlin, swordfish and tuna. Game fishing is best between December and August.

Golfers have a choice of around 70 courses in the Philippines, although most don't conform to championship specifications and you need to be a member to play on the best courses. Further information and prices are available from the Federation of Golf Clubs Philippines (⌨ www.federationgolf.com).

Restaurants

The Philippines isn't one of the region's culinary capitals, but there's more to sample than the fare peddled by the many western fast food restaurants found throughout the country. Particularly recommended for carnivores is lechon, the local version of suckling pig.

Nightlife

Manila's main attractions for many visitors are probably its bars, clubs and other entertainment venues, the more notorious catering for sex tourists. Manila's nightlife reflects the Filipino love of music, with many music bars, discos and concerts, both traditional and western.

Shopping

Shopping attractions include fabrics, handmade clothes, guitars (from Cebu), cigars, brassware, tribal wood carvings and cane furniture. Avoid anything made from objects that come from under the sea, as the Philippines' marine life is suffering from decades of overharvesting. Flea markets usually offer the country's best shopping buys, and bargaining is expected everywhere except in department stores and supermarkets.

Singapore

Singapore is sometimes portrayed as a huge, landscaped shopping centre and can give just that impression. However, while much of it is sleek and modern, Singapore retains relics of its colonial past and hints of oriental exoticism. Raffles Hotel, The Empress Palace Building and several cathedrals and churches are testament to Singapore's colonial past, while Chinatown still has an atmosphere of 'the East', although much of it unfortunately has been pulled down.

Culture

Arab St is the heart of Muslim Singapore, with some interesting mosques and good places to eat, while Little India is a lively, colourful antidote to the blander, more anodyne parts of Singapore. The country's most popular attraction is probably Sentosa Island, a park area with museums, beaches, sports facilities and a camping ground, and the infamous Changi Prison is also worth visiting.

The northern island of Pulau Ubin is a tranquil contrast with most of the rest of Singapore, offering quiet beaches and temples. Tranquillity can also be found on some of the southern islands, while the Bukit Timah Nature Reserve (to the north of Singapore's Central Business District) is the country's largest remaining area of primary rainforest, home to over 800 species of plant.

Sport

Sports enthusiasts are reasonably well catered for. Badminton is the unofficial national sport and ten-pin bowling is also very popular, with over 20 centres, some open 24 hours. Singapore Cricket Club is one of the world's oldest sporting associations and hockey, rugby and football (soccer) are played there as well as cricket. Polo matches are held regularly at the Singapore Polo Club, while the Singapore Turf Club holds race meetings at weekends. Golfers are catered for at a number of golf clubs, many allowing non-members to play on weekdays, but at a price: up to S$200 (US$116) for a round!

Cycling is popular and cycle paths link many parts of Singapore, although some people find the hot, humid climate uncomfortable for life on a bicycle. The waters off parts of Singapore are polluted, which restricts the practice of watersports, particularly swimming. The waters are cleaner off the outlying islands, where scuba-diving, windsurfing, sailing, fishing and waterskiing are popular.

Restaurants

Singapore has recently become a destination for discerning gourmands. The choice of restaurants and cuisines is wide, including the full range of Indian and Chinese cuisines, Nonya, which is a combination of Chinese and Malay styles, and sophisticated French and Italian restaurants. Restaurants in Singapore appear and disappear with great frequency, and staff turnover is similarly rapid. Prices vary from the modest to the stratospheric.

Nightlife

Singapore used to have a (partially justified) reputation as an over-cossetted nanny state, whose people didn't know how to have fun. The last ten years have seen changes, and Singapore now has a wide choice of bars and clubs. Drinks, however, are usually expensive, although many establishments have 'happy hours'.

Shopping

Singapore's primary leisure activity is shopping, with a vast range of goods available. Much of the shopping is in large, rather soulless centres, but the air-conditioning is welcome in Singapore's steamy climate.

Taiwan

Taiwan's two most popular leisure activities are shopping and hiking. The capital, Taipei, is definitely not a relaxing city, but as well as its frenetic pace of life, crowding and choking pollution, the city offers friendly people, great food and some interesting sites.

Culture

Taipei: Much to the annoyance of the mainland Chinese, Taiwan's National Palace Museum has the world's largest collection of Chinese artefacts. Of the total of around 725,000 items, only 15,000 can be displayed at any time, on a three-month rotation, which means that you must visit quarterly for 12 years to see them all!

Taipei has much more concrete than greenery, but an oasis of calm is provided by the Botanical Gardens, which are near to other attractions, including the National Arts Hall, the Museum of Natural History and the National Science Hall. For those wanting to reinforce the view that the Chinese eat anything, a visit to the vibrant Huashi Night Market is recommended. It's also called Snake Alley, with all manner of snakes and snake products for sale.

Taipei has a new claim to fame: since 17th October 2003, it has boasted the world's tallest building, a 91-storey office block (enigmatically called the Taipei 101 Tower or Building, or simply the Taipei 101) which rises to an alarming 508m (1,667ft), a full 56m (185ft) higher than the previous tallest building, Malaysia's Petronas Towers. It has apparently been designed to endure high winds, earthquakes of over seven on the Richter scale and an attack similar to that on New York's World Trade Centre. The building, which is due to remain the world's tallest building for only around three years, houses a shopping mall, offices for around 12,000 people and the Taiwan Stock Exchange.

Other Sites: You can see animals in their natural environment close to Taipei. To the south-east of the city lies the large, beautiful Sungshan Nature Reserve; heavily forested and mountain-studded, it's a magnet for hikers and climbers. At the northern end of the island, the Yangmingshan mountains provide another opportunity to breathe fresh air. Also close to the capital is one of Taiwan's most beautiful locations, Taroko Gorge, 19km (12mi) of cliffs towering above a white water river. These sites help to justify Taiwan's nickname of *Ilha Formosa* (the beautiful island).

Tainan is on the south-west coast of Taiwan and is the island's 'temple town' – the best place to observe Buddhist culture and festivals. Off the south-east coast lies the beautiful volcanic island of Lanyu, peopled by Yami aborigines who are closer to the peoples of the Philippines than to those of China. The Penghu Islands lie halfway between Taiwan and the Chinese mainland and are a contrast to Taiwan, being flat and beach-fringed.

Sport

Much of Taiwan is mountainous, accounting for the popularity of hiking. You can also indulge in grass skiing, sledding and tobogganing, appropriate for a place with plenty of mountains but little snow. Watersports are practised, particularly diving off the islands surrounding Taiwan. The island has several golf courses and ten-pin bowling has become very popular.

Restaurants

The Taiwanese love to eat and the island's cuisine is becoming a draw for visitors. The food is similar to Chinese, with an added sub-tropical flavour, plenty of seafood and the use of sugar in many dishes. A speciality is the *haw gwau* (fire pot), and Taipei has thousands of *haw gwau* restaurants, where you sit at a table in the middle of which is a pot of boiling water. You choose the ingredients you want for a stew, either from waiters or a buffet, and it's cooked in the pot. The major cities also have a wide choice of foreign restaurants, offering food from all over the world.

Nightlife

The island also offers vibrant nightlife, particularly in Taipei. As well as plenty of western-style pubs, bars and clubs, KTVs (the local version of karaoke bars) are popular.

Shopping

Shopping hours are generally 9am to 10pm, Monday to Saturday, giving ample opportunity for buying. The night markets offer particular choice and value.

Thailand

Thailand's leisure attractions are sometimes portrayed as little more than lounging on the designer beaches and visiting the dubious 'entertainment' bars, but the country offers much more. Thailand probably has more surviving evidence of its past than any other south-east Asian country. It also has friendly people and one of the region's best cuisines. The capital city Bangkok is itself an attraction and, despite being sticky, crowded, traffic-choked and polluted, it's one of the region's great cities. Night markets, cheap clothes shops and the notorious go-go bars of Patpong are among its diverse attractions.

Culture

Bangkok: There are plenty of oases of calm away from the frenetic maelstrom of the capital, including 400 *wats* (temple-monasteries). One of them is the Temple of the Golden Buddha, which houses a 5.5-tonne gold Buddha. Another of Bangkok's great sites is the Wat Sai floating market (markets are often held at temples – hence the use of the word *wat*), which is touristy but vibrant and colourful.

The National Museum on the river bank in Bangkok has one of the region's best collections, with items from all periods of Thai history as well as from surrounding countries and cultures.

Slightly north of Bangkok lies Ko Kret, one of Thailand's oldest Mon settlements. The Mon dominated the country between the 6th and 10th centuries and are famous for their pottery. South of Bangkok is the Ancient City, touted as the world's largest open-air museum; it covers a huge 80 hectares (200 acres) and is includes scale models of over 100 of Thailand's most famous monuments. Lying around 86km (53mi) north of Bangkok is Ayuthaya, the former capital, full of ruins and museums, and declared a World Heritage Site.

Chiang Mai: Chiang Mai is Thailand's second-largest city, in the far north-west of the country. Its climate (particularly at night) is fresher than Bangkok's, it doesn't have the traffic and pollution problems, and it's a great place to eat. Attractions include 300 *wats*, the Night Bazaar, the Tribal Museum and the surrounding hill country, which is ideal for hiking and visiting the hill tribes.

Other Sites: Ko Samui is a beautiful holiday island off south-east Thailand. Although increasingly invaded by tourists, there are still stretches of tranquillity, as well as fine beaches, swimming and snorkelling. Phuket lies off Thailand's south-west coast and is connected to the mainland by a bridge. It's known as the 'pearl of the south' but, although the beaches and forests are still attractive, tourist development is threatening the island's calm.

North-east Thailand is the site of Phanom Rung, the largest Khmer monument in Thailand, a temple dating from the 10th century and the peak of the culture's architecture (it's almost as 'important' as the Angkor Wat in Cambodia). Its site, on an extinct volcano, adds to its majesty. In the far south, the Thaleh Ban National Park on the Thai/Malaysian border contains spectacular rainforest and fauna.

Sport & Other Activities

As well offering beautiful beaches, Thailand's long coastline (2,710km/1,694mi) and offshore islands are ideal for watersports. Diving and snorkelling are well catered for in many places (particularly Pattaya and Phuket), the islands of Chumphon Province having well-preserved coral reefs to explore. Sea-canoe tours of the limestone formations and caves around Phuket are popular. Windsurfing is practised, the windiest season being February to April in the Gulf of Thailand, September to December in the Andaman Sea. Sailing between Thailand's islands is popular and Phuket holds the King's Cup Regatta in December. Game fisherman can pursue barracuda, marlin, swordfish and tuna in Thailand's waters.

Northern Thailand specialises in trekking (or 'wilderness walking', as it's called by trek organisers). Meditation study is popular throughout Thailand, with scores of temples and meditation centres, some giving instruction in English; *vipassana* (insight) meditation is a speciality. Courses in Thai boxing (*muay thai*), Thai cooking and traditional massage are becoming more popular.

There are horse races every two weeks at the Royal Bangkok Sports Centre on a Saturday and at the Royal Turf club on a Sunday.

Restaurants

The food served in Thailand's plentiful, generally inexpensive restaurants is many people's favourite Asian cuisine, known for its balance: many dishes manage to be hot, sweet, sour and spicy, all at the same time. Dining out is one of the country's many visitor attractions, and the food includes liberal use of garlic, ginger and lemon grass, famed for their health benefits as well as their flavours.

Nightlife

Thailand's nightlife is also plentiful, with a huge range of bars, discos and clubs to serve the many holidaymakers, as well as the locals. An uncomfortable fact of life in Thailand is the sex industry, with some bars and clubs selling 'flesh' as well as alcohol. The government is becoming aware of the bad publicity this has generated and has periodic crackdowns, especially on those establishments offering underage girls and boys. Other places of dubious entertainment value include the notorious 'go-go' bars of Patpong.

Shopping

Thailand's best shopping buys include silk, laquerware (ubiquitous in much of the region), pottery, tribal handicrafts, custom-made shoes and clothes (off-the-peg items in the shops and markets are on the small side for most westerners) and jewellery (although there are plenty of conmen selling worthless 'gems'). Bargaining is common in markets, but not in shops.

PETS

If you plan to take a pet to the Far East, it's important to check the latest regulations. Make sure that you have the correct papers, not only for your country of destination, but for any countries you might pass through to reach it, e.g. when travelling overland between different Far Eastern countries. Particular consideration must be given before exporting a pet from a country with strict quarantine regulations, such as the UK. If you need to return prematurely, even after a few hours abroad, your pet may need to go into quarantine, e.g. for six months in the UK.

Many countries operate a quarantine period, which may be in the owner's own home, and some have a 'pet passport' scheme allowing pets to travel freely provided certain conditions are met. Most countries require pets to have a health certificate issued by an approved veterinary surgeon and vaccination certificates for rabies and possibly other diseases. A rabies vaccination must usually be given not less than 20 days or more than 11 months before the date of issue of the health certificate. Pets aged under 12 weeks are usually exempt but must have a health certificate and a certificate stating that no cases of rabies have occurred for at least six months in the local area. Note that there's no quarantine period (or only a token one) in many countries when pets are exported from countries without rabies.

If you're transporting a pet by ship or ferry, you should notify the shipping company. Some companies insist that pets are left in vehicles (if applicable), while others allow pets to be kept in cabins. If your pet is of a nervous disposition or unused to travelling, it's best to tranquillise it on a long sea crossing. **Note that long journeys can be far more stressful for animals even than for humans.** Pets can also be transported by air. Contact airlines for information. Animals may be examined at the port of entry by a veterinary officer in the country of destination.

In many countries, pets must be registered and may be issued with a disc to be worn on a collar around their neck, while other countries require dogs to be tattooed on their body or in an ear as a means of registration. In recent years, some countries have introduced a microchip identification system for dogs (which has replaced tattooing), whereby a microchip is inserted under the skin. Registration can be expensive. Irrespective of whether your dog is tattooed or microchipped, it's recommended to have it fitted with a collar and tag with your name and telephone number on it and the magic word 'reward'.

Most countries have rules regarding the keeping of dogs, which may require a health card if they're older than three months. In public areas, a dog may need to be kept on a lead (and muzzled if it's dangerous) and wear a health disc on its collar. Dogs are usually prohibited from entering places where food is manufactured, stored or sold, and may also be barred from sports and cultural events, and banned from beaches. Note that in some countries the keeping of dogs may be restricted or banned from long-term rental or holiday accommodation (so check when renting an apartment). Some countries also have strict laws regarding cleaning up after pets in public places (so-called 'poop-scoop' laws) and you can be heavily fined for not doing so.

If you intend to live in the Far East permanently, dogs should be vaccinated against certain diseases in addition to rabies, which may include hepatitis, distemper and kennel cough. Cats should be immunised against feline gastro-enteritis and typhus. Pets should also be checked frequently for ticks and tapeworm. **Note that there are a number of diseases and dangers for pets in some countries that aren't found in North America and Northern Europe.** Obtain advice about these and other diseases from a veterinary surgeon in your home country or on arrival in the Far East. In areas where there are poisonous snakes (including much of the Far East), some owners keep anti-venom in their refrigerator (which must be changed annually). Take extra care when walking your dog in country areas, as hunters sometimes put down poisoned food to control natural predators. **Don't let your dog far out of your sight, as dogs may be stolen or mistakenly shot by hunters.**

Health insurance for pets is available in most countries (vets' fees can be astronomical) and it's wise to have third party insurance in case your pet bites someone or causes an accident. Country-specific information is given below.

Brunei

Before coming to Brunei with a pet, you must obtain an entry form from The Veterinary Officer, Department of Agriculture, Bandar Seri Begawan, Brunei Darussalem (☎ 673-2-382080). Include with your request letter a health certificate for the animal and a certificate from the veterinary authority of the exporting country stating that the country has been free from rabies for the previous six months. You must obtain permission for your pet's entry from the Brunei authorities at least two weeks in advance.

Quarantine isn't required for pets from the UK, Ireland, Australia, New Zealand, Singapore and other parts of Borneo. Pets from anywhere else (including the US) must undergo six months' quarantine, although cases are considered individually and the required period is sometimes reduced. There's no fee for importing pets, which must arrive in Brunei as cargo. **Note that Bruneians consider dogs to be unclean, and won't touch a dog or enter a house in which there's a dog.**

China

Bringing a pet into China is relatively straightforward. You need a vaccination certificate (or multiple certificates, depending on the type of animal) and a health certificate. Vaccinations (which naturally vary from animal to animal) must have been given within 30 days of departure; **note that China doesn't recognise three-year rabies vaccinations.** The health certificate should be issued by a vet in your home country. China doesn't have its own form, so the standard international certificate should be used. It's helpful to have all documentation translated into Chinese before arrival in the country. Ask your nearest Chinese Embassy about this and ensure that translations are certified.

When you arrive in China, take your pet, documentation and the fee of RMB150 (US$18) to the Customs and Immigration Plant and Quarantine Office. There's a mandatory 30-day quarantine period, although you're often allowed to keep your pet at home during this period; quarantine officers come to examine the pet, and charge a nominal fee for their services.

If your pet is a dog, you must register it with the local police station, and obtain a dog licence. The price varies according to where you live but is high: usually between RMB1,000 (US$120) and 2,000 (US$240).

Hong Kong

Dogs and cats cannot be imported into Hong Kong unless a Special Permit is obtained in advance. An application form (AF240) can be downloaded from the Agriculture and Fisheries website (see below) or obtained by fax (☎ 2708-8885). You must pay a fee at the time of application, which is currently HK$432 (US$55) for one animal and HK$102 (US$13) for each additional animal. Fees should be paid by bank draft in HK$, made payable to 'The Government of the Hong Kong Special Administrative Region'. Submit your application to the Permit Issuing Desk (Counter No. 10), 5th Floor, Agriculture, Fisheries and Conservation Department, Cheung Sha Wan Government Offices, 303 Cheung Sha Wan Road, Kowloon, Hong Kong. Apply well in advance and allow plenty of time for compliance with any health requirements, e.g. vaccinations and blood tests.

Dogs and cats imported from the UK, Ireland, Australia, New Zealand, Fiji and Hawaii are usually exempted from quarantine, subject to compliance with the permit conditions. Full information about bringing animals and pets into Hong Kong can be obtained from The Veterinary Officer, Director of Agriculture and Fisheries, 8th Floor, 393 Canton Road, Hong Kong (☎ 2733-2165, 💻 www.afcd.gov.hk).

Indonesia

The rules regarding the import of pets to Indonesia are complex and subject to change. Indeed, different 'authorities' have different ideas of what's required and it's recommended to check with your nearest embassy for the latest regulations. The following are currently (late 2003) required for the import of dogs and cats:

- A rabies vaccination certificate issued by a veterinary surgeon (vet) in the country of origin;

- A health certificate issued by an Animal Quarantine Office at the place of departure or by an authorised government vet;

- A letter of recommendation for importation issued by the Provincial Veterinary Service at the place of entry (ask at an Indonesian embassy for details of how to contact them and the Directorate below);

- An import permit issued by the Directorate of Animal Health, Directorate General of Livestock Services, Jl. Harsono, Rm No 3, Building C, 9th Floor, Jakarta 12550, Indonesia;

- An export permit issued by the Convention on International Trade in Endangered Species of Wild Fauna and Flora (CITES, 💻 www.cites.org) authority in the country of origin, although this might not be required for 'normal' types of cat and dog (i.e. not rare or endangered species).

When the above have been obtained, you must inform the local Quarantine Office at least two days before your arrival and submit an application for quarantine inspection.

Japan

It's possible to take pets to Japan, but expatriates doing so severely limit their chances of finding rented accommodation because **the vast majority of Japanese landlords don't allow pets**, even those renting out houses with gardens. If you decide to transport a pet to Japan, note the following requirements:

- All animals entering Japan must be examined to check that they're free from communicable diseases.

- The original rabies vaccination certificate DD208 and two copies must accompany the animal. The vaccination must have been given over 30 days but less than 365 days before the animal's entry into Japan.

- The original health certificate DD2209 and two copies must accompany the animal. It must have been issued by a vet within ten days of the animal's arrival in Japan.

- The two above-mentioned certificates must be stamped by the Department of Agriculture, or the equivalent government body, in the case of animals coming from certain countries (e.g. the US).

- Before animals are inspected, you must fill in form 380EJ, available from customs when you enter Japan.

Animals less than 90 days old don't require a rabies vaccination but will be placed in quarantine for 120 days. When they're 90 days old, they're given a rabies vaccination. A further 14-day period of 'home quarantine' is required.

Korea

It's straightforward to bring most pets into Korea. They can pass through customs after the production of the bill of lading, a health certificate issued by a vet in the country of origin and the owner's passport. If dogs and cats are older than 90 days and have a certificate to confirm that they've been vaccinated against rabies at least a month before entry into Korea, they aren't subject to quarantine.

Malaysia

Breeds of dog considered to be dangerous cannot be imported into Malaysia, and the import of 'exotic' pets is subject to CITES conditions (see **Indonesia** above); check with a Malaysian embassy for current details of what constitutes a dangerous dog and an exotic pet. Dogs and cats must be at least three months old before they can be imported into Malaysia.

You must obtain an import permit before importing your pet, which must be produced at your point of entry into Peninsular Malaysia (for entry to Sabah and Sarawak, enquire at a Malaysian embassy, as requirements might be different). Forms for import permits can be obtained by writing to The Director, Jabatan Perkhidmatan Haiwan (Department of Veterinary Services, Malaysia), Negeri Johor, Jalan Kebun The, Peti Surat 734, 80250 Johor Bahru, Johor Darulta'zim (☎ 07-228-2851) or you can download them from 🖳 http://agrolink.moa. my/iph/dvs/import/pet-imp/impexpform/html.

Submit the application form with a copy of the animal's vaccination records and the import permit fee of RM5 (US$1.30) per dog or cat. The fee can be paid in cash or by bank draft, money order or postal order, payable to the Director General of Veterinary Services of Malaysia. Import permits are valid for 30 days from their date of issue.

Dogs and cats coming from the Australia, Brunei, Ireland, New Zealand, Japan, Singapore, Sweden and the UK aren't subject to quarantine, provided that they're healthy and their documents are in order. Dogs and cats from other countries must be quarantined for at least seven days. Quarantine charges are around RM79 (US$21) per week for a dog and RM72 (US$19) for a cat, exclusive of food and any treatment required.

Philippines

In order to import a cat or dog into the Philippines, you must have an import permit. Fax a request for one to the Animal Health Division in Quezon City (🖷 632-928-1778), including details of the number of animals, their species, sex, age and expected arrival date. You must have a health certificate issued by a vet within ten days of shipping, confirming that the animal is free from communicable diseases. In countries with rabies you must also have a certificate stating that there have been no rabies cases within a 20km (12.5mi) radius in the last six months. You also need a vaccination certificate for rabies, canine distemper, infectious hepatitis, leptsopirosis, canine parvovirus or feline panleucopenia and proof that the animal has been treated for internal and external parasites. A permit will be posted to you and you will be charged a P50 (90¢) issuing fee when you arrive at the airport, where quarantine personnel examine the animal and issue a landing permit costing P165 (US$3). If everything is in order, there's no quarantine period.

Singapore

To bring a cat or dog into Singapore, you must obtain an import licence from the City Veterinary Centre, 25 Peck Seah Street, Singapore 079315 (☎ 6227-0670). The licence must be completed and delivered at least two weeks before importing the animal and a fee of S$50 (US$29) per animal applies. In order to secure the licence, you must demonstrate that the animal is in good health and has up-to-date vaccinations. Cats and dogs coming from Australia, Ireland, New Zealand and the UK aren't subject to quarantine, but animals from elsewhere are subject to quarantine of at least 30 days at the owner's expense.

The following breeds of dog are banned from Singapore: Akita, Dogo Argentino, Fila Braziliero, Neapolitan Mastiff, Pit Bull (including the American Pit Bull Terrier, American Staffordshire Terrier, Staffordshire Bull Terrier and the American Bulldog), Tosa and crosses of these breeds. If you're living in a Housing Development Board property (see page 104), only one dog is allowed; not more than three dogs are allowed in non-HDB premises. No cats are allowed in HDB properties.

Taiwan

In order to import a cat or dog into Taiwan, you must apply for an import permit two weeks before departure, from Hsin-Chu Office, Bureau of Animal and Plant Health Inspection and Quarantine, No 25, Hung Ching N Road, CKS International Airport, Tao Yuan, Taiwan, ROC. You must supply the following:

- An application form;
- A copy of a health certificate from a vet, including the pet's breed, sex, age, fur colour, physical characteristics, the vet's signature, the date of rabies vaccination and the type of vaccine given (it must have been at least 30 days and no more than 365 days before entry);
- Four 6x4in (15x10cm) photographs of the pet in full body;
- A copy of the applicant's passport or identity card.

Animals from countries with rabies are subject to at least 21 days' quarantine. Rabies-free areas currently include Australia, Iceland, Japan, New Zealand, Sweden and the UK.

Thailand

As with most aspects of life in Thailand, the rules and regulations concerning the import of pets are subject to regular change (and occasional confusion). It's therefore recommended that you check the current requirements with a Thai embassy or the Bangkok Airport Customs Office (☎ 535-1269 or 535-1153 or 535-1680). The following procedure applied in late 2003. If you're entering the country for six months or more and bringing a cat or dog, you can obtain permission to import it at Bangkok airport, subject to having the following:

- An identity certificate issued by a registered vet in your home country describing the animal's age, breed, sex and colour;

- A rabies vaccination certificate, the vaccination having been administered at least 15 days before arrival in Thailand;

- A leptospirosis vaccination certificate, the vaccination having been made at least 21 days before arrival.

The animal must appear to be in good general health and free of any signs of infectious or contagious disease.

RELIGION

Most countries have a tradition of religious tolerance and citizens and foreigners alike generally have total freedom of religion without hindrance by the state or community. However, in some countries certain sects have been declared to be dangerous to the community and have been banned. Note that in certain countries there have been violent clashes between religious groups, notably in parts of Indonesia and the Philippines, between Muslims and Christians, which have resulted in civil wars and massacres. You should be aware of any religious tensions in a country where you're planning to live and how they will affect your lifestyle.

It's necessary to take care not to offend anyone's religion and watch what you wear when visiting religious sites and holy places, where there are often strict rules regarding dress (particularly in Muslim countries). Note also that many Muslim countries ban alcohol (its importation and consumption) and the import of certain types of literature and videos, and impose severe penalties for blasphemy against the Islamic religion. For details of the principal religions in each territory, see **Religion** in the Country Profiles (**Chapter 9**). For religion-related restrictions and conventions in each of the 11 territories, see **Social Customs & Rules** on page 285.

SHOPPING ABROAD

Shopping by mail-order, phone, fax or via the internet is popular among expatriates in the Far East, particularly where it's difficult or impossible to buy certain western goods (or they're prohibitively expensive). Direct retailing by manufacturers has become much more widespread in recent years and many companies sell goods and services by post, often via their own websites.

Many major stores publish catalogues and will send goods anywhere in the world, particularly American and British stores. Many companies provide account facilities or payment can be made by credit card. Although some foreign mail-order companies won't send goods abroad, there's nothing to stop you obtaining catalogues via friends or relatives and ordering through them. Buying goods mail-order from the US can result in huge savings, even after paying postage and local taxes. One company of interest to avid mail-order shoppers is Shop the World by Mail, PO Box 1599, Sarasota, FL 34230-1599, US (☎ 941-365 2419), which publishes a catalogue of US mail-order companies.

When buying goods overseas you should ensure that you're dealing with a bona fide company and that the goods will work in your country of residence (e.g. electrical equipment or video games). You should also check the vendor's returns policy. Note that you may not be covered by consumer protection legislation when shopping abroad and, should anything go wrong, it can take eons to get it resolved. If possible, always pay by credit card when buying by mail-order or via the internet, as you have more security and the credit card issuer may be jointly liable with the supplier. When you buy expensive goods abroad, always have them insured for their full value.

When you purchase a large item abroad, it's wise to have it shipped by air freight to the nearest international airport. The receiving freight company will notify you when it has arrived and you must usually provide them with details of the contents and cost so that they can clear it through customs. They will deliver the goods to you with the bill for taxes, duty and freight, payable on the spot, unless you make alternative arrangements.

Internet Shopping

Retailers and manufacturers in most countries offer internet shopping, but the real benefit comes when shopping abroad, when savings can be made on a wide range of products (you can buy virtually anything via the internet). However, when comparing prices, take into account shipping costs, insurance, duty and VAT (see **Taxes & Duty** below). Shopping via the internet is very secure (secure servers, with addresses beginning https:// rather than http://, are almost impossible to crack) and in most cases safer than shopping by phone or mail-order. However, it isn't completely safe and credit card fraud is a growing problem.

To find companies or products via the internet, simply use a search engine such as Altavista, Google or Yahoo. Useful websites include 🖳 http:// ukonlineshop.about.com, www.myprimetime.com, www.pricewatch.com, www.mytaxi.co.uk (which contains the Internet addresses of 2,500 worldwide retail and information sites), www.amazingemporium.co.uk, www.abargain. co.uk, www.shopsmart.com, www.enterprisecity.co.uk, www.buy.com, www.iwanttoshop.com, www.shopguide.co.uk, www.grouptrade.com, www. euroffice.co.uk, www.usecolor.com and www.virgin.net/shopping/index.html (which has a good directory of British shopping sites). Many websites offer online auctions, including www.qxl.com, www.ebay.com (and www.ebay. co.uk), www.auctions.yahoo.com and www.loot.com. Many websites also provide useful advice about shopping abroad.

With internet shopping the world is literally your oyster and savings can be made on a wide range of goods, including CDs, clothes, sports equipment, electronic gadgets, jewellery, books, wine and computer software, and services such as insurance, pensions and mortgages. Savings can also be made on holidays and travel. Small high-price, high-tech items (e.g. cameras, watches and portable and hand-held computers) can usually be purchased cheaper somewhere abroad, particularly in the US, with delivery by courier worldwide within as little as three days.

Taxes & Duty

When buying overseas, take into account shipping costs, duty, VAT and other taxes. Carefully calculate the total cost in local currency or the currency in which you're paying – you can do this with the universal currency converter (🖳 www.xe.com/ucc). Most countries levy no taxes on goods imported from abroad below a certain nominal value. Don't buy alcohol or cigarettes abroad, as the duty is usually too high to make it pay (and it may be illegal!). When VAT or duty is payable on a parcel, the payment is usually collected by the post office or courier company on delivery.

SOCIAL CUSTOMS & RULES

When moving to a foreign country, it's important to know the local 'ropes' in order not to offend the natives and to make your integration smoother and quicker. This is particularly important when moving from a western to an eastern country, where the local culture, lifestyle, religion, customs and regulations are likely to be very different from what you're used to.

In Muslim and Hindu countries, women should cover arms, legs and heads when visiting a mosque or temple. Some Muslims might be uncomfortable if alcohol is served at social or business functions. Be aware that Muslims have to pray five times per day and be careful not to arrange meetings or appointments at prayer times (which are published in newspapers).

As in many parts of the world, bribery is an accepted 'social' function in many parts of the Far East, particularly when dealing with low-ranking officials and customs officers in remote regions. **Take care, however, before offering anybody a bribe.** If possible, obtain advice from someone who knows the 'customs' of the country and the type of official you're dealing with. Failing that, a subtle approach is invariably the best, especially in a region where maintaining your cool and the other person's 'face' are crucial. Adopt a euphemistic air and ask how you can 'speed things up', perhaps by making a donation to the official's favourite charity. Some people argue that offering bribes only encourages officials and others to ask for more, but when bribes are necessary officials don't need any encouragement. Always maintain your composure and sense of humour, and be polite but firm. The offer of around US$20 (in US currency) works wonders in many places.

The following country-by-country guide will help you to avoid committing faux pas or getting on the wrong side of the law, wherever you choose to live. For details of business etiquette, see the Country Profiles (**Chapter 9**).

Brunei

Religion: Brunei is a Muslim country and the religion pervades and informs all aspects of life. There's even a Ministry of Religious Affairs, which fosters and promotes Islam, although other religions are allowed to be practised.

Dress: Revealing clothes are considered immodest and therefore unacceptable in Brunei. Dress, however, is informal, except for special occasions, and men should wear lightweight shirts and long trousers, while the rules are more stringent for women, who should ensure that their heads, knees and arms are covered. Topless or nude sunbathing or swimming are illegal. Always remove your shoes when entering a Muslim home or institution, and never pass in front of somebody at prayer or touch the Koran.

Alcohol: Alcohol cannot be legally bought or sold in Brunei. Non-Muslims travelling from abroad (which is never far in tiny Brunei) can bring up to 12 cans of beer and two bottles of wine or spirits, but only for personal use; you mustn't give alcohol to a Muslim. It's an offence to fail to declare any alcohol you import to customs officials. Retain the customs slip, as goods are sometimes inspected. Drunkenness is unacceptable in Brunei and can lead to arrest.

Drugs: Avoid any involvement with drugs. Offenders are punished severely in Brunei, with a heavy fine if you're lucky, the death penalty if you aren't. It's therefore very unwise to carry anything through customs for somebody else unless you know exactly what it is.

Meeting & Greeting: When a foreign man meets a Bruneian man, a light handshake is traditional, but physical contact between members of the opposite sex is avoided. Non-Muslims aren't allowed in the company of a Muslim of the opposite sex in private, and any form of compromising behaviour or sexual contact between Muslims and non-Muslims is punishable by deportation.

Forms Of Address: Many Bruneians, particularly prominent ones, have around 20 words to their full name and titles, and working out who they are and how to address them can be tricky for foreigners. Bruneians realise this and are invariably tolerant of any mistakes in protocol in conversation, but it's very important to address a person correctly in correspondence. Failure to do so is regarded as an insult and will probably result in the letter being thrown away or returned unopened. The structure of a Bruneian's name is usually as follows: title, family name, son/daughter of. *Bin* means 'son of', *Binte* means 'daughter of'. Titles are as follows:

- *Pengiran* – Similar to Duke and is a hereditary title given to relations of the royal family. The words following *Pengiran* describe how close a relation to the Sultan the person is, for example:

  - *Penigran Perdana Wazir* - The Sultan's brother, His Royal Highness Mohamed Bolkiah;

  - *Penigran Muda* - The Sultan's eldest son, His Royal Highness Crown Prince;

  - *Penigran Anak* - Immediate Royal Family, for example daughters or sisters of the Sultan.

  If nothing follows Penigran, the person is a more distant relation, e.g. a cousin.

- *Awangku* – Used for distant male relations of the royal family. If an *Awangku* has a child, his title automatically changes to *Pengiran*, to reflect his impact of continuing the royal line, which explains why there are a lot of people with the title *Pengiran*. The child is automatically given the title *Awangku* or *Dyangku*.

- *Dyangku* – The title of distant female relations of the royal family. Their title isn't converted if they have a child, unless they're married to an *Awangku*.

- *Pehin* – Similar to Lord and the highest title given to commoners, usually for a long period of service.

- *Dato* – The first step towards *Pehin* status, this title and has many different levels, shown by the words that follow it: for example, *Dato Paduka, Dato Seri Paduka, Dato Seri Setia, Dato Paduka Seri Setia, Dato Laila Utama, Dato Paduka Seri Laila Jasa*.

- *Haji/Hajah* – *Haji* (male) and *Hajah* (female) are titles that people who have been on the pilgrimage to Mecca are allowed to use.

Hands & Feet: Avoid pointing the soles of your feet (which are considered unclean) towards other people, so be careful when crossing your legs or, perhaps better, don't cross them. The left hand is considered as being for 'private bathroom functions' and you should therefore avoid giving or receiving anything with your left hand. Food is sometimes eaten without cutlery and you should be particularly careful to use only your right hand to pass and eat food.

Pointing with the index finger is regarded as impolite (use the right thumb instead), as is beckoning somebody with your fingers. The right fist shouldn't be smacked into the left palm, which is regarded as an obscene gesture, and avoid patting anybody on the head (even children), which is considered to be the 'seat of the soul'. It's rude to refuse refreshment when it's offered by a host, but you should avoid eating and drinking in public places, particularly during Ramadan, when Muslims fast during daylight hours.

China

Religion: Unlike religious Brunei, China is officially atheistic, although there are five state-registered religions: Daoism, Buddhism, Islam, Catholic Christianity and Protestant Christianity. However, foreigners should be aware that there are restrictions on certain religious activities, including preaching and distributing religious materials, and the detention and harassment of religious practitioners is quite common. The Falun Gong movement was banned in 1999 and its followers have been singled out for particularly harsh treatment.

Demonstrations, Drugs & Photography: Public demonstrations are allowed only with the approval of the authorities and if you're involved in or caught up in a demonstration that isn't 'official', you can be imprisoned and then deported. All drug offences are dealt with harshly in China, sometimes by the death penalty. Also be careful with photography. It isn't permitted at airports and permission should be sought before photographing military installations, government buildings and any other potentially sensitive sights.

Dress: China's new tolerance falls down on the question of dress: revealing, skimpy clothes are deemed offensive and the rule is for understated, casual clothes.

Meeting & Greeting: When addressing people in China, the family name comes first (and is usually one syllable), so Hung Man Sing is addressed as Mr Hung. Avoid using the given name unless you've known the person for some time. Avoid trying to be too friendly too quickly and don't worry if Chinese people don't address you by your first name for some time after becoming acquainted with you. The quick informality of some Americans, Australians and Europeans is rarely found in China.

When visiting people, handshakes might be the greeting offered by your hosts (soft handshakes rather than the bone crunching favoured by some westerners), but visitors are sometimes applauded as a sign of welcome (most common if you visit a school or workplace), in which case you should respond by applauding back. A nod is also a common form of greeting, whereas bowing is increasingly restricted to ceremonies. Take your lead from the person you're meeting.

If you're invited to a social occasion, it's usual and polite to arrive a little early, rather than 'fashionably late' as in some western countries. If you're invited to somebody's home, it's customary to take a modest gift, such as sweets (candy) or a small souvenir from your home country. Stamps are also popular presents, China being a nation of stamp collectors. The present should be wrapped, but avoid plain black or white paper because these are mourning colours. Don't be offended if the present isn't opened in front of you. This shows that it's the thought that counts more than the material value of the present. Presents **never** to buy include clocks, handkerchiefs, umbrellas and white flowers (particularly chrysanthemums), as these all signify tears or death. Also avoid sharp objects like knives and scissors, which indicate the severing of a relationship.

Social Interaction: It's difficult to generalise about around 1.3 billion individuals (a fifth of the world's population), but the nation's people are often understated or actively reserved in manner, and formal courtesy rather than familiarity is the norm. Modesty is valued and if somebody pays you a compliment it's seemly to deny it politely. Avoid making exaggerated or unusual facial expressions, and note that smiling is less common in China than in many places because there's a tradition of hiding emotion. Try to avoid using your hands while speaking because the Chinese don't and can become annoyed with people who do. And rather than pointing with the index finger, use the whole hand. To gain attention, the palm is turned down and the fingers fluttered towards your body.

Note that the country's full title – The People's Republic of China – is often used, and must be used in all formal communications, although in casual conversation 'China' can be used.

The Chinese rarely volunteer information, so foreigners must become accustomed to asking questions. Foreigners in China are often followed by small crowds, particularly outside the main cities and tourist areas, where foreigners are still a novelty. Don't be put off or threatened by this; it's merely curiosity.

As is the case in much of the Far East, it's important to avoid expressing anger and arguing with people in public. Also avoid criticising or upbraiding Chinese people in front of others or putting them in a difficult position, because this will cause them to lose 'face', i.e. dignity and self-respect. Public displays of affection between the sexes are disliked.

Although China is more open and tolerant than it was, politics and religion are still controversial topics (as in many countries) and it's best to avoid expressing political and religious views, especially with relative strangers. Particular topics to be avoided are the thorny question of Taiwan (which China lays fierce claim to) and China's population control measures. Instead, stick to the safe (and inexhaustible) topics of food, sport and places that you should visit.

Try to learn at least a handful of Chinese words, as this shows an interest in the country and its culture. You can safely begin with these four: *Nin haoi* (hello); *Shay shay* (thank you); *Gan pei* (cheers – as a toast); *Jai jian* (goodbye).

Eating: Toasting at a meal is common, as is smoking, the consumption of vast quantities of cigarettes being very popular in China. As a foreigner, you simply have to get used to and tolerate it.

Hong Kong

Although it's part of China (only since 1997 politically, but always from a cultural point of view), Hong Kong has been exposed to western people and ways for much longer than the rest of The People's Republic and its more relaxed social conventions reflect this. The rules of etiquette and custom are similar to those detailed for China, but more diluted and with far more tolerance of 'strange' foreign ways.

Dress: Western fashion is much more common in Hong Kong than it is in China and, while the attitude is more tolerant, revealing clothing is still frowned upon, certainly by older people. Casual clothing is acceptable for most occasions, but certain restaurants and social functions require formal clothing. If in doubt about what to wear to an occasion, check beforehand. Please note that it's usual to invite your hosts for dinner at your home.

Meeting & Greeting: As in the rest of China, a person's family name is given first and handshaking is the usual form of greeting, a reflection of the long western influence.

Eating: Entertaining is usually in restaurants rather than at people's homes, partly for reasons of practicality; homes are small in crowded, expensive Hong Kong. Toasts often accompany each course of a meal – and there can be 10 or 12 courses – and a 'healthy' appetite is well received, so you should attempt at least to sample each course on offer, although it isn't (as is sometimes supposed) regarded as an insult to the host not to eat a lot. As in China, you will have to put up with people smoking enthusiastically before, during and after the meal.

Indonesia

Dress: Women should observe the Islamic dress code, and keep their arms, heads and knees covered. For men, the dress code in Indonesia is informal and, in a sensible bow to the hot, humid climate, a safari suit (or similar) is acceptable for most business and formal social occasions. Always remove your shoes when entering a Muslim house or institution. Avoid walking in front of people when they're at prayer and don't touch copies of the Koran. Never point the soles of your feet at anybody (they're also considered to be unclean) and similarly avoid putting your feet on desks or tables.

Meeting & Greeting: With Indonesian Chinese people, the handshake is the standard greeting. As in many parts of the Far East, however, handshakes in Indonesia aren't the macho shows of strength sometimes indulged in by westerners. Rather, the Indonesian handshake is more like a handclasp, a limp affair that lasts 10 to 15 seconds. For subsequent meetings, the bow sometimes replaces the handshake, accompanied by the Indonesian greeting *selamat* (peace).

The usual Indonesian Hindu greeting is a small bow with the palms together, as when praying. Handshakes are sometimes used when greeting westerners. Shaking hands with Chinese and Hindu Indonesian women is usually acceptable, but check beforehand if possible, and certainly check with regard to Muslim women. Stricter followers of Islam frown on any contact between men and women, except family members.

If you're invited to somebody's home, it's considered polite to bring a modest gift (although remember to carry and give it with your right hand).

Social Interaction: Social interaction and courtesies are usually stately and formal in Indonesia, being carried out in a deliberate, slow manner. To hurry matters is seen as disrespectful.

With the exception of handshakes, public contact between the sexes is frowned upon in Indonesia. Public displays of affection and kissing in public are particularly taboo. During conversation, however, touching people of the same sex – even strangers – is common. And it's usual to see men holding hands or even walking with their arms around each other. This is strictly friendly, with no sexual connotations.

Pointing with the index finger is considered to be rude in Indonesia, as is losing your temper. When pointing, do so with an open hand. Standing with your hands on your hips is to be avoided, as it's perceived as angry or aggressive. (In fact, this pose is used to symbolise anger in Indonesian shadow puppet theatre.) Avoid pounding one fist into the palm of the other hand because some Indonesians regard this as an obscene gesture. Don't touch Indonesians on the head, even children, as many people consider the head to be the 'seat of the soul'. Smiling, however, is a cultural tradition and Indonesians smile through most situations, even uncomfortable ones, which can be confusing for the foreigner who's unused to this.

Eating: When food or drink are served, don't touch anything until invited to do so by the host. As in all predominantly Muslim countries, never pass or take anything with the left hand, which is deemed to be for private, 'bathroom' tasks (Hindus also regard the left hand as unclean). Avoid eating or drinking in public during Ramadan, when Muslims fast during daylight hours. Chewing gum in public is frowned upon, as it is in Singapore.

Japan

Japan is sometimes portrayed as a social minefield for the foreigner and, although this is an exaggeration, Japanese people are very conscious about manners and etiquette, and are sensitive to many subtleties of behaviour. However, they're also well aware of the difficulty that foreigners have in adapting to Japanese ways of doing things and make allowances accordingly. Nevertheless, the more you manage to comply with Japanese social customs, the quicker you will be accepted in the country.

Dress: Avoid wearing overly colourful or ostentatious clothes to work and women should avoid too much jewellery (men should wear only a watch and a wedding ring).

Meeting & Greeting: When meeting and dealing with Japanese people, avoid a lot of eye and physical contact. The bow is usual when greeting people, although handshakes are becoming more common with the Japanese when they're dealing with foreigners. Don't, however, indulge in back-slapping or putting your arm around people. Also avoid pointing at people with your finger.

It's considered polite to put *san* after another person's name (*kun* after a boy's name, *chan* after a girl's), but never do this after your own name. The Japanese are very punctual and you should be likewise.

Always remove your shoes when visiting somebody's home (and for this reason, try to wear shoes that are easy to slip on and off rather than ones with elaborate laces or ties. Also be sure that your socks don't have holes!). Put your shoes neatly inside the entrance, with the toes facing the door. Your host will provide slippers for you to wear during the visit. Never, however, wear slippers on *tatami* mats. There are special slippers for visits to the toilet. Change your house slippers for these when necessary and, importantly, remember to change back afterwards.

It's traditional to sit on the floor in a *tatami* room. Women should avoid sitting cross-legged with people they don't know well. Instead, adopt the more formal position of kneeling and sitting back on your heels. Note that Japanese buildings usually have thin walls, so in your own home, moderate the volume of your television and stereo.

Social Interaction: The following list includes some of the more common Japanese social conventions:

- Japanese people sometimes use silence as much as words in order to communicate. It isn't dissimilar to the English idea that it isn't only what you say but also what you don't say that counts.

- The Japanese are effusive in their use of compliments, in order to foster a good atmosphere. The polite response is to deny how well you look, how well you understand Japanese, or whatever is being complimented.

- When somebody offers you help, it's polite to refuse the offer at first. An offer is usually made three times, so accept on the third.

- The sarcasm used by some Britons and Australians to emphasise a point isn't understood in Japan.

- Don't shout to attract somebody's attention. Either wave or go to them.

- To indicate themselves, the Japanese point at their noses rather than their chests.

- The Japanese indicate 'no' by fanning a hand sideways in front of the face a couple of times.

- Japan doesn't follow the tradition of 'ladies first'.

- Japanese women often cover their mouths with a hand when they laugh. Foreign women aren't, however, obliged to do so.

- When blowing your nose, it's best to leave the room and do so in private. If you cannot, do it discreetly and be sure to use a tissue not a handkerchief.

- In a car, the traditional custom is for the senior passenger to sit behind the driver. The junior sits next to the driver (sometimes called 'riding shotgun'). For this reason, taxi drivers open and close the rear left hand door for passengers.

Gifts: Gift giving (*omiyage*) is an established part of Japanese life. The traditions surrounding it are complex and foreigners aren't expected to take part. However, if you do, it's very much appreciated, and you aren't under pressure to understand all the intricacies. The main occasions on which gifts are exchanged are as follows:

- New Year (*oshogatsu*) sees the exchange of postcards between friends and associates.
- Valentine's Day on February 14th sees the exchange of modest gifts between men and women.
- *Ochugen* between 1st and 13th July sees gifts of beer, coffee, fruit and nuts given to people who've given you help or support. The response is to send a thank-you card and perhaps a gift at the next opportunity.
- *Oseibo* in mid-December is effectively another *ochugen*.
- *Hikkoshi aisatsu* is when you move into a new home and visit the neighbours to give them a modest present, perhaps a tea towel.
- *Kekkon iwai* is a wedding, when a cash gift is usual (up to around ¥20,000/US$183).
- *Nyugaku iwai* is a gift to a child starting school, usually consisting of school items such as stationary up to the value of around ¥2,500 (US$23).
- *Ososhiki* is a funeral, at which a condolence gift of up to around ¥12,000 (US$110) is given.
- *Shussan iwai* is a gift to celebrate a new baby, normally up to around ¥5,000 (US$46).
- When you return from holiday (vacation), it's usual to bring a modest gift for your work colleagues.
- Cash gifts are given in a special envelope (*noshibukuro*), which is tied with different coloured cords according to the nature of the event being marked. For a funeral, use black and white or yellow and grey; for a wedding and other occasions, use red and white. Gifts of ¥4,000 (US$36.65) are never given. The amount is considered to be bad luck because the word for four (*shi*) can also mean death.

Eating: Eating and drinking involve a list of dos and don'ts, which often takes the newcomer some time to ingest. These include the following:

- It's polite to say *itadakimasu* before eating and *gochisosama deshita* after eating.
- Never gobble your food and, when taking food from a shared dish, put it on your plate before eating it (i.e. don't put food from the shared dish straight into your mouth).

- It's usual and not considered impolite to lift your rice or soup bowl and hold it under your chin when eating from it. This sensible practice makes it much less likely that you will spill food on yourself.

- Japanese food is invariably served on a series of small plates. It's usual to alternate dishes, rather than to clear one dish at a time.

- Never use your chopsticks to stab or skewer food (instead, pick it up or move it with them), never leave them standing up in your food and never use your chopsticks to point at anybody. When taking food from a communal dish, use the non-eating end of your chopsticks.

- It's considered rude to pour your own drink when eating with other people. You pour your neighbour's drink and he pours yours. If you don't want any more to drink, leave your glass full.

- Making noise isn't always considered uncouth when eating and drinking. It's usual, in fact, to make slurping sounds when eating noodles and gulping noises when drinking.

- When you've finished eating, fold your napkin neatly and try not to leave a messy plate.

- If you need to use a toothpick, cover your mouth with your other hand while you do so.

- When offered an *oshibori* (a small, moist, rolled-up towel) use it to wipe your hands, but don't wipe your face and neck with it, which is considered vulgar.

- In restaurants, it's usual to pay the bill at the cash register rather than paying the waiting staff; tips aren't expected. It's rude to examine your change closely; give it no more than a quick glance.

- Avoid eating and drinking when walking down the street.

- Chewing gum is considered unacceptable at work and in other formal situations.

As in China, be prepared to be surrounded by chain smokers at work and in bars and restaurants!

Korea

Western newcomers to Korea sometimes find Koreans rude, but this is simply due to cultural differences. For example, whereas westerners are used to queuing in shops, ticket offices, etc., this isn't the norm in Korea, where a certain amount of self-assertion is taken for granted. If you form a queue, locals are likely to push in front of you. Similarly in crowds (which are common in Korea, one of the world's most densely populated countries), it's normal to be jostled and pushed; don't take this personally because it's the same for everybody and pushing isn't considered rude.

But not all the behaviour and customs of Korean people are eye-popping for the average westerner. For example, Koreans are often very helpful to foreigners and, if you're looking lost or confused, somebody will invariably stop to ask if you need help. It's common to be walked to your destination by a helpful Korean, to have a cab hailed for you, and even to be driven to where you want to go in a person's car, even if it's out of his way. Koreans are also eager to talk to foreigners, particularly to tell them about their country and its achievements, of which they're very proud. They're also tolerant of strange foreign ways and errors and will happily advise you on how to behave in their country.

Meeting & Greeting: The usual greeting between men is a slight bow, sometimes accompanied by a (weak) handshake, while keeping eye contact. By supporting your right forearm with your left hand during the handshake, you confer added respect. Women rarely shake hands in Korea and westerners shouldn't shake hands with Korean women. Western women have to initiate a handshake with Korean men.

In a group of new people, wait to be introduced rather than introducing yourself to people ('cold calls' of any kind are unpopular in Korea, where people like to deal with strangers via mutual acquaintances). The junior person present usually initiates the introductions, with a bow, while the senior person present will offer the first handshake.

As in China, Korean surnames are given first, followed by the given name. Given names are only used between very close friends. In business situations, the standard Far Eastern formality regarding the exchange of business cards is observed. Bilingual cards are recommended and they should be exchanged with both hands. Never give or receive anything with the left hand, as this is disrespectful. Take a little time to read the card.

When speaking to Koreans, maintain eye contact because this shows attentiveness and sincerity. Keep your voice quiet and, if you laugh, keep it restrained, as most Koreans do. Age is respected in Korea, so be sure to converse with the older people first. Complimenting their good health is well regarded.

Social Interaction: Be wary of any physical contact apart from a handshake, as many forms of contact are regarded as disrespectful, particularly with older people, members of the opposite sex and people you don't know very well. Avoid touching anybody on the back or arm. On the other hand, you will often see people of the same sex holding hands. Another Korean habit that is common throughout the Far East is to smile not simply when something is funny, but also as a way of hiding discomfort or embarrassment, which can be confusing for foreigners. Note also the following customs:

● As is common throughout the Far East, conflict and criticism aren't for public places; engage in them in private so that the other person does not lose face.

● Feet are regarded as dirty and the soles should be hidden (always point them down) and never used to touch anything.

● Public nose blowing is considered to be vulgar (especially in restaurants).

- Be sure to cover your mouth when yawning or using a toothpick.
- Don't signal or beckon people by using a single finger (stationary or moving) because this is seen as particularly rude.
- If the Korean national anthem is played in a public place, stand to attention as a sign of respect.

Foreigners aren't expected to learn to speak fluent Korean, but people appreciate the effort of saying hello (*an yang ha say so*) and thank you (*gam sa ham ni da*) in their language. In conversation, avoid the infamous matter of the Korean treatment and consumption of dogs. Westerners sometimes view this as awful, regarding the dog as man's best friend, but to Koreans, westerners' treatment of old people is often equally disgraceful.

Eating: Korean table manners can also be something of a surprise to the newcomer. Slurping noodles, holding your soup bowl close to your mouth while eating and gnawing meat off bones before throwing or spitting the bones onto the table are common. Other aspects of dining are more formal and it's polite to wait for the oldest person at dinner to start eating before you do and not to leave the table before the oldest person has finished eating. It's very bad form to pour your own drink; neighbours do it for each other.

Malaysia

Meeting & Greeting: When Malays meet westerners, the most common greeting is the handshake, sometimes with both hands. Indian Malays might use the *namaste* greeting, which is touching both palms together at heart level and making a gentle bow. This sometimes takes place after a handshake. When meeting a Malaysian woman, only shake hands if she extends her hand first. If she doesn't, greet her with a smile and a nod.

When introducing a man and a woman, use the woman's name first. When introducing an older or more senior person to a younger or more junior person, use the older or more senior person's name first. If dealing with royalty, be on your best behaviour. Take a gift and stand with your hands at your sides, except when greeting the royal. Do this by bowing with your palms pressed together at chest level. Don't leave a room before a royal person.

Social Interaction: Except for handshakes, there's no public contact between the sexes in Malaysia, and hugging and kissing are forbidden, even between married couples. Physical contact between members of the same sex, however, is common. You often see men holding hands or with their arms around each other; this is purely friendly, with no sexual connotations. Note also the following conventions:

- When leaving a room, say 'excuse me' and give a slight bow.
- Keep your hands out of your pockets in public.

- Don't point a finger to indicate something, but use the entire right hand, palm up. Similarly, use the hand rather than a finger to beckon somebody. Malays use the forefinger to point at animals.

- Pounding the fist into the palm of the other hand is considered to be obscene.

- Do as much as you can with your right hand because the left hand is considered to be unclean, as are the feet, which should never be used to point at anything; never show the soles. If your shoes or feet accidentally touch somebody, you should apologise.

- Never cross your legs in the presence of royalty.

- Don't touch anybody on the head, even children.

- Avoid standing with your hands on your hips because this is regarded as aggressive.

- With Indian Malays, moving the head from side to side indicates agreement, rather than 'no' as in much of the west (although the Indian gesture is slightly different, being more of a head toss).

- Indian Hindus have a sense of personal space and are most comfortable around a metre from other people.

As in most of the Far East, westerners aren't expected to learn to speak the language, but the attempt to speak a few words of Malay is appreciated and marks you out from the throng, who don't bother. When greeting a Malaysian in the morning say *salamat pagi*, otherwise *salamat petang*.

Philippines

The Philippines has a culture in which maintaining friendly relations with people is essential. This is best achieved by being positive all the time; negative remarks of any kind can cause loss of face, which leads to the end of friendships and sometimes the cutting of all ties between people. Despite the country's great economic inequalities, it's believed that everybody should be treated civilly. In fact, the more senior and successful a person becomes in the Philippines, the more modest, thoughtful and polite he is expected to be, particularly towards those less fortunate than himself.

Meeting & Greeting: Westerners are normally greeted with a handshake by Filipino men, which is firmer than in much of the rest of the region, where a limp handshake is the norm. Only shake hands with a Filipino woman if she extends her hand first. It's acceptable for western women to offer a handshake to Filipino men and women. (Filipino women often greet their female friends with a hug and a kiss.) Filipinos often greet each other by making eye contact and lowering and raising their eyebrows. If this is done to a foreigner, it means that he has been understood.

Social Interaction: As in much of the Far East, smiling communicates many things in the Philippines. As well as amusement, Filipinos sometimes smile to cover embarrassment, distress or nerves, which is confusing for newcomers. Here are some other common social conventions:

- Physical contact in public between men and women is invariably avoided.

- Raising your voice in the Philippines is best avoided, being considered unacceptable. Using a low, even tone of voice conveys confidence and authority.

- Filipino men commonly hold hands with their male friends or walk with an arm around each other.

- It's important not to stare at Filipinos. Staring is sometimes regarded as hostile and if you're stared at, look away. As a result, it's wise to break eye contact regularly when speaking to people.

- If you walk between two people, lower your head and clasp your hands in front of you as you pass, a sign of respect.

- Pointing with the middle finger at anybody or anything is the Philippines' most obscene gesture. And because pointing is such a taboo, Filipinos rarely indicate anything with any form of hand gesture, preferring to glance or purse their lips.

- Don't stand with your hands on your hips in the Philippines; as in much of the Far East, this is considered to be aggressive and challenging, which is particularly unwise in the sometimes-violent Philippines.

- Another custom that at first seems strange is the sound of hissing in restaurants, which is a popular way to summon a waiter.

Singapore

Some people regard Singapore as an excessively ordered, even repressive, society. This is unfair; although Singapore is certainly formal and regulated in many ways, in others it's more relaxed than neighbouring Indonesia and Malaysia. Nevertheless, perhaps the strongest cultural tradition in Singapore is that of strict adherence to the law. This has resulted in an enviably low crime rate, but also in a culture where you can be fined for actions considered acceptable or inconsequential in most western countries, most notably the following:

Action	Fine (S$)
Jaywalking	20
Failing to flush a toilet	150
Failing to give a pedestrian the right of way	150

Disposing of chewing gum in public	500
Littering	1,000
Spitting in public	1,000
Selling chewing gum (see below)	2,000

The import, manufacture and sale of chewing gum was banned in Singapore in 1992 and the penalty for smuggling it into the country has since been a year in prison and a fine of around US$5,500 (S$10,000)! The ban was supposedly introduced because chewing gum was preventing doors from closing on MRT trains, disrupting the system . . . or, according to others, because it was blocking the storm drains (unlikley in view of their size). Recent US lobbying has resulted in a partial lifting of the ban due to be introduced in 2004: sugarless gum prescribed by doctors and dentists as having therapeutic benefits (including nicotine gum to help smokers quit) will be sold by chemists.

It's widely thought that smoking in public is also forbidden in Singapore, but that isn't true. In fact, most of the many public litter bins have an ashtray on top.

Social Interaction: Handshakes are the normal greeting and, with Indians, tossing the head from side to side indicates agreement, not 'no'. Here are some of the dos and don'ts of Singaporean life:

- Ostentatious contact between the sexes is discouraged in public.
- Your voice should be kept low in Singapore (shouting is vulgar).
- Don't maintain long periods of eye contact with people.
- Avoid using the left hand if possible, as the Muslim and Hindu tradition that the left hand is unclean has left its mark in Singapore.
- Similarly, avoid moving or touching anything with your feet, and avoid pointing at things with a finger; Malays do this only with animals, while Indians find pointing with two fingers impolite.
- Avoid touching people on the head.
- As in much of the region, avoid standing with your hands on your hips, which is seen as an aggressive gesture.

Taiwan

Meeting & Greeting: When meeting Taiwanese people for the first time, a nod is the usual greeting, although handshakes are sometimes offered to westerners, particularly by younger and foreign-educated Taiwanese. The Taiwanese handshake is the limp, lingering kind rather than the robust version usual in the west; avoid a trial of strength. Taiwanese women rarely shake hands, and western women need to initiate a handshake with a Taiwanese man. Bowing is rarely used as a greeting in Taiwan.

As in China, the family name comes before the given name, but westernised Taiwanese sometimes reverse the names when dealing with westerners; if in doubt, ask which is the family name. Avoid calling somebody by his given name until you've known him for a long time.

Social Interaction: Taiwanese people sometimes come across as overly reserved, even cold, to foreigners. This is partly because it's usual not to smile or even to acknowledge people when you pass them in the street. This 'understatement' is continued in the reluctance of Taiwanese people to say a direct 'no' to anything. Foreigners need to analyse responses like 'maybe' and 'I'll think about it' to discern what is actually meant: learn to read between the lines and pick up on non-verbal signs of reluctance. In Taiwan, the amount and type of eye contact, tone of voice, facial expression and physical gestures are as important in communication as what is actually said.

Emotions should always be kept in check in Taiwan, where calm, composed behaviour is respected. When dealing with older Taiwanese or people in senior positions, it's respectful to minimise direct eye contact. Don't point with a finger, but use an open hand. Pointing at your nose indicates yourself, the western equivalent of pointing at your chest. Don't wink at people, even light-heartedly. Feet are regarded as dirty and should be kept away from people and objects. Women may cross their legs, but men should try to keep their feet flat on the floor.

The Taiwanese have a highly developed sense of personal space, so try to stay around 1.5m (5ft) away from people and avoid touching them. Expansive gestures are also to be avoided. The concept of 'saving face' is important in Taiwan. Don't raise your voice to anybody in public, or embarrass or criticise them. If necessary, this should be reserved for a private meeting between the two of you.

Eating: When eating with Taiwanese people, it's usual and polite to sample at least a little of every dish served. Leave something on your plate at the end to show that you're no longer hungry.

Thailand

Thais rightly have a reputation as friendly, tolerant, charming people but, contrary to the view of some foreigners, Thailand isn't a country where anything goes and there are rules to be observed.

Religion & Dress: Thailand is a Buddhist country, and Buddhism is regarded as one of the most tolerant religions (or philosophies more accurately, Buddhism being non-theistic). Images of the Buddha, however, should be treated respectfully, because all are regarded as sacred, whatever their age, size or artistic value (or lack of it). Don't touch or clamber on statues of the Buddha or pose for photographs in front of them.

Buddhist temples (*wats*) are open to all, but you must wear modest clothing. Men should wear long trousers and a shirt that covers the shoulders (no vests or cut-off t-shirts), women should wear a skirt or dress that covers the knees and a top that covers the shoulders and which isn't transparent. Take off your shoes before entering the temple; there are usually racks outside. Be careful with photography: don't take pictures while people are praying and (it bears repeating) don't have your picture taken with any Buddha image. Some monks don't object to being photographed, but others do, and it's recommended to ask permission before doing so. Women can talk to monks, but may not touch them and monks cannot receive anything directly from a woman's hand.

Meeting & Greeting: Shaking hands is unusual in Thailand (although more common in Bangkok, particularly in business circles involving westerners), and the common greeting involves pressing the palms together, prayer-like, which is known as *wai*. The younger or junior person *wais* the older or senior person. Thais often address people with a title and the first name, for example Mr Steve, because family names are a recent arrival in Thailand and are often surprisingly long and difficult to pronounce.

Social Interaction: The feet are regarded as dirty in much of the Far East, but perhaps most of all in Thailand. Never point at anything with the foot and avoid showing the soles of your shoes or feet to people. It's recommended that men lose the habit of crossing their legs (it's bad for the circulation anyway). Shoes aren't worn in Thai homes and in some other buildings. If you see a pile of shoes outside where you're visiting, take yours off and add then to the pile.

Conversely, the highest part of the body – the head – is revered in Thailand, and you should avoid touching anybody on the head. Because of the head's importance, it's usual for Thais to try to keep their heads lower than those of older people, as a sign of respect and to avoid looking down on them. This is sometimes all-but impossible – particularly for westerners, who are invariably taller than Thais, sometimes much taller – but being seen to try to do so is what's important.

Public displays of affection between the sexes are frowned upon, while losing your temper is bad manners. It's particularly important for foreigners to show respect towards the Thai royal family, which is deeply revered in the country. If you're at an event where a royal is present, watch how Thais behave and copy them. Respect for the royals is such that you have to be careful about how you treat banknotes, which carry a picture of the king; **defacing or tearing banknotes is a criminal offence and you should even avoid crumpling them**. Also, when putting stamps (which show the king's head) on cards and letters, stick them neatly and the right way up. **Being disrespectful to the royal family in any way is the one thing almost guaranteed to make all Thais angry.**

TELEVISION & RADIO

Although most people complain endlessly about the poor quality of television (TV) programmes in their home countries, many find they cannot live without a TV when they're in the Far East. Fortunately the growth of satellite and cable TV in the last few decades has enabled people to enjoy TV programmes in English and a variety of other languages almost anywhere in the world. The quality of local radio (including expatriate stations in some countries) is generally excellent, and if you have a high quality receiver (or a satellite TV system) it's possible to receive radio stations from around the globe. For details of English-language television and radio broadcasting in each territory, see the **English-Language Media** sections under **Communications** in the Country Profiles chapter (**Chapter 9**).

Television

The standards for TV reception aren't the same in all countries. For example, TVs and video cassette recorders (VCRs) operating on the PAL system or the North American NTSC system won't function in some countries.

Cable TV

Cable TV is available in all 11 territories. There are a number of cable TV companies in most countries, although if you live in an apartment or townhouse with a communal aerial you will usually be billed automatically for the services of the communal satellite TV service (unless you have no TV). All you need to do to receive cable TV is connect your TV aerial to a special wall socket. Cable TV consists of cable relays of local and foreign TV stations, dedicated cable-only stations and satellite stations. The number of stations available varies and may run from 20 to over 100, according to the package you (or your community/development) choose.

In much of the Far East, English-language cable TV stations are widely available and include BBC World News, Bloomberg, CNBC, CNN, Eurosport, ITN News, MTV and Sky News. In addition to unscrambled TV channels, scrambled TV channels are available in many areas. Like some satellite TV stations (see below), you require a decoder (which can be hired from and installed by most TV shops) to receive some stations and must pay a monthly subscription. Cable companies also offer pay-per-view services, where you pay to watch a particular live event, such as a sporting event or concert.

Satellite TV

Wherever you live in the region, it's likely that you will be able to receive satellite TV, although the signal strength and number of stations that can be received will depend on your equipment and location. The use of satellite dishes to receive foreign broadcasts is allowed or tolerated throughout the region, although periodic bans or restrictions are possible in the mainly Islamic states (Brunei, Indonesia and Malaysia) and China, to protect citizens from 'subversive' foreign influences.

Equipment: A satellite receiver should have a built-in Videocrypt decoder (and others such as Eurocrypt, Syster or SECAM if required) and be capable of receiving satellite stereo radio. A system with an 85cm dish (to receive Astra stations) costs from around US$300, plus installation, which may be included in the price. A digital system is more expensive: for example, a BSkyB system costs around US$1,000. Shop around, as prices can vary considerably. With a 1.2 or 1.5m motorised dish, you can receive hundreds of stations in a multitude of languages from around the world. If you wish to receive satellite TV on two or more TVs, you can buy a satellite system with two or more receivers. To receive stations from two or more satellites simultaneously, you need a motorised dish or a dish with a double feed antenna (dual LNBs).

There are satellite sales and installation companies in most countries, some of which advertise in the expatriate press. Shop around and compare prices. Alternatively, you can import your own satellite dish and receiver and install it yourself. Before buying a system, ensure that it can receive programmes from all existing and planned satellites.

Location: To receive programmes from any satellite, there must be no obstacles between the satellite and your dish, i.e. no trees, buildings or mountains must obstruct the signal, which you should check before renting or buying a home. Before buying or erecting a satellite dish, check also whether you need permission from your landlord, development or local municipality. Some towns and buildings (such as apartment blocks) have regulations regarding the positioning of antennae, although in some countries owners can mount a dish almost anywhere. Dishes can usually be mounted in a variety of unobtrusive positions and can also be painted or patterned to blend in with the background. Note, however, that in some countries, private dishes in apartment blocks are prohibited and have been replaced by a single communal antenna with a cable connection to individual homes.

Programme Guides: Many satellite stations provide teletext information and most broadcast in stereo. Satellite programme listings are provided in a number of British publications such as *What Satellite* and *Satellite Times*, which are available on subscription and from local newsagents in some countries. Satellite TV programmes are also listed in expatriate newspapers and magazines in most countries. The annual *World Radio TV Handbook* edited by David G. Bobbett (Watson-Guptill Publications) contains over 600 pages of information and the frequencies of all radio and TV stations worldwide.

BSkyB Television: You must buy a receiver with a Videocrypt decoder and pay a monthly subscription to receive BSkyB or Sky stations except Sky News (which isn't scrambled). Various packages are available costing from around GB£12 to around GB£35 per month for the premium package offering all movie channels plus Sky Sports. To receive scrambled channels such as Movimax and Sky Sports, you need an address in the UK. Subscribers are sent a coded 'smart' card (similar to a credit card), which must be inserted in the decoder to activate it (cards are periodically updated to thwart counterfeiters). Sky won't send smart cards to overseas viewers, as they have the copyright only for a British-based audience (expatriates need to obtain a card through a friend or relative in the UK). However, satellite companies (some of which advertise in the expatriate press) in most countries can supply genuine BSkyB cards.

Digital Television: English-language digital satellite TV was launched on 1st October 1998 by BSkyB in the UK. The benefits include a superior picture, better (CD) quality sound, wide-screen cinema format and access to many more stations (including around ten stations that show nothing but movies). To watch digital TV you require a Digibox and a (digital) dish. In addition to the usual analogue channels (see above), BSkyB digital provides BBC1, BBC2, ITV, Channel 4 and Five, plus many digital channels (a total of 200 with up to 500 possible later). Further information about BSkyB digital is available on the Internet (🖳 www.digiguide.co.uk).

BBC Worldwide Television: The BBC's commercial subsidiary, BBC Worldwide Television, broadcasts two 24-hour channels: BBC Prime (general entertainment) and BBC World (24-hour news and information), transmitted via the Eutelsat Hotbird 5 satellite (13° East). BBC World is unencrypted (clear) while BBC Prime is encrypted and requires a D2-MAC decoder and a smartcard, available on subscription from BBC Prime, PO Box 5054, London W12 0ZY, UK (☎ 020-8433 2221 or 020-8433 3040, ✉ bbcprime@bbc.co.uk). For further information and a programming guide contact BBC Worldwide Television, Woodlands, 80 Wood Lane, London W12 0TT, UK (☎ 020-8576 2555). A programme guide is also available on the Internet (🖳 www.bbc.co.uk/ schedules) and both BBC World and BBC Prime have their own websites (🖳 www. bbcworld.com and www.bbcprime.com). When accessing them, you need to enter the name of the country so that schedules are displayed in local time.

Radio

Radio flourishes in most countries, where it's often more popular than TV with a much larger audience. Numerous public and private, local, regional, national and foreign radio stations can be received throughout the Far East, with programme standards varying from excellent to agonisingly amateurish. There's a wealth of excellent FM (VHF stereo) and AM (medium waveband) stations in the major cities and resort areas in most countries, although in remote rural areas (particularly mountainous ones) you may be unable to receive any FM stations clearly. The long wave (LW) band is little used in most countries. A short wave (SW) radio is useful for receiving international stations.

Foreign Radio Stations

There are English-language and other foreign-language commercial radio stations in the major cities and resort areas in many countries; the emphasis is usually on music and chat with some news. Some expatriate stations broadcast in a variety of languages (not simultaneously), including English, Dutch, German and various Scandinavian languages, at different times of the day. Unfortunately (or inevitably), expatriate radio tries to be all things to all men (and women) and, not surprisingly, usually falls short, particularly with regard to music, where it tries to cater for all tastes. However, it generally provides a good service and is particularly popular among retirees. The main drawback of expatriate radio (and most commercial radio) is its amateurish advertisements, which are obtrusive and repetitive and make listening a chore.

English-language radio and other foreign radio programmes are published in the expatriate press in many countries. The BBC (see below) and many other foreign stations, including Radio Australia, Radio Canada, Denmark Radio, Radio Nederland, Radio Sweden International and the Voice of America, publish programme listings and frequency charts for expatriates keen for news from home. Don't forget to check for websites, where you can often download and hear broadcast material as well as view schedules. More and more people are listening to radio via their computers.

BBC World Service: The BBC World Service is broadcast on short wave on several frequencies (e.g. 12095, 9760, 9410, 7325, 6195, 5975 and 3955 kHz) simultaneously and you can usually receive a good signal on one of them. The signal strength varies according to where you live, the time of day and year, the power and positioning of your receiver, and atmospheric conditions. The BBC World Service and BBC Radio 1, 2, 3, 4 and 5 are also available via the Astra (Sky) satellite.

For a free BBC World Service programme guide and frequency information, write to BBC World Service, BBC Worldwide, PO Box 76, Bush House, Strand, London WC2B 4PH, UK (☎ 020-8752 5040). The BBC publishes a monthly magazine, *BBC On Air*, containing comprehensive programme listing for BBC World Service radio, BBC Prime TV and BBC World TV. It's available on subscription from the BBC, On Air Magazine, Room 207 NW, Bush House, Strand, London WC2B 4PH, UK (☎ 020-7240 4899, ✉ on.air.magazine@ bbc.co.uk) and from news-stands in some countries.

Cable & Satellite Radio: If you have cable or satellite TV, you can also receive many radio stations via your cable or satellite link. For example, BBC Radio 1, 2, 3, 4 and 5, BBC World Service, Sky Radio, Virgin 1215 and many foreign-language stations are broadcast via the Astra satellites (see page 302). Satellite radio stations are listed in British satellite TV magazines such as *Satellite Times*. If you're interested in receiving radio stations from further afield, you should obtain a copy of the *World Radio TV Handbook* edited by David G. Bobbett (Watson-Guptill Publications).

TIME DIFFERENCE

When living in the Far East it's important to be aware of the difference between local time and the time in countries where you have friends or family or do business (one sure way to upset friends and relatives is to phone them at 3am for a chat!). World time is expressed in relation to Greenwich Mean Time (GMT), which is the time at Greenwich in England between November and March. The difference between GMT and standard time in the 11 countries covered in this book is as follows:

Country	GMT+ (hours)
Brunei	8
China	8
Hong Kong	8
Indonesia (western)	7
Indonesia (central)	8
Indonesia (eastern)	9
Japan	9
Korea	9
Malaysia	8
Philippines	8
Singapore	8
Taiwan	8
Thailand	7

Indonesia's three time zones are as follows: Western Indonesia Time applies in Sumatra, Java and west and central Kalimantan; Central Indonesia Time applies in Bali, south and east Kalimantan, Sulawesi and Nusa Tenggara; Eastern Indonesia Time covers Maluku and Irian Jaya. None of the 11 territories uses 'summer' or 'daylight saving' time.

If you don't know how many hours ahead of or behind GMT the country you're calling is, you can usually find out by looking in the 'International Dialling' section of telephone books or on websites such as ⌨ www.world timeserver.com/country.asp, www.timeanddate.com/worldclock, www. time anddate.com, www.worldtime.com and www.worldtimezone.com.

Times in timetables are usually written using the 24-hour clock. Note, however, that the 24-hour clock is rarely referred to in speech. In some countries, times are given using the 12-hour clock ('am' and 'pm'), in which case they may be printed in timetables in light type to indicate before noon (am) and in bold type to indicate after noon (pm).

9.

COUNTRY PROFILES

This chapter contains profiles of the 11 territories covered by this book, summarising information detailed elsewhere in the book and including additional details.

BRUNEI

General Information

Capital: Bandar Seri Begawan.

Population: 340,000, comprising around 69 per cent Malays, 18 per cent Chinese, and 7 per cent indigenous tribes.

Foreign Community: There's a large expatriate population in Brunei, mostly working in the private sector, where around 75 per cent of employees are foreigners. The largest group is British, numbering around 20,000.

Area: 5,765km² (2,226mi²).

Geography: Brunei consists of two small enclaves on the coast of northern Borneo, 277mi (443km) north of the equator. It borders Sarawak (part of Malaysia) on all sides except the north coast, which is on the South China Sea. The country is mainly humid plains and forested mountains, cut by rivers, and is rich in oil. Human activity is concentrated in coastal areas and at estuaries. Around 70 per cent of Brunei is covered by virgin rainforest, which is rich in flora and fauna.

Climate: Brunei has a typically tropical climate with high temperatures and humidity throughout the year. Average temperatures range from 26°C (79°F) to 31°C (88°F) all year.

Health: Brunei is one of the region's safest countries from a health point of view (and also because of its low crime rate), although there's a slight risk of malaria in border areas. A cholera vaccination is recommended and a yellow fever vaccination is required for travellers aged one year and over who have visited an endemic or infected area in the week prior to entering Brunei. Take precautions against insect bites.

Health facilities are adequate for basic medical conditions but a lack of materials and some types of medical staff mean that many people travel to Malaysia or Singapore for complicated care or surgery. Therefore it's strongly recommended that your medical insurance specifically includes cover for such an eventuality and emergency medical evacuation. Although residents qualify for free treatment, non-residents must pay, in public as well as private hospitals.

Language: The official language is Malay. English and Chinese dialects are widely spoken.

Religion: 65 per cent Muslim (mainly Sunni), 15 per cent Buddhist, 10 per cent Christian, the rest others.

Government: Independent Sovereign Sultanate.

Political Stability: Very good. The country was once a British protectorate, gaining independence in 1983, and is still a close ally of the UK. The Sultan of

Brunei is the supreme authority and acts as President, Minister of Finance and Minister of Defence. The current Sultan is one of the world's richest men and Brunei has one of the highest standards of living in the world.

Economy

Overview: Brunei has a stable economy based on its oil and gas industries, as well as earnings from the Brunei Investment Agency overseas. Annual economic growth is steady and the country has no external debt. The Brunei government has recently made some important economic changes with a view to widening the country's economic base and diversifying its industries. The newly established Brunei Economic Development Board's (BEDB) principal aim is to attract foreign investment and industry.

GDP Per Head (2002): US$17,600.

Growth (2002): 3 per cent.

Target Industries: Aviation, land transportation, oil and gas, and ports (services and construction).

Ranking Among UK's Trade Partners: Outside top 50.

Ranking Among US's Trade Partners: Outside top 50.

Employment Market

Overview: Around 65 per cent of the active work force of approximately 80,000 is employed by the government, and many of the remainder are employed in Brunei Shell Petroleum or Brunei Royal Airlines. Three-quarters of employees in the private sector are foreigners and recruitment is generally straightforward and government approval forthcoming.

Unemployment Rate (2002): 4.6 per cent.

Work Permits: All foreign nationals require a work permit (known as a 'labour licence' or 'employment pass'), which must be applied for by the employer on the employee's behalf from the Labour Department. There's usually no difficulty in obtaining a permit, as Brunei needs foreign labour to satisfy the demands of the private sector, where some 75 per cent of employees are foreign.

Labour Relations: Brunei has a very good labour relations record and disputes are rare. Collective bargaining isn't usual, except in the oil industry.

Employment Conditions: Employment conditions are good and you can expect many fringe benefits. The working week is around 42 hours and employees are entitled to at least 15 days' annual holiday.

Finance

Currency: Brunei Dollar (BD$), comprising 100 cents. Notes are in denominations of BD$10,000, 1,000, 500, 100, 50, 25, 10, 5 and 1 dollars. Coins are in denominations of 50, 20, 10, 5 and 1 cents. Note that the Brunei Dollar is linked to the Singapore Dollar. Singapore Dollars may also be used in Brunei and most major currencies are convertible at banks, hotels and official money changers. Credit cards are accepted by most major establishments but not by many small retailers. Travellers' cheques can be cashed at banks and larger hotels. Cheques in currencies other than US$ and GB£ attract additional exchange charges.

Exchange Rate (2003): US$1 = BD$1.6.

Exchange Controls: None.

Banks: The banking system is stable and well organised. There's no central bank, although the Ministry of Finance supervises all banking activity. There are currently eight local commercial banks and several foreign banks.

Cost/Standard Of Living: Brunei has one of the highest standards of living in the world and its inhabitants live very well, with high wages and no personal taxation. Food and transport are more expensive than in neighbouring Malaysia, but not much. Accommodation, however, can be very expensive (see **Accommodation** below).

Loans: Loans are available from the Economic Development Board, which is responsible for assisting businessmen through the provision of loans at favourable rates of interest for both start-up and expansion of business. The scheme provides loans for a maximum amount of BD$1.5 million at a 4 per cent interest rate repayable within 12 years. Commercial banks also provide loans.

Interest Rate (2002): 5.5 per cent.

Taxation

Corporate Tax: 30 per cent.

Personal Income Tax: None.

Capital Gains Tax: None.

Wealth Tax: None.

Inheritance & Gift Tax: Inheritance tax is levied at a flat rate of 3 per cent on estates valued at over BD$2 million.

Value Added/Sales/Purchase Tax: None.

Social Security & Pensions: There are no social security contributions, and benefits such as health and medical care are free for residents; there's a non-contributory pension scheme for the retired and disabled.

Withholding Taxes: Interest is subject to 20 per cent withholding tax.

Tax Filing: Companies must file an annual return for tax purposes and business organisations are required to submit accounting data annually to the Economic Planning Unit for statistical purposes. Branches of foreign companies are required to file the annual financial accounts of the company with the Registrar of Companies.

Departure Tax: BD$12 for most departing passengers (BD$5 to Malaysia and Singapore), payable in cash in local currency at the airport check-in desk.

Doing Business

Forming A Company: Foreigners may set up branches, partnerships or companies in Brunei, a process that is generally straightforward. Companies must be registered with the Register of Companies and Business Names, and shareholders need not be Brunei citizens. Private companies (*Sdn. Bhd*) must have a minimum of two and a maximum of 50 shareholders. Foreigners cannot set up sole proprietorships.

Investment: Brunei welcomes foreign investment and setting up is generally straightforward.

Government Incentives: Numerous incentives are available for qualifying companies, including tax exemption or tax 'holidays', exemption from taxes on imported goods and exemption from tax on imported raw materials if they're unavailable in Brunei.

Business Hours: Offices and business are open from 9am to 5pm Mondays to Fridays and from 9am to noon on Saturdays. Banking hours are from 9am to noon and from 2pm to 3pm Mondays to Fridays, and from 9am to noon on Saturdays.

Public Holidays: 12 per year as follows:

Day/Date	Holiday
1st January	New Year's Day
A day in late January or early February	Chinese New Year
A day in February	Hari Raya Haji (Feast of the Sacrifice)
23rd February	National Day
A day in late February or early March	Hijriah (Islamic New Year)
A day in May	Maulud (Birth of the Prophet)
31st May	Anniversary of the Royal Brunei Malay Regiment
15th July	The Sultan's Birthday
A day in September	Israk Mikraj (Ascension of the Prophet)
A day in October	Start of Ramadan
A day in November	Hari Raya Puasa (End of Ramadan)
25th December	Christmas Day

Holidays not assigned particular dates vary from year to year, usually according to local sightings of the phases of the moon.

Business Etiquette: Before doing business in Brunei, it's wise to take some time to study local customs and social behaviour (see page 286). Bear in mind that Brunei is considerably more conservative than Indonesia and Malaysia, and business etiquette is very different. First impressions and appearance are extremely important in Brunei and you should dress and behave appropriately. Under government directive, all male civil servants are required to wear long-sleeved shirts and ties, and businessmen should wear the same plus a jacket. Businesswomen should wear long sleeves and a long shirt or trousers. A light handshake is the accepted greeting between members of the same sex. Avoid direct eye-contact when addressing people, particularly the opposite sex.

Accommodation

Restrictions On Foreign Ownership: Foreigners aren't permitted to own any property in Brunei, so the only accommodation option for expatriates is renting.

Building Standards: Good.

Renting: There's a vast rented accommodation market in Brunei and property can generally be found easily. Service apartments are available, although they can be expensive, especially for long-term stays.

Personal Effects: If you have a work permit, you're permitted to import personal effects duty-free, although certain items (e.g. videos) may be subject to censorship.

Utilities: The electricity supply (230V) is generally reliable and charges are reasonable, although electricity bills can be high if you have air-conditioning. Bottled gas is available for cooking. Tap water is generally safe to drink, although many people prefer to drink bottled water.

Communications

Postal Services: Post offices are open between 7.45am and 4.30pm from Mondays to Thursdays and on Saturdays. On Fridays, they're open between 8 and 11am and from 2 to 4pm. Most hotels provide postal services. Brunei's post is generally reliable. Letters to Europe take from two to five days, postcards cost 20 cents to Singapore and Malaysia, 35 to 60 cents to other destinations. Registered post and express post are also available.

Telecommunications: Telecommunications are among the best in South-east Asia. The country has fixed and satellite links for worldwide IDD, as well as telex links. Most hotels offer these services. Public phones operate with local coins (10 and 20 cents) and phonecards for card-operated phones are available from many retailers. A pre-paid card called a Hallo Kad (!) allows calls to be made to over 130 countries from Brunei. The card can be bought at the airport and from many retailers. International call charges are high in Brunei. DSTCom

(💻 www.dst-group.com), Brunei's mobile system server, offers the GSM 900 system. It has a hotline for further information (☎ 151).

International Dialling Code: 673.

Internet: The internet has gained in popularity in recent years and email is widely used by companies in Brunei. Internet services are through the Brunet section of Jabatan Telekom Brunei and two speeds are currently available: 33.6Kb/s and 56Kb/s. See the website 💻 www.brunet.bn for current services, prices and offers in this ever-changing field.

Transport Infrastructure: Most people in Brunei own a car (or cars) and public transport is thin on the ground.

Getting There: Brunei's airport has recently been expanded and upgraded, and is served by flights from many countries. Royal Brunei Airlines (RBA), Garuda Indonesia, Malaysian Airlines, Philippine Airlines, Singapore Airlines and Thai Airways International offer the most services. Note, however, that it's usually cheaper to fly via Malaysia than direct to Brunei. There are also express ferry services from neighbouring countries (e.g. Singapore).

Import/Export Restrictions: Generally none. Some items are subject to import duty.

Miscellaneous

Crime & Legal Restrictions: Very low crime rate and violent crime is virtually unknown. Note that alcohol cannot be sold in Brunei and visitors are allowed to import two bottles of alcohol and 12 cans of beer. There are serious penalties for drug smuggling, including death.

Education: Education is compulsory for all children aged from 5 to 16 and free in state schools, although most expatriates send their children to a boarding school in their home country. There are several good schools in Brunei, but facilities are limited for secondary education.

English-Language Media: The national television network, Radio and Television Brunei (RTB), transmits local and international programmes for around eight hours on weekdays and 15 at weekends. It shows some English-language programmes, and news bulletins are broadcast in Malay and English. Malaysian television can also be received in Brunei. International satellite and cable TV are widely available.

Radio Brunei has two networks, one in Malay (the National Network), one in English, Chinese and Gurkhali (the Pilihan Network). The latter broadcasts between 6am and midnight. Pelangi and Kristal FM are bilingual stations, broadcasting in Malay and English. The *Borneo Bulletin* is Brunei's only independent daily English-language newspaper. The Government publishes a *Daily News Digest* and a *Brunei Darussalem Newsletter* fortnightly, both in English.

Time Difference: GMT +7.

Weights & Measures: Metric.

Reference

Useful Addresses

British High Commission, PO Box 2197, Bandar Seri Begawan BS 8674 (☎ 02-673 222 231, 🖳 www.britain-brunei.org).

Embassy of Brunei, 19/20 Belgrave Square, London SW1X 8PG, UK (☎ 020-7581 0521).

Embassy of Brunei, Watergate Suite, 2600 Virginia Ave, NW, Washington DC 20037, US (☎ 202-342 0159, 🖳 www.bruneiembassy.org).

National Chamber of Commerce and Industry (🖳 www.nccibd.com). Provides useful information and latest business updates for investors in Brunei.

US Embassy, 3rd Floor, Teck Guan Plaza, Jalan Sultan, Bandar Seri Begawan (☎ 02-220 384, 🖳 http://bandar.usembassy.org).

Further Reading

A Short History of Malaysia, Singapore and Brunei, C Mary Turnbull

Brunei Darussalam (Brunei Shell)

By God's Will - A Portrait of the Sultan of Brunei, Lord Chalfont

White Rajah: a Dynastic Intrigue, Cassandra Pybus

Useful Websites

Britain Brunei (🖳 www.britain-brunei.org) – The website of the British High Commission Brunei.

Brunei Air (🖳 www.bruneiair.com) – The website of Royal Brunei Airlines.

The Government of Brunei Darussalam (🖳 www.brunei.gov.bn) – Most useful for its links to the websites of the various government ministries.

CHINA

General Information

Capital: Beijing.

Population: 1,295,000,000. China is by far the world's most populated country and one in five of the world's citizens is Chinese. Around 93 per cent are Han Chinese, the rest are split between around 55 ethnic minorities.

Foreign Community: China has traditionally been closed to foreigners, although this is gradually changing and the western population, albeit small, is increasing, particularly in cities such as Shanghai.

Area: 9,500,000km^2 (3,668,236mi^2).

Geography: China is the world's third-largest country, occupying most of East Asia, and its geography has encouraged isolation from the rest of the world. On the northern, western and southern borders, vast deserts, forests and mountain ranges make overland access difficult, while to the east is the Pacific Ocean. There are two main mountain ranges, running north-south and east-west. The vast majority of the population lives in the low-lying lands in the east around the agricultural plains of Manchuria and the North China Plain, and in the Yangtze basin and delta further south. China is divided into 22 provinces and five autonomous regions, and has around 5,000 islands.

Climate: China can be divided into three climatic zones: the north has a continental climate with severe winters and hot, dry summers; the central area is milder, although winters are still cold and summers hot; the south of the country is generally much milder, with rain all year. Average temperatures for Beijing are 1°C (33°F) in January and 28°C (82°F) in July.

Health: Malaria is present in much of China. Hepatitis B is common throughout the country and hepatitis E is common in the north. Japanese encephalitis is found in the rural north of China between May and September, and in the rural south between April and October. Schistosomiasis is common in many of China's rivers and lakes, and tuberculosis is common throughout the country. Bengal cholera has been found in western China and rabies from dogs is a risk everywhere. China's cities and industrial regions have some of the highest levels of air pollution in the world. The only mandatory vaccination for entry to China is yellow fever, applicable to travellers coming from infected areas. If you intend to stay in China for longer than six months, you need to pass an HIV test.

Due to the outbreak of Severe Acute Respiratory Syndrome (SARS), the World Health Organisation (WHO) in June 2003 advised foreigners against travel to some parts of China, although warnings have since been lifted. Check with your country's foreign office for the latest information.

The country's major cities have plenty of doctors and hospitals and, since foreign doctors have been allowed to practise in China, there are increasing numbers of international health clinics staffed by highly trained doctors in the larger cities, many of whom speak at least some English. However, Chinese state hospitals are sometimes very basic and their lack of facilities (and hygiene) comes as a shock to many foreigners.

The vast majority of expatriates (if they have any sense) have extensive medical insurance, including emergency evacuation to specialist hospitals in Hong Kong.

Language: The official language is Mandarin, and there are many local and regional dialects. Large groups in the south speak Cantonese, Fukienese, Hakka and Xiamenhua. The autonomous regions of Mongolia, Tibet and Xinjiang have their own languages. English is spoken only in main cities (not widely and not always well).

Religion: Confucianism, Buddhism (around 100 million) and Taoism are the major religions/philosophies, and there are also around 50 million Muslims and around 9 million Christians.

Government: Single-party, communist republic.

Political Stability: Reasonably good. The People's Republic of China was founded in 1949 and until 1979 China and its citizens were subject to strict government control, with the country virtually isolated internationally. In 1979 an 'Open Door Policy' was introduced whereby China's economy was opened up to the world, bringing greater prosperity and wealth. China has a very poor human rights record and it's hoped that with greater economic expansion it will become more democratic and liberal. Wen Jiabao, a reformer, became China's Premier in March 2003.

Economy

Overview: China has made enormous economic progress over the last two decades and is now the world's sixth largest economy, although the country still faces huge economic challenges, particularly in the areas of finance and state owned enterprises (SOEs), a significant number of which are loss-making. Local and provincial governments are often reluctant to close SOEs for fear of loss of influence and social unrest, such as that seen in industrial cities in the north-east during 2002. In 2002 China joined the World Trade Organisation and, as a result, foreign direct investment rose sharply, although WTO reforms will take place very slowly. In 2003 the mismanaged SARS crisis seriously disrupted policy making and will probably lead to a noticeable reduction in GDP growth for the year. Foreign investment, however, continues to grow and consumer spending increases annually.

GDP Per Head (2002): US$1,070.

Growth (2002): 8 per cent. This figure is considerably higher than most other countries, but the figure was lower than expected and China must maintain an annual GDP growth of at least 7 per cent in order to keep urban unemployment at levels that don't threaten social stability.

Target Industries: Agriculture, communications, construction, consumer services, education and training, environment (particularly water), financial services, fire and security, food and drink, healthcare, leisure and tourism, power, railways (including metro and light railway) and textiles. There's an ambitious investment programme in preparation for the 2008 Beijing Olympics and numerous investment opportunities are available.

Ranking Among UK's Trade Partners: 11.

Ranking Among US's Trade Partners: 1.

Employment Market

Overview: Many Chinese in urban areas are well-trained and educated, although many foreign investors find that there's a lack of business managers of international standard and experience in China and prefer to hire expatriate staff. However, the cost of hiring expatriates is high and can amount to as much as 40 per cent of a basic salary. Note also that most Chinese enterprises have more employees than they need. In negotiating an acquisition or joint venture transaction, the Chinese party will often attempt to transfer all the existing employees. It's important that all the surplus employees be excluded from the transaction because of the level of protection offered to employees in China.

Unemployment Rate (2002): 9.6 per cent.

Work Permits: All foreign nationals require a work permit, which can be difficult to obtain, as Chinese nationals take priority. To obtain a work permit you must have an official invitation from a Chinese Government Agency or a government authorised company, as well as a Foreign Specialist's Licence from the Chinese authorities for some jobs. These documents must be attached to your work visa application.

Labour Relations: Labour unrest is uncommon, although the closure of SOEs in provinces in the north-east led to unrest in 2003, particularly among agricultural workers. China permits only unions that belong to the All-China Federation of Trade Unions (ACFTU), and independent trade unions are illegal. Although a union presence in foreign companies isn't compulsory, the ACFTU is increasing its presence in them.

Employment Conditions: Employment conditions are strictly controlled by the state. The working week is usually 45 hours and employees are generally entitled to between three and five weeks' annual holiday. If you wish to live and work in China, a good knowledge of Chinese is essential. **Most foreigners find the culture very difficult to adapt to.**

Finance

Currency: Renminbi (RMB), also known as the Yuan (Y) or the Renminbi Yuan (RMBY), divided into 10 chiao/jiao or 100 fen. Bank notes come in denominations of RMB100, 50, 10, 5, 2 and 1, and of 5, 2 and 1 chiao/jiao. Coins come in denominations of RMB1, 1.5 chiao/jiao and 5, 2 and 1 fen. Chinese currency isn't traded outside China.

Foreign currency and travellers' cheques (US$ cheques are recommended) can be exchanged at main branches of the Bank of China, tourist hotels, Friendship Stores and some other retail outlets. Scottish and Northern Irish banknotes cannot be exchanged. Keep exchange receipts if you wish to change RMB back into foreign currency. Credit cards are accepted more and more in China.

Exchange Rate (2003): US$1 = RMB8.25.

Exchange Controls: Foreign Exchange Certificates were phased out on 1st January 1994, greatly simplifying currency matters for travellers to China. Renminbi issued in exchange for foreign currency can be converted back into foreign currency on presentation of the original exchange receipt.

Banks: Banking activity is controlled by the People's Bank of China and there are several commercial banks (all state-owned) but, although banking is now computerised, transactions are very slow. Foreign banks are gradually establishing themselves in China.

Cost/Standard Of Living: Compared to the west, China is a cheap country but there are variations within the country, and the east is generally more expensive than the west, sometimes twice as much. Shanghai is an expensive city and tourists and westerners are generally charged more than locals throughout China. Imported goods are very expensive.

Loans: Short-term loans for working capital are available from China's state-owned commercial banks, although priority is usually given to investments that bring in advanced technology or produce goods for export. Chinese interest rates are generally lower than those overseas, making Chinese-financing attractive. Foreign-invested firms, which can keep foreign currency accounts in commercial banks, can only borrow funds from abroad and must register all foreign loans with the State Administration for Foreign Exchange (SAFE).

Interest Rate (2002): 0.72 per cent.

Taxation

Chinese taxation is a complicated matter and expert advice is necessary.

Corporate Tax: 30 per cent plus 3 per cent levied by local authorities.

Personal Income Tax: You're liable for income tax in China if you have a permanent home there. If you don't, you're taxed according to the length of residence in China. Foreigners who reside in China for less than a year are taxed on their Chinese-source income only. Foreigners who reside in China for more than a year but less than five years are liable for tax on both Chinese-source and worldwide income, although the taxation of foreign-source income can be limited to Chinese entities only if approval is given by the Chinese tax authorities. Income tax rates range from 5 to 45 per cent and the tax exemption is RMB100,000 (US$12,120). Foreign expatriates are exempt from tax on the first RMB48,000 (US$5,820) of annual earnings. Taxpayers must register with their local tax office.

Capital Gains Tax: CGT is levied at the same rates as income tax except for gains on property (real estate), which is levied at between 30 and 60 per cent. Permanent residences are exempt.

Wealth Tax: None.

Inheritance & Gift Tax: None.

Value Added/Sales/Purchase Tax: VAT is levied at a standard rate of 17 per cent and a reduced rate of 13 per cent for necessities.

Social Security & Pensions: Foreigners working in China don't need to contribute to the social security system. Companies employing Chinese nationals are required to make contributions to the state housing fund (around 10 per cent of the payroll) and to local pension and unemployment funds, maximum amounts of which can total 20 per cent of the total payroll.

Withholding Taxes: Dividends and interest are subject to 20 per cent withholding tax.

Tax Filing: Individuals must file monthly returns and make tax payments within seven days of the end of each month. Companies make provisional tax payments after every quarter and a final settlement within five months of the calendar year's end.

Doing Business

China has changed many of its foreign investment requirements since accession to the WTO in 2002. As a consequence many new areas have been opened up. However, associated legislation is still in its infancy and before making any investments you should research them thoroughly and take advice from professional experts who have access to current information. Note that foreign investors often find it difficult to know how certain rules will be interpreted and implemented by the government. This problem is compounded by the fact that most regulations are constantly changing! Furthermore, administrative interpretations and implementation of rules are sometimes left to the various layers of provincial government and industry bureaucracy. It's therefore virtually essential to use a competent lawyer.

Forming A Company: Foreigners may set up a 100 per cent foreign-owned company in China, although there are restrictions. Equity Joint Ventures and China Joint Ventures are also permitted. In recent years, numerous private firms have been established and currently employ more than 150 million people.

Investment: The investment climate is continually changing in China, where billions of US dollars have been invested over the last few years by foreign businesses. Although investment is welcomed in theory, in practice there are numerous obstacles and large business sectors where foreign investment is prohibited or severely restricted. Seek professional advice.

Government Incentives: Incentives are available, although many aren't automatically conferred and to obtain them you may have to negotiate with the relevant government authorities. Incentives include substantial reductions in national and local income taxes, import and export duties, and priority treatment to obtain basic infrastructure. High-technology and export-orientated industries are given priority.

Business Hours: Most offices and businesses (including state-owned companies) open from 8.30am to 5.30pm Mondays to Fridays, although many close on Friday afternoon. Banking hours are generally from 9am to noon and from 1.30pm to 5.30pm Mondays to Fridays.

Public Holidays: Around 12 national holidays per year as follows:

Day/Date	Holiday
1st January	New Year
Late January or early February	Chinese New Year/Spring Festival – government departments and most companies close for a week
Early May	International Labour Day – lasts around a week!
Early October	National Day – government departments and most companies close for a week

Other holidays are celebrated locally or by certain groups, including:

Day/Date	Holiday
8th March	International Women's Day
4th May	National Youth Day
1st June	International Children's Day
1st August	Army Day

Business Etiquette: Dress is formal in China and women should take care to dress modestly, as 'traditional gender concepts' prevail in many businesses. Introductions are formal and usually made in order of superiority. A handshake is the accepted form of introduction. Business cards are essential and should be printed in both English and Chinese. You should present the card with both hands, Chinese-side up. English isn't widely spoken in business circles and you should take an interpreter with you. **Westerners doing business with the Chinese should refer to China as the People's Republic of China rather than just China.**

Accommodation

Restrictions On Foreign Ownership: Ownership of property by foreigners is restricted in most parts of China, where foreigners can only purchase 'foreign approved for sale' housing, which is very difficult and expensive to buy. Title deeds aren't permanent and you can usually only use the property for 70 years before title reverts to the state. There's no freehold in China. **You should exercise extreme caution and obtain expert advice before embarking on any purchase of property in China.** In Shanghai, however, the situation is generally more open and foreigners can now buy properties anywhere in the city (in 2002 over 40 per cent of property transactions were made by foreign investors). The situation elsewhere in the country is also undergoing change and you should consult an expert for the latest information.

Cost Of Housing: In Shanghai prices vary greatly according to the location and age of the property; houses built before 1940 (known as 'old houses') are particularly expensive. Apartments in a desirable area with two to four bedrooms are available from US$1,000 to US$3,600 per m². 'Old houses', which are often large with gardens, cost from US$1,200 to US$5,000 per m².

Local Mortgages: Mortgages are now available from Chinese state commercial banks for up to 80 per cent of a property's value, for up to 30 years if the loan is in RMB, or up to 10 years for foreign currency loans.

Purchase Fees & Taxes: As property purchase is a recent phenomenon in China, fees and taxes have yet to be established in most areas.

Building Standards: Variable.

Renting: The vast majority of foreigners rent accommodation in China, where compounds for foreigners are popular but expensive. An apartment in a compound costs between RMB16,500 to RMB66,000 (US$2,000 and US$8,000) per month. If you work for the Chinese government, you're likely to be provided with low-cost housing, although this is usually basic. Other options include renting a room from a Chinese family, which costs from RMB1,200 (US$145) per month depending on the facilities and type of board.

Personal Effects: Personal and household effects can generally be imported duty-free, although electronic equipment and computers may be subject to duty.

Utilities: The electricity supply (230V) is generally reliable in the larger cities and isn't expensive. Note, however, that the supply is erratic or non-existent in many rural areas. Mains gas for cooking and heating is available in most large cities. Tap water is best avoided and bottled water is widely available.

Communications

Postal Services: The postal system is efficient but delivery is slow, particularly in rural areas. **There are strict regulations regarding post and you must use regulation envelopes, the correct postcode and Chinese characters for domestic post, or it won't be delivered.** All postal communications to China should be addressed to the People's Republic of China.

Telecommunications: The telephone service is run by several state-owned companies and is old but generally reasonably efficient, although call charges are high and it can be easier to make international calls than internal ones. IDD is available. Mobile phones are extremely popular in the cities. GSM 1800 and 900 networks provide coverage in Beijing, Guangzhou and Shanghai. GSM 900 networks also cover major towns and cities in the south and east. Networks are operated by China Mobile (🖳 www.chinamobile.com) and China Unicom (🖳 www.netchina.com.cn).

International Dialling Code: 86.

Internet: The internet is fast gaining in popularity and many companies are online and have email facilities. Connections, including ADSL, are improving and competition growing between internet service providers (ISPs), leading to a welcome price reduction; one of the leaders is Eastnet China Ltd (🖳 www.

eastnet.com.cn). **Note that internet usage is subject to strict government control and access to some sites is restricted.** In 2003 numerous internet cafés were closed as a result of a government clampdown on internet usage.

Transport Infrastructure: China has extensive and cheap public transport services, although buses can be crowded and stuffy.

Getting There: The cities of Beijing, where a new terminal has recently been completed, and Shanghai both have large international airports served by flights from most major cities worldwide. Construction starts in 2004 on a new international airport in Guangzhow in Canton. China can also be entered via Hong Kong, which is often the cheapest route. The country's national carrier is the Civil Aviation Administration of China (CAAC), usually known as Air China. It also has a joint venture with Hong Kong's Cathay Pacific called Dragonair.

There are plenty of points of entry by land into China, including the Trans-Siberian railway and rail and road routes from Vietnam, Tibet, Pakistan, Kazakhstan and Kyrgystan. There's also the option of the famous 'slow boat to China', often from Japan or South Korea, and popular ports of entry include Hong Kong, Macau, Shanghai, Xiamen (opposite Taiwan) and Tanggu (near Tianjin).

Import/Export Restrictions: China frequently makes changes to its import-export regulations and you're advised to check with shipping agents for up-to-date information. Many imported products must carry the new China Compulsory Certification (CCC), the introduction of which has caused numerous obstacles for foreign companies, although the procedure is transparent. For up-to-date information on the CCC, including which products require it and the correct import procedure, you should contact Certification and Administration of China (🖥 www.cnca.gov.cn) or its Chinese representation in your home country. Costs for the application for a CCC range from RMB5,000 to RMB50,000 (US$600 to US$6,000), plus the agent's commission (a high 30 to 40 per cent of the total cost) and takes from around two to six weeks.

China has duty-free zones in Dalian, Tianjin, Shanghai, Guangzhou, and Hainan and free-trade zones offering similar privileges, usually in economic development zones and open cities throughout China.

Miscellaneous

Crime & Legal Restrictions: China has a low crime rate, due no doubt to its severe penalties, including the death penalty for relatively minor offences.

Education: There aren't many educational facilities for expatriate children and there's only one international school, in Beijing, although there are American schools in Guangzhou and Shanghai.

English-Language Media: Unless you live in a foreign compound with a licence for satellite TV, it's illegal to receive foreign broadcasts. Satellite broadcasts in compounds include most channels available in the US and Europe.

The main English-language daily is the appropriately-named *China Daily*. *Beijing Review* is weekly, with editions in English, French, German, Japanese and Spanish.

Time Difference: GMT +7

Weights & Measures: Metric.

Reference

Useful Addresses

American Chamber of Commerce, China Resources Building 1903, 8 Jianguomenbei Dajie, Beijing 100005 (☎ 10-8519 19220, 🖳 www.amcham-china.org). Publishes the monthly magazine *China Brief*, available by email.

British Embassy, 11 Guang Hua Lu, Jianguomenwai, Beijing 100600 (☎ 10-6532 1961, 🖳 www.britishembassy.org.cn).

China-Britain Business Council (CBBC), Abford House, 15 Wilton Road, London SW1V 1LT (☎ 020-7827 5176, 🖳 www.cbbc.org). Publishes the useful guide to doing business, *China Guide* and the 'e-zine' (email magazine) *China-Britain Trade Review*.

Chinese Embassy, 2300 Connecticut Avenue, NW, Washington DC 20008, US (☎ 202-328 2500, 🖳 www.china-embassy.org).

Chinese Embassy, 31 Portland Place, London W1N 3AG, UK (☎ 020-7636 9375, 🖳 www.chinese-embassy.org.uk).

US Embassy, 3 Xiu Shui Bei Jie, Beijing 100600 (☎ 10-6532 3831, 🖳 http://beijing.usembassy.gov).

Further Reading

Titles prefaced by an asterisk are recommended by the author.

A Last Look: Western Architecture in Old Shanghai, Deke Erh and Tess Johnson

Behind the Wall, Colin Thubron

Biking Beijing, Diand Kingsbury

Bitter Winds: A Memoir of My Years in China's Gulag, Harry Wu

China Wakes, Nicholas D Kristof and Sheryl Wudunn

Deng Xiaoping and the Making of Modern China, Richard Evans

Doing Business Guide: China (PriceWaterhouseCoopers)

Doing Business in China (Ernst & Young Publications)

Dragon Lady: The Life and Legend of the Last Empress of China, Sterling Seagrave

Eldest Son: Zhou Enlai and the Making of modern China, 1898-1976, Han Suyin

Empire of the Sun, J G Ballard

Evening Chats in Beijing, Perry Link

Life and Death in Shanghai, Nien Cheng

Mandate of Heaven, Orville Schell

Old Peking: City of the Ruler of the World, Chris Elder

Riding the Iron Rooster, Paul Theroux

Shanghai: the Rise and Fall of a Decadent City, 1842-1940, Stella Dong

Son of the Revolution, Liang Heng and Judith Shapiro

Sowing the Seeds of Democracy in China: Political Reform in the Deng Xiaoping Era, Merle Goldman

The Great Chinese Revolution 1800 to 1985, John King Fairbank

The Private Life of Chairman Mao, Zhisui Li

The Search for Modern China, Jonathan Spence

The Walled Kingdom: A History of China from 2000 BC to the Present, Witold Rodzinsky

The White Boned Demon: A Biography of Madame Mao Zedong, Ross Terrill

Wild Swans, Jung Chang

Useful Websites

Beijing Scene (⌨ www.beijingscene.com) – Bills itself as 'Beijing's best bi-lingual lifestyle magazine'.

Chinese Business World (⌨ www.cbw.com) – Has information about most aspects of work, trade and travel within China.

Expats in China (⌨ www.expatsinchina.com) – A useful general resource, including a list of international schools in the major cities.

Shanghai Expat (⌨ http://shanghaiexpat.com) – A website for foreign workers and students in Shanghai.

HONG KONG

General Information

Population: 7.3 million. Hong Kong is one of the most densely populated places in the world with 17,250 people per km² (6,650 per mi²).

Foreign Community: Hong Kong has a foreign population of almost 500,000, with large groups from North America, South-east Asia, Australia, the UK and India.

Area: 1,098km² (424mi²).

Geography: Hong Kong lies just south of the Tropic of Cancer in southern China. It consists of 235 tiny islands and a section of mainland in the Chinese province of Guangdong. Hong Kong is divided into four areas: Kowloon, Hong

Kong Island, the New Territories and the Outlying Islands. Kowloon and The New Territories are on a peninsula of the Chinese mainland, Hong Kong Island is south of Kowloon, the Outlying Islands are the other 234 islands. There's little undeveloped land remaining and high-rise tower blocks dominate.

Climate: Hong Kong has a tropical climate for most of the year, when it's warm and humid. Winter lasts a couple of months and can be surprisingly cold for the latitude. Average temperatures are 28°C (82°F) in summer and 16°C (61°F) in winter.

Health: Hong Kong has fewer health threats than most of the Far East. Malaria occurs occasionally in border regions, and Japanese encephalitis is a low risk in the New Territories between April and October. There are no vaccination requirements for international travellers.

Due to the outbreak of Severe Acute Respiratory Syndrome (SARS), the World Health Organisation (WHO) in June 2003 advised foreigners travelling to Hong Kong to take appropriate precautions, although warnings have since been lifted. Check with your country's foreign office for the latest information.

Hong Kong enjoys a wide range of excellent health facilities, catering for most eventualities, the equal of the best in most western cities. While Hong Kong residents receive subsidised medical treatment (they pay a modest charge), non-residents must pay for all treatment, often up-front. This can be very expensive and it's essential to have extensive private medical insurance. Hong Kong has no reciprocal health agreements.

Language: The official languages are Chinese (Cantonese is the most commonly spoken form) and English.

Religion: Buddhism, Confucianism, Taoism, Christianity and Islam.

Government: Formerly a British Crown Colony, Hong Kong became a Special Administrative Region of China on 1st July 1997, with a three-tier system of representative government. Under this arrangement, Hong Kong is responsible for its own affairs (with the exception of foreign affairs and defence) for 50 years from 1997.

Political Stability: Very good, although there's some tension between Hong Kong's administration and Chinese central government in Beijing.

Economy

Overview: Hong Kong is one of the world's leading trade and financial centres and, despite its size, the world's tenth-largest trader and fourth source of foreign direct investment. The world's largest container port and its busiest air cargo centre are found on the island. In 2002, however, the traditionally strong economy began to show signs of slowing down, mainly due to the poor economic situation throughout the world, competition from China, particularly Shanghai, and in 2003 the effects of the SARS epidemic. GDP growth in 2003 is expected to be around 0.3 per cent, although forecasts are better for 2004. Hong Kong is generally considered to be a good gateway to the more challenging Chinese market.

GDP Per Head (2002): US$23,140.

Growth (2002): 1.9 per cent.

Target Industries: Building and construction, clothing and footwear, creative and media, environmental industries, food and drink, giftware, healthcare, IT and electronics, property services, railways, recreation and leisure goods, security, sports and leisure infrastructure, telecommunications and textiles.

Ranking Among UK's Trade Partners: 10.

Ranking Among US's Trade Partners: Outside top 50.

Employment Market

Overview: There's a strong work ethic and desire to do well in life. Over 80 per cent of the workforce is employed in the service sector. Rising unemployment is a problem.

Unemployment Rate (2002): 7.3 per cent (a considerable increase from 4.9 per cent in 2001).

Work Permits: Work permits are required by all foreign nationals and may be difficult to obtain, as the authorities have a policy of recruiting from the local workforce whenever possible. Alternatively, the employer must show that the employee will contribute substantially to the economy.

Labour Relations: Generally excellent and few days are lost to industrial action.

Employment Conditions: Employment conditions are regulated by the Employment Ordinance law, although there are no restrictions on the number of working hours nor is there a minimum wage. The working week is generally 44 hours, from Mondays to Saturday afternoons, although offices are gradually introducing a five-day week. Employees rarely take more than the statutory minimum 12 days of holiday per year (see **Public Holidays** below), even if their contract allows it.

Finance

Currency: Hong Kong Dollar (HK$), comprising 100 cents. Notes are in denominations of HK$1,000, 500, 100, 50, 20 and 10. Coins are in denominations of HK$10, 5, 2 and 1, and 50, 20 and 10 cents. Foreign currency can easily be exchanged in banks, hotels and bureaux de change. Banks usually offer the most favourable rates. Credit cards are widely accepted, and travellers' cheques can be exchanged in a variety of places. GB£, US$ and Euros are the preferred cheque currencies.

Exchange Rate (2003): US$1 = HK$7.8.

Exchange Controls: None.

Banks: Hong Kong is one of the world's most important financial centres with over 170 banks. The banking system is state-of-the-art and efficient, and foreigners can easily open a bank account.

Cost/Standard Of Living: The standard of living is high. Consumer goods are relatively expensive but food and transport are inexpensive.

Loans: Loans are readily available from local banks.

Interest Rate (2002): 5 per cent.

Taxation

Corporate Tax: 17.5 per cent.

Personal Income Tax: Income tax rates range from 2 to 20 per cent, although most income is taxed at 16 per cent. There are several deductible allowances for individuals and their dependants. Hong Kong has very few double-taxation agreements and you may also find yourself liable for income tax in your home country. You should therefore take expert advice on how to plan your taxation.

Capital Gains Tax: None.

Wealth Tax: None.

Inheritance & Gift Tax: Estate tax is levied on property situated in Hong Kong at 5, 10 or 15 per cent. Property valued at under HK$7.5 million is exempt.

Value Added/Sales/Purchase Tax: None except for hotel accommodation, which is subject to 3 per cent tax.

Social Security & Pensions: There's no social security scheme in Hong Kong, although the government provides many social services and in 2000 introduced the implementation of a privately-managed retirement fund, known as the mandatory provident fund (MPF) system, to which all employees and employers are obliged to contribute 5 per cent of their gross salary, up to a maximum contribution of HK$1,000. Some foreigners may be exempt from payments, although there are strict conditions, such as that their employment in Hong Kong must last for less than a year or they must be a member of a similar scheme in a country outside Hong Kong.

Withholding Taxes: Only royalties are subject to withholding taxes, which are levied at rates from 4.8 to 17.5 per cent, depending on the relationship between payer and payee.

Tax Filing: The tax year in Hong Kong is from 1st April to 31st March. Income tax isn't deducted at source; instead, both companies and individuals pay an estimated amount at the beginning of the tax year and at the end of the tax year receive a bill for the amount due or a refund.

Doing Business

Forming A Company: Setting up a company is generally straightforward and foreigners may choose from a variety of business options for their investment, although the most commonly used by foreign investors are private limited companies and registered branches. Companies are required to register with the Company Register. Hong Kong has a well-educated and skilled workforce with an abundance of labour available at all levels, including senior management. Many people speak English and are computer literate.

Investment: The Hong Kong government welcomes foreign investment and there are no restrictions or trade barriers.

Government Incentives: Incentives are available, although they tend to be limited to funds for innovation and technology. The government will refund up to 75 per cent of the cost of training employees in new technology.

Business Hours: Offices open from 9am to 5pm Mondays to Fridays and from 9am to 12.30pm on Saturdays. Banking hours vary but are generally from 9am to 5pm Mondays to Fridays and some banks open from 9am to 1pm on Saturdays.

Public Holidays: 14 per year as follows:

Day/Date	Holiday
1st January	New Year's Day
Late January or early February	Chinese New Year
5th April	Ching Ming Festival
Late March or early April	Good Friday and Easter Monday
1st May	Labour Day
8th May	Buddha's Birthday
4th June	Tuen Ng (Dragon Boat)
1st July	Hong Kong Special Administrative Region Establishment Day
1st October	National Day; October 4th, Chung Yeung Festival
12th October	Chinese Mid-Autumn Festival
25th and 26th December	Christmas Day and Public Holiday

Note that the dates of some holidays are set according to a lunar calendar and vary from year to year.

Business Etiquette: Business is conducted formally and the exchange of business cards is essential. A handshake is the accepted form of greeting. Hong Kong business people wear dark suits all year. English is the usual business language.

Accommodation

Restrictions On Foreign Ownership: None.

Cost Of Housing: Property in Hong Kong is very expensive, with prices comparable to New York and London. Houses are particularly expensive but apartments are more reasonably priced, although most apartments are smaller than in western countries. Many new apartments have pools, gymnasiums and clubhouse facilities. The price for a 40 to 70m^2 (430 to 750ft^2) apartment (two to three bedrooms) is from HK$4.75 million (US$600,000) in the New Territories to from HK$14 million (US$1.8 million) on Hong Kong island. Luxury apartments are considerably more expensive.

Local Mortgages: Local banks provide mortgages for property purchase and usually lend up to 70 per cent of the purchase price.

Fees: Taxes on property purchase are levied on a sliding scale, with a maximum of 3.75 per cent of the purchase price on properties costing HK$6 million (US$770,000) or over.

Property Taxes: Annual property tax is levied on land and buildings at a standard rate of 16 per cent of the rateable value, less a statutory deduction of 20 per cent for repairs and out-goings.

Building Standards: Very good.

Renting: Almost half of Hong Kong's population lives in rented accommodation, of which the majority live in public housing provided for those in financial need. There's a high demand for quality accommodation, which is in short supply and costs an astronomical HK$30,000 to HK$80,000 (US$3,850 to US$10,250) per month.

Personal Effects: Personal effects can be imported duty-free.

Utilities: The electricity supply (220V) is reliable and charges are reasonable. Mains gas is available for cooking and heating. Tap water is generally safe to drink, although bottled water tastes better.

Communications

Postal Services: The postal system is inexpensive and generally reliable. There are two main post offices, open from 8am to 6pm, Mondays to Fridays, and 8am to 2pm on Saturdays.

Telecommunications: The telephone service is provided by Hong Kong Telecom and is modern and efficient. Full IDD is available, charges are reasonable and local calls are free. Mobile phones are very popular and GSM 900 and 1800 networks provide excellent coverage, even of the outlying islands. Mobiles function in the underground system thanks to transmitters installed in the tunnels. Major operators include New World Mobility (💻 www.nw mobility.com), Orange Dual-Band (💻 www.orangehk.com), Peoples' Telephone Co. (💻 www.peoplesphone.com.hk), SmarTone Mobile Comms (💻 www.smartone.com.hk) and Sunday (💻 www.Sunday.com).

International Dialling Code: 852.

Internet: Hong Kong businesses make wide use of the internet, particularly email, and there's been a huge growth in networking hardware. There are over 120 ISPs in Hong Kong, including ABC Net (💻 www.hkabc.net), HKNet (💻 www.hknet.com) and Hong Kong Internet Service (💻 www.hkis.com).

Transport Infrastructure: Hong Kong's public transport system is one of the world's best and is invariably efficient, inexpensive and quick, although it's currently poorly integrated.

Getting There: Hong Kong is China's major entry point and one of the busiest in Asia. Regular flights connect Hong Kong with many international destinations, and the new airport (opened in June 1998) Chek Lap Kok (CLK) on the north side of Lantau Island has made landing and take-off less 'dramatic' than they used to be (the old airport's runway was flanked by blocks of flats, close enough for passengers to have a worryingly clear view of what people were doing inside their apartments). Hong Kong and Macau are connected by frequent daily jetfoil and fast catamaran services, and there's also a regular helicopter service to Macau. The only land entry to Hong Kong is via China, but land links have improved since the hand-over.

Import/Export Restrictions: Hong Kong is a free port with very few trade restrictions. Import and export licences are required only to protect consumer health and safety or for security reasons.

Miscellaneous

Crime & Legal Restrictions: Very low crime rate. Hong Kong is one of the safest cities in the world.

Education: Places in schools in Hong Kong are in high demand and short supply, so it's vital to apply well in advance. Most schools on the peninsula cater for the local population and the teaching language is usually Chinese, although there are a number of private international schools based on the British curriculum.

English-Language Media: There's a wide choice of English-language programmes, both on TV and radio, and satellite and cable TV are also available. There's no TV licence. There's a selection of English-language daily newspapers, including *Asian Wall Street Journal, Hong Kong Mail, International Herald Tribune* and *South China Morning Post*.

Time Difference: GMT +7.

Weights & Measures: Metric, although imperial and Chinese measures are sometimes used.

Reference

Useful Addresses

British Consulate General, 1 Supreme Court Road, Central, Hong Kong PO Box 528 (☎ 2901-3000, 💻 www.britishconsulate.org.hk).

Hong Kong Consulate, 2300 Connecticut Avenue, NW, Washington DC, US (☎ 202-328 2500, 💻 www.china-embassy.org).

Hong Kong Government Office, 6 Grafton Street, London W1X 3LB, UK (☎ 020-7499 9821, ✉ general@hketolondon.gov.uk).

Immigration Department, Immigration Tower, 7 Gloucester Road, WAN CHAI (☎ 2824-4055, 💻 www.info.gov.hk/immd).

Invest Hong Kong, The Government of the Hong Kong Special Administrative Region, 15/F, One Pacific Place, Queensway, Hong Kong (☎ 3107-1000, 💻 www.investhk.gov.hk). The official government agency for foreign investment. London Office: 6 Grafton Street, London W1S 4EQ (☎ 020-7499 9821). Washington Office: 1520 18th Street, NW, Washington DC, 20036 (☎ 202-331 8947). Publishes the useful *Investment Hong Kong* handbook, available in PDF.

US Consulate, 26 Garden Road, Mid-Levels, Central, Hong Kong (☎ 2523-9011, 🖳 http://hongkong.usconsulate.gov).

Further Reading

Titles prefaced by an asterisk are recommended by the author.

An Insular Possession, Timothy Mo

*Borrowed Time, Borrowed Place, Richard Hughes

Chinese Gods, Johnathan Chamberlain

Doing Business Guide: Hong Kong (PriceWaterhouseCoopers)

Foreign Mud, Maurice Collin

History of Hong Kong, G B Endacott

Kowloon Tong, Paul Theroux

*Hong Kong: Epilogue to an Empire, Jan Morris

Useful Websites

Business HK (🖳 www.business.gov.hk) – A comprehensive website offering information for those arriving and settling in Hong Kong.

Expat Hong Kong (🖳 www.expathongkong.com) – An excellent expatriate website with a wealth of useful information.

First Choice Hong Kong (🖳 www.firstchoicehongkong.gov.hk) – Information for those arriving and settling in Hong Kong.

INDONESIA

General Information

Capital: Jakarta.

Population: 216 million. Indonesia is the fourth most-populated country in the world (after China, India and the US). There are around 365 ethnic and tribal groups in the country, the main ones being Acehnese, Bataks and Minangkabaus on Sumatra, Balinese on Bali, Javanese and Sundanese on Java, Dani on Irian Jaya and Sasaks on Lombok.

Foreign Community: There's quite a large expatriate population in Indonesia, concentrated around Jakarta.

Area: 1,900,000km² (733,647mi²).

Geography: Indonesia is situated between the Indian and Pacific Oceans in South-east Asia, and is the world's largest archipelago, consisting of over 17,000 islands, around 6,000 of them inhabited. It has land frontiers with Malaysia and Brunei on the island of Borneo and with Papua-New Guinea, plus sea 'boundaries' with East Timor, Malaysia, Singapore, Vietnam, the Philippines and Australia. Indonesia is mountainous and susceptible to earthquakes, and has more active volcanoes than any other country. Mangrove swamps line the coast and tropical rainforests are the major feature of the less-populated islands, although many larger islands have been cleared by logging and for cultivation. Three-quarters of the area and population of the country are contained in just five islands: Java (home to half the population), Sumatra, Sulawesi, Kalimantan (Indonesian Borneo) and Irian Jaya.

Climate: Indonesia has a typical tropical monsoon climate, with high temperatures and humidity common throughout the year. It rains at all times of year, but the main wet season is from October to April and the driest part of the year is May to September. Coastal average temperatures vary little during the year and range from 29 to 32°C (84 to 90°F).

Health: Malaria is found year-round in Indonesia, but mainly in rural areas. A combination of chloroquine and proguanil is the standard prophylaxis (preventive treatment), but in higher risk Irian Jaya, mefloquine is usually prescribed because there's chloroquine resistance. Japanese encephalitis is also found in rural areas. A yellow fever vaccination is required for entry into the country for travellers coming from infected areas. Vaccination against dengue fever, giardiasis, hepatitis, Japanese encephalitis, malaria, paratyphoid, rabies and typhoid is recommended.

Levels of health care and sanitation in Indonesia are much lower than in western countries. General medical care is available in most Indonesian cities, but for anything serious or specialised, most expatriates elect to travel abroad for treatment, usually to Singapore or Australia.

Immediate cash payment is invariably required by doctors and hospitals, and **it's therefore vital for foreigners to have extensive medical insurance, including coverage for transportation and medical care abroad if necessary, and emergency repatriation coverage**.

Language: The official language is Bahasa Indonesia, although many local languages and dialects are also spoken (around 580). Bahasa Indonesia is similar to Malay and written in the Roman alphabet. English and Dutch are spoken too, the latter by older people.

Religion: Around 88 per cent of the population is Muslim, with 9 per cent Christian, 2 per cent Hindu (mainly on Bali) and small Buddhist groups. Animist beliefs are still held in remote regions.

Government: Democratic Republic.

Political Stability: Very unstable. Indonesia, once a Dutch colony and occupied by the Japanese during the second world war, gained independence in 1945 and has since had a traumatic political history characterised by military intervention and authoritarian rule. The Asian crisis in 1997 hit Indonesia particularly hard, since when the country has suffered high inflation and public sector debt. Democracy was introduced in 1999, but it's extremely fragile and civil unrest is commonplace in many parts of the country.

In late 2003, foreigners were advised against all non-essential travel to all parts of Indonesia, as there was a high risk of terrorist attacks against westerners throughout the country. Check with the Foreign Office in your home country for the latest information. If you travel to Indonesia you're strongly advised to register with your home country's embassy and to inform your embassy if you're leaving Indonesia for more than ten days, and to notify the embassy when you return.

Economy

Overview: Over the last 30 years Indonesia has experienced rapid economic growth, but the Asian economic crisis in 1997 had a crippling effect on the country, with drastic devaluation of the currency and inflation at over 80 per cent. Civil unrest followed and the President was forced to resign. Indonesia's first democratic elections were held in 1999 and, although there have since been positive changes, the country still faces serious political and social problems. Progress on economic reforms has been slow and the economy has suffered further from the after-effects of the September 2001 attacks in New York. In 2002, however, Indonesia's economy stabilised – both the currency and inflation – and the outlook is better.

GDP Per Head (2002): US$848.

Growth (2002): 3.6 per cent.

Target Industries: Investment opportunities are currently somewhat limited given the current political and security situation: the agribusiness sector, particularly acquaculture, fish, shrimp and duck farming, dairy, pig and poultry management, and second-hand agricultural machinery.

Ranking Among UK's Trade Partners: 33.

Ranking Among US's Trade Partners: 15.

Employment Market

Overview: Women make up over half the workforce. Education standards have dropped considerably since 1997 and many young people leave school early in order to work.

Unemployment Rate (2002): 10.3 per cent. Official unemployment figures are generally thought greatly to underestimate the actual situation and a large percentage of the workforce is underemployed.

Work Permits: Work permits are compulsory for all foreign employees and can be difficult to obtain, as there are strict regulations regarding the employment of foreigners and high unemployment means that priority is given to locals. To obtain a work permit, your sponsor must have permission from the Expatriate Placement Plan, who will authorise the issue of a limited stay visa to the Indonesian consulate or embassy where you make your application. Once you arrive in Indonesia, you must go to the Immigration Office within three to seven days to complete the paperwork. Work permits are issued for one year and are valid only for one person. Spouses must obtain their own work permit if they wish to work. Note that before a work permit is issued, proof of payment of US$1,200 for a year's DPKK fee (see **Social Security** below) is required.

Labour Relations: In recent years, trade unions have grown in strength and strikes have been commonplace, some of which have forced the government to postpone or abandon the introduction of economic reforms.

Employment Conditions: The working week is generally 44 hours, from Sundays to Thursdays or Friday mornings. Labour regulations have undergone major reforms and in 2001 a minimum wage was introduced, which varies according to the region. Indonesia has one of the lowest average wage rates in Asia.

Finance

Currency: Rupiah (Rp). Notes are in denominations of Rp100,000, 50,000, 20,000, 10,000, 5,000, 1,000, 500 and 100. Coins are in denominations of Rp1,000, 500, 100, 50 and 25. Foreign currencies are easy to exchange in major cities and tourist centres but may not be elsewhere. The US$ is the easiest currency to exchange. Credit cards are widely accepted in Jakarta and tourist areas, but elsewhere cash is required. Travellers' cheques can be exchanged at banks and larger hotels, and US$ and GB£ cheques are favoured.

Exchange Rate (2003): US$1 = Rp8,500.

Exchange Controls: None.

Banks: Since the Asian crisis in 1997 and the subsequent dramatic devaluation of the rupiah, Indonesian banks have been undergoing substantial restructuring. The Indonesian Bank Restructuring Agency (IBRA) is conducting a process of re-capitalisation and merger. **Until this process is completed, you're advised not to deposit any assets in Indonesia and if possible, bank abroad or with a local branch of a reputable foreign bank.** Note that credit card fraud is rife and you should not lose sight of your card during transactions.

Cost/Standard Of Living: Very low. Economic predictions are cautious about a recovery in the Indonesian economy, although the situation improved in 2002, with higher growth than many countries. Imported goods are expensive.

Loans: Loans are available from Indonesian and foreign banks, although they're uncommon and until the banking system reaches international standards of accounting and bank disclosure, you're advised not to take out loans with Indonesian banks. Interest rates are also considerably higher than in many other countries.

Interest Rate (2002): 18 per cent.

Taxation

Corporate Tax: Up to 30 per cent.

Personal Income Tax: Income tax is generally deducted at source (PAYE) and if you have only one source of income you aren't obliged to file a tax return.

Rates range from 10 to 35 per cent and the tax exemption is Rp200 million (US$2,350).

Capital Gains Tax: Capital gains are taxed at the same rates as income tax.

Wealth Tax: None.

Inheritance & Gift Tax: None.

Value Added/Sales/Purchase Tax: The standard rate of VAT is 10 per cent. Some 'luxury' items are taxed at up to 35 per cent.

Social Security & Pensions: Contributions to the workers' accident insurance and provident fund are the only form of social security in Indonesia, and expatriate workers aren't obliged to contribute. Employers must contribute 9 per cent of earnings for single employees and 12 per cent for married employees. Note that companies employing foreigners are charged US$100 per month per expatriate employee to offset the costs of training Indonesian nationals through the Skill and Development Fund (DPKK).

Withholding Taxes: Interest is subject to 20 per cent withholding tax and interest on bonds on Indonesian stock exchanges to 15 per cent.

Tax Filing: The Indonesian tax year is the calendar year and the majority of expatriates must file annual income tax returns. Individual taxpayers are required to pay tax by March 25th. In addition to the annual filing requirement, many expatriates may be required to file monthly tax returns and pay monthly tax instalments. Individual taxpayers who are required to file monthly must do so by the 20th of the following month. Tax instalments must be paid by the 15th of the following month.

Doing Business

Forming A Company: There are several options open to foreign investors. The first is to set up a representative office, although these cannot carry out direct business activities. They're used for promotion and market research. You can also set up as an agent or distributor. A joint venture company (*Penanaman Modal Asing/PMA*) is the corporate entity permitted under the foreign investment law. A *PMA* takes the form of a limited liability company (*Perseroan Terbatas/PT*) having the venture partners as shareholders.

Indonesia has an abundance of semi-skilled and unskilled labour, but skilled labour and management personnel are in short supply. Note that foreign investors must contribute to the training and development of Indonesian nationals, with a view to replacing expatriate workers with Indonesians.

Investment: Despite its economic and political difficulties, Indonesia has maintained a relatively open foreign investment policy. In recent years, political instability and corruption have forced foreign investors out of Indonesia, although in 2002 the outlook improved and current levels of investment are being maintained, particularly as the government's policy is to encourage private sector growth and foreign investment. Official approval is always required, but for investment of under US$100 million approval need only be sought from the Capital Investment Coordinating Board (BKPM), which can be done via a limited number of Indonesian representatives abroad. Larger investments need approval from the President of Indonesia. Some business sectors, listed on the 'Negative Investment List', are closed to all private or foreign investment. Check with your country's embassy in Indonesia for the latest information.

Government Incentives: Numerous incentives are available, including tax holidays and exemption from customs duties.

Business Hours: Office and business hours are from 8am to 5pm Sundays to Thursdays and from 8am to noon on Fridays. Local banks open from 8 to 11am and from 2 to 3pm Mondays to Fridays. Foreign banks open from 8.30am to 3.30pm Mondays to Fridays.

Public Holidays: Around 20 per year as follows:

Day/Date	Holiday
1st January	New Year's Day
February	Chinese New Year – around a week
February	Eid al-Adha (Feast of the Sacrifice)
Late February or March	Muharram (Islamic New Year)
March or April	Nyepi (Hindu New Year)
March or April	Good Friday
May	Mouloud (Prophet's Birthday)
May	Waisak (Buddha's Birthday)
May	Ascension
August 17th	Indonesian Independence Day
September	Lailat al-Miraj (Ascension of the Prophet)
Three or four days in October or November	Eid al-Fitr, (End of Ramadan) – three or four days
25th December	Christmas Day

Most holiday dates vary, as they're determined by local sightings of various phases of the moon.

Business Etiquette: Business dealings are usually conducted through an agent and tend to be slow. Personal relationships are very important in the country and most Indonesians are friendly. Shaking hands is the accepted form of greeting and business cards are exchanged after introductions. English is spoken in most business circles and prices are generally quoted in US dollars. Men should wear suits and women should dress modestly, with long-sleeved shirts and long skirts or trousers.

Accommodation

Restrictions On Foreign Ownership: Except in the Batam area, where there are no restrictions, foreigners are currently permitted to buy apartments, although only for residence (not investment purposes) and foreigners cannot own land, meaning that the purchase of a house is impossible. The subject of foreign property ownership is unclear and, although there are several loopholes, it's generally recommended not to buy property in Indonesia unless you obtain expert legal advice and are 100 per cent certain that the property will be legally yours.

Cost Of Housing: A typical Indonesian house with two or three bedrooms costs between Rp650 million and Rp1.2 billion (US$75,000 to US$100,000), but they can be found for as little as Rp200 million (US$25,000) in outlying rural regions. Some of Indonesia's most sought-after and expensive property is on the holiday island of Bali, where a two-bedroom house costs around Rp2 billion (US$175,000) and a three-bedroom house with a swimming pool around Rp15 billion (US$1.35 million).

Building Standards: Variable.

Renting: Jakarta has experienced a building boom in recent years and there's a vast range of apartment accommodation available, particularly in large complexes with facilities and services designed specifically for expatriates. Apartments are usually large and often include staff quarters. You can rent a serviced or unserviced, furnished or unfurnished apartment. Rent for the entire period of a rental contract (a minimum of a year) must usually be paid in advance, although after the recent economic crisis concessions are increasingly made and prices have dropped. Two-bedroom apartments cost from Rp8.5 million to Rp25.25 million (US$1,000 to US$3,000) per month and three-bedroom apartments from Rp12.75 million to Rp42.5 million (US$1,500 to US$5,000) depending on the location and facilities.

Personal Effects: Personal and household effects can be imported duty-free, provided they've been in your possession for at least 12 months and you have both a residence and a work permit. You must provide an inventory of goods, which must be imported in a maximum of two consignments.

Utilities: The electricity supply is generally 220V, although in some rural areas it's 110V. The service is reasonably reliable, although violent storms sometimes interrupt supplies. There's no mains gas in Indonesia, although bottled gas is available. Tap water isn't safe to drink but bottled water is readily available.

Communications

Postal Services: The postal service is efficient and the delivery of domestic post is fast and secure, particularly by the express service, Pos KILAT. Post to the outer islands can take a considerable time to arrive. Airmail to Western Europe takes around ten days.

Telecommunications: Telecommunications are reliable and reasonably modern, with IDD available. Calls are expensive, particularly when made from hotels. State-operated phone booths (WARTEL) are found throughout Indonesia and you pay when you finish your call. Mobile telephones are popular and GSM 900 and 1800 networks operate, although coverage is usually restricted to major urban areas. Major operators include Excelcomindo (💻 www.excelcom.co.id), Lippo Telecom (💻 www.lippotel.com) and Telkomsel (💻 www.telkomsel.com).

International Dialling Code: 62.

Internet: The internet is popular and many companies are online, particularly those in rural areas, where physical access to the company is difficult. Internet service providers include Indobiz (💻 www.indobiz.com) and Indosat (💻 www.indosat.net.id).

Transport Infrastructure: The best way to travel long distances within Indonesia is by air and the domestic flight service is generally good. Islands are also linked by ferries and government-owned ships. The rest of the public transport system is poor and the railway network is limited to Java and some parts of Sumatra. Buses are slow, unreliable and overcrowded. Taxis are the best way to travel around cities. In Jakarta, metered air-conditioned taxis wait at major hotels and they can be hired on an hourly basis (a useful service for long journeys). Note that you should only hire official taxis, preferably booked by phone. Road conditions are generally good on the main islands, particularly Java, although driving standards are poor and traffic is very congested. Traffic drives on the left. **You should avoid travelling alone at night and for longer journeys you should notify friends of your itinerary. Theft from cars is common on motorways.**

Getting There: Indonesia has several international airports, including Jakarta, Bali and Medan, with flights from many international destinations. The only open land crossing is at Entikong, between Kalimantan and Sarawak. There are sea connections on high-speed ferries, most of them between Malaysia and Sumatra but also one between Manado on northern Sulawesi and Davao in the Philippines.

Import/Export Restrictions: There are numerous restrictions regarding imports for foreign companies and for Indonesian companies with foreign shareholders; domestic companies can import goods only if they have an import licence. Customs duties, VAT and possibly income tax are payable on imports. Certain goods are also restricted. Regulations and classification are subject to change and you should contact the Indonesian Ministry of Trade (see **Useful Addresses** below) or an Indonesian embassy for up-to-date information.

Miscellaneous

Crime & Legal Restrictions: Civil unrest and separatist tensions are currently a serious problem in Indonesia and foreigners are advised to take all possible precautions, including avoiding night travel, crowds and demonstrations, and being extremely vigilant with belongings (particularly credit cards).

There was a terrorist bomb attack on a nightclub in Bali in 2002 and violent crime is on the increase. Kidnappings of foreigners also occur. Nowhere in the country is safe from separatist and sectarian unrest. You're recommended to register with your local embassy as soon as you arrive in Indonesia and to advise it of your movements.

Education: The standard of education in Indonesian state schools isn't particularly high and lessons are in the Indonesian language, so most expatriate families send their children to international schools, of which there are many, particularly in Jakarta. Note, however, that many schools cater only for children up to junior school age.

English-Language Media: TV broadcasts are generally in Indonesian, although there's a daily news bulletin in English. Satellite TV is available throughout the country and is popular. Cable TV is limited to some areas of Jakarta. Both systems are expensive to install, although most expatriate apartment blocks have cable or satellite TV installed. There's a monthly TV tax, which is a minimal amount and depends on the size and number of TVs owned. The leading English-language newspapers are the *Bali Post*, *Indonesian Observer*, *Jakarta Post* and *The Indonesia Times*.

Time Difference: GMT +6.

Weights & Measures: Metric.

Reference

Useful Addresses

British Chamber of Commerce, World Trade Centre, 8th Floor, Jl Jend Sudirman Kav. 31, Jakarta 12920 (☎ 21-522 9453, 💻 www.britcham.or.id).

British Embassy, 80 Jalan Imam Bonjoi, Jakarta 10310 (☎ 21-390 7484, 💻 www.britain.in.indonesia.or.id).

Department of Foreign Affairs (💻 www.deplu.go.id). Provides useful information on visas and permits.

Indonesian Chamber of Commerce & Industry (KADIN), Menara Kadin, 29th Floor, JI H R Rasuna Said X-5, Kac 2-3, Jakarta (☎ 21-527 4486, 💻 www.kadin.net.id).

Indonesian Embassy, 2020 Massachusetts Avenue, NW, Washington DC 20036, US (☎ 202-775 5200, 💻 www.embassyofindonesia.org).

Indonesian Embassy, 38 Grosvenor Square, London W1X 9AD, UK (☎ 020-7499 7661, 💻 www.indonesianembassy.org.uk).

Indonesian Ministry of Trade, J1 Gatot Subroto Kav. 52-53, Jakarta 12950 (☎ 21-525 5509, 💻 www.dprin.go.id).

Jakarta Chamber of Commerce & Industry, Majapahit Permai Blok B 21-22-23, Majapahit No 18-20-22, Jakarta 10160, PO Box 3077 Jkt (☎ 21-380 8089, ✉ kadinjkt@indosat.net.id).

Jakarta Chamber of Commerce & Industry, Majapahit Permai Blok B 21-22-23, Majapahit No 18-20-22, Jakarta 10160, PO Box 3077 Jkt (☎ 21-380 8089, ✉ kadinjkt@indosat.net.id).

US Embassy, JL Merdeka Selatan 4-5, Jakarta 10110 (☎ 21-344 2211, 💻 www. usembassyjakarta.org).

Further Reading

Titles prefaced by an asterisk are recommended by the author.

An Empire of the East, Norman Lewis

A History of Modern Indonesia, M C Ricklefs

Doing Business Guide: Indonesia (PriceWaterhouseCoopers)

Drums of Tonki, Helen and Frank Schreider

Historical Sights of Jakarta, Adolf Heuken

Jakarta: A History, Susan Abeyasekere

The Year of Living Dangerously, C J Koch

Twilight in Jakarta, Mochtar Lubis

Useful Websites

Bali Paradise (💻 www.bali-paradise.com) – Contains information about everything from airlines to property and medical facilities.

Expat (💻 www.expat.or.id/info/info.html) – A comprehensive website, covering most aspects of expatriate life in Indonesia.

Promoting Bali (💻 www.promotingbali.com) – A comprehensive guide to all aspects of living and working on the island of Bali.

The Jakarta Post (💻 www.thejakartapost.com) – The newspaper's online edition.

JAPAN

General Information

Capital: Tokyo.

Population: 127 million. Japan is one of the most densely populated countries in the world. The vast majority of the population is Japanese, with some Koreans and indigenous Ainu and Okinawans.

Foreign Community: There are over 1.5 million foreigners in Japan, mostly from other Asian countries, although there's also a reasonably large western community.

Area: 378,000km² (145,957mi²).

Geography: The Japanese archipelago is situated 160km (100mi) off the east coast of Asia and consists of four main islands (Hokkaido, Honshu, Shikoku and Kyushu) and over 4,000 much smaller islands. Much of the terrain is mountainous (around 70 per cent), including many volcanic cones, and there are frequent earthquakes. In central Japan there are large areas of forest, while small cultivated plains dominate the coast.

Climate: Japan can be divided into two broad climatic regions: the north has long, cold and wet winters that last from October to April, when the mountains are usually snow-capped, and hot summers; the south is milder in winter, but summers are very hot and wet, and typhoons can occur in September and October. Average temperatures in Tokyo are 1°C (30°F) in January and 35°C (95°F) in July.

Health: Health risks in Japan are among the region's lowest. Japanese encephalitis is a low risk in rural areas between April and October, and eating the much-loved raw fish carries the risk of paragonamiasis. Otherwise, the main health risk is from pollution in Japan's large cities and industrial areas. There are no vaccination requirements for international travellers.

Medical care and facilities in Japan are excellent. English-speaking doctors, however, are difficult to find in Japan and their services are invariably expensive.

Everybody is required by law to contribute to a health insurance policy, meaning that subsidised (usually 70 per cent) medical treatment is available.

Language: The official language is Japanese. English is spoken by some people in the main cities.

Religion: Japan is one of the world's most secular countries, although many Japanese pay at least lip service to the philosophies of Buddhism and Shintoism. There's also a Christian minority, while on Okinawa some people believe in Niraikanai, the realm of the dead beyond the sea.

Government: Constitutional monarchy with bicameral legislature.

Political Stability: Unstable. Japan has a system of proportional representation and many political parties, leading to fragile political coalitions and frequent general elections – only on one occasion has a coalition served the full four-year electoral term. This political fragility, however, hardly affects daily life or the country's economy.

Economy

Overview: Japan is the world's second-largest economy and, despite the effects of the Asian economic crisis in 1997, it managed to register economic growth in 2000, although growth has since been very slow and 2002 registered a negative figure. The financial sector is currently very unstable, with problems of debt and deflation, and in desperate need of reform. Radical financial reforms, including the closure of insolvent banks, were made in 2003, but the economic climate isn't expected to improve substantially. Many of Japan's major manufacturers are relocating to China, where there are lower costs and a rapidly expanding market. However, many Western investment experts consider that there has never been a better time to invest in Japan since market entry conditions are excellent. Property prices have fallen by up to 75 per cent, and in some cities, including Tokyo and Osaka, are at mid-1980s levels, and there's a good support structure for investors from western countries already in the country.

GDP Per Head (2002): US$30,990.

Growth (2002): -1 per cent.

Target Industries: Aerospace, automotive, biotechnology, building and construction, communications, creative and media, education, fashion and footwear, fire, police and security, food and drink, giftware, healthcare, household goods, IT and electronics, leisure and tourism, oil and gas, power and textiles.

Ranking Among UK's Trade Partners: 7.

Ranking Among US's Trade Partners: 2.

Employment Market

Overview: The original Oriental Tiger has lost its bite of late and rising unemployment is making it increasingly difficult for foreigners to find work.

Unemployment Rate (2002): 5.4 per cent.

Work Permits: All foreign nationals require a work permit, which is issued only if you have a firm offer of work or a contract from a Japanese employer/sponsor, who must apply on your behalf. Once the Ministry of Justice has issued a Certificate of Eligibility, this is sent to the Japanese consulate or embassy where you make your application for a work visa. Note that you can only obtain a work visa from outside the country, even if you're in Japan when an offer of employment is made.

Labour Relations: Generally good. The Japanese are a disciplined workforce and tend to be loyal to their employer. Unions play an important role in the annual collective wage bargaining, but only 21.5 per cent of Japanese workers are union members. In firms with less than 100 employees, a mere 1.4 per cent are members.

Employment Conditions: The Japanese work long hours with few holidays. The working week is often 50 hours and employees rarely take more than nine days' annual holiday, whatever their entitlement. To obtain a job, a good working knowledge of Japanese or at least the willingness to learn is essential.

Finance

Currency: Japanese Yen (¥). Notes are in denominations of ¥10,000, 5,000, 2,000 and 1,000. Coins are in denominations of ¥500, 100, 50, 10, 5 and 1. Japan still has a strong cash culture. This and the low crime rate mean that people commonly carry large amounts of cash. Credit cards are becoming more popular, but have been slow to catch on. Foreign currency must be exchanged by authorised banks or money changers. Travellers' cheques can be exchanged at major banks, large hotels and some duty-free shops. Yen and US$ cheques attract the lowest commission charges.

Exchange Rate (2003): US$1 = ¥110.

Exchange Controls: None.

Banks: The Japanese banking system is one of the most modern and efficient in the world, although it's currently in the process of restructuring after the Asian crisis in 1997 and is in chronic need of reform, which began in 2003. Numerous commercial banks and several foreign banks operate in the country, but note that some foreign banks aren't agents of the Bank of Japan and therefore cannot be used for paying taxes or making certain other payments. Foreigners can open an account with a Japanese bank, but the paperwork can take time and you should know in advance exactly which documents the bank will require from you. You need a Alien Registration Card.

Cost/Standard Of Living: The standard of living is very high in Japan, around double the EU average, and Tokyo is usually ranked as the world's most expensive city. You should make sure that your salary is sufficient to live on.

Loans: Loans are available but Japanese banks are unlikely to provide a loan until you've established a credit record with them. There are numerous venture capital companies operating in the country.

Interest Rate (2002): 0.06 per cent.

Taxation

The Japanese tax system is very complicated and you should obtain expert advice on all aspects of taxation.

Corporate Tax: There are three levels of corporate income tax: national corporate tax with rates ranging from 22 to 30 per cent, depending on turnover; enterprise tax ranging from 5 to 10.08 per cent, depending on capital and location (note that enterprise tax is deductible from taxable income when paid); and local corporate tax ranging from 4.55 to 6.21 per cent, depending on turnover. There's a further levy of between ¥70,000 and ¥3.8 million (US$635 and US$34,550), depending on capitalisation and number of employees.

Personal Income Tax: The Japanese income tax system is complicated and rates are high. You're recommended to obtain expert advice regarding tax planning in order to ease your tax burden. There are three groups of taxpayer, classified according to residential status. Rates range from 10 to 50 per cent and an additional local income tax is levied at between 5 and 10 per cent. Expatriate employees are taxed only on income arising in or remitted to Japan. There are a number of permitted deductions and tax allowances.

Capital Gains Tax: CGT is levied at a flat rate of 15 per cent after a deduction of ¥500,000 (US$4,550) and residents are subject to a further 5 per cent local CGT. Property is subject to long or short-term capital gains, depending on how long it has been owned.

Wealth Tax: None.

Inheritance & Gift Tax: Inheritance tax is levied at rates ranging from 10 to 70 per cent, with a statutory basic deduction of ¥50 million (US$455,000), plus other reductions for spouses and dependants aged under 20. Gift tax is levied at rates ranging from 10 to 70 per cent, after an annual deduction of ¥600,000 (US$5,450).

Value Added/Sales/Purchase Tax: A 5 per cent purchase tax is levied on most goods and services except for the hotel and catering industries, where a 7 per cent consumption tax is levied.

Social Security & Pensions: All residents of Japan must contribute to a Japanese insurance programme. The two main types are health insurance, referred to as 'social insurance' (Kenko-Hoken), and national health insurance (Kokumin-Kenko-Hoken). Generally, social insurance is for company employees and national health insurance is for students and the self-employed. Premiums are based on taxable income, the actual costs being calculated using your previous year's tax filing. During the first year, you pay the minimum contribution.

Withholding Taxes: Interest and dividends are subject to 20 per cent withholding tax, unless exempted by double-taxation treaties.

Tax Filing: Company filing requirements are extremely complex and you should consult an expert. Individuals are required to file tax returns unless their income is below ¥200,000 (US$1,820) per year. The tax year is the calendar year and returns must be filed by 15th March.

Doing Business

Forming A Company: Westerners should bear in mind that doing business in Japan may be quite unlike what they're used to and setting up a business can be costly and time-consuming, although the rewards can be substantial. The main company structures are a domestic corporation (either limited liability (YK) or joint-stock (KK), and branch or liaison offices. Limited liability companies must have between 1 and 50 investors and a minimum capital of ¥3 million (US$27,270).

The Japanese workforce is highly skilled and well-educated. Young people are usually well-qualified, with fluency in foreign languages, and are increasingly seeking employment with foreign companies. It's no longer difficult to find skilled staff at middle management levels, as many domestic companies have been restructured and employees can now transfer benefits such as pension plans.

Employing an expert in accountancy and Japanese paperwork to assist you in running a company is essential if you don't have a strong command of Japanese.

Investment: Japan welcomes foreign investment and has now eliminated most of the formal restrictions governing its FDI regime. Government approval is no longer required for most foreign investment except in certain restricted sectors, including aerospace, agriculture, electricity/gas/water utilities, forestry, petroleum and telecommunications. Approval in these sectors depends on how the Japanese government considers the investment would effect the economy and national interests.

Government Incentives: There are a number of central government incentive schemes, particularly for information and technology-based companies. They're usually property-related and take the form of long-term low interest loans and local land tax subsidies. Some regions provide subsidies of up 50 per cent or a maximum of ¥3 million (US$27,250) to cover the cost of investigation into setting up an enterprise. Further information about incentives can be obtained from the local government office in your planned area of investment. Local governments offer a range of incentives, including direct subsidies and assistance in paying for worker training and even worker salaries. Note, however, that by international standards, the incentives are modest.

Business Hours: Businesses and offices generally open from 9am to 5pm Mondays to Fridays. A few open on Saturday mornings. Banks open from 9am to 3pm Mondays to Fridays.

Public Holidays: 17 days per year as follows:

Day/Date	Holiday
1st January	New Year's Day
2nd and 3rd January	Bank Holidays
Mid-January	Coming of Age Day
11th February	National Foundation Day
20th or 21st March	Vernal Equinox
29th April	Greenery Day
3rd May	Constitution Memorial Day
5th May	Children's Day
Late July	Maritime Day
Mid-to-late September	Respect for the Aged Day
23rd September	Autumnal Equinox
Mid-October	Health and Sports Day
3rd November	Culture Day
23rd November	Labour Thanksgiving Day
23rd December	Birthday of the Emperor
31st December	Bank Holiday

Business Etiquette: At formal introductions, the exchange of business cards is *de rigueur*. The correct way to do this is to pass the card to the other person with both hands, with the writing facing him. Receive his card with both hands and look at it before putting it in a shirt or jacket pocket. Avoid putting it in a trouser pocket and sitting on it.

The Japanese are very punctual and you should be likewise. Never be late for appointments and be sure to start work at the official hour. At the end of the working day, white collar workers are expected not to leave the office before their boss, so don't expect to be able to leave at the official end of business.

A study of Japanese business etiquette is recommended before arrival in the country and an understanding of Japanese culture will have positive effects on your business. The way personal and business relationships are established and maintained is very different to that in the western world.

Accommodation

Restrictions On Foreign Ownership: None.

Cost Of Housing: Property (real estate) is very expensive in Japan, where a two-bedroom apartment costs from ¥195 million (US$1.75 million) and a small house from ¥230 million (US$2.1 million), although property prices have been falling over the last 12 years, a trend that's expected to continue in the near future.

Local Mortgages: Local mortgages are theoretically available for foreigners, but in practice are exceptionally difficult to obtain.

Fees: Fees total around 9 per cent of the purchase price and include a 4 per cent property acquisition tax and 5 per cent of the assessed value for registration of ownership. Note that this figure doesn't include legal fees.

Property Taxes: Property taxes are usually included in income tax payments and range from 5 to 12 per cent, depending on the locality and the amenities provided. The Tokyo district levies the highest rates.

Building Standards: Variable but generally good.

Renting: Rented accommodation can be difficult to find and properties are often much smaller than in the west. Rents are high and when you sign the contract you must pay usually pay at least two months' rent as a deposit and non-refundable 'key-money'. Rents are from ¥300,000 (US$2,725) for a (very) small one-bedroom apartment and from ¥500,000 (US$4,550) for a small two-bedroom apartment.

Personal Effects: If your stay in Japan will be longer than a year, you may import your personal effects duty-free. You may also import a car, but must prove that it's at least a year old.

Utilities: The electricity supply is reliable and is 100V and 50Hz in eastern Japan and 100V 60Hz in the west of the country. Mains gas is available for cooking and heating in most of the country. Tap water is safe to drink, although many Japanese prefer bottled water.

Communications

Postal Services: The postal service is generally very good and reasonably fast. To avoid confusion over Japanese characters, it's recommended to have a post box number for post delivery. The Central Post Office and International Post Office in Tokyo have some English-speaking staff. Post office hours are 9am to 5pm, Mondays to Fridays. The Central Post Office and International Post Office are open until 7pm on weekdays, and also on Saturdays from 9am to 5pm. Airmail to Europe and the US takes between four and seven days.

Telecommunications: Telecommunications are excellent and there's a full IDD service. The telephone system is operated by three main companies, KDDI, IDC and ITJ, all of which offer competitive prices. Japan has the highest number of mobile phones in the world, but note that GSM telephones cannot be used. **The Japanese mobile network uses PDC (Personal Digital Cellular system), which is incompatible with other services.** Handsets are easy to hire in Japan, for example from Japan Handy Phone (🖥 www.japanphone.com) and Rentafone Japan (🖥 www.rentafonejapan.com).

International Dialling Code: 81.

Internet: The internet is extremely popular in Japan and the country is currently registering one of the world's fastest growth rates in usage. Charges are competitive and the government has invested heavily in internet technology. Major internet service providers include ASCII (🖥 www.ascii.co.jp).

Transport Infrastructure: Japan's communications are excellent and its public transport system is one of the world's best. The domestic flight network is comprehensive and operated by three airlines offering competitive prices. Other public transport is efficient and generally fast, especially trains, although it can be very crowded, particularly at peak times. Road conditions are excellent and Japan has a very low accident rate. Traffic congestion, however, is chronic, particularly in the cities. Japanese and Korean cars are reasonably priced, but others are expensive.

Getting There: Japan is easily reached by air, with frequent flights from most worldwide destinations to its main international airports, Narita for Tokyo and Kansai for Kyoto. There are also a number of ferry services connecting Japan with China, Korea, Russia and Taiwan.

Import/Export Restrictions: Very few and generally there are no special qualifications or licensing requirements. Quota restrictions may be applied on certain products, particularly foodstuffs. Japan has no free-trade zones.

Miscellaneous

Crime & Legal Restrictions: Japan has one of the lowest crime rates in the world and is a very safe place to live.

Education: Many expatriate families send their children to a boarding school in their home country, because, although there are schools in Japan catering for English-speaking pupils, they usually follow a Japanese rather than an American or British curriculum. There are international schools, but fees are high.

English-Language Media: Cable and satellite TV are readily available and are already installed in many rental apartments. Note also that most new TVs have a special bilingual function, allowing you to select English-language audio for certain programmes. Tokyo's English-language newspapers include *The Asahi Shimbun*, *The Daily Yomiuri*, *The Japan Times* and *The Mainichi Daily News*.

Time Difference: GMT +8.

Weights & Measures: Metric.

Reference

Useful Addresses

British Chamber of Commerce, Kenkyusha Eigo Centre Building (3rd Floor), 2 Kagurazaka 1 Chome, Shinjuku-Ku, Tokyo 162-0825, Japan (☎ 3267 1901, 🖳 www.uknow.or.jp).

British Embassy, 1 Ichiban-cho Chiyoda-ku, Tokyo 102-8381 (☎ 03-5211 1100, 🖳 www.uknow.or.jp).

Japan External Trade Organisation (JETRO), Leconfield House, Curzon Street,

Japanese Embassy, 101-104 Piccadilly, London W1V 9FN, UK (☎ 020-7465 6500, 🖳 www.embjapan.org.uk).

Japanese Embassy, 2520 Massachusetts Avenue, NW, Washington DC 20008, US (☎ 202-238 6700, 🖳 www.embajapan.org).

Japan External Trade Organisation (JETRO), Leconfield House, Curzon Street, London W1Y 8LQ, UK (☎ 020-7470 4700, 🖳 www.jetro.go.jp). JETRO publishes many useful guides to different aspects of doing business in Japan.

US Embassy, 1-10-5 Akasaka Minato-ku, Tokyo 107-8420 (☎ 03-3224 5000, 🖳 http://tokyo.usembassy.gov).

Further Reading

Titles prefaced by an asterisk are recommended by the author.

Appreciations of Japanese Culture, Donal Keane

Doing Business Guide: Japan (PriceWaterhouseCoopers)

Doing Business in Japan (Ernst & Young Publications)

Exploring Kyoto, Judith Clancy

In the Realm of the Dying Emperor, Norma Field

Inside Japan, Peter Tasker

Kyoto-A Cultural Guide to Japan's Ancient Imperial City, John and Phyllis Martin

Japan: A Short Cultural History, George B Sansom

Japanese Religion: A Cultural Perspective, Robert S Elwood and Richard Pilgrim

Lost Japan, Alex Kerr

The Outnation - A Search for the Soul of Japan, Jonathan Rauch

The Roads to Sata, Alan Booth

Tokyo for Free, Susan Pompian

Tokyo Nightlife Guide, (Tokyo Journal)

You Gotta Have Wa, Robert Whiting

Zen and Japanese Culture, Daisetzu T Suzuki

Useful Websites

Action Japan (🖥 www.actionjapan.org.uk) – Offers a wealth of export information, provided by Tradepartners UK.

EU-Japan Centre (🖥 www.eujapan.com) – A joint venture funded by the EU and the Ministry of International Trade and Industry of Japan, providing details of free training courses on various aspects of Japanese business.

Gaijin Pot (🖥 www.gaijinpot.com) – A comprehensive website for expatriates, including job advertisements.

International Tourist Centre of Japan (🖥 www.itcj.or.jp) – A useful guide to accommodation and travel within Japan.

Japan Guide (🖥 www.japan-guide.com) – A general guide to living in Japan, a website which claims over 400,000 visitors per month. It covers everything from accommodation to employment and etiquette, plus useful links to various services.

KOREA

General Information

Capital: Seoul.

Population: 48.8 million.

Foreign Community: There's a large expatriate community in Korea, particularly in the capital, comprising mainly US nationals.

Area: 99,000km^2 (38,279mi^2).

Geography: The Korean peninsula borders China and the Soviet Union to the north, the Yellow Sea to the west, the Korean Straits to the south and the Sea of Japan to the east. South Korea occupies the southern half of the peninsula and is separated from the Democratic People's Republic of Korea by a 4km/2.5mi-wide Demilitarised Zone (DMZ), which runs roughly along the 38th parallel. Around two-thirds of the terrain is mountainous and rugged, especially in the east, and the principal lowland areas are located in the west. Over 70 per cent of the population lives in cities.

Climate: There are four distinct seasons, of which spring and autumn are the most pleasant. Summer is hot and humid with July and August the hottest and wettest months, and temperatures up to 32°C (90°F). Winter is cold with moderate snowfall and an average temperature of 0°C (32°F).

Health: Like Japan, Korea is a relatively safe destination from a health point of view. There's a risk of malaria (vivax) in some northern regions, but because most of the affected zone is militarised the risk to visitors is negligible. Japanese encephalitis is sometimes a risk in rural areas between July and October. Long-stay visitors to Korea must take an HIV test. There are no vaccination requirements for international travellers, but it's recommended to have vaccinations for hepatitis, tetanus, polio, cholera, malaria and typhoid, particularly if you plan to visit rural areas.

Korean medical facilities are reasonable but inferior to those in most western countries. People who've been resident in the country for at least a year and who have a job that's registered with the Korean Labour Union have access to state-subsidised (around 80 per cent) medical facilities (otherwise, you need private medical cover). You might have trouble finding doctors who speak fluent English in Korea and are recommended to take a Korean-speaker with you.

Language: The official language is Korean. English is widely spoken.

Religion: Mahayana Buddhism, with Christian, Confucian and Shamanistic minorities.

Government: Democratic Republic.

Political Stability: Following 25 years of authoritarian and military rule, a new constitution and democracy were introduced in October 1987. Kim Dae-Jung won the presidential election in 1997 and has since had to deal with the economic crisis that affected Korea at the start of his term. He also put in place a 'Sunshine' policy towards North Korea, his goal being to establish communications with the North and its President on the issue of reunification. The result of this policy saw the historic meeting of the two leaders on 15th June 2000 in Pyongyang, North Korea. However, for the time being, the north and south remain divided. Foreigners staying in the country for longer than two weeks are advised to register with their embassy.

Economy

Overview: Korea's economy previously concentrated mainly on the export market and growth was strong until the Asian crisis of 1997 when the weakness of the domestic economy became apparent. The government was quick to react and introduced major reforms designed to strengthen the economy. As a result, Korea has emerged as one of the strongest and most resilient countries in the area. The economy received a welcome boost from the 2002 World Cup and economic growth has been stable over the last few years, with consistent business investment. The domestic consumer market is now particularly strong and the number of shopping facilities (including mail-order) has grown spectacularly.

GDP Per Head (2002): US$10,880.

Growth (2002): 5.6 per cent.

Target Industries: Aerospace, automotive, business services, chemicals, clothing, creative and media, education and training, environment, financial services, IT and electronics, and marine.

Employment Market

Overview: Korea is in the process of introducing a five-day week, which is currently causing numerous problems such as labour shortages in small and medium companies, and difficulties over wage negotiation.

Unemployment Rate (2002): 3 per cent (note that this figure hides the fact that unemployment among people aged 15 to 29 is at least double the average rate).

Work Permits: All foreign nationals require a work permit, which must be applied for from outside Korea, even if you're offered a job while visiting. The process is long and complicated and requires a lot of paperwork, which includes a firm offer of employment from a Korean 'sponsor'. All paperwork must be signed by representatives from various government agencies in Seoul.

Labour Relations: Reasonable, although the introduction of the five-day week is causing a certain amount of friction between management and workforce, particularly with wage negotiations. Strikes are now relatively common.

Employment Conditions: Employment conditions are regulated by the Labour Standards Act, and major issues such as hours, overtime and wages are agreed by collective bargaining. The working week is 40 hours (reduced from 45 in 2003) and male employees are entitled to 22 days' annual holiday and females 32 days. Note that under Korean Civil Law, an offer of employment, once made, cannot be withdrawn.

Ranking Among UK's Trade Partners: 19.

Ranking Among US's Trade Partners: 8.

Finance

Currency: South Korean Won (SKW). Notes are in denominations of SKW10,000, 5,000 and 1,000. Coins are in denominations of SKW500, 100, 50 and 10. Credit cards are widely accepted, but it can be difficult to change travellers' cheques in smaller towns. US$ travellers' cheques attract the lowest commission.

Exchange Rate (2003): US$1 = SKW1,175.

Exchange Controls: There are a few controls on foreign exchange transactions made by individuals. You can send only two-thirds of your salary out of the country.

Banks: During the Asian crisis, the Korean government nationalised the main banks, which remain under state control. Numerous foreign banks, particularly American, operate in the capital. All banking activity is supervised by the Financial Supervisory Commission (FSC) and is generally secure and efficient.

Cost/Standard Of Living: Seoul is one of most expensive cities in the world and the cost of living is very high, particularly accommodation. However, food is inexpensive and outside the capital city costs are generally lower.

Loans: Short and medium-term loans are available from both Korean and foreign banks in the country. Long-term debt financing is provided by the Korea Development Bank, although this is generally only for high priority industries.

Interest Rate (2002): 4.8 per cent.

Taxation

Corporate Tax: 27 per cent, although companies whose tax base is below SKW100 million (US$8,500) are subject to a rate of 15 per cent. Corporate tax will be reduced by 4 per cent over the next five years.

Personal Income Tax: Income tax is divided into Class A earned income (from a Korean company or Korean branch of a foreign company), generally withheld at source (PAYE) and Class B income (employment income received in foreign currency from a foreign company outside Korea), which may be withheld and declared or paid through a licensed taxpayers' association. Income tax is levied at rates ranging from 9 per cent on annual earnings under SKW10 million (US$8,500) to 36 per cent on annual earnings over SKW80 million (US$68,000). There are numerous personal exemptions and deductions. A local income tax of 10 per cent is also levied.

Capital Gains Tax: Gains on shares are subject to 20 per cent CGT (non-residents pay 10 per cent of the total price or 25 per cent of profits, whichever is smaller). Gains on assets transferred without registration are subject to 65 per cent CGT. Property gains are levied at rates ranging from 20 to 40 per cent, the top level on gains in excess of SKW60 million (US$51,000).

Wealth Tax: None.

Inheritance & Gift Tax: None.

Value Added/Sales/Purchase Tax: The standard rate is 10 per cent, which is levied on most goods and services.

Social Security & Pensions: Employers and employees make contributions to the medical insurance and pension funds of around 4.5 per cent of the employee's gross salary.

Withholding Taxes: Interest and dividends are subject to 16.5 per cent withholding tax.

Tax Filing: The Korean tax year is the calendar year. Individuals whose income is derived from both Class A and B or Class B only if not declared through a licensed taxpayers' association (see **Personal Income Tax** above) must file annual returns by 31st May. Corporate tax returns must generally be filed within 15 days of the date when the company's accounts are finalised. Any taxes still owed at that time must be paid within the filing period for the company's tax return. Domestic companies are also required to publish a copy of their balance sheets in a local daily newspaper within the same period.

Doing Business

Forming A Company: Setting up is generally straightforward and can be done via the KISC (see **Reference** below), which provides assistance and support. Foreign investor ventures require registration and investor visas. The Korean workforce is generally highly educated and has a strong work ethic. Employees are available at all levels.

Investment: Korea encourages foreign investment and in 2002 introduced generous financial incentives to foreign companies setting up in the country (see below). Korea also encourages the development of foreign investment zones (FIZ), mainly for manufacturing and R&D industries, which enjoy additional financial and economic advantages. Note that certain sectors of the economy are 'closed' or 'partly closed' to foreign participation. Check with your country's embassy for an up-to-date list of restricted sectors.

Government Incentives: In 2002 the Korean government introduced a comprehensive package of tax incentives for foreign investors designed to attract FDI to the country. The incentives for large scale investments (at least US$50 million) include 100 per cent exemption from corporate tax for seven years and a 50 per cent reduction for the following three years. The incentives for medium scale investments (at least US$10 million in manufacturing and tourism) are exemption from corporate tax for three years and a 50 per cent reduction for the following two years.

The non-taxable limit for overseas allowances for expatriate employees was recently increased to 40 per cent of gross monthly salary. Note that foreign companies that set up in Foreign Investment Zones (FIZ) are also entitled to further financial incentives.

Business Hours: Businesses and offices open from 9am to noon and from 1pm to 7pm Mondays to Fridays and from 9am to 1pm on Saturdays, although in the near future most will no longer open on Saturdays. Banking hours are from 9am to 4.30pm Mondays to Fridays and from 9.30am to 1pm on Saturdays.

Public Holidays: 17 per year as follows:

Day/Date	Holiday
1st and 2nd January	New Year
Late January to early February	Sollal (Lunar New Year) – three days
1st March	Independence Movement Day
5th April	Arbor Day
5th May	Children's Day
Early to mid-May	Birth of Buddha
6th June	Memorial Day
17th July	Constitution Day
15th August	Liberation Day
Late September or October	Chusok (Harvest Moon) – three days
3rd October	National Foundation Day
25th December	Christmas Day

Business Etiquette: Business is generally conducted very formally and it's usually necessary to have a formal introduction to a company you plan to do business with in Korea. Business cards are always exchanged at the beginning of a meeting. Many Korean business people speak English, but it's wise to go over key points and issues twice to ensure understanding. Personal relationships are very important when doing business.

Accommodation

Restrictions On Foreign Ownership: New legislation introduced in 1998 allows 100 per cent foreign ownership, but it's generally difficult for foreigners to buy property in Korea and most expatriates who own property have the title deeds in a Korean national's name (e.g. their spouse).

Cost Of Housing: Property in Seoul is expensive and prices have risen sharply in recent months. Prices of new apartments and villas in some areas have increased by more than half and most prices have now regained their pre-1997 levels. If you're planning to spend five or more years in Korea, property may be a good investment. Note that property is mostly apartments, and houses are few and far between.

Mortgages: In an attempt to control rising property prices, from the Korean government tightened the rules on mortgage lending in November 2003, limiting banks' lending to 40 per cent of the market value of a property.

Fees: Fees include a 2 per cent acquisition tax and a 3.6 per cent registration tax, plus legal expenses.

Property Taxes: Property taxes vary from 0.3 to 7 per cent of the property's value, depending on its location.

Building Standards: Variable.

Renting: Rented property is expensive and limited almost exclusively to apartments. Monthly rents start at SKW1.5 million (US$1,275) for a small, modest apartment. Western-style larger apartments (known as 'villas') with more amenities cost from SKW5 million (US$4,250). Houses are also sometimes available from SKW5 million. Note that many Korean landlords prefer rental payment using the *chonsei* system, whereby the tenant pays a large deposit called 'key money' (several tens of thousands of dollars), then lives in the place rent-free for the duration of the contract. The landlord collects the interest from the payment in lieu of monthly rent, then returns the deposit at the end of the contract. **Be aware that some landlords invest the key money and then 'lose' it!** The western style of rent payment is gradually becoming more accepted.

Personal Effects: Personal effects can be imported duty-free if you're in possession of a long-term visa.

Utilities: The electricity supply (220V in new buildings and 110V in old properties) is generally reliable. Tap water is officially safe to drink but most Koreans and expatriates drink bottled water.

Communications

Postal Services: The postal service is generally efficient and provides banking services as well as the payment of bills and money transfers. Airmail to Western Europe can take up to ten days. Post office hours are from 9am to 5pm on Mondays to Fridays, 9am to 1pm on Saturdays.

Telecommunications: The telephone service is provided by three companies and is generally efficient, although call charges are high. IDD is available. Mobile phones are popular and GSM 900 and 1800 networks are used.

International Dialling Code: 82.

Internet: The government is investing heavily in IT and use of the internet has increased enormously in recent years. There's fierce competition between service providers (ISPs), many of which offer unlimited access and online time. Leading ISPs include Korea-Afis (💻 www.korea-afis.co.kr), Korea Telecom (💻 www.kornet.net) and Shinbiro (💻 http://english.shinbiro.com). Most large companies are online and have websites.

Transport Infrastructure: The domestic flight service run by Korean Air and Asiana Airlines is generally good and connects main cities. All main towns and cities are linked by rail and the service is generally very good, although first-class fares can be expensive. Seoul has a good public transport network, including an underground (subway), although at peak times the transport system is crowded. Seoul suffers from chronic traffic congestion and journey times should be adjusted accordingly.

Getting There: The new international airport at Incheon, outside Seoul, is well served by international flights from many worldwide destinations.

Import/Export Restrictions: Generally none.

Miscellaneous

Crime & Legal Restrictions: Very low crime rate and few legal restrictions other than those usual in the west.

Education: Education is taken seriously by Koreans, who have a high literacy rate, and is compulsory for children aged from 5 to 17. There are several international schools in Seoul.

English-Language Media: Korean TV broadcasts mainly in Korean, except for films, which tend to be in the original language with subtitles. The US forces broadcast on one channel in English. Satellite and cable TV are popular and widely available. English radio broadcasts are provided only by US forces stations. English-language national daily newspapers are *The Korea Herald* and *The Korea Times*.

Time Difference: GMT +8.

Weights & Measures: Metric, but the *pyong* (3.3m²) is still used to measure floor area.

Reference

Useful Addresses

American Chamber of Commerce, 4501 Trade Tower 159-1, Samsung-dong, Kangnam-gu, Seoul 135-731 (☎ 564-2040, 💻 www.amchamkorea.org).

British Chamber of Commerce, 21/F Seoul Finance Centre, 84 Taepyoung-ro 1 ga, Choong-gu, Seoul 100-101 (☎ 720-9406, 🖥 www.bcck.or.kr).

British Embassy, 40 Taepyung-ro, 4 Chung-dong, Chung-ku, Seoul 100-120 (☎ 3210-5500, 🖥 www.britishembassy.or.kr).

Korean Embassy, 2370 Massachusetts Avenue, NW, Washington DC 20008, US (☎ 202-797 6343, 🖥 www.koreaemb.org).

Korean Embassy, 60 Buckingham Gate, London SW1E 6AJ (☎ 020-7227 5500, 🖥 www.mofat.go.kr/uk).

Korean Investment Services Centre (🖥 www.kisc.org). The KISC provides comprehensive information and assistance and publishes the useful *Guide to Living in Korea*, available in hard copy or in PDF.

Korean Trade Investment Promotion Agency (KOTRA, 🖥 www.kotra.or.kr). Provides assistance to foreign investors.

National Tax Service (🖥 www.nta.go.kr). Provides a useful *Income Tax Guide for Foreigners*, published annually.

US Embassy, 82 Sejong-ro, Chongro-ku, Seoul 110-050 (☎ 397-4221, (🖥 http:// seoul.usembassy.gov).

Further Reading

Titles prefaced by an asterisk are recommended by the author.

Doing Business Guide: South Korea (PriceWaterhouseCoopers)

*Korea Old and New-A History of Korea (Harvard University)

*Korea, Tradition and Transformation, Andrew C Nahm

Korea's Cultural Roots, John Carter Covell

Silver Stallion, Ahn Cheong-hyo

The Confucian Transformation of Korea, Martina Deuchler

The Shadow of Arms, Hwang Suk-Young

*To Dream of Pigs, Clive Leatherdale

Useful Websites

English Spectrum (🖥 www.englishspectrum.com) – For English teachers in Korea, with general advice about living in Korea and a job centre.

Korean Information Service (🖥 http://korea.net) – A government website with plenty of information about everything from Korean culture to the media and education.

Life in Korea (🖥 www.lifeinkorea.com) – Contains extensive information about all aspects of life in the country, including an online therapist for those experiencing culture shock!

MALAYSIA

General Information

Capital: Kuala Lumpur.

Population: 23.5 million. 50 per cent Malay, 33 per cent Chinese, 9 per cent Indian and indigenous tribes, including the Iban and Orang Asli.

Foreign Community: There's a large expatriate community in Malaysia, particularly in the capital, comprising mainly Australians, British and New Zealanders.

Area: 330,000km^2 (127,422mi^2).

Geography: Malaysia is divided into two distinct areas: Peninsular Malaysia, extending from the Thai border in the north to the island of Singapore in the south, and East Malaysia, which is 440km (275mi) away across the South China Sea in the north of the island of Borneo, consisting of Sabah and Sarawak. Peninsula Malaysia is dominated by several large mountain ranges and 70 per cent of the landmass is forest. Over two-thirds of Malaysia's population lives in cities.

Climate: The climate is tropical, i.e. hot and humid for most of the year, and there's little temperature difference between the 'seasons'; the average lowland temperature is 31°C (88°F). Rainfall in the form of short intense thunderstorms occurs all year, especially from November to March.

Health: Malaria (mainly falciparum) is present in Sabah, where because of chloroquine resistance mefloquine is the usual prophylaxis, and in Peninsular Malaysia and Sarawak, where the risk is lower, as the disease is mainly present in remote, forested areas. Cholera has been a problem in some regions, and there's a low risk of Japanese encephalitis. The high humidity and heat may produce fatigue and health problems. The only mandatory vaccination is yellow fever, for travellers over the age of one coming from infected areas.

Western-trained doctors and facilities can be found in most of Malaysia's cities and offer good-quality treatment. Payment is usually expected immediately, often in cash, although credit cards are becoming more accepted. Free medical treatment is often provided in expatriate employment packages in Malaysia and to government employees. If it isn't, extensive private medical insurance is essential, as treatment can be expensive.

Language: The official language is Bahasa Malaysia. English is widely spoken, while Cantonese, Hokkien, Iban, Tamil and indigenous languages are spoken by minorities.

Religion: The largest religions are Islam (53 per cent) and Buddhism (19 per cent), the rest of the population split between Animism, Christianity, Confucianism and Taoism.

Government: Parliamentary monarchy.

Political Stability: Excellent, although the retirement in 2003 of Mahathir Mohamad, the country's prime minister for 23 years, may herald some political instability. In 1867, Malaya and neighbouring states became British colonies. The bilateral relationship between the UK and Malaysia is strong.

Economy

Overview: Malaysia's economy is generally stable and in recent years the government has introduced a number of initiatives to try to diversify the economy, which is generally considered to be over-dependent on the merchandise trade. Competition from China in the export market is strong and, although Malaysia managed to avert the spread of Severe Acute Respiratory Syndrome (SARS) in 2003, the disease had a negative economic effect on income from both tourism and trade.

GDP Per Head (2002): US$10,300.

Growth (2002): 5.2 per cent.

Target Industries: Aerospace, agriculture, creative and media, education and training, environment, fire and security, IT and electronics, oil and gas, and power and energy.

Ranking Among UK's Trade Partners: 23.

Ranking Among US's Trade Partners: 9.

Employment Market

Overview: The Malaysian workforce is generally young, educated and has a strong work ethic. There's a willingness to learn new techniques and skills, particularly in the field of technology. Unemployment is generally low. Note that it's Malaysian government policy to ensure that training exists for Malaysian nationals at all levels, and companies are often required to provide this training. The government has also taken measures to increase the number of engineering and technical graduates from the country's universities.

Unemployment Rates In 2002: 3.8 per cent.

Work Permits: All foreign nationals require a work permit, which an employer must apply for on your behalf. A permit will generally be issued only if there's a shortage of trained Malaysians, although foreign companies are permitted a quota of expatriate workers to fulfil key positions. Dependants wishing to work in Malaysia must also obtain permission from the immigration authorities.

Labour Relations: Generally excellent and there's a high degree of co-operation and understanding between management and workers. Labour costs are relatively low and productivity is high.

Employment Conditions: The working week is 48 hours, usually from Mondays to midday on Saturdays, although in some states the Muslim week is worked (from Saturdays to midday on Thursdays) and there's a growing trend towards a 40-hour week, from Mondays to Fridays. Employees are entitled to at least eight days' annual holiday.

Finance

Currency: Ringgit (RM), also called the Malaysian Dollar, made up of 100 sen. Notes are in denominations of RM1,000, 500, 100, 50, 10, 5, 2 and 1. The RM1,000 and 500 notes are being phased out. Coins are in denominations of RM1 and 50, 20, 10 and 5 and 1 sen. Foreign currencies are easy to exchange in major cities and tourist centres, but there can be problems elsewhere. Travellers' cheques in GB£, US$ and Australian Dollars attract the lowest charges.

Exchange Rate (2003): US$1 = RM3.8.

Exchange Controls: None, although the export of sums over RM10,000 (US$2,630) requires permission from the Controller of Foreign Exchange.

Banks: Banking is generally efficient and modern, and a number of banking groups have embarked on massive reorganisation programmes in recent years. Foreign banks are represented in Malaysia, although for the last decade there has been a freeze on the opening of foreign commercial banks.

Cost/Standard Of Living: The cost of living is generally quite low, although the state of Sabah is considerably more expensive than Peninsular Malaysia.

Loans: Loans are generally available from local banks.

Interest Rate (2002): 4.5 per cent.

Taxation

Corporate Tax: 28 per cent on all businesses except those in the petroleum sector, which are subject to tax at a rate of 38 per cent.

Personal Income Tax: Income tax is deducted at source (PAYE), with rates ranging from 0 to 28 per cent after certain deductions. There are generous allowances for dependants. If you're employed for less than 182 days in Malaysia, you aren't liable for income tax. Non-residents are taxed at 28 per cent on Malaysia-source income only.

Capital Gains Tax: CGT is levied only on immovable property and rates range from 30 per cent, if the property is disposed of within two years after acquisition, to 5 per cent for companies and 0 for individuals if it has been owned for over five years. There's a one-time exemption for the sale of a principal residence and permanent residents and Malay nationals qualify for an exemption on the first RM5,000 (US$1,315) or 10 per cent of a gain (whichever is higher).

Wealth Tax: None.

Inheritance & Gift Tax: None.

Value Added/Sale/Purchase Tax: Malaysia levies a sales tax at various rates, e.g. 5 per cent on fruit, certain other foods and some construction materials, 10 per cent on most goods and services, and 15 per cent on cigarettes and alcohol. Certain items such as basic foodstuffs, books and printed matter are exempt.

Social Security & Pensions: There are various funds in Malaysia's limited social security system. The first is the pension fund, to which contributions are a minimum of 12 per cent for employers and 11 per cent for employees from gross monthly salary. Note that foreigners and their employers are exempt from these contributions, although employers may contribute if they wish at the rate of RM5 (US$1.30) per employee and employees at 11 per cent of gross monthly salary. The second fund is the employment injury and invalidity scheme for employees earning less than RM2,000 (US$560) per month, to which the employer must contribute 1.75 per cent of the employee's gross monthly wage and the employee 0.5 per cent. Third, there's the Human Resources Development Fund, to which contributions are 1 per cent of all employees' wages if the company employs more than 50 Malaysian workers or employs between 10 and 50 workers and has a paid-up capital of RM2.5 million (around US$675,000). There are no welfare or unemployment benefits.

A separate pension fund is usually contributed to privately by employees. Companies employing expatriates are also liable for annual levies, which vary according to the expatriate's salary and length of contract.

Withholding Taxes: Interest is subject to 5 per cent withholding tax.

Tax Filing: From 2004, Malaysia will introduce a self-assessment tax regime for companies and self-employed individuals, who will be required to make advance tax payments and file an annual tax return. Employed individuals aren't generally required to file a return.

Doing Business

Forming A Company: Setting up a company in Malaysia is generally straightforward foreign investors can choose between a company under sole proprietorship and a partnership with a minimum of 2 and a maximum of 20 shareholders, and between a local or foreign company. All companies are required to register with the Companies Commission of Malaysia (CMM).

Investment: Malaysia welcomes foreign investment, which is seen as necessary to diversify the country's economy. The Malaysia Investment Development Agency (MIDA) was established in order to offer information about requirements.

Government Incentives: Various incentives are available both from the government and state authorities, and companies which have made contributions to the Human Resources Development Fund (see **Social Security** below) are eligible for grants and subsidies for employee training. Contact MIDA (see **Reference** below) for further information. State Development Corporations offer further incentives.

Business Hours: Opening hours for businesses are generally 8.30am to 5.30pm Mondays to Fridays and from 8.30am to 1pm on Saturdays. Banking hours are from 9.30am to 3.30pm Mondays to Fridays and some banks open on Saturdays from 9.30am to 11.30am. Note that in the states of Johor, Kedah, Kelantan, Perlis and Terengganu, Thursday afternoons and Fridays aren't working periods, but Saturdays and Sundays are.

Public Holidays: 16 per year as follows:

Day/Date	Holiday
1st January	New Year's Day
Late January or February	Chinese New Year – three days
February	Hari Raya Haji (Feast of the Sacrifice)

Late February or March	Hari Raya Tussa (Islamic New Year)
1st May	Labour Day
May	Birth of the Prophet Mohammed
May	Wesak Day (Birth of the Buddha)
Early June	Official Birthday of HM the Yang di-Pertuan Agong
31st August	National Day;
October or November	Deepavali Festival
November	Hari Raya Puasa (End of Ramadan) – three days
25th December	Christmas Day

Most dates vary according to local sightings of the moon's phases.

Business Etiquette: You should always bear in mind that nothing is done in a hurry in Malaysia and many westerners become frustrated at the time taken to achieve anything. Note that meetings are frequently postponed and that the first meeting about any matter rarely deals with the business in hand! Politeness is essential and you should seek advice beforehand about how to address your business partners.

Accommodation

Restrictions On Foreign Ownership: Regulations regarding property ownership by foreigners vary between states. In the capital, foreigners are allowed to purchase a maximum of two apartment units priced at RM250,000 (US$65,750) or more, sometimes reduced to RM150,000 (US$39,500).

Cost Of Housing: Property costs vary considerably according to the area of the country and the facilities provided. In the capital, an apartment costs from RM140,000 (US$36,800) upwards and a small bungalow from RM610,000 (US$160,500).

Local Mortgages: Local mortgages are available, but only for residential properties valued at over RM250,000 (US$65,800).

Fees: Fees include stamp duty of 1 to 4 per cent of the purchase price, tax levied at 1 per cent on the first RM100,000 (US$26,300) and 0.5 per cent on the remainder, plus legal fees and expenses.

Building Standards: Variable.

Renting: The rental market in the capital is strong and prices are relatively low. A two-bedroom apartment in an attractive area costs from RM1,000 to RM5,000 (US$265 to US$1,315) per month and a house from RM8,500 (US$2,235) per month.

Personal Effects: Personal effects can be imported duty-free but you must provide customs with a packing list, i.e. an inventory of the goods to be imported. It's recommended to pack videos separately, as they're checked by the authorities and may be confiscated if they appear to contain unacceptable material. Note that there's a high import duty on cars (from 100 to 350 per cent!).

Utilities: The electricity supply (230V) is generally reliable; stormy weather frequently causes blackouts but power is usually quickly restored. Mains gas isn't available but bottled gas is widely used. Water can be drunk from the tap, but most people prefer bottled.

Communications

Postal Services: The postal service is generally reliable and fast, with post offices open between 8am and 5pm Mondays to Saturdays.

Telecommunications: Malaysia has one of the most advanced telecommunications networks in the developing world, with Telekom Malaysia and Maxis Communications the main providers of fixed lines, although more competitors are expected in the near future. Competition is intense, resulting in ever-lower call charges. IDD is available. Mobile phones are popular and GSM 900 and 1800 networks cover the vast majority of the country. Operators include Celcom (🖥 www.celcom.com.my), DiGi (🖥 www.digi.com.my), Maxis Mobile (🖥 www.maxis.com.my) and TIMECel (🖥 www.time.com.my).

International Dialling Code: 60.

Internet: The internet is widely used by most companies, although outside the major population centres usage is much lower. Service providers include Jaring (🖥 www.jaring.net.my) and Tmnet (🖥 www.tm.net.my).

Transport Infrastructure: The domestic flight service in Malaysia is good and fares are competitive. Peninsula Malaysia has an excellent and comprehensive bus service and a limited rail network. Sarawak has a limited bus service. The best way to get around is by car, although road conditions vary and driving standards are poor. Petrol is cheap but spares and mechanical expertise are in short supply.

Getting There: The main international airport is at Sepang, which is served by flights from most international destinations. There are also several smaller international airports with more limited services. Malaysia can be reached by road and rail from Thailand, by train along the causeway or ferry from Singapore, and by ferry from Indonesia.

Import/Export Restrictions: Generally none, although some goods require a licence.

Miscellaneous

Crime & Legal Restrictions: Low crime rate and no special restrictions.

Education: State schools in Malaysia give priority to local nationals and there are few places for expatriate children, who may in any case find it difficult to adapt to the Malaysian curriculum. There are some private schools but you must to apply well in advance, as places are in high demand and short supply.

English-Language Media: Malaysian TV's four stations broadcast a significant number of programmes in English and satellite TV is readily available. There are plenty of English-language newspapers in Malaysia, including *Borneo Mail, Borneo Post, Daily Express, Business Times, Malay Mail, Malaysiakini, New Straits Times, Sabah Times, Sarawak Tribune, The Star* and *The Sun*.

Time Difference: GMT +7.

Weights & Measures: Metric.

Reference

Useful Addresses

British High Commission, 185 Jalan Ampang, 50450 Kuala Lumpar (☎ 03-2170 2200, 💻 www.britain.org.my).

British Malaysian Chamber of Commerce (BMCC), 2nd Floor, Bangunan MIDF, 195A Jalan Tun Razak, 50400 Kuala Lumpur (☎ 03-2163 1784, ✉ bmita@ppp.nasionet.net).

Federation of Malaysian Manufacturers, Wisma FMM, 3 Persiaran Dagang, PJU 9 Bandar Sri Damansara, PO Box 28, Jinjang, 52200 Kuala Lumpur (☎ 03-636 1211, 💻 www.fmm.org.my). In London: 17, Curzon Street,London W1J 5HR (☎ 020-7493 0616, ✉ midalon@btconnect.com). In New York: Consulate General of Malaysia (Investment Section), 313 East, 43rd Street, New York, NY 10017 (☎ 212-687 2491, ✉ mida@midany.org).

Malaysian Embassy, 2401 Massachusetts Avenue, NW, Washington DC 20008, US (☎ 202-328 2700).

Malaysian Embassy, 45 Belgrave Square, London WC2N 5DU, UK (☎ 020-7235 8033).

Malaysian Industrial Development Authority (MIDA), Plaza Sentral, Jalan Stesen Sentral 5, 50470 Kuala Lumpur (☎ 03-2267 3633, 💻 www.mida.gov.my).

US Embassy, 376 Jalan Tun Razak, 50400 Kuala Lumpar (☎ 03-2168 5000, 💻 http://usembassymalaysia.org.my).

Further Reading

A Short History of Malaysia, Singapore and Brunei, C Mary Turnbull

A Stroll Through Borneo, James Barclay

Borneo Stories, Somerset Maugham

Culture Shock Malaysia, Jo Ann Craig

The Consul's File, Paul Theroux

The Malayan Trilogy, Anthony Burgess

Turtle Beach, Blanche d'Alpuget

Useful Websites

Allo Expat (💻 www.alloexpat.com) – A useful resource for everything to do with living in Malaysia describing itself as 'a one-stop expatriate information centre in Malaysia'.

Journey Malaysia (💻 www.journeymalaysia.com) – An extensive resource, with information about everything from accommodation to etiquette and public transport.

Tourism Malaysia (💻 www.tourism.gov.my) – The website of a government agency, with plenty of information and useful links, including links to various government ministries.

PHILIPPINES

General Information

Capital: Manila. Note that the term Manila properly applies to the central part of the capital only. The whole conurbation, comprising three 'cities' and 13 municipalities is called Metro Manila. However, Manila is used in this book to refer to the whole of Metro Manila, unless otherwise specified.

Population: 78.4 million, mainly descendants of Chinese, Malaysian and Islamic peoples, with a minority of mestizos (Filipino/Spanish or Filipino/American).

Foreign Community: There's a small expatriate, community mainly consisting of US nationals, concentrated around Manila.

Area: 300,176km^2 (115,907mi^2).

Geography: The Philippines consists of over 7,100 islands, of which around 1,000 are inhabited. The two largest islands, Luzon and Mindanao, comprise over 66 per cent of the land area, and between them lie the Visaya islands. The terrain of much of the Philippines is mountainous, with several active volcanoes, one of which, Mount Apo (2,954m/9,691ft), is the country's highest peak. Much of the land is fertile and narrow coastal plains give way to forested plateaux, with over 33 per cent of the islands forested. The Philippines is in an earthquake zone.

Climate: The climate is tropical, the heat tempered by sea breezes. Average annual temperatures range from 20 to 35°C (68 to 95°F), with high humidity. Rainfall occurs throughout the year and, in the north of the country, the monsoon season lasts from June to December and can produce typhoons. The monsoon doesn't affect the south.

Health: Malaria (primarily falciparum) is found in lower lying (below around 600m) rural areas, but there's little risk in Manila. The highest risk is in the Palawan, Luzon and Mindanao. Japanese encephalitis is a risk in some regions, and chikungunya fever is common in some cities, including Manila. A stubborn, penicillin-resistant strain of gonorrhoea is a problem in the

Philippines, particularly in the large cities. A yellow fever vaccination certificate is required by travellers aged one and over coming from infected areas. Permanent residence applicants must pass an HIV test.

Standards of health care are good in Manila and some of the large cities, but elsewhere levels of care and supplies are inadequate. Foreigners must pay for all medical treatment (often immediately and in cash) and private medical insurance is therefore essential. Medical treatment in the Philippines can be very expensive.

Language: The official language is Filipino, which is based on the Tagalog dialect, and there are some 70 other dialects. English is widely spoken, particularly in Manila and other major cities, and Spanish to a lesser extent.

Religion: Roman Catholic (around 84 per cent), with minorities of other Christian denominations, Muslims, Buddhists and Taoists.

Government: Democratic republic.

Political Stability: Reasonable. High inflation is a problem and President Estrada was ousted from government in January 2001 by popular pressure amid charges of bribery and corruption, and President Gloria Macapagal-Arroyo appointed. **In June 2003 foreigners were advised against travel to central, southern and western Mindanao, Basilan and the Sulu archipelago. Care should be taken in the rest of Mindanao, Manila, throughout Palawan and at coastal resorts and tourist centres in the country, where there is a danger of kidnapping and terrorist attack. Check with your country's foreign office for the latest information.**

Economy

Overview: The Philippines has seen a remarkable economic recovery since democracy was restored in 1985; the country was largely unaffected by the Asian financial crisis in 1997, but since then political events have had serious effects on the economy and foreign investment has declined sharply. In early 2001, however, the appointment of the new president brought economic stability, the peso recovered and inflation dropped sharply. Growth in 2002 was considerably higher than in many countries and the best since 1997. The Philippines' main challenge is to continue economic reform and restore foreign confidence in the country. Over the last ten years, the UK has been the largest investor in the Philippines (US$17.2 billion) and in 2000 accounted for nearly 30 per cent of all investment in the country.

GDP Per Head (2002): US$3,800.

Growth (2002): 4.6 per cent.

Target Industries: Agribusiness, chemicals, consumer goods, development of infrastructure (including power, transport, water, construction and oil and gas), education and training, financial services, IT and electronics.

Ranking Among UK's Trade Partners: 31.

Ranking Among US's Trade Partners: 21.

Employment Market

Overview: Unemployment is a growing social problem and in 2002 reached an all-time high.

Unemployment Rate (2002): 15.4 per cent (up from 11 per cent in 2001).

Work Permits: All foreign nationals require a work visa. Once you've received a firm offer of employment, you must apply for a visa from a Philippines consulate or embassy in your home country. Once you enter the Philippines, you must apply for a work permit from the Immigration Bureau.

Labour Relations: The union movement is quite strong in the Philippines, although the large number of different unions rarely pursue the same objective! In recent years, strikes have been reduced and there's a growing understanding and co-operation between management and workers.

Employment Conditions: Employment conditions are highly regulated under the Labour Code, the working week is around 45 hours and employees are generally entitled to at least two weeks' annual holiday.

Finance

Currency: Philippine Peso (P), known locally as the *piso*, divided into 100 centavos. Notes are in denominations of P1,000, 500, 100, 50, 20, 10 and 5. Coins are in denominations of P5, 2 and 1, and 50, 25 and 10 centavos. Outside Manila, it can be difficult to exchange foreign currency. Credit cards are widely accepted in the large cities. Travellers' cheques can be exchanged at many banks and are accepted by many businesses. US$ cheques attract the lowest charges.

Exchange Rate (2003): US$1 = P55.

Exchange Controls: Some restrictions apply for capital account transactions. Note that foreign currency of over US$3,000 (or the equivalent) must be declared at the Central Bank of the Philippines counter, which is behind the customs examination area. Departing passengers aren't permitted to take out foreign currency exceeding the amount that was declared and brought into the country. A maximum of P1,000 (US$18) in local currency can be taken out of the country.

Banks: There are many commercial banks in the Philippines and banking is reasonably efficient, although some transactions take a long time. Foreigners may open bank accounts, although you need confirmation of employment or your certificate of registration, and must maintain a minimum deposit of around US$1,000.

Cost/Standard Of Living: There's a huge disparity in standards of living in different parts of the country. Income per head in Manila is seven times that of the poorest region and the richest 10 per cent of the population have an income 24 times that of the poorest 10 per cent. Approximately one-third of the population live at or below the poverty level. The Philippines is generally more expensive than its neighbours.

Interest Rate (2002): 7 per cent (down from 25 per cent in 2001).

Taxation

All taxpayers require a Tax Identification Number, obtainable from local tax offices.

Corporate Tax: 32 per cent.

Personal Income Tax: Income tax is levied at rates ranging from 0 to 32 per cent and the tax exemption is P500,000 (US$9,100). Non-residents are subject to a flat rate of 25 per cent.

Capital Gains Tax: CGT is levied at 6 per cent on property. Gains under P100,000 (US$1,800) on shares and dividends are taxed at 5 per cent and at 10 per cent above this amount.

Wealth Tax: None.

Inheritance & Gift Tax: There's no inheritance tax on estates worth less than P2 million (US$36,350). Gift tax is levied at 30 per cent unless the donor is a direct relative, in which case it's zero.

Value Added/Sales/Purchase Tax: The standard rate is 10 per cent. Some items, such as education, health and books, are exempt.

Social Security & Pensions: Social security contributions apply only to employers and Philippine nationals. Monthly contributions must be made towards the social security and health insurance funds and vary according to the employee's salary. The maximum monthly amount payable by the employer is P975 (US$17.70) and by the employee P525 (US$9.55). Employers must also contribute a minimum of P100 (US$1.80) per month per employee towards the Home Development and Mutual Fund.

Withholding Taxes: Interest from bank accounts is subject to 20 per cent withholding tax. Dividends are exempt.

Tax Filing: The tax year is the calendar year and annual tax returns must be filed by individuals and companies by the middle of April each year.

Doing Business

Forming A Company: Setting up a business has been greatly simplified and is now generally straightforward. Foreign investors may choose from a variety of options, including branches, companies and representations. The Philippines has one of the highest literacy rates in the world and there's an abundance of skilled and semi-skilled labour available. Filipinos have shown themselves to be easily trainable and to adapt well to new technologies.

Investment: The Philippines government is very keen to attract foreign investment and to this end allows foreign participation in practically all sections of the economy. Many sectors have been deregulated and foreign investors now have greater participation in areas that were previously a government monopoly.

Government Incentives: Numerous incentives are available, particularly for companies that set up in disadvantaged areas, including income tax holidays of up to six years, tax credits and exemptions from taxes and duties on imports and exports.

Business Hours: Businesses and offices open from 8am to noon and from 1pm to 6pm Mondays to Fridays and from 8.30am to noon on Saturdays. Banking hours are from 9am to 4pm Mondays to Fridays.

Public Holidays: 12 per year as follows:

Day/Date	Holiday
1st January	New Year's Day
9th April	Bataan Day
March or April	Maundy Thursday
March or April	Good Friday
1st May	Labour Day
12th June	Independence Day
31st August	National Heroes' Day
1st November	All Saints' Day
30th November	Bonifacio Day
25th December	Christmas Day
30th December	Rizal Day
31st December	New Year's Eve

Business Etiquette: The Philippine business culture is very much influenced by the US. Personal contact is very important and business is generally conducted in a friendly and open manner. English is the business language.

Accommodation

Restrictions On Foreign Ownership: Foreigners aren't permitted to own land and therefore cannot buy houses, only apartments. Note that in an apartment development, foreigners can own a maximum of 40 per cent of the total number of properties.

Cost Of Housing: Apartments in Manila cost between P4 million and P25 million (US$73,000 and US$450,000), depending on the area.

Local Mortgages: Local banks rarely give mortgages to foreigners, who must have a strong US$ deposit account in order to be considered for one. Loans are usually for a maximum of 50 per cent and, given the erratic Filipino lending rates, it's recommended to obtain a loan from a foreign bank.

Fees: Fees total at least 9 per cent of the purchase price and include 6 per cent transfer tax, 1.5 per cent stamp duty and 1.5 per cent legal fees. There are also registration and processing fees.

Property Taxes: Transfer taxes and costs (paid by the buyer) vary with the region between 5 and 7 per cent of a property's price. There are also agent's fees of around 5 per cent (paid by the vendor), although these are negotiable.

Building Standards: Variable.

Renting: Rented accommodation is the only viable option for expatriates, due to property ownership restrictions. Apartment compounds rented exclusively by westerners, often with many amenities and sports facilities, are popular with expatriates. In Manila, a fully furnished two-bedroom apartment costs between P20,000 and P180,000 (US$365 and US$3,250) per month and a house from P35,000 to P250,000 (US$635 to US$4,500), depending on the location and amenities.

Personal Effects: Personal and household effects can be imported duty-free.

Utilities: The electricity supply (110V or 220V) is generally reliable in the capital, although charges are high. **Note that some older properties may have dangerous wiring.** Mains gas isn't available in the Philippines, but you can buy bottled gas at petrol stations for cooking. **Tap water shouldn't be consumed** and bottled water is widely available.

Communications

Postal Services: The postal service is generally efficient, with post offices open between 8am and 5pm Mondays to Fridays. Airmail to Europe takes between five and ten days.

Telecommunications: Telecommunications have been deregulated and are modern and efficient, although call charges are high and IDD isn't always available outside the main towns. Mobile telephones are popular and the GSM 900 and 1800 networks are in operation, although coverage is limited to the major urban areas. Operators include Digitel (🖳 www.digitelone.com), Globe (🖳 www.globe.com.ph) and Smart Gold GSM (🖳 www.smart.com.ph).

International Dialling Code: 63.

Internet: Internet use is fairly widespread and many companies and government departments are online, although the level of personal use is low. IT parks are currently being established in Manila. Service providers include Cyber Space (🖳 www.cyberspace.com.ph), Internet Manila (🖳 www.i-manila.com.ph) and Inter.net Philippines Inc (🖳 www.ph.inter.net).

Transport Infrastructure: The domestic flight service is good and there are some 80 domestic airports, meaning that most of the country is linked by air. This is probably the best way to travel, as other forms of public transport are limited throughout most of the country. Within cities, taxis provide the best means of transport, as well as the ubiquitous jeepneys – a type of jeep-taxi. A light railway system has been constructed in Manila. Road conditions are extremely variable in the country and driving is often dangerous.

Getting There: The Philippines can be reached by air from many major cities, mainly flying to Ninoy Aquino Airport near Manila, although there are also international airports on other islands.

Import/Export Restrictions: Import licences are no longer required, although before goods can be cleared through customs, a release certificate signed by an authorised bank is necessary. Pre-shipment inspections have been abolished and a new advance processing facility (known as the 'Super Green Lane') introduced, which makes customs release easier. Further details are available from the Bureau of Customs (🖥 www.boc.gov.ph). There are Special Economic Zones, such as Subic Bay Freeport and the Clark Special Economic Zone, where investment incentives are available.

Miscellaneous

Crime & Legal Restrictions: The crime rate is high but falling. Violence is fairly prevalent, although visitors are rarely targeted; however, you should be vigilant and beware of being drugged in bars, as well as of bogus policemen, car-jackings and hotel theft. Political insurgency occurs in some areas, particularly in the south.

Education: Ten years of education is compulsory for children, usually from the ages of 6 to 16. School standards vary and are generally higher in Manila. Instruction is in English. There are many private schools, usually of a religious denomination, and there are several international schools in Manila.

English-Language Media: Television programmes are in English and native languages. Satellite TV is widely available and popular. English-language newspapers include *Manila Bulletin, Manila Times, Philippine Daily Inquirer* and *Philippine Star*.

Time Difference: GMT +7.

Weights & Measures: Metric.

Reference

Useful Addresses

Annexus International Inc, 1 Vernida I Building, 120 Amorsolo St, Makati City, 1221 Philippines (☎ 817-2457, 🖥 www.annexusinternational.com). An experienced relocation company.

Board of Investments, Industry & Investments Building, 385 Sen Gil Puyat AvenueMakati, Metro Manila (☎ 890-9332, (🖥 www.boi.gov.ph).

British Chamber of Commerce, Floors 15-17, LVV Locsin Building 6752 Ayala Avenue, Makati City, 1226 Makati (☎ 580-1158, 🖥 www.bccphil.com).

British Embassy, Floors 15-17, LVV Locsin Building 6752 Ayala Avenue, Makati City, 1226 Makati (☎ 816-7116/7, 🖥 www.britishembassy.org.ph).

European Chamber of Commerce (ECCP), 19th Floor, PS BANK Tower, Sen Gil Puyat Avenue cor. Tindalo Street, Makati City (☎ 759-6680, 🖥 www.eccp.com).

Philippine Chamber of Commerce and Industry, 14/f Multinational Bancorporation Centre, 6805 Ayala, Makati City (☎ 844-3424, 🖥 www. philcham.com).

Philippine Embassy, 1600 Massachusetts Avenue, NW, Washington DC 20036, US (☎ 202-467 9300, 🖥 www.philippineembassy-usa.org).

Philippine Embassy, 9A Palace Green, London W8 4QE, UK (☎ 020-7937 1600).

US Embassy, 1201 Roxas Boulevard, 1000 Manila (☎ 523-1001, 🖥 http:// manila.usembassy.gov).

Further Reading

Titles prefaced by an asterisk are recommended by the author.

A Short History of the Philippines, Teodoro Agoncillo

America's Boy, James Hamilton-Paterson

Brownout on Breadfruit Boulevard, Timothy Mo

Corazon Aquino and the Brushfire Revolution, Eileen Guerrero and Robert Reid

Doing Business Guide: Philippines (PriceWaterhouseCoopers)

Doing Business in the Philippines (Ernst & Young Publications)

For Every Tear A Victory, Hartzell Spence

Reading in Philippine History, Horacio de la Costa

The Philippines, Horacio de la Costa

Useful Websites

The Manila Bulletin Online (🖥 www.mb.com.ph) – The newspaper's online edition.

The Philippine Star (🖥 www.philstar.com) – The newspaper's online edition.

SINGAPORE

General Information

Capital: Singapore.

Population: 4.15 million. 77 per cent Chinese, 14 per cent Malay, 8 per cent Indian.

Foreign Community: There's a large expatriate community – mainly British, who number around 13,000.

Area: 683km^2 (266mi^2).

Geography: Singapore's geographical position has helped it to become one of the main centres of trade for South-east Asia. It lies just north of the equator and the main island is situated off the south of the Malay Peninsula, to which it's joined by a 1km-wide causeway known as the Johor Strait. It's a mainly flat country, with some low hills. In the north-east of the island large areas have been reclaimed and much of the original jungle and swamp has been cleared. As well as the main island, there are 64 islets.

Climate: Singapore has a tropical climate, hot and humid for most of the year with year-round temperatures averaging of 30°C (86°F) during the day and 24°C (75°F) at night. There are two monsoon periods, one in summer and one in winter.

Health: Singapore is a very low risk destination health-wise. A yellow fever vaccination is required for travellers aged one and over coming from infected areas. All workers who earn less than S$1,250 (US$725) per month and applicants for permanent residence are required to pass an HIV test.

In late 2003, Singapore had been removed from the WHO list of SARS-affected countries. The authorities, however, are still applying a strict regime of quarantine and control, and there are large fines for breaching these. Travellers should check with their country's foreign office for the latest information.

Singapore has state-funded medical facilities (paid for by employee contributions from their salaries), which foreign workers can use if they contribute; charges are low. Standards of care are high, including those of specialist treatment, but not as high as in the private sector, which is state-of-the-art, although expensive. Medical insurance is often included in expatriate employee packages; many foreigners who aren't offered insurance by their employers choose to buy it.

Language: The four official languages are Malay (the national language), English (the language of business and administration, which most Singaporeans speak, in addition to another language), Cantonese and Tamil.

Religion: Buddhism (42 per cent), Islam (15 per cent), Christianity (14 per cent), Taoism (9 per cent) and Hinduism (4 per cent).

Government: Republic within the British Commonwealth.

Political Stability: Very good. Singapore has been governed by the People's Action Party (PAP) since 1959. It has recovered well from the Asian financial crisis and has maintained strong economic growth in the last few years.

Economy

Overview: Singapore is one of the Asian 'tigers', with more than 30 years of annual GDP growth at over 8 per cent. It's among the world's wealthiest nations and has a strong economy. The country suffered a recession in 2001 and the government took action to reduce production costs and the country's dependence on the electronics sector. The results have been positive and there are strong signs that the economy is on the road to recovery. Singapore is one of the UK's largest export markets outside the EU and exports amounted to over £1.6 billion in 2001. More than 700 British companies are represented in the country.

GDP Per Head (2002): US$22,180.

Growth (2002): 2.3 per cent.

Target Industries: Education and training, electronics, environmental technology, healthcare and life sciences, IT, telecommunications and transport infrastructure.

Ranking Among UK's Trade Partners: 21.

Ranking Among US's Trade Partners: Outside top 50.

Employment Market

Overview: The Singapore workforce is generally well-educated and the country has one of the highest literacy rates in Asia (around 93 per cent). There's little unemployment in spite of the 2001 recession.

Unemployment Rate (2002): 4.7 per cent.

Work Permits: Work permits (known as 'employment passes') are required by all foreigners and must be obtained by your employer on your behalf. Your employer must also apply for a pass for your dependants.

Labour Relations: Generally excellent and there are few strikes.

Employment Conditions: Employment conditions are regulated by the Employment and Industrial Relations Acts. There are national guidelines for annual wage adjustments, but these aren't mandatory.

Finance

Currency: Singapore Dollar (S$), which is divided into 100 cents. Notes are in denominations of S$10,000, 1,000, 500, 100, 50, 20, 10, 5 and 2. Coins are in denominations of S$1, and 50, 20, 10, 5 and 1 cents. Brunei currency is also legal tender in Singapore. Credit cards are widely accepted in Singapore. GB£ travellers' cheques attract the lowest charges.

Exchange Rate (2003): US$1 = S$1.7.

Exchange Controls: None.

Banks: There are over 140 commercial banks in Singapore and most foreign banks are represented. Banking services are comprehensive, modern and efficient. The Post Office Savings Bank (POSBank) has the largest number of branches on the island, as well as offering tax-free interest on savings. To open a bank account you usually need to make a minimum deposit.

Cost/Standard Of Living: The standard of living in Singapore is high and similar to that of Australia or Italy. The cost of living is high too, one of the highest in South-east Asia.

Loans: Loans are available from local banks as well as from the Economic Development Board (see **Reference** below).

Interest Rates in 2002: 5.35 per cent.

Taxation

Taxes are currently being reduced by the Singapore government.

Corporate Tax: Currently 20 per cent, although rates are progressively being reduced by the Singapore government.

Personal Income Tax: Income tax rates range from 2 to 26 per cent, the top rate applying to annual income in excess of S$400,000 (US$235,000), with allowances for dependants. Tax returns are filed annually. If employment is for less than 60 days per year, no income tax is payable. Non-residents are generally taxed at the rate of 24.5 per cent, although Singapore employment income is taxed at a flat rate of 15 per cent or at resident rates, whichever is higher.

Capital Gains Tax: None.

Wealth Tax: None.

Inheritance & Gift Tax: None.

Value Added/Sales/Purchase Tax: Goods and Services Tax (GST) is levied at a flat rate of 3 per cent on most goods and services.

Social Security & Pensions: The Central Provident Fund (CPF) is a social security savings scheme to which employers contribute around 16 per cent and employees contribute around 20 per cent of their gross salary. The CPF provides retirement pensions and the fund can also be used to buy homes, pay for health care and invest in stocks and shares. Expatriate employees are required to contribute only if they're permanent residents. A Supplementary Retirement Scheme (SRS) was introduced in 2001; contributions are voluntary and are made only by employees, who may contribute up to 15 per cent (Singapore nationals and permanent residents) or 35 per cent (foreigners).

Withholding Taxes: Interest from bank accounts and securities is exempt. Other sources of interest and dividends are subject to withholding taxes and rates depend on the residence status of the recipient and whether a double-taxation treaty exists.

Tax Filing: The Singapore tax year is the calendar year and all individuals and companies are required to file annual tax returns by 15th April.

Doing Business

Forming A Company: Foreigners may choose from a variety of structures, such as sole proprietorship or partnership with up to 20 shareholders, a limited liability company, a branch or representative office. The choice should be based on the activity and tax considerations, and you should take expert advice before making a decision. Skilled and executive employees are readily available and most speak good English. Semi-skilled and unskilled labour is generally provided by foreigners, usually from Singapore's neighbouring countries. All businesses in Singapore must be registered with the Registry of Companies and Businesses (RCB).

Investment: Singapore welcomes foreign investment and there are generally few restrictions, although some sectors, such as banking, finance, insurance and stock broking, require a special licence from the government.

Government Incentives: Several financial incentives are available for certain business sectors. Procedures for applying for incentives have recently been simplified.

Business Hours: Businesses and offices are generally open from 8.30am to 5.30pm Mondays to Fridays and from 8.30am to 12.30pm on Saturdays. Banking hours are from 10am to 3pm Mondays to Fridays and from 11am to 4pm on Saturdays.

Public Holidays: 13 per year as follows:

Day/Date	Holiday
1st January	New Year's Day
Late January or February	Chinese New Year – three days
February	Hari Raya Haji (Feast of the Sacrifice)
March or April	Good Friday
1st May	Labour Day; one day in May, Vesak (Birth of Buddha)
9th August	National Day
October or November	Diwali
November or December	Hari Raya (End of Ramadan) – three days
25th December	Christmas Day

Note that the dates of some holidays vary according to local sightings of the moon's phases.

Business Etiquette: Singapore is a cosmopolitan country and business practice is similar to that in many western countries. Business dress is formal and punctuality is important. Appointments should be made in advance and you should arrange to see someone as senior as possible in the first instance, as it can be difficult to make contact with a higher-ranking person later. Business cards are essential and should be presented with both hands.

Accommodation

Restrictions On Foreign Ownership: You must be a permanent resident and, to buy certain kinds of property, you require permission from the Controller of Residential Property Land Dealings.

Cost Of Housing: Most Singapore citizens live in public housing, known as HDB apartments, which are built and maintained by the Housing and Development Board. Property is expensive owing to the lack of building land: a two-bedroom apartment costs from S$500,000 (US$295,000), a small house from S$800,000 (US$470,000).

Local Mortgages: Mortgages are available from local banks for residents with an adequate income.

Property Taxes: Property taxes are generally 4 per cent of the rateable value of a property and are included in your utility bills from the Public Utilities Board. They include a small charge for sewage maintenance and S$8 to S$20 (US$4.70 to US$11.75) for refuse collection, depending on the type of property.

Building Standards: Good.

Renting: Rented property is usually widely available, although it's more difficult to rent HDB apartments, which rarely become available. Rates vary enormously from S$1,500 (US$880) per month for a three-bedroom HDB apartment to from S$18,000 (US$10,000) per month for a large house with a garden.

Personal Effects: Personal effects can be imported duty-free, provided you've owned and used them for three months previously and continue to do so for six months after your arrival in Singapore. **There's strict import censorship of printed material, videos and CDs, and if you wish to import these items they will be subject to scrutiny by the censors, and a high import duty levied.**

Utilities: Electricity (230 to 250V), mains gas and water are supplied by the Public Utilities Board. When you register, you must pay a refundable deposit and monthly charges are reasonable. Note that there's also a monthly fee for each sanitary appliance in your home.

Communications

Postal Services: Singapore Post provides a fast and reliable postal service and numerous other services, such as bill and licence payment and renewal. Post office hours are 8.30am to 5pm Mondays to Fridays, 8.30am to 1pm on Saturdays. Airmail to Western Europe takes between five and seven days.

Telecommunications: Telecommunications are modern and efficient and are currently operated by three companies: M1, SingTel and Starhub. Full IDD is available. Competition is intense and call charges are constantly falling. Singapore has among the world's highest ownership of mobile phones. Singapore has GSM 900 and 1800, and network operators include MobileOne (Asia) Pte (💻 www.m1.com.sg), Singapore Telecom (💻 www.singtel.com) and StarHub Pte (💻 www.starhub.com).

International Dialling Code: 65.

Internet: The use of the internet in Singapore is widespread, with a penetration rate of over 50 per cent. However, e-commerce is yet to develop to the same extent as in the US and some European countries (partly because of concerns over set-up costs and security), although Singapore is expected to close the gap quickly. Internet service providers include Cyberway Pte (💻 starhub. com) and Singnet (💻 www.singnet.com).

Transport Infrastructure: The Singapore public transport system is one of the cheapest in the world and is generally reliable and efficient. MRT trains in particular provide a fast and reliable means of getting around the island. Within the city, taxis are the best way to travel and fares are low. Road conditions are good, although traffic congestion is commonplace and the government has introduced a number of measures designed to reduce this, including high import duty, high car prices and limitations on car use. Note that driving standards are sometimes poor, but better than in much of the region.

Getting There: Singapore's international airport – Changi – is served by flights from many international destinations and is often voted the world's 'best' airport.

Import/Export Restrictions: Generally none, since Singapore is to all intents and purposes a free port. Import goods are subject to GST at 3 per cent and certain items are controlled. Further information can be obtained from the Singapore Customs and Excise Department (🖳 www.gov.sg/customs).

Miscellaneous

Crime & Legal Restrictions: Low crime rate but many (petty) legal restrictions.

Education: Expatriate children whose parents are resident and in possession of an employment pass may attend state schools, for which there's an initial S$5,000 (US$3,000) contribution to the Education Fund and a monthly fee of S$3 to $5 (US$1.75 to US$3). There are many international schools catering for various nationalities, although British schools cater only for primary-school-age children. Many expatriates send their children to boarding schools in their home country.

English-Language Media: Channel 5 broadcasts in English and other channels broadcast mainly in local languages with English subtitles. Private satellite dishes aren't permitted (because of censorship) but you can receive programmes via cable TV, to which most households subscribe. There are several radio stations broadcasting in English. A TV and radio licence (including car radios) is compulsory and renewable annually. English-language newspapers include *The Business Times, The New Paper* and *The Straits Times*.

Time Difference: GMT +7.

Weights & Measures: Metric.

Reference

Useful Addresses

British Chamber of Commerce, 138 Cecil Street, 11-01 Cecil Court, Singapore 069538 (☎ 6222-3552, 🖳 www.britcham.org.sg).

British Embassy, Tanglin Road, Singapore 247919 (☎ 6424-4200, 🖳 www.britain.org.sg).

Economic Development Board (EDB), 250 North Bridge Road, 24-00 Raffles City Tower, Singapore 179101 (☎ 336-2288, 🖳 www.sedb.com).

Singapore Embassy, 3501 International Place, NW, Washington DC 20008, US (☎ 202-537 3100, 🖳 www.gov.sg).

Singapore Embassy, 9 Wilton Crescent, London SW1X 8SP, UK (☎ 020-7235 8315, 🖳 www.gov.sg/mfa/london).

US Embassy, 27 Napier Road, Singapore 258508 (☎ 6476-9100, 🖳 http:// singapore.usembassy.gov).

Further Reading

Titles prefaced by an asterisk are recommended by the author.

A Short History of Malaysia, Singapore and Brunei, C Mary Turnbull

Doing Business Guide: Singapore (PriceWaterhouseCoopers)

Fistful of Colours, Suchen Christine Lim

King Rat, James Clavell

Lee Kuan Yew – The Struggle for Singapore, Alex Josey

*Lord Jim, Joseph Conrad

Saint Jack, Paul Theroux

Useful Websites

American Association of Singapore (🖳 http://aasingapore.com) – A useful resource for those living, working or studying in Singapore.

British Club Singapore (🖳 www.britishclub.org.sp) – The club and its website are a social club and support network for expatriates and Singaporeans.

Contact Singapore (🖳 www.contactsingapore.org.sg) – A comprehensive general website covering all aspects of life in Singapore.

E-Citizen (🖳 www.ecitizen.gov.sg) – A government-run website providing a very useful guide to starting a business in Singapore as well as comprehensive advice on other aspects of business.

Expat Singapore (🖳 www.expatsingapore.com.sg) – Has English, French and German versions and includes information about all aspects of life in Singapore. Singapore Government (🖳 www.gov.sg) – The government website includes a useful section called 'Information and Services for non-Singaporeans'.

The Straits Times (🖳 http://straitstimes.asia1.com.sg) – The website of the Pacific Area Newspaper of the Year.

TAIWAN

General Information

Capital: Taipei.
Population: 22.5 million.

Foreign Community: There are around 330,000 foreign workers based in Taiwan, mainly in the capital and in the export-processing zones.

Area: 35,751km² (13,804mi²).

Geography: The island of Taiwan is east of China and is separated from the Chinese mainland by the Taiwan Strait. The South China Sea lies to the south, the Philippines Sea to the east and the East China Sea to the north. Taiwan is 394km (245mi) long and 142km (88mi) wide. Most of the island is mountainous, with the exception of the west coast, where there are plains used for agriculture.

Climate: Taiwan has a monsoon climate, with tropical and sub-tropical zones. Average temperatures are 20°C (68°F) in December and 30°C (86°F) in July, although humidity of over 80 per cent makes it seem considerably hotter, and rainfall is heavy. Tropical storms and typhoons are common from July to September.

Health: Japanese encephalitis and filariasis are low risks in rural areas and even lower in urban areas; the odd case of the former has been reported in Taipei. A cholera vaccination certificate is required of travellers arriving from infected areas, a yellow fever vaccination is necessary for travellers coming from affected areas, and anybody staying in the country for longer than 90 days must pass an HIV test. Vaccination against polio, tetanus, typhoid and hepatitis A and B is highly recommended.

The outbreak of Severe Acute Respiratory Syndrome (SARS) caused the World Health Organisation in June 2003 to advise foreigners against travel to Taiwan, although warnings have now been lifted.

Taiwan has a National Health Insurance Scheme, mainly subsidised by the government, to which employers pay a contribution of around 4.5 per cent of a worker's salary and employees around 1.3 per cent on monthly salaries of up to NT$60,800 (US$1,785). This makes medical costs in Taiwan among the cheapest in the region. To receive National Health Insurance, you must either be a citizen of Taiwan or hold and Alien Residence Certificate (see page 36). Even without National Health Insurance, medical bills for 'standard' illnesses are reasonable in Taiwan. Nevertheless, private health insurance is recommended.

Most doctors in Taiwan speak some English, although nurses and other medical staff tend not to. As well as plenty of public hospitals and health clinics, Taiwan has a number of private ones. Private clinics and hospitals are usually smaller and less well-equipped than public facilities, but they're more convenient, being more widespread and having longer opening hours.

Language: Mandarin, Taiwanese and other Chinese dialects are spoken on the island. English is widely used in business, although negotiations also take place in Mandarin (the official language).

Religion: Mainly Buddhism, with Christianity, Islam and Taoism.

Government: Parliamentary democracy.

Political Stability: Good. Taiwan's political spectrum changed dramatically in 2000, when the Democratic Progressive Party came to power, ending more than 50 years of Kuomintang (KMT) party rule. Taiwan is expected to hold a referendum on independence in the near future.

Economy

Overview: Taiwan's economy is one of the strongest in Asia and was virtually unaffected by the Asian crisis of 1997. Annual growth is strong and the government has introduced a number of political and economic measures in recent years to maintain the competitiveness of Taiwanese industries. These included the creation of the Asia-Pacific Regional Operations Centre to attract businesses operating globally to the island. In 2003 the crisis caused by SARS took a toll on the economy and GDP growth for 2004 will be reduced considerably.

GDP Per Head (2002): US$12,940.

Growth (2002): 3.4 per cent.

Target Industries: The manufacturing industry remains strong, as do the food processing and textile industries. In recent years, high-technology industry has become increasingly important and now accounts for more than half Taiwan's exports.

Employment Market

Overview: The Taiwanese workforce is highly skilled and well-educated, although there are labour shortages in several fields, including IT and software, and engineering. The supply of unskilled workers is maintained by workers from neighbouring countries and in recent years the number of foreign workers in Taiwan has grown significantly. A rising unemployment rate among Taiwanese nationals, however, has forced the government to reduce the number of foreign workers in some sectors and the construction industry cannot now employ foreign workers.

Unemployment Rate (2002): Around 5.3 per cent.

Work Permits: All foreign nationals wishing to work in Taiwan require an employment authorisation or work permit. Employers must fulfil certain conditions in order to obtain work permits for foreign personnel. **Foreigners cannot be self-employed in Taiwan.**

Labour Relations: Generally good, although in 2003 there was an increase in the number of workers involved in industrial action. Trade unions are active, particularly in the public sector.

Employment Conditions: The working week is 48 hours, from Monday to Friday, and annual holiday entitlement varies according to the profession. A minimum wage applies to most sectors. Note that there's a strong work ethic in Taiwan.

Ranking Among UK's Trade Partners: 17.

Ranking Among US's Trade Partners: 6.

Finance

Currency: New Taiwan dollar (NT$), made up of 100 cents. Notes are in denominations of NT$1,000, 500, 200, 100 and 50. Coins are in denominations of

NT$50, 10, 5 and 1, and 50 cents. Credit cards are widely accepted, and US$ travellers' cheques attract the lowest commission.

Exchange Rate (2003): US$1 = NT$34.

Exchange Controls: The controls depend on several factors, such as status and purpose or origin of the funds. Qualified importers and exporters generally have no limits but businesses and individuals are subject to certain controls.

Banks: Banking in Taiwan is controlled by the Central Bank of China and is now liberalised (until 1992 all banks were state-owned), with numerous commercial banks operating on the island. Foreigners may open a bank account, although high-rate deposit accounts can be held by foreigners only if they have an Alien Residence Certificate.

Cost/Standard Of Living: Taiwan has one of the highest standards of living in Asia. The cost of living is similar to Western Europe.

Loans: Short and medium-term loans are available from local banks and the Chiao Tung Bank assists with long-term financing for industry.

Interest Rate (2002): Around 1 per cent.

Taxation

Corporate Tax: Ranges from 0 to 25 per cent on net income from Taiwan sources in excess of NT$100,000 (US$2,950).

Personal Income Tax: Individuals are liable for personal income tax on all income derived from Taiwan. Certain expenses, such as rental payments for expatriates, are tax deductible and residents are entitled to numerous tax deductions and exemptions. Non-residents are taxed at a flat rate of 20 per cent and resident rates range from 6 per cent on taxable income below NT$370,000 (US$10,880) to 40 per cent on taxable income over NT$3,720,000 (US$109,400).

Capital Gains Tax: Residents are subject to CGT at the same rates as income tax (see above). Sales of land are exempt from CGT, although they're subject to a 'land value increment tax' (rates range from 10 to 30 per cent). Property sales aren't exempt from CGT.

Wealth Tax: None.

Inheritance & Gift Tax: For foreign nationals, estate tax is imposed on assets in Taiwan only and rates range from 2 to 50 per cent. There are generous deductions, but Taiwan has forced inheritance rules. Gift tax is levied at rates of between 4 and 50 per cent, with an annual exemption of NT$1 million (US$29,400).

Value Added/Sale/Purchase Tax: VAT is levied at 5 per cent on most goods and services.

Social Security & Pensions: Taiwan has two schemes which apply to businesses. Under the government labour insurance plan, which is mandatory except for service industries and applies to monthly salaries up to NT$42,000 (US$1,235), the employer contributes 3.85 per cent and the employee 1.1 per cent. Under the national health insurance scheme, which applies to monthly salaries up to NT$60,800 (US$1,790), contributions are around 4.5 per cent for employers and 1.3 per cent for employees.

Withholding Taxes: Dividend rates are 35 per cent for non-resident corporations, 30 per cent for non-residents and 0 per cent for residents. Interest is subject to 10 per cent for residents and 20 per cent for non-residents.

Tax Filing: The tax year is the calendar year and returns must be filed in the fifth month following the close of the tax year (i.e. from 1st to 31st May). Individuals who spend more than 183 days in Taiwan in any year must file a tax return. Married couples may file jointly after their first year of marriage.

Doing Business

Forming A Company: There are several options available to foreign investors, although the most common among foreigners not involved in manufacturing is a foreign branch or subsidiary. The establishment of any sort of company in Taiwan is subject to approval from the Ministry of Economic Affairs (MOEA).

Investment: Taiwan generally welcomes foreign investment, particularly in high-technology industries, although **the petroleum sector is prohibited to foreign investors**. The island is set to create numerous intelligent industrial parks in its bid to become a global logistics centre and a 'green silicon island'. There are currently four export-processing zones, where there are numerous business incentives, such as tax holidays and competitive leases.

Government Incentives: Incentives include tax credits for spending on certain products such as automation technology, recycling equipment and energy-saving devices, and research and development. Tax holidays are also available. Employers who replace foreign workers with Taiwanese nationals receive a monthly subsidy of NT$10,000 (US$2,950).

Business Hours: Banks are open from 9am to 3.30pm Mondays to Fridays, and businesses open from 9am to 5.30pm Mondays to Fridays. Saturday is no longer a working day.

Public Holidays: 16 per year as follows:

Day/Date	Holiday
1st to 3rd January	Founding of the Republic of China and New Year's Day
January or February	Chinese New Year – three days
29th March	Youth Day
5th April	Tomb-Sweeping Day and Anniversary of President Chiang Kai-Shek's Passing
June	Dragon Boat Festival
September	Mid-Autumn Moon Festival
September	Teacher's Day (Confucius' Birthday)
10th October	National Day
25th October	Taiwan's Retrocession Day

31st October	Birthday of Chiand Kai-Shek
October or November	Birthday of Dr Sun Yat-Sen
25th December	Constitution Day.

Business Etiquette: The Taiwanese are very formal and polite people, and your dress and business approach should reflect this. Business cards are essential (make sure you take plenty) and should be printed in Mandarin as well as English.

Accommodation

Restrictions On Foreign Ownership: Generally none in towns and cities, but foreigners cannot purchase property in restricted areas, such as forested land and near Taiwan's borders.

Cost Of Housing: Accommodation in Taiwan is generally very expensive and is mainly apartments, with very few houses. Small apartments in Taipei start at around NT$9 million (US$265,000).

Local Mortgages: Taiwan's banks have been very keen to offer mortgages to property buyers in recent years and the resultant intense competition has meant that in 2003 some banks started to lose money on mortgages! Mortgages are generally available for up to 80 per cent of the property price, for periods of up to 25 years.

Fees: Fees include deed tax at 6 per cent of the purchase price, stamp duty levied at 0.5 per cent and legal fees.

Property Taxes: Property taxes are payable annually and range from 1.38 to 5 per cent of the assessed value of the property.

Building Standards: Variable.

Renting: Rented accommodation is quite widely available. Most rental contracts are in Chinese and you should make sure that you understand all the conditions. **When you sign a contract, you will be required to pay between two and four months' damage-deposit.** A two-bedroom apartment costs from NT$9,000 to NT$30,000 (US$265 to US$900) per month, a three-bedroom apartment from NT$12,000 to NT$35,000 (US$350 to US$1,000), depending on the location and amenities.

Personal Effects: Personal effects and household goods can generally be imported duty-free, provided they're for personal use only and not sold. Some items less than a year old, e.g. new furniture, electrical appliances and antiques, may be subject to import duty. Note that you can import only two bottles of alcoholic drink.

Utilities: The electricity supply (110V) is reliable and efficient. Many apartments are connected to the gas supply. Tap water isn't drinkable in Taiwan, but bottled mineral water is widely available.

Communications

Postal Services: The postal service is generally efficient and delivery is reasonably fast. However, airmail to Western Europe sometimes takes ten days.

Telecommunications: The telephone service is provided mainly by the China Telephone Company, although there are other smaller companies. IDD is available and charges are reasonable. Mobile phones are popular and call charges reasonable for local calls but very high for international calls. GSM 900 and 1800 are in use, and operators include Far Eastone Telecommunications (🖳 www.fareastone.com.tw), KG Telecom (🖳 www.kgt.com.tw) and Taiwan Cellular Corporation (🖳 www.twngsm.com.tw).

International Dialling Code: 886.

Internet: Internet use is widespread in Taiwan, where the government has invested heavily in new technology. All government departments and the majority of companies are online and have email. Internet service providers include Asia Pacific Online (🖳 www.apol.com.tw) and Chunghwa Telecom/Hinet (🖳 www.hinet.net).

Transport Infrastructure: Taiwan has a good domestic flight service and Taipei's domestic airport serves most of the island's cities. Taipei itself has a metropolitan rail system, which is currently being expanded, and a comprehensive bus network. Taiwan has good roads, with freeways linking most cities, although traffic congestion is chronic and journey times slow.

Getting There: Taiwan has two international airports, Kaohsiung in the south and Chiang Kai Shek in the north, some 30km (19mi) from Taipei and the island's main airport. There are weekly flights from international destinations, although many travellers take flights via another Asian city, such as Hong Kong. Note that the journey from Chiang Kai Shek airport to Taipei takes at least an hour and that taxi drivers often speak no English. It's recommended to take a printed card in Mandarin with your destination address on it.

Import/Export Restrictions: Certain dangerous goods are subject to restrictions, but otherwise there are few. Tariffs are imposed, although the system is under review and soon to change. There are four 'export-processing' zones on the island from which exporting is considerably easier than from other areas.

Miscellaneous

Crime & Legal Restrictions: Very low crime rate and few restrictions.

Education: There are several private, foreign-curriculum schools in Taipei, including American, British, French, German and Japanese schools. State schools are open to resident foreigners, although all instruction is in Chinese.

English-Language Media: Taiwan television broadcasts mainly in Chinese, although several cable operators provide some channels in English. There is one

English-language radio station. English-language publications include *China Post, Taipei Journal, Taipei Review* and *Taiwan News*.

Time Difference: GMT +8.

Weights & Measures: Metric.

Reference

Useful Addresses

American Chamber of Commerce, Suite 1012, Chia Hsin Building, Annex, 96 Chung Shan N. Rd., Sec 2., Taipei 104 (☎ 02-2581 7089, 🖥 www.am cham.com.tw).

British Embassy in China, 11 Guang Hua Lu, Jianguomenwai, Beijing 100600 (☎ 10-6532 1961, 🖥 www.britishembassy.org.cn).

Chinese Embassy, 2300 Connecticut Avenue, NW, Washington DC 20008, US (☎ ?202-328 2500, 🖥 www.china-embassy.org).

Chinese Embassy, 31 Portland Place, London W1N 3AG, UK (☎ 020-7636 9375, 🖥 www.chinese-embassy.org.uk).

European Chamber of Commerce, 11F, 285 Zhongxiao East Road, Sec 4, Taipei (☎ 02-2740 0236, 🖥 www.ecct.com.tw).

Ministry of Economic Affairs (MOEA), 15 Fu Chou St, Taipei (☎ 02-23221 2200).

US Embassy in China, 3 Xiu Shui Bei Jie, Beijing 100600 (☎ 10-6532 3831, 🖥 http://beijing.usembassy.gov).

Note that there is no American or British diplomatic representation on the island.

Further Reading

Titles prefaced by an asterisk are recommended by the author.

Arts & Culture in Taiwan, B Kaulbach and B Proksch

Doing Business in Taiwan (Ernst & Young publications)

Taipei (Times Edition)

Taiwan with a View, (Independence Evening Post)

**The 100 Best Bars in Taipei*, Jim Ehrhart and Anthony Watts

Useful Websites

Forumosa (🖥 http://forumosa.com) – A Taiwan-oriented online community.

THAILAND

General Information

Capital: Bangkok.

Population: 62.4 million. 75 per cent Thai, 11 per cent Chinese, 3.5 per cent Malay, with Karen, Khmer, Mon and Phuan minorities.

Foreign Community: Before the Asia crisis of the late 1990s, it was estimated that there were some 400,000 foreigners living in Bangkok alone. There are fewer now but still a substantial expatriate population, mainly of Americans, Australians and New Zealanders.

Area: 513,115km^2 (200,000mi^2).

Geography: Thailand is situated in South-east Asia, with Burma to the west and north, Laos to the north and east, and Cambodia to the east. Southern Thailand consists of a long peninsula which is bounded on the west by the Indian Ocean and on the east by the South China Sea and the Gulf of Thailand, while to the south lies Malaysia.

Climate: Thailand has a tropical climate with three distinct seasons: the wet (monsoon) season from around June to October; the cool season from November to February (although 'cool' is a relative term in the south); and the hot season from March to June. The annual mean temperature in Bangkok is 28°C (82°F), although it can drop as low as 11°C (52°F) in the cool season and as high as 41°C (106°F) in the hot season. Humidity is quite high.

Health: The risk of malaria in Bangkok, Chiang Mai and the tourist areas of Ko Samui, Pattaya, Phuket and Songhkla is very low, but it's higher in areas bordering Cambodia and Myanmar (Burma). The risk of Japanese encephalitis is generally quite low, but there are occasional outbreaks in the Chiang Mai region and there have been cases in Bangkok. Sexually transmitted diseases are rife in Thailand, particularly HIV among the prostitutes of the cities and tourist resorts (see below). A yellow fever vaccination certificate is required by travellers over the age of one arriving from infected areas.

Thailand has some public health provision and it's of a reasonable standard (fees are charged according to a patient's income), but private sector treatment is much better, although expensive, and private health insurance is essential. Hospitals?80 Medical facilities in Bangkok are of a particularly high standard, the equal of many western cities for most types of healthcare. Outside the capital, however, standards are lower and in some places barely adequate, especially on the islands.

Medical fees aren't regulated in Thailand and doctors and hospitals set their own charges, which vary very widely. Fees in Bangkok can be as much as four times as high as those in the provinces, although standards are often much higher. Many Thai doctors speak English.

Language: The official language is Thai. English is widely spoken.

Religion: 95 per cent Theravada Buddhist, with 4 per cent Muslim and Christian minorities.

Government: Constitutional monarchy with bicameral legislature.

Political Stability: Very good. Thailand, known as Siam until 1939, is the only Asian country never to have been colonised or occupied by a western power. The King of Thailand, King Bhumibol Adulyadej (Rama IX), is one of the longest-serving monarchs in the world and a much-loved and influential head of state, providing stability and continuity.

Economy

Overview: Like many Asian countries, Thailand was badly hit by the Asian crisis in 1997 and in 1998 registered negative GDP growth of minus 10 per cent. Since then, however, the Thai economy has made a dramatic recovery, mainly owing to major economic reform introduced by the government, a more user-friendly foreign investor climate and a move towards the high-tech sector. Thailand, once a country heavily dependent on agriculture, is now one of the most diverse markets in the region. The UK is Thailand's fifth largest investor.

GDP Per Head (2002): US$12,940.

Growth (2002): 4.9 per cent.

Target Industries: Airports, communication, education and training, environment technologies and services, financial services, food and drink, IT, power and water.

Ranking Among UK's Trade Partners: 28.

Ranking Among US's Trade Partners: 13.

Employment Market

Overview: The Thai workforce has an abundance of unskilled workers, many of whom emigrate to the cities from the countryside, where over 35 per cent of the workforce is employed in agriculture. Education standards have risen dramatically in the last two decades and the literacy rate is over 90 per cent, but there's a shortage of skilled workers, particularly technical, management and engineering staff. Many foreign employers bring in expatriate employees for these positions. Despite economic problems in the late 20th and early 21st centuries, the number of expatriates coming to Thailand has increased, although their profile has changed. The majority used to work in the construction sector, but many now work in insurance, telecommunications and for legal and consultancy firms, and often have higher housing allowances than the construction employees used to receive. But many now come without their families, for short or medium-term projects, rather than being given permanent contracts. Unemployment is traditionally low in Thailand.

Unemployment Rate (2002): 2.9 per cent.

Work Permits: All foreign nationals require a work permit. Before entering the country you must apply for a non-immigration visa that entitles you to work and live in the country. You should apply in your home country and must provide proof of a firm offer of employment. Once in Thailand, you need to provide a medical certificate and proof of your qualifications.

Labour Relations: Generally very good and there are few strikes. Less than 2 per cent of the workforce belongs to a trade union.

Employment Conditions: Working conditions are regulated by the Labour Protection Act and there's a minimum daily wage. The working week is 48 hours and employees are entitled to national public holidays plus at least six extra days after one year's service. Expatriate employees can expect substantially more than this, plus a range of fringe benefits.

Finance

Currency: Baht (Bht), divided into 100 satang. Notes are in denominations of Bht1,000, 500, 100, 50, 20 and 10. Coins are in denominations of Bht10, 5 and 1, and 50 and 25 satang. Foreign currency can be exchanged at a range of banks, hotels and bureaux de change. Banks usually offer the most competitive rates. Credit cards are widely accepted and travellers' cheques in US$, € and GB£ attract the lowest commission.

Exchange Rate (2003): US$1 = Bht40.

Exchange Controls: Foreign currency transactions are regulated by (and require the permission of) the Bank of Thailand, although since 1990 regulations have been relaxed considerably. Note that all foreign currency earned by a resident, whether or not derived from employment or business in Thailand, and brought into Thailand, must be changed into local currency or deposited with a commercial bank within 15 days, unless permission for an extension is granted.

Banks: Thai banking is efficient and modern, and there are several foreign banks operating (mainly in Bangkok). Thailand is a popular base for offshore banking in Asia and banks are particularly oriented to the needs of foreigners. Non-residents can open only savings accounts; to open a current account you must be in possession of a valid work permit.

Cost/Standard Of Living: The standard of living is generally low, although there are vast differences between the cities (particularly Bangkok) and rural areas, where poverty is endemic. The cost of living is high and luxury goods relatively expensive.

Loans: Loans are available, although after the financial crisis in 1997 and the closure of more than 50 finance companies, Thai banks are somewhat reluctant to provide new credit and it may be some time before full confidence is restored. Many foreign investors use offshore financing.

Interest Rate (2002): Around 10 per cent.

Taxation

Corporate Tax: Incorporated companies are liable for 30 per cent corporate tax. Newly listed companies registered with the Thai Stock Exchange are liable for

25 per cent and those listed on the Market for Alternative Investment are liable for 20 per cent. Small and medium-size enterprises whose paid-up capital at the end of the financial year is less than Bht5 million (US$125,000) are subject to 20 per cent corporate tax on net profits up to Bht1 million (US$25,000), 25 per cent on profits between Bht1 million and Bht3 million (US$25,000 to US$75,000), and 30 per cent on amounts above Bht3 million.

Personal Income Tax: Income tax rates are from 5 per cent on annual earnings under Bht100,000 (US$2,500) to 37 per cent on earnings in excess of Bht4 million (US$100,000). There are numerous tax allowances for dependants and housing, and Thailand has double-taxation treaties with many countries. Residents are taxed on Thai-source income only.

Capital Gains Tax: None.

Wealth Tax: None.

Inheritance & Gift Tax: None.

Value Added/Sales/Purchase Tax: VAT is levied at 7 per cent on most goods and services. Certain services, such as education and financial transactions, are exempt. Note that some businesses, such as commercial banks and insurance companies, are subject to Specific Business Tax (SBT) at 3 per cent instead of VAT.

Social Security & Pensions: Social security payments are compulsory for all employers and employees, who each contribute 3 per cent of the employee's gross monthly salary (up to a monthly wage of Bht45,000/US$1,125). Benefits are limited.

Withholding Taxes: Interest is subject to withholding tax at 15 per cent and dividends at 10 per cent.

Tax Filing: The Thai tax year is the calendar year and all individuals are required to file annual returns by 31st March. Companies file returns every six months and are required to pay 50 per cent of the estimated annual income tax within 150 days of the close of a six-month accounting period.

Doing Business

Forming A Company: Thailand offers three options for foreign businesses: sole proprietorships, partnerships and public and private limited companies. The private limited company is the most popular option among foreign investors and requires a minimum of seven shareholders. All companies must be registered and require a company income tax identity card. Setting-up is generally straightforward.

Investment: Thailand generally welcomes foreign investment but there are numerous restrictions and company activity is divided into three lists: activities included in List 1 (such as media, farming and dealing in land) are totally prohibited to foreigners; those in List 2 (generally those concerning national security, art and culture, customs, local handicrafts, and those having an impact on natural resources and the environment) are prohibited to foreigners unless permission is obtained from the Ministry of Commerce after the appropriate cabinet resolution. List 2 activities must have a minimum of 40 per cent Thai participation and 40 per cent of the board must be Thai nationals. Activities on List 3 (by far the most numerous and classed as those where Thais aren't ready for competition) are prohibited to foreigners unless permission is obtained from the Department of Commercial Registration and the Ministry of Commerce. Approval from the Foreign Business Board is also necessary. All foreigners must invest between Bht2 million and Bht3 million (US$50,000 and US$75,000) depending on the activity. Contact the Thai Board of Investment (see **Reference** below) for further information.

Government Incentives: Several financial incentives are available, particularly for those foreign companies who choose to set up their Regional Operating Headquarters (ROH) in Thailand, for whom incentives are especially generous, including 10 per cent corporate tax and 15 per cent personal income tax for expatriate employees. The BCCT (see **Reference** below) and the British Embassy have introduced a new programme to assist British companies in gaining entry to the Thai market by matching companies with Thailand business executives in the same sector.

Business Hours: Businesses and offices generally open from 8am to 5pm Mondays to Fridays with an hour's break for lunch from noon to 1pm. Banking hours are from 9.30am to 3.30pm Mondays to Fridays.

Public Holidays: 16 per year as follows:

Day/Date	Holiday
1st January	New Year's Day
One day in February	Magha Bucha Day
6th April	Chakri Day
13th to 15th April	Songkran (Thai New Year)
1st May	Labour Day
One day in May	Visakha Bucha
5th May	Coronation Day
1st July	Mid-Year Bank Holiday
One day in July	Khao Phansa Day (Buddhist Lent)
12th August	HM The Queen's Birthday
23rd October	Chulalongkorn Day
5th December	HM The King's Birthday
10th December	Constitution Day
31st December	New Year's Eve

Dates for some holidays vary, as they're determined by the lunar calendar.

Business Etiquette: Before travelling to Thailand, it's worth studying Thai social customs and learning a few basic phrases of the language. Thai people place great emphasis on polite, respectful behaviour, and strong feelings should never be expressed. A handshake is an accepted form of greeting, although Thai women may be reluctant to shake hands.

Accommodation

Restrictions On Foreign Ownership: Foreigners cannot own land in Thailand and to purchase property you must obtain approval from the Ministry of the Interior. Foreigners are allowed to own up to 49 per cent of apartments in a block. The purchase price must be paid in full with funds brought into Thailand for this purpose. **You should obtain expert legal advice before committing yourself to a purchase.**

Cost Of Housing: In the aftermath of the Asian financial crisis of the late 1990s, property prices in Thailand fell dramatically, although in recent years prices have stabilised. Property is a reasonable long-term investment and in Bangkok two or three-bedroom apartments cost from Bht2 million (US$50,000) and houses from Bht2.5 million (US$62,500), depending on their location and age.

Local Mortgages: Local mortgages aren't available to foreigners and funds for the entire purchase price must be imported.

Purchase Fees: Stamp duty is charged at 0.5 per cent, a business tax at 0.11 per cent, income tax at 1 to 3 per cent and transfer fees at 0.01 per cent. The vendor pays the estate agent commission of between 3 and 5 per cent. Some agents try to charge a fee to the buyer and you should beware of this.

Property Taxes: Annual property tax rates vary according to the rateable value of land, although the average rate is 12.5 per cent. Owner-occupied residences are exempt.

Building Standards: Variable, although good in new properties.

Renting: Rental accommodation can be found easily in Bangkok, although it's recommended to rent through a reputable agent rather than independently. Rental contracts are usually for a minimum of a year and are generally written in English. Monthly rental fees range from Bht25,000 to Bht34,000 (US$625 to US$850) per m^2 according to the size, location and facilities. Most accommodation is spacious with air-conditioning. Serviced apartments are available for short-term rentals, but are considerably more expensive.

Personal Effects: A limited amount of personal effects can be imported duty-free if you have a residence permit; effects must be imported within six months of your arrival.

Utilities: The electricity supply (220V) is generally reliable except in bad weather, when power cuts are frequent. Charges are usually reasonable, although in some rented accommodation charges are high. Gas isn't available.

Tap water isn't generally safe to drink, but bottled water is widely available and can be delivered to your home. Water rationing is common in summer.

Communications

Postal Services: The postal service is reasonably efficient but can be slow, and many international companies prefer to use couriers. Airmail to Europe takes around a week.

Telecommunications: The telephone service is reasonably reliable and is operated by two companies, one state-owned and one private (the latter is generally better and provides a quicker service). Local calls are charged at a fixed rate of Bht3 (7.5¢), but other call charges are quite high. Note that in order to make IDD calls, you must register with the communications authorities. Mobile phones operate on GSM900, 1800 and 1900, and operators include Advanced Info Service (⌨ www.ais900.com), the Digital Phone Company (⌨ www.dpc1800.com) and Total Access Comms Co (⌨ www.dtac.co.th).

International Dialling Code: 66.

Internet: Internet use is widespread within the business community but private access isn't common, although this is changing and the internet is increasingly popular in Thai homes. Service providers include Asia Infonet (⌨ www.asianet.co.th) and Internet Thailand (⌨ www.inet.co.th).

Transport Infrastructure: Thailand has a comprehensive domestic flight service connecting the main cities. The country-wide bus network is excellent and one of the best ways to travel. The rail service is limited mainly to the area north of Bangkok. Bangkok itself has a good bus service and air-conditioned taxis are a popular and economical. River taxis also operate, as a means of crossing the river and of travelling to Bangkok's suburbs. Road conditions are generally reasonable, although congestion can be horrendous and driving standards are often poor.

Getting There: Thailand is well serviced by international flights and Thai Airways is regularly voted one of the world's 'best' airlines.

Import/Export Restrictions: Import controls have been greatly reduced in recent years, but there are still more than 50 classes of goods that require a licence, which is available from the Ministry of Commerce (see **Reference** below) and may be for a set period rather than for a specific product. The Ministry may also designate the port for arrival and unloading.

Miscellaneous

Crime & Legal Restrictions: Low crime rate and few restrictions.

Education: In recent years, several international schools have opened in and around Bangkok to cater for the needs of the expatriate population. Local educational standards aren't particularly high, although they've improved greatly over recent years. Instruction is in Thai.

English-Language Media: Cable TV is available in most rented accommodation in Bangkok and can be installed in other accommodation, although it's quite expensive. English-language newspapers include *Bangkok Post, Thailand Times* and *The Nation*.

Time Difference: GMT +6.

Weights & Measures: Metric.

Reference

Useful Addresses

British Chamber of Commerce Thailand (BCCT), 7th Floor, 208 Wireless Road, Bangkok 10330 (☎ 2665-153 503, 🖳 www.bccthai.com).

British Embassy, 1031 Wireless Road, Lumpini Pathumwan, Bangkok 10330 (☎ 2-305-8333, 🖳 www.britishemb.or.th).

Ministry of Commerce, Thanon Samamchai, Pranakorn, Bangkok 10200 (☎ 282-61719, 🖳 www.moc.go.th).

Royal Thai Embassy, 1024 Wisconsin Avenue, NW, Washington DC 20007, US (☎ 202-944 3600, 🖳 www.thaiembdc.org).

Royal Thai Embassy, 29-30 Queensgate, London SW7 5JB, UK (☎ 020-7589 2944).

Thailand Board of Investment, 55 Vibhavadi-Rangsit Road, Chatuchak, Bangkok 10900 (☎ 537-811 155, 🖳 www.boi.go.th). The website provides a wealth of economic and financial information.

US Embassy, 22 Wireless Road, Bangkok 10330 (☎ 2-205-4000, 🖳 http://bangkok.usembassy.gov).

Further Reading

A Woman of Bangkok, Jack Reynolds

Bangkok, (Lonely Planet)

Culture Shock! Thailand & How to Survive it, Robert and Nanthapa Cooper

Doing Business in Thailand (Ernst & Young Publications).

Hill Tribes of Northern Thailand, Gordon Young

Patpong Sisters, Cleo Odzer

Thailand, (Lonely Planet)

Thailand: A Short History, David Wyatt

Useful Websites

2 Bangkok (⌨ www.2bangkok.com) – A general guide to news and developments in Thailand.

Bangkok Post (⌨ www.bangkokpost.net) – The online edition of the newspaper, including a property guide.

Into Asia (⌨ www.into-asia.com) – A general guide to Bangkok, including everything from the cost of living to local scams.

Thailand Guidebook (⌨ www.thailandguidebook.com) – Travel guide site.

10.

ARRIVAL & SETTLING IN

On arrival in the Far East your first task is to negotiate immigration and customs (see below). Fortunately this presents few problems for most people. However, a visa is required to enter many countries, irrespective of the purpose of your visit (see page 19). You may also be required to entered via a particular airport, port or land border.

In addition to information about immigration and customs and adapting to life abroad, this chapter contains checklists of tasks to be completed before or soon after arrival in the Far East, plus suggestions for finding local help and information.

IMMIGRATION

When you arrive in the Far East, the first thing you must do is pass through immigration. **If you require a visa to enter a country and attempt to enter without one you will be refused entry.** If you have a single-entry visa, it will be cancelled by the immigration official. Some people may wish to get a stamp in their passport as confirmation of their date of entry into a country. If you're going to the region to work, study or live, you may be asked to show documentary evidence. Visitors may also be asked to produce a return ticket and proof of accommodation, health insurance and financial resources, e.g. cash, travellers' cheques or credit cards. Immigration officials aren't required to prove that you will break the law and can refuse you entry on the grounds of suspicion. **The onus is on visitors to prove that they're genuine and won't violate immigration laws.**

Immigration officials in most countries are usually polite and efficient, although they're occasionally a little over-zealous in their attempts to exclude illegal immigrants, and certain nationalities or racial groups may experience harassment or even persecution.

CUSTOMS

Customs regulations vary considerably according to the country, your nationality, and whether your home country has an agreement with the country where you're planning to live. The rules regarding the importation of furniture and personal effects usually vary according to whether you will be a temporary or permanent resident. **Before making any plans to ship goods to any country, check the latest regulations with a local embassy or consulate in your home country.** You may need to obtain an application form (available from local embassies) and provide a detailed inventory of the items to be imported and their estimated value in local currency. All items to be imported should be included on the list, even if some are to be imported at a later date. Customs documents may need to be signed and presented to an embassy or consulate in the Far East with your passport.

It's usually necessary to show proof of having rented or purchased a home, and in some countries you may need to pay a deposit or obtain a bank guarantee equal to the value (or a percentage) of the personal effects to be imported. The deposit is returned after a specified period, e.g. one or two years, or when the goods are exported or you've obtained a residence permit. Belongings imported duty-free mustn't be sold within a certain period of their importation, e.g. one or two years, and, if you leave the country within this period, everything imported duty-free must be re-exported or duty paid.

If you use a shipping company to transport your belongings, the company will usually provide all the necessary forms and complete the paperwork. Always keep a copy of all forms and communications with customs officials, both those in the Far East and those in your 'home' country. If the paperwork isn't in order, your belongings may end up incarcerated in a customs storage depot for a number of weeks or months. If you personally import your belongings, you may need to employ a customs agent at the point of entry to clear them. You should have an official record of the importation of valuables in case you wish to export them later. For information about importing cars, see **Importing A Car** on page 219.

Prohibited & Restricted Goods

Certain goods are subject to special regulations in all countries and in some cases their import and export is prohibited or restricted. These may include the following:

- Animal products;
- Plants, bulbs and seeds;
- Wild fauna and flora and products derived from them;
- Live animals;
- Medicines and medical products (except for prescribed medicines);
- Firearms and ammunition;
- Certain goods and technologies with a dual civil/military purpose;
- Works of art and collectors' items.

If you're unsure whether anything you're importing falls into one of the above categories, check with the local customs authorities. If you wish to import sporting guns, you may require a certificate from an embassy or consulate abroad, which is usually issued on production of a local firearms licence. Those travelling to the Far East from other 'exotic' regions, e.g. Africa, South America and the Middle East, may find themselves under close scrutiny from customs and security officials searching for illegal drugs. The following sections describe specific restrictions that apply in each territory.

Brunei

The following can be imported into Brunei by travellers aged 17 and over without incurring customs duty:

- 200 cigarettes or 250g of tobacco products;
- A one litre bottle of spirits or wine (only by non-Muslims and it must be declared at customs);
- 60ml of perfume and 250ml of eau de toilette.

Prohibited items are drugs (narcotics), firearms and pornography. All medicines must be declared. **The penalty for drug trafficking is death, while the possession of drugs carries a 20-year jail sentence and punishment by caning.**

China

The following can be imported into China by travellers staying less than six months without incurring customs duty:

- 400 cigarettes (600 for stays of over six months);
- Two bottles (up to 75cl) of alcoholic drinks (four bottles for stays of over six months);
- A 'reasonable' amount of perfume for personal use.

Prohibited items are arms, ammunition, 'pornography' (which includes material that would seem innocuous in the west), radio transmitters and receivers, exposed but undeveloped film, fruit and some vegetables, political and religious pamphlets (a modest amount of religious material for personal use is allowed), and any printed material 'directed against the public order and the morality of China' (a very loose definition, open to interpretation).

Please note that Chinese customs officials can be over-zealous. They sometimes seize audio and video tapes, books and CDs to check for political, pornographic or religious material. Be sure to complete the baggage declaration forms on arrival noting all valuables (e.g. cameras, watches and jewellery), because these are sometimes checked when you leave the country. Keep receipts for any valuables you buy in China, which are necessary to obtain export certificates when you leave.

Hong Kong

The following can be imported into Hong Kong by non-residents aged over 18 without incurring customs duty:

- 200 cigarettes or 50 cigars or 250g of tobacco;
- A one-litre bottle of wine or spirits;
- A 'reasonable' amount of other items for personal use.

Residents may import only 60 cigarettes or 15 cigars or 75g of tobacco, 75cl of still wine, and a 'reasonable' amount of other items for personal use. Prohibited items are counterfeit goods, firearms, drugs, copyright-infringed goods, plants and endangered species (dead or alive) and products derived from them. Antibiotics are prohibited unless accompanied by an explanation of their use from your doctor, and the import of animals is strictly controlled.

Indonesia

The following can be imported into Indonesia by travellers aged over 18 without incurring customs duty:

- 200 cigarettes or 50 cigars or 100g of tobacco;
- One litre of alcohol;
- A 'reasonable' quantity of perfume and gifts up to a value of US$250.

Cameras must be declared upon arrival in Indonesia and video tapes, laser discs, computer software and motion-picture film are invariably screened for content by the censor board.

Prohibited items are ammunition, weapons, non-prescribed medicines, TV sets, cordless telephones and other electrical equipment, fresh fruit, Chinese medicines and publications, and 'pornography' (which includes a wide variety of material).

Japan

The following can be imported into Japan without incurring customs duty:

- 400 cigarettes or 100 cigars or 500g of tobacco;
- Three bottles of spirits (75cl each);
- 57ml of perfume;
- Gifts up to the value of ¥200,000 (US$1,835).

Alcohol and tobacco allowances apply to people aged over 20. Prohibited items are anything that infringes a patent, trademark or copyright, counterfeit or altered coins, banknotes or securities, plants with soil attached, most meats, animals without health certificates, ammunition and firearms, drugs and obscene articles and publications.

Korea

The following can be imported into Korea by travellers aged over 20 without incurring customs duty:

- 200 cigarettes or 50 cigars or 250g of other tobacco products;
- One litre of alcoholic drink;
- 2oz of perfume;
- Gifts valued up to US$400.

Prohibited items are drugs, fruit, hay, seeds, products originating from communist countries, and printed material, films, records or cassettes deemed to be obscene, subversive or harmful to national security or public interest. Restricted items are firearms, explosives and other weapons, textiles, radio equipment and anything considered to be for commercial use, and some animals and plants.

Malaysia

The following can be imported into Malaysia without incurring customs duty:

- 200 cigarettes or 50 cigars or 225g of tobacco;
- One litre of alcoholic drink;
- One bottle of perfume up to a value of RM200 (US$52.65);
- 100 matches;
- Gifts and souvenirs up to a total value of RM200 (US$52.65).

Prohibited items are anything from Israel and South Africa, non-prescribed medicines, drugs, pornography, weapons, any cloth bearing the imprint or reproduction of any verses of The Koran and any imprint or reproduction of any currency note or coin.

Philippines

The following can be imported into the Philippines without incurring duty:

- 400 cigarettes or 50 cigars or 250g of tobacco;
- Two litres of alcoholic drinks, in bottles of not more than one litre.

The items that are prohibited are explosives, firearms, pornography, seditious or subversive material, drugs, gambling items and machines, and adulterated or misbranded foodstuffs.

Singapore

The following can be imported into Singapore (from everywhere except Malaysia) by travellers who are aged 18 or older without incurring any customs duty:

- One litre of spirits, one litre of wine and one litre of beer;
- Gifts and food items valued at up to S$150 (US$87.50) if away from Singapore for less than 48 hours, S$300 (US$175) if away for 48 hours or more.

Duty-free cigarettes are forbidden, and chewing gum and tobacco products must be declared on arrival in Singapore. Prohibited items are firearms, non-prescribed medicines, drugs, pornography, meat and meat products. Export permits are needed for arms, ammunition, explosives, animals, telecommunications equipment, film and video tapes and discs, precious metals and stones, drugs and poisons.

Taiwan

The following can be imported into Taiwan by travellers aged over 20 without incurring customs duty:

- 200 cigarettes or 25 cigars or 454g of tobacco;
- One bottle (one litre or less) of alcoholic drink;
- 'Reasonable' quantities of perfume;
- Other goods for personal use up to a value of NT$20,000 (US$587.20).

Travellers aged under may import goods up to a value of NT$10,000 (US$293.50) duty-free. Prohibited items are arms, drugs, ammunition, gambling articles, meat products (unless tinned), fresh fruit and toy pistols, publications promoting communism and items originating in Albania, Bulgaria, Cambodia, China, Cuba, North Korea, Laos, Romania, Vietnam and members of the CIS. All luggage must be itemised and declared in writing.

Thailand

The following can be imported into Thailand by all travellers, irrespective of age, without incurring customs duty:

- 200 cigarettes or 250g of tobacco or the same weight of cigars;
- One litre of wine or spirits;
- One still camera with five rolls of film or one movie camera with three rolls of 8mm or 16mm film.

Prohibited items are non-prescribed medicines, drugs, ammunition, firearms and meat from countries affected by BSE.

RESIDENCE

Foreigners (legally) residing in a Far Eastern country for longer than 90 or 180 days must usually either obtain a visa extension or apply to become a resident. If you don't have a regular income or adequate financial resources, your application may be refused. Failure to apply for a residence permit within the specified time is a serious offence and can result in a heavy fine or even deportation. **Permission to reside in a country may depend on your nationality and whether a reciprocal agreement exists between your home country and the country where you're planning to live.** For details, see **Permits & Visas** on page 19.

EMBASSY REGISTRATION

Nationals of some countries are required to register with their local embassy or consulate after taking up residence in the Far East. Registration isn't usually mandatory, although most embassies like to keep a record of their country's citizens abroad. Many countries maintain a number of consulates in the region; for example, most major European countries maintain consulates in the major cities where their nationals reside. Consulates are an important source of local information and can often provide useful contacts.

FINDING HELP

One of the major problems facing new arrivals in any foreign country is where to get help with day-to-day problems. How successful you are at finding local help depends on the town or area where you live (e.g. those in cities and resort areas are far better served than those living in rural areas), your nationality, your language proficiency and your sex (women are usually better catered for than men, through women's clubs). There's often an abundance of information available in the local language, but less in English and little in other foreign languages. An additional problem is that much of the available information isn't intended for foreigners and their particular needs. You may find that your friends, neighbours and colleagues can offer advice based on their own experiences and mistakes. But take care! Although they mean well, you're likely to receive as much unreliable and conflicting information as accurate (it may not be wrong but may not apply to your particular situation).

If a woman lives in or near a major town, she can turn to many English-speaking women's clubs and organisations for help. The single foreign male (who, of course, cannot possibly have any problems!) must usually fend for himself, although there are men's expatriate clubs in some areas and mixed social clubs in most countries. Among the best sources of information and help for women are the American Women's Clubs (AWC) located in major cities. AWCs provide comprehensive information in English about local matters and topics of more general interest, and many provide data sheets, booklets and orientation programmes for newcomers. Membership of the organisation is sometimes limited to Americans or those with active links to the US, e.g. through study, work or a spouse who works for a US company or the US government, but most publications and orientation programmes are available to others for a fee. AWCs are part of the Federation of American Women's Clubs Overseas (FAWCO), which can be contacted via its website (🖥 www.fawco.org).

In addition to the above, there are many social clubs and expatriate organisations for foreigners in most of the region's countries, whose members can help you find your way around. They may, however, be difficult to locate, as most clubs are run by volunteers and operate out of the president's or secretary's home, and they rarely bother to advertise or take out a phone book listing. If you ask among your neighbours or colleagues, it's possible to find various Anglophone 'friendship' clubs or English-speaking organisations. Finally, don't neglect to check the internet, where local newspapers, government offices, clubs and organisations often have websites. Contacts can also be found through expatriate magazines and newspapers.

Your town hall may be a good source of information, but you usually need to speak the local language to benefit and may still be sent on a wild goose chase from department to department. However, some town halls in countries where there are many foreign residents have a foreigners' department, where staff may speak English.

Many businesses (particularly large multinational companies) produce booklets and leaflets containing useful information about clubs or activities in the area. Book shops may have some interesting publications about the local region, and tourist and information offices are also good sources of information. Most embassies and consulates provide their nationals with local information, which may include the names of local lawyers, interpreters/translators, doctors, dentists, schools, and social and expatriate organisations.

Home Help

If you spend long periods at a home in the Far East or live there permanently, you may wish to employ someone to help around the home such as a cleaner, housekeeper, maid, nanny, cook, gardener, chauffeur, nurse or baby-sitter. If you have young children, you can also employ an au pair in many countries. In some countries you're permitted to take a 'servant' with you, although this may depend on your status.

If you need or wish to hire a full-time employee, there are a number of important points to take into consideration. In some countries there are strict regulations concerning the employment of full-time domestic staff, including minimum salaries, time off and paid holidays. Minimum salaries may vary considerably according to the nationality, age and experience of an employee. You may need to apply for a work or residence permit and pay an employee's pension, accident and health insurance (or part). It may also be necessary to deduct tax at source from your employee's income (including lodging and meals, if part of his salary) and complete all the associated official paperwork.

In some countries, an employer and a domestic employee must have a written contract of employment; if there's no written contract, the law may assume that there's a verbal agreement for a minimum period, e.g. a year. If you break the law regarding the hiring and firing of employees, an employee may have redress to a labour court, which can result in a substantial compensation award. Most regulations apply to full-time staff only and not to temporary staff employed for less than a specified number of hours per week, e.g. 15 or 20.

In many countries you should ensure that employees are covered by social security, as you can be held responsible should they have an accident on your property. Always ask to see an employee's social security card and obtain legal advice if you're unsure of your obligations under the law. Note that if you're found to be employing someone who isn't paying social security (and income tax), you can be heavily fined and may have to pay any unpaid social security payments. In some countries you should ask for a written quotation from temporary staff stating the work to be done and the cost, as this will then make them legally responsible for their own insurance and social security.

Although there are statutory minimum wages in some countries for full-time employees, you may need to pay a higher rate for a temporary employee who's employed by the hour, half-day or day. Enquire among your neighbours and friends to find out the going rate; if you pay too much, you could find yourself unpopular. If you need to hire someone who speaks English or another foreign language, you may need to pay a premium.

ADAPTING TO LIFE IN THE FAR EAST

Although many expatriate workers are single, experiencing life in the Far East before they settle in their home countries, many are accompanied by their families, who, usually because of the man or woman's profession or career, find themselves relocating abroad (for an average of around four years), possibly several times in their life. The implications are far-reaching, particularly for family members who are being uprooted for reasons alien to them and who may not want to leave what they regard as home.

Family life may be completely different in the Far East and relationships can become strained under the stress of adapting and culture shock (see page 414). You shouldn't underestimate the consequences of culture shock, the effects of which can be lessened if you accept the condition rather than deny it – a popular tactic that's often used to save face in front of others. Your family may find itself in a completely new and possibly alien environment, your new home may scarcely resemble your previous one (it may be much more luxurious or significantly smaller) and the climate and way of life may be dramatically different from those of your home country.

Your new country may be much richer or poorer than your home country and you will need to adapt to this. Bear in mind that this will be much more difficult if the country or region is significantly poorer, when the images and experiences confronting you may initially be distressing. You may find yourself with servants, a novelty at first but one that can bring additional problems. If possible, you should prepare yourself for as many aspects of the new situation as you can and explain to your children the differences they're likely to encounter, while at the same time dispelling their fears.

Family members, particularly parents, often find that they assume a new role during a posting abroad. The spouse who was the instigator of the relocation (in most cases the man) becomes the most important member of the family. Decision-making may be almost entirely in his hands and he will probably manage all financial matters, particularly if his wife doesn't work and banking transactions are performed through his company. The man will probably also be working longer hours than he was at home, as his overseas posting may be a promotion involving increased responsibility and demanding more time and dedication to his job, and he will therefore be spending less time with his family than previously.

The woman, particularly if she worked before moving abroad, will therefore find herself in a new situation where she is financially dependent on her partner, and where her children (through lack of time with their father) become much more dependent on her than previously. The mother may find herself alone, a solitude intensified by the fact that there are no close relations or friends on hand. The resulting situation can put tremendous strain on a family. However, if you're aware that this may arise beforehand, you can act to lessen its effects. Good communication between family members is vital and you should make time to talk about your experiences and feelings, both as a couple and as a family. Questions should always be raised and, if possible answered, particularly when asked by children.

However difficult the situation may appear at the beginning, it will help to bear in mind that it's by no means unique and that most expatriate families have experienced exactly the same problems and have managed to triumph over them and thoroughly enjoy their stay in the Far East.

There are numerous resources for families planning a move abroad, including *Women Abroad* magazine (🖳 www.womanabroad.com), *Living &*

Working Abroad: A Wife's Guide (Kuperard), *Living & Working Abroad: A Parent's Guide* (Kuperard) and *Homeward Bound* (Expatriate Press), all written by Robin Pascoe, *The Third Culture Kid Experience* by David C. Pollock & Rurh E. Van Reken (Intercultural Press), plus many websites, including 💻 www.expats pouse.com, www.outpostexpat.nl, www.expatexchange.com and www. brookes.ac.uk/worldwise. See also **Appendices A, B** and **C**.

Children

Expatriate children (known as 'third culture kids' by sociologists) run into hundreds of thousands in the region. In general, children under 12 adapt much faster to new surroundings and tend to accept new realities and situations far more readily than adults. However, this doesn't mean that children will take to living in a new country immediately, nor that they won't suffer similar culture shock and feelings of displacement to those of their parents.

Before Arrival

In order to make your children's move to another country as problem-free as possible, you should consider the following before leaving home:

- Provide them with as much information as possible about the country you're going to. Look at maps, books, videos and websites together, and talk about what you're going to discover.

- Talk to your children and try to discover their expectations and fears (children's imaginations are vivid, particularly about the unknown). Answer all the questions that you can and try to correct any misconceptions they have.

- It will help if you can find your children pen friends in the new country a few months before you go.

- If the move involves learning a new language, it will help enormously if your children have language lessons beforehand and even, if time permits, arrange a cultural exchange (where your child changes places with a child in the country that you're moving to). This is particularly important for teenage children.

- Try to find out about potential new schools and share the information with your children. If possible, contact other expatriate parents with children at the same school and ask their advice. Note that most international schools have a higher academic level and a greater sense of competitiveness than their equivalent at home, so you may need to prepare your children for this. If possible, try to find a family locally who have been to the country you're moving to and arrange a meeting with them and encourage your children to ask as many questions as possible.

- If they're old enough, allow your children to organise their own farewell party for friends and make sure that they say goodbye to everyone (and everything) before you leave. Bear in mind that it may be difficult or impossible to take pets with you (see page 276) and you may need to leave them with friends or relatives or have them 'adopted'.

- Above all, try to be positive about the move – even if you aren't! Children are quick to pick up on any negative undercurrents or tensions in their parents and, if you're openly nervous and apprehensive about a move, they will be too.

Although families may be given relatively short notice before a relocation and you often don't have a lot of choice about when you can arrive in a new country, you should try to arrive a few weeks before the start of a new term or school year. This will give your children time to settle into their new home and surroundings, possibly time to visit their new school, but not so much time that they will become bored without school (and friends). They will then quickly get back into the school routine, albeit a different one. Be aware that your children's school(s), as well as being totally new, may also have a different educational system or curriculum from what they're used to. Your children may therefore find themselves immersed in two new cultures, that of the country and the school – to say nothing of possibly having to learn another language!

While health and safety issues are of paramount importance for any expatriate, they're even more important when you have children, and they should be planned for thoroughly before leaving your home country. They may include the following:

Insurance: Make sure that your health insurance covers your children for all eventualities and that it includes evacuation when treatment isn't available locally.

Vaccinations: Find out well in advance of your departure the vaccinations your family will need and whether there are any optional but recommended vaccinations; it's wise to have those also. Check how long the vaccinations are valid for and keep them up to date.

Medicines: Take useful medicines and a first-aid kit with you. In many countries some medicines aren't always available or are difficult to find, so it's recommended to take a good supply of infant analgesic and anti-fever medicines with you. You may also wish to take a supply of anti-diarrhoea and other general medicines for your children. Find out what other medication you may require, such as malaria tablets.

Hygiene: Scrupulous hygiene can often prevent illness, particularly in hot and/or developing countries, and its importance must be impressed upon your children at an early stage. In particular, unless the tap water is absolutely safe to drink, they should get used to drinking bottled water (from a reliable source) – even for cleaning their teeth. They should wash all fresh produce (fruit and vegetables), fish and meat thoroughly in boiled or bottled water, and avoid using ice made from tap water in drinks unless they're certain it's drinkable. Teach your children not to drink from public water supplies and not to buy food from street vendors.

Local Dangers: Prepare your children for the possible dangers of their new environment, which may include people, animals and traffic. Inform them about no-go areas and teach them what to do in threatening situations.

Unwelcome Attention: If your children are fair-haired, prepare them for the fact that they (particularly teenagers) may receive a lot of unsolicited attention. Teach them what to do if they find themselves the centre of unwelcome attention and how to deal with it.

Teenagers: Teenagers will probably react negatively at first to the idea of relocation and certainly very differently from their younger siblings. The thought of leaving friends and familiar references will usually be more overwhelming the older a child is. Teenagers will also have a much better idea of the world as it really is than younger children, whose experience is limited. A teenager will probably already know something about the country and may have preconceived ideas or even prejudices. You will need to provide exact information for teenagers, as well as give them precise assurances to dispel their fears and apprehensions.

For example, you will need to know in advance what sort of independence you will be able to offer a teenager once you're settled in the new country and will need ready-prepared answers to questions such as: Will I be able to go shopping on my own or with my friends? Will I be able to get the bus on my own (or drive a car) and what sort of things will I be able to do with my friends? If you're going to live in an expatriate compound in the country you're relocating to, you will have to explain the implications of this to a teenager, who will probably be used to considerably freedom and lack of restriction. Teenage daughters will need particular information and explanations if you're moving to a country where women have restrictions imposed on them (see **Women** on page 41).

After Arrival

Once you've arrived in your new country, try to establish a routine for your children as soon as possible. Children need routine, which is essentially their point of reference in life and their way of keeping a grip on reality. Whatever circumstances you find yourself in, develop a daily routine so that your children feel more stable and secure (this will also be beneficial for parents!).

You should ensure that your children retain plenty of contact with home and their friends. It may be possible for them to communicate by email with their friends and previous school class. It also helps to encourage letter writing to friends and relatives (and replying to letters!). When you arrive, ensure that your children have plenty of photos and reminders of life back home in their new home, particularly in their bedrooms. However, be aware that your children may quickly consider the new country to be 'home' – probably well before you do!

Language: Encourage your children to learn a new language (see page 185), a task younger children find astonishingly easy compared to adults. Pre-teenage children quickly pick up a foreign tongue and if they're at a local school rather than an international establishment (where English is the main teaching language), they will usually quickly become fluent. You should encourage this, as it has been proved that bi-lingual children are generally more intelligent, culturally aware and tolerant. However, you should take care that your children don't lose their mother tongue. It's recommended to speak to them and have a ready supply of books and videos in their native tongue, and to encourage visits to their home country. When children attend a local school where they're taught in a foreign language, expatriate parents often arrange for private lessons in their mother tongue during school holidays, if possible with other expatriate children.

Culture: Expatriates in some countries tend to live their lives in a sanitised 'expatriate bubble', inside which everything is orientated towards expatriate needs and demands, and where there's little or no contact with the host country's culture or people. You should encourage your children to experience the new culture so that they can understand the real country, rather than seeing it through (rose-tinted?) expatriate spectacles. This will undoubtedly mean greater effort on your part, as you will need to find extra motivation to learn the language, to travel and to take part in local customs and traditions. However, if you endeavour to integrate (even to a small extent), it will be much easier for your children to experience the new culture. Research has shown that expatriate children who are exposed to another culture benefit far more from relocation than those who are constrained by the 'expatriate bubble'.

Medical Services: When you arrive at your destination, one of your first priorities should be to find out where the nearest local doctor and hospital are and how to get there. It's recommended to register with a doctor soon after arrival. Children are accident-prone and you never know when you may need medical help, so you should keep a list of emergency numbers by the telephone. Embassies can usually provide the names and addresses of reputable local doctors and clinics, and other expatriates may be able to make recommendations.

Teenagers: With teenagers, you must take care that they don't find their lives too sheltered in their new home. Teenagers, especially older ones, will be used to the freedom afforded them at home, where they probably hung out with their friends at weekends, went shopping at the local mall on their own or with friends, and popped down to the local sports centre for a swim or a game of tennis. The ground rules may be very different in your part of the Far East and need to be established from the start. If you've moved to a country where teenage children cannot feasibly go on a shopping trip by themselves, you need to provide an acceptable alternative, preferably one that you've discussed and agreed upon beforehand. Depending on the country and the situation there, you may also need to discuss with your children the dangers of drugs, alcohol, prostitution and crime (etc.) in the context of the new culture. If you have a teenage daughter, discuss thoroughly with her the implications of the new culture for women, if applicable.

Further Information: An excellent book about moving abroad and adjusting to expatriate life written specifically for children is *Let's Make a Move* published by BR Anchor Publishing (⌨ www.branchor.com). For parents, *The Third Culture Kid Experience* by David C. Pollock & Rurh E. Van Reken (Intercultural Press) is a useful guide, and *Living & Working Abroad, A Parent's Guide* by Robin Pascoe (Kuperard) provides practical advice on all aspects of your stay.

CULTURE SHOCK

Although often used loosely to refer to the period of adjustment to a new country, the term 'culture shock' properly describes a particular psychological and physical state often experienced by people who relocate abroad. The symptoms are essentially psychological and are caused by the sense of alienation that you feel when bombarded on a daily basis by cultural differences in an environment where there are few, if any, familiar references (see below). It's thought that culture shock has five components:

1. Stress caused by the obvious changes that travel involves, including the adjustment to a new climate and language.

2. A sense of deprivation that you feel when away from your home, possessions, family and friends (etc.), i.e. those things that anchor and define us and give us a sense of place, status and continuity.

3. A feeling of rejection by people in the country that you're visiting, which is sometimes experienced.

4. Confusion as to what you're doing and why.

5. Powerlessness and the inability to cope with all of the above.

Culture shock is also said to have physical symptoms, which usually manifest themselves in the form of an increased incidence of minor illnesses (e.g. colds and headaches), but can also lead to more serious psychosomatic illnesses brought on by depression. Individuals may experience any or all of the above symptoms and to varying degrees. The word 'shock' implies a sudden impact, but in fact culture shock is usually felt as a series of experiences, which can be broken down into the following five stages:

1. The first stage is known as the 'honeymoon stage' and usually lasts between a few days and a few weeks after arrival. This stage is positive, when the newly arrived traveller finds everything an exciting and interesting novelty. It's characterised by the making of enjoyable (but superficial) acquaintances

and friendships. Most travellers don't stay anywhere long enough to move beyond the honeymoon stage, which is why holidays are usually pleasant experiences (and why it's often unwise to visit the same place twice!).

2. The second stage is very different from the first: it's negative and comes as the initial excitement and feelings of holiday euphoria wear off. It's characterised by a general feeling of disorientation and confusion, as well as loneliness. Physical exhaustion brought on by jet lag and extremes of hot and cold weather are characteristic of this stage.

3. The third stage is sometimes called the 'flight' stage, because of an overwhelming desire to escape. It usually lasts the longest and is the most difficult to cope with. The traveller feels depressed and angry, as well as resentful towards the new country and its people. Depression is worsened by a person's inability to see anything positive or attractive about the country. Instead, he focuses on the negative aspects, refusing to acknowledge any plus points.

4. The fourth stage sees the traveller begin to relax, find it easier to fit in and adjust to the location, culture and language.

5. The final stage finds the traveller enjoying and benefiting from the cultural and social differences that he encounters and avoiding negative aspects of the country. He synthesises the foreign culture with his own, taking the best from both.

It's generally agreed by psychologists that it takes around six months for travellers to reach the fifth stage, which is therefore only relevant to those who are away from home for a long time, although some people adjust much earlier than this, while those who never get over the 'flight' stage are forced to return home early.

Non-working spouses and teenage children appear to be most affected by culture shock, as they rarely have any choice about a relocation and therefore feel most resentment when they find themselves in a situation in which they have little control or any familiar references. These two groups may also feel alone and isolated – the expatriate wife left behind in the new 'home' while the husband goes to his new office to meet new people who all speak his language, or the expatriate teenager at a new school trying desperately to be accepted by a new peer group. Younger children are also victims of culture shock, although they will probably suffer its effects for a shorter time than their older siblings and parents.

Although some degree of culture shock is unavoidable, there are certain things that you can do to minimise its adverse effects, both before travelling and while you're away:

● The key to reducing the negative effects of culture shock is to generate a positive attitude towards your trip and the country that you're visiting. If you approach the trip with confidence and convince yourself that the new experience is going to be 'different' rather than 'bad', it will go a long way towards helping you to feel less negative and resentful and to cope with and move on from any mishaps or unpleasant experiences.

- In order to feel positive about a trip, remind yourself of the benefits you will derive from it. Obtain as much information as possible about your destination. Immerse yourself in it before you go – not simply the country's culture and history, but its geography, transport systems, government and how the country operates (see **Appendices A** to **C**). This will smooth your integration and ensure that your arrival and settling in periods don't contain too many surprises. There are dozens of useful websites where you can obtain information, many of which also provide free 'notice boards' where you can post messages and questions. Before you go, try to find someone in your area who has visited the country and talk to them about it.

- Learn at least some of the language. The ability to speak the local language isn't just a practical and useful tool (one that will allow you to buy what you need, find your way around, etc.), but it's also the key to understanding a country and its culture. If you can speak the local language, even at a basic level, your range of possible friends and acquaintances is immediately widened beyond the usual limited circle of expatriates and fellow-travellers. Obviously, learning a language can take time and requires motivation. With sufficient perseverance, however, virtually anyone can learn enough to participate in the local culture. See also **Language Schools** on page 196.

- The relationship between the sexes is one of the most noticeable and important differences between cultures. Learning the rules before or early in your stay will ease your path and make you less likely to cause offence.

- Make a conscious effort to involve yourself in the new culture, even if you're somewhere for a relatively short time. You can do this by joining clubs, societies and organisations, whether meetings are in English or the local language.

- Get out and see the country and visit the tourist sites and attractions. If possible, make sure your family has plenty of weekend 'tourist' breaks – you may never get the chance again!

- Talk to other expatriates and share experiences. Although they may deny it, they've all been through exactly what you have and faced the same feeling of disorientation. Even if they may not be able to provide you with advice, it helps to know that you aren't alone and that it gets better in the end.

There are a number of books designed to help you understand and overcome culture shock, including *Breaking Through Culture Shock – How to Survive an International Assignment* by Dr. Elizabeth Marx (Nicolas Brealey), and many expatriate websites offer advice and help, including several of those listed in **Appendix C**.

RETURNING HOME

For a variety of reasons (e.g. end of assignment, political unrest, children's schooling) you will almost certainly return home sooner or later; those who have spent a number of years in the Far East may find this a daunting prospect, especially younger children, who may have spent a major part of their lives in the region or may not even remember their 'home'. Since you left your home country, your family will have changed and the return may not be an easy experience, as family members re-adjust to a lifestyle that has existed only in their memories for a number of years, and one that has probably been idealised, particularly if their life in the Far East has been in a developing country.

Your family will suffer from reverse culture shock as they discover that daily existence at home isn't quite what they imagined when abroad. You may even find that life at home is dull and monotonous, and that people quickly lose interest in your tales of life in the exotic East. The transition can be particularly confusing for children, who find themselves confronted with a culture that's supposed to be normal to them, although the one they've just left was their norm. According to experts, teenagers find the return home most difficult and they will probably need the most help and guidance as they try to find their place again among a new peer group, while trying to cope with one of the most difficult stages of their life.

To make your return home as smooth as possible, you should follow the same advice as for moving abroad, but above all you should allow yourself and your children plenty of time to settle back into your home country. It may take as long as a year for everyone to feel properly settled – by which time there may well be another posting abroad in the offing!

CHECKLISTS

Before Arrival

The checklists on the following pages list tasks which you need (or may need) to complete before and after arrival in the Far East:

- Check that your family's passports are valid!
- Obtain a visa, if necessary, for all your family members. Obviously this must be done before travelling to the Far East.
- Arrange health and travel insurance for your family. This is essential if you aren't already covered by a private insurance policy and won't be covered by a country's national health service.
- Open a local bank account and transfer funds – you can open an account with many banks from abroad or even via the internet.

- Obtain some local currency (if possible) before your arrival, which will save you having to change money immediately on arrival. Failing this, take some US$ or GB£, which are readily accepted in most countries.
- Obtain an international driving permit, if necessary.
- If you don't already have one, it's recommended to obtain an international credit card, which will prove invaluable during your first few months in the Far East.

If you plan to become a permanent resident, you may also need to do the following:

- Arrange schooling for your children.
- Organise the shipment of your personal and household effects.
- Obtain as many credit references as possible, e.g. from banks, mortgage companies, credit card companies, credit agencies, and companies with which you've had accounts, and references from professionals such as lawyers and accountants. These will help you establish a credit rating in the region.
- Take your family's official documents with you. These may include birth certificates, driving licences, marriage certificate, divorce papers or death certificate (if a widow or widower), educational diplomas and professional certificates, employment references and curricula vitae, school records and student identity cards, medical and dental records, bank account and credit card details, insurance policies (plus no-claims records), and receipts for any valuables, as well as any additional documents necessary to obtain a residence permit plus certified copies, official translations and numerous passport-size photographs (students should take around a dozen).

After Arrival

The following checklist contains a summary of the tasks to be completed after arrival in the Far East (if not done before arrival):

- On arrival at an airport, port or land border post, have your visa cancelled and your passport stamped, as applicable.
- If you aren't taking a car with you, you may wish to hire or buy one locally. Note that it's difficult to get around in many countries without a car if you don't live in a major city and it's practically impossible in rural areas.
- Open a bank account at a local bank and give the details to your employer and any companies that you plan to pay by direct debit or standing order.

- Arrange whatever insurance is necessary, such as health, car and home.
- Contact offices and organisations to obtain local information.
- It's recommended to make courtesy calls on your neighbours and the local mayor within a few weeks of your arrival. This is particularly important in villages and rural areas if you want to be accepted and integrate into the local community.

If you plan to become a resident in the region, you may need to do the following within the next few weeks (if not done before your arrival):

- Apply for a residence permit.
- Register for membership of the state national health service.
- Register with a local doctor and dentist.
- Apply for a local driving licence.
- Arrange schooling for your children.

Moving House

When moving to the Far East permanently there are many things to be considered and a 'million' people to be informed. Even if you plan to spend only a few months per year in the region, it may still be necessary to inform a number of people and companies in your home country. The checklist below is designed to make the task easier and help prevent an ulcer or a nervous breakdown – provided of course you don't leave everything to the last minute!

- Arrange to sell anything you aren't taking with you (e.g. house, car and furniture). If you're selling a home or business, you should obtain expert legal advice, as you may be able to save tax by establishing a trust or other legal vehicle. If you own more than one property, you may need to pay capital gains tax on the profits from the sale of second and subsequent homes. An alternative to selling a home is letting it, particularly if you may be returning to the country in a few years; arrange letting well in advance of your move.
- Give notice to the following:
  - Your landlord (if you live in rented accommodation – check your contract);
  - Your children's schools. Try to give a term's notice and obtain copies of any relevant reports or records from current schools.
  - Your employer;

- Your electricity, gas, water and telephone companies. Contact companies well in advance, particularly if you need to get a deposit refunded.

● Inform the following:

- Your local town hall or municipality. You may be entitled to a refund of your local property or other taxes.

- The police (if it was necessary to register with the police in your home country);

- Your insurance companies (for example health, car, home contents and private pension), banks, post office (if you have a post office account), stockbroker and other financial institutions, credit card, charge card and hire purchase companies, lawyer and accountant, and local businesses where you have accounts. Check whether you're entitled to a rebate on your road tax, car and other insurance and obtain a letter from your motor insurance company stating your no-claims discount.

- Your local tax and social security offices. You may qualify for a rebate on your tax and social security contributions. If you're leaving a country permanently and have been a member of a company or state pension scheme, you may be entitled to a refund or may be able to continue payments to qualify for a full (or larger) pension when you retire. Contact your company personnel office as appropriate.

- Your family doctor, dentist and other health practitioners. Health records should be transferred to your new doctor and dentist in the Far East.

- All regular correspondents, publications to which you subscribe, social and sports clubs, and friends and relatives. Give them your new address and telephone number in the Far East and arrange to have your post redirected by the post office or a friend (or a property management company).

● Arrange shipment of your furniture and belongings by booking a shipping company well in advance. International shipping companies usually provide a wealth of information and can advise on a wide range of matters regarding an international relocation. Find out the procedure for shipping your belongings to your new home from a local embassy or consulate.

● If you're exporting a car, complete the relevant paperwork in your home country and re-register it in the Far East after your arrival. You may also need to return the registration plates. Contact a local embassy or consulate for information.

● Arrange vaccinations, documentation and shipment for any pets that you're taking with you.

● Arrange health, dental and optical check-ups for your family before leaving your home country and have any necessary or recommended vaccinations.

- Obtain a copy of health records and a statement from your private health insurance company stating your present level of cover.
- Terminate any outstanding loan, lease or hire purchase contracts and pay bills (allow plenty of time as some companies may be slow to respond).
- Return any library books or anything borrowed.
- Check whether you need an international driving permit or a translation of your foreign driving licence(s) for your new country. Note that some foreign residents are required to take a driving test to drive in some countries.
- If you will be living in the region for an extended period (but not permanently), you may wish to give someone 'power of attorney' over your financial affairs in your home country so that they can act for you in your absence. This can be for a fixed period or open-ended and can be for a specific purpose only. Note, however, that you should take expert legal advice before doing this!
- Allow plenty of time to get to the airport, register your luggage, and clear security and immigration.

Have a good trip!

APPENDICES

Appendix A: Useful Addresses

The British Association of Removers (BAR) Overseas, 3 Churchill Court, 58 Station Road, North Harrow, Middlesex, HA2 7SA, UK (☎ 020-8861 3331).

The British Council, 10 Spring Gardens, London SW1A 2BN, UK (☎ 020-7930 8466, ☐ www.britishcouncil.org).

The Centre for International Briefing, Farnham Castle, Farnham, Surrey, GU9 0AG, UK (☎ 01252-721194, ☐ www.cibfarnham.com). Organises briefing courses for people moving overseas.

Corona Worldwide, Commonwealth Institute, Kensington High Street, London, W8 6NQ, UK (☎ 020-7610 4407). Provides information for women expatriates.

Employment Conditions Abroad, Anchor House, 15 Britten Street, London, SW3 3TY, UK (☎ 020-7351 5000, ☐ www.eca@eca-international.com). Publishes information for expatriates on over 75 countries.

English Contacts Abroad, PO Box 126, Oxford, OX2 6UB, UK.

The Experiment in International Living, Kipling Road, PO Box 676, Brattleboro, Vermont 05302-0676, US (☎ 802-257-7751, ☐ www.experiment.org).

Going Places, 84 Coombe Road, New Malden, Surrey, KT3 4QS, UK (☎ 020-8949 8811). Organises tailor-made expatriate briefing courses.

International Living, PO Box 1598, Newburg, NY 12551-9983, US (☎ 800-643 2479).

Medical Advisory Service for Travellers Abroad (MASTA), London School of Hygiene and Tropical Medicine, Keppel Street, London, WC1E 7HT, UK (☎ 020-7631 4408). 24-hour Travellers Healthline.

The Retirement Letter, 28 Eccleston Square, London, SW1V 1PA, UK. Voluntary Service Overseas, 317 Putney Bridge Road, London, SW15 2PN, UK (☎ 020-8789 1331, ☐ www.vso.org.uk).

Wexas International, 45–49 Brompton Road, London, SW3 1DE, UK (☎ 020-7589 3315, ☐ www.wexas.com). Provides a comprehensive range of travel insurance.

APPENDIX B: FURTHER READING

English-Language Publications

Condé Nast Traveller, Vogue House, 1 Hanover Square, London, W1S 1JU, UK (☎ 020-7499 9080, 💻 www.cntraveller.co.uk) and 4 Times Square, New York, NY 10036, US (☎ 212-286 2860). Glamorous travel magazine for the well-heeled.

The Expatriate, 175 Vauxhall Bridge Road, London, SE1 1ER, UK (☎ 020-7233 8595, ✉ 106044.1374@compuserve.com).

Home and Away, Expats, International Ltd., Expats House, 29 Lacon Road, London SE22 9HE, UK (☎ 020-8299 4986, 💻 www.expats.co.uk). Monthly magazine for expatriates.

National Geographic, National Geographic Society, 1145 17th St, NW Washington, DC 20036-4688, US (☎ 202-857 7000, 💻 www.national geographic.com). Also publish **National Geographic Traveller**.

Nexus Expatriate Magazine, Expat Network Limited, International House, 500 Purley Way, Croydon, CR0 4NZ, UK (☎ 020-8760 5100, 💻 www.expatnetwork. co.uk).

Official Airlines Guide, Church Street, Dunstable, Bedfordshire, LU5 4HB, UK (☎ 01582-600111, 💻 www.oag.com). Monthly airline pocket timetable.

Overseas Jobs Express, Premier House, Shoreham Airport, Sussex, BN43 5FF, UK (☎ 01273-440220, 💻 www.overseasjobs.com).

South East Asia Traveller, Compass Publishing, 336 Smith Street, 04-303 New Bridge Centre, Chinatown, Singapore 0105 (☎ 221-1111).

Thomas Cook Magazine, 7 St. Martin, UK (☎ 020-7499 9080, 💻 www.cntraveller.co.uk) and 4 Times Square, New York, NY 10036, US (☎ 212-286 2860). Glamorous travel magazine for the well-heeled.

Transitions Abroad, PO Box 1300, Amherst, MA 01004-1300, US (☎ 413-256 3414, 💻 www.transitionsabroad.com).

Traveller, Wexas International, 45-49 Brompton Road, Knightsbridge, London, SW3 1DE, UK (☎ 020-7581 4130, 💻 www.traveller.org.uk). Long-established, quality travel magazine.

Wanderlust, PO Box 1832, Windsor, SL4 6YP, UK (☎ 01753-620426, 💻 www. wanderlust.co.uk). Excellent monthly practical magazine for avid travellers.

Woman Abroad, Postmark Publishing Ltd., 1 Portsmouth Road, Guildford, Surrey, GU2 4YB, UK (💻 www.womanabroad.com).

Books

The books listed below are just a small selection of the many books written for those planning to live, work or retire in the Far East. Some titles may be out of print, but may still be obtainable from bookshops and libraries. Books prefixed with an asterisk (*) are recommended by the author. See also the list of books published by Survival Books (see page 444).

The Adventure of Living Abroad: Hero Tales from the Global Frontier, Joyce Sautters Osland (Jossey-Bass)

*Americans Living Abroad, J. Kepler (Praeger)

*Directory of Jobs and Careers Abroad, E. Roberts (Vacation Work)

Executives Living Abroad, Deloitte Touche Tohmatsu International (Kluwer Law)

Getting a Job Abroad, Roger Jones (How To Books)

*Getting a Job in Europe, Mark Hempshell (How To Books)

Guide to Living Abroad, Michael Furnell & Philip Jones (Kogan Page)

Guide to Working Abroad, Godfrey Golzen & Helen Kogan (Kogan Page)

*Home from Home (Central Bureau)

International Jobs: Where They Are and How to Get Them, E. Kocher (Perseus Press)

**Living and Working Abroad, David Hampshire (Survival Books)

Living & Working Abroad: A Parent's Guide, Robin Pascoe (Kuperard)

Living & Working Abroad: A Wife's Guide, Robin Pascoe (Kuperard)

Look Ahead: A Guide to Working Abroad, Alan Vincent (Heinemann)

*Money Mail: Moves Abroad, Margaret Stone (Kogan Page)

Moving and Living Abroad, Sandra Albright, Alice Chu & Lori Austin (Hippocrene Books, Inc.).

Opportunities in Overseas Careers, B. Camenson (Vgm Opportunities Series)

Relocation: Escape from America, R. Gallo (Manhattan Loft Publishers)

Summer Jobs Abroad, David Woodworth (Vacation Work)

Survival Kit for Overseas Living: For Americans Planning to Live and Work Abroad, L. Robert Kohis (Nicholas Brealey)

*Teach Abroad (Central Bureau)

*US Expat Handbook Guide to Living & Working Abroad, John W. Adams

Work & Study in Developing Countries, Toby Milner (Vacation Work)

*Work Your Way Around the World, Susan Griffith (Vacation Work)

Working Abroad, Alan Vincent (Heinemann)

*Working Abroad, Peter Gartland (Financial Times)

*Working Abroad, William Essex (Bloomsbury)

*Working Holidays (Central Bureau)

*Working Holidays Abroad, Mark Hempshell (Trotman)

Working Overseas, Bryan Havenhand (Global Exchange)

*A Year Between (Central Bureau)

Health & Safety

The ABC of Healthy Travel (British Medical Journal)

Business Smarts – Business Travel Safety Guide, Aura Lee O'Banion (Safety First)

*How to Stay Healthy Abroad, Dr. R. Dawood (Oxford University Press)

International Travel and Health 2004 (World Health Organization)

Keeping Your Life, Family and Career Intact While Living Abroad, Cathy Tsang-Feign (Hamblan)

*Travellers' Health, Richard Dawood (Oxford Paperbacks)

*A Travellers' Medical Guide, Paul Zakowich (Kuperard)

Immunization – Childhood and Travel Health, Kassianos (Blackwell)

*Merck Manual of Medical Information: Home Edition (Merck)

*Rough Guide to Travel Health, Dr. Nick Jones (Rough Guides)

*Safety and Security for Women Who Travel, Sheila Swan (Travelers' Tales)

*Survivor's Guide to Business Travel, R. Collins (Kogan Page)

Travel Can be Murder: A Business Traveler's Guide to Personal Safety, Terry Riley (Applied Psychology Press).

*Travel with Children**, Mike Wheeler (Lonely Planet)

Travel in Health, Graham Fry & Vincent Kenny (Gill and Macmillan)

Travel and Health in the Elderly, I.B. McIntosh (Quay)

*Travel Medicine and Migrant Health**, Cameron Lockie MBE (Churchill Livingstone)

*Travel Safety**, Adler (Hippocrene)

*The Travellers Handbook** (Wexas)

*Traveller's Health**, Dr. R. Dawood (OUP)

Understanding Travel and Holiday Health, Bernadette Carroll (Family Doctor)

*World Wise - Your Passport to Safer Travel**, Suzy Lamplugh (Thomas Cook)

Retirement

*The Good Retirement Guide**, Rosemary Brown (Kogan Page)

How to Retire Abroad, (How To Books)

Making the Most of Retirement, Michael Barratt (Kogan Page)

Retirement Abroad, Robert Cooke (Robert Hale)

APPENDIX C: USEFUL WEBSITES

There are literally dozens of expatriate websites and as the internet increases in popularity the number grows by the day. Most information is useful and websites generally offer free access, although some require a subscription or payment for services. Relocation and other companies specialising in expatriate services often have websites, although these may only provide information that a company is prepared to offer free of charge, which although it can be useful may be rather biased. However, there are plenty of volunteer sites run by expatriates providing practical information and tips. A particularly useful section found on most expatriate websites is the 'message board' or 'forum', where expatriates answer questions based on their experience and knowledge, and offer an insight into what a country or city is really like.

Below is a list of some of the best expatriate websites. Note that websites are listed under headings in alphabetical order and the list is by no means definitive. Websites relating to specific countries are listed in **Chapter 9** under individual countries.

General Websites

Direct Moving (⌨ www.directmoving.com) – The first worldwide relocation portal with a plethora of expatriate information, tips and advice with good links.

ExpatAccess (⌨ www.expataccess.com) – Unlike other 'expat' sites, ExpatAccess is specifically for those planning to move abroad, with free online moving guides to help you through the relocation process.

ExpatBoards (⌨ www.expatboards.com) – The mega site for expatriates, with very popular discussion boards and special areas for Britons, Americans, expatriate taxes, and other important issues.

Escape Artist (⌨ www.escapeartist.com) – An excellent website and probably the most comprehensive, packed with resources, links and directories covering most expatriate destinations. You can also subscribe to the free monthly online expatriate magazine, Escape from America.

Expat Exchange (⌨ www.expatexchange.com) – Reportedly the largest online community for English-speaking expatriates, provides a series of articles on relocation and also a question and answer facility through its expatriate network.

Expat Forum (💻 www.expatforum.com) – Provides interesting cost of living comparisons as well as over 20 country-specific forums and chats.

Expat Network (💻 www.expatnetwork.com) – The leading expatriate website in the UK, which is essentially an employment network for expatriates, although there are also numerous support services plus a monthly online magazine, Nexus.

Expat World (💻 www.expatworld.net) – 'The newsletter of international living.' Contains a wealth of information for American and British expatriates, including a subscription newsletter.

Expatriate Experts (💻 www.expatexpert.com) – A website run by expatriate expert Robin Pascoe, providing invaluable advice and support.

Expats International (💻 www.expats2000.com) – The international job centre for expats and their recruiters.

Gap Year (💻 www.gapyear.co.uk) – A website mainly targted at students doing a gap year, but full of useful information and advice about countries and travelling.

Global People (💻 www.peoplegoingglobal.com) – Provides interesting country-specific information with particular emphasis on social and political aspects.

Living Abroad (💻 www.livingabroad.com) – Provides an extensive and comprehensive list of country profiles, although they're available only on payment.

Outpost Information Centre (💻 www.outpostexpat.nl) – A website containing extensive country specific information and links operated by the Shell Petroleum Company for its expatriate workers, but available to everyone.

Real Post Reports (💻 www.realpostreports.com) – Provides relocation services, recommended reading lists and plenty of interesting 'real-life' stories containing anecdotes and impressions written by expatriates in just about every city in the world.

World Travel Guide (💻 www.wtgonline.com) – A general website for world travellers and expatriates.

American Websites

Americans Abroad (💻 www.aca.ch) – This website offers advice, information and services to Americans abroad.

American Teachers Abroad (🖳 www.overseasdigest.com) – A comprehensive website with numerous relocation services and advice plus teaching opportunities.

US Government Trade (🖳 www.usatrade.gov) – A huge website providing a wealth of information principally for Americans planning to trade and invest abroad, but useful for anyone planning a move abroad.

British Websites

British Expatriates (🖳 www.britishexpat.com and www.ukworld wide.com) – These websites keep British expatriates in touch with events and information about the UK.

Trade Partners (🖳 www.tradepartners.gov.uk) – A government sponsored website whose main aim is to provide trade and investment information on just about every country in the world. Even if you aren't planning to do business abroad, the information is comprehensive and up to date.

Worldwise Directory (🖳 www.suzylamplugh.org/worldwise) – This website run by the Suzy Lamplugh charity for personal safety, providing a useful directory of countries with practical information and special emphasis on safety, particularly for women.

Australian & New Zealand Websites

Australians Abroad (🖳 www.australiansabroad.com) – Information for Australians concerning relocating plus a forum to exchange information and advice.

Kiwi Club (🖳 www.kiwiclub.org) – Information and support for New Zealanders in Austria, Switzerland, Singapore and North America.

Southern Cross Group (🖳 www.southern-cross-group.org) – A website for Australians and New Zealanders providing information and the exchange of tips.

Websites For Women

Career Women (🖳 www.womenconnect.com) – Mainly contains career opportunities for women abroad plus a wealth of other useful information.

Women Abroad (🖳 www.womanabroad.com) – Offers the chance to subscribe to a monthly magazine of the same name and access to advice on careers, expatriate skills and the family abroad.

Spouse Abroad (🖳 www.expatspouse.com) – Designed with the expatriate spouse in mind with particular emphasis on careers and working abroad. You need to register and subscribe to the standard or premium membership.

Expatriate Mothers (🖳 http://expatmoms.tripod.com) – Provides help and advice on how to survive as a mother on relocation.

Third Culture Kids (🖳 www.tckworld.com) – A website designed for expatriate children living abroad.

Travel Information & Warnings

The websites listed below provide daily updated information about the political situation and natural disasters around the world, plus general travel and health advice and embassy addresses.

Australian Department of Foreign Affairs and Trade (🖳 www.dfat.gov.au/consular/advice/advices_mnu.html).

British Foreign and Commonwealth Office (🖳 www.fco.gov.uk/travel).

Canadian Department of Foreign Affairs (🖳 http://voyage.dfait-maeci.gc.ca/menu-e.asp). They also publish a useful series of free booklets for Canadians moving abroad.

Gov Spot (🖳 www.govspot.com/ask/travel.htm) – US Government Website.

New Zealand Ministry of Foreign Affairs and Trade (http://www.mft.govt.nz/ travel/report.html).

SaveWealth Travel (🖳 www.save wealth.com/travel/warnings)

The Travel Doctor (🖳 www.tmvc.com.au/info10.html) – Contains a country by country vaccination guide.

Travelfinder (🖳 www.travelfinder.com/twarn/travel_warnings.html).

US Department of State (🖳 http://travel.state.gov/travel_warnings.html and http:// travel.state.gov/warnings_list.html). This website also contains warnings about drugs (🖳 http://travel.state.gov/drug_warning.html) – and a list of useful travel publications (🖳 http://travel.state.gov/travel_pubs.html).

World Health Organization (🖳 www.who.int).

Appendix D: WEIGHTS & MEASURES

The metric system of measurement is in general use throughout the Far East. Those who are more familiar with the imperial system of measurement will find the tables on the following pages useful. Some comparisons shown are only approximate, but are close enough for most everyday uses. In addition to the variety of measurement systems used, clothes sizes often vary considerably with the manufacturer (as we all know only too well). Try all clothes on before buying and don't be afraid to return something if, when you try it on at home, you decide it doesn't fit (most shops will exchange goods or give a refund).

Women's Clothes

Continental	34	36	38	40	42	44	46	48	50	52
UK	8	10	12	14	16	18	20	22	24	26
USA	6	8	10	12	14	16	18	20	22	24

Pullovers

	Women's						Men's					
Continental	40	42	44	46	48	50	44	46	48	50	52	54
UK	34	36	38	40	42	44	34	36	38	40	42	44
USA	34	36	38	40	42	44	sm	med		lar	xl	

Men's Shirts

Continental	36	37	38	39	40	41	42	43	44	46
UK/USA	14	14	15	15	16	16	17	17	18	-

Men's Underwear

Continental	5	6	7	8	9	10
UK	34	36	38	40	42	44
USA	sm	med		lar	xl	

Note: sm = small, med = medium, lar = large, xl = extra large

Children's Clothes

Continental	92	104	116	128	140	152
UK	16/18	20/22	24/26	28/30	32/34	36/38
USA	2	4	6	8	10	12

Children's Shoes

Continental	18	19	20	21	22	23	24	25	26	27	28	29	30	31	32
UK/USA	2	3	4	4	5	6	7	7	8	9	10	11	11	12	13

Continental	33	34	35	36	37	38
UK/USA	1	2	2	3	4	5

Shoes (Women's and Men's)

Continental	35	36	37	37	38	39	40	41	42	42	43	44
UK	2	3	3	4	4	5	6	7	7	8	9	9
USA	4	5	5	6	6	7	8	9	9	10	10	11

Weight

Avoirdupois	Metric	Metric	Avoirdupois
1oz	28.35g	1g	0.035oz
1lb*	454g	100g	3.5oz
1cwt	50.8kg	250g	9oz
1 ton	1,016kg	500g	18oz
2,205lb	1 tonne	1kg	2.2lb

Length

British/US	Metric	Metric	British/US
1in	2.54cm	1cm	0.39in
1ft	30.48cm	1m	3ft 3.25in
1yd	91.44cm	1km	0.62mi
1mi	1.6km	8km	5mi

Capacity

Imperial	Metric	Metric	Imperial
1 UK pint	0.57 litre	1 litre	1.75 UK pints
1 US pint	0.47 litre	1 litre	2.13 US pints
1 UK gallon	4.54 litres	1 litre	0.22 UK gallon
1 US gallon	3.78 litres	1 litre	0.26 US gallon

Note: An American 'cup' = around 250ml or 0.25 litre.

Area

British/US	Metric	Metric	British/US
1 sq. in	0.45 sq. cm	1 sq. cm	0.15 sq. in
1 sq. ft	0.09 sq. m	1 sq. m	10.76 sq. ft
1 sq. yd	0.84 sq. m	1 sq. m	1.2 sq. yds
1 acre	0.4 hectares	1 hectare	2.47 acres
1 sq. mile	2.56 sq. km	1 sq. km	0.39 sq. mile

Temperature

°Celsius	°Fahrenheit	
0	32	(freezing point of water)
5	41	
10	50	
15	59	
20	68	
25	77	
30	86	
35	95	
40	104	
50	122	

Notes: The boiling point of water is 100°C / 212°F.

Normal body temperature (if you're alive and well) is 37°C / 98.6°F.

Temperature Conversion

Celsius to Fahrenheit: multiply by 9, divide by 5 and add 32. (For a quick and approximate conversion, double the Celsius temperature and add 30.)

Fahrenheit to Celsius: subtract 32, multiply by 5 and divide by 9. (For a quick and approximate conversion, subtract 30 from the Fahrenheit temperature and divide by 2.)

Oven Temperatures

Gas	Electric	
	°F	°C
-	225–250	110–120
1	275	140
2	300	150
3	325	160
4	350	180
5	375	190
6	400	200
7	425	220
8	450	230
9	475	240

Air Pressure

PSI	Bar
10	0.5
20	1.4
30	2
40	2.8

Power

Kilowatts	Horsepower	Horsepower	Kilowatts
1	1.34	1	0.75

INDEX

G

H

I

J

Q

R

S

LIVING AND WORKING SERIES

Living and Working books are essential reading for anyone planning to spend time abroad, including holiday-home owners, retirees, visitors, business people, migrants, students and even extra-terrestrials! They're packed with important and useful information designed to help you **avoid costly mistakes and save both time and money.** Topics covered include how to:

- Find a job with a good salary & conditions
- Obtain a residence permit
- Avoid and overcome problems
- Find your dream home
- Get the best education for your family
- Make the best use of public transport
- Endure local motoring habits
- Obtain the best health treatment
- Stretch your money further
- Make the most of your leisure time
- Enjoy the local sporting life
- Find the best shopping bargains
- Insure yourself against most eventualities
- Use post office and telephone services
- Do numerous other things not listed above

Living and Working books are the most comprehensive and up-to-date source of practical information available about everyday life abroad. They aren't, however, boring text books, but interesting and entertaining guides written in a highly readable style.

Discover what it's really like to live and work abroad!

Order your copies today by phone, fax, mail or e-mail from: Survival Books, PO Box 146, Wetherby, West Yorks. LS23 6XZ, United Kingdom (☎/🖨 +44 (0)1937-843523, ✉ orders@ survivalbooks.net, 🖳 www.survivalbooks.net).

BUYING A HOME SERIES

Buying a Home books are essential reading for anyone planning to purchase property abroad and are designed to guide you through the jungle and make it a pleasant and enjoyable experience. Most importantly, they're packed with vital information to help you **avoid the sort of disasters that can turn your dream home into a nightmare!** Topics covered include:

- Avoiding problems
- Choosing the region
- Finding the right home and location
- Estate agents
- Finance, mortgages and taxes
- Home security
- Utilities, heating and air-conditioning
- Moving house and settling in
- Renting and letting
- Permits and visas
- Travelling and communications
- Health and insurance
- Renting a car and driving
- Retirement and starting a business
- And much, much more!

Buying a Home books are the most comprehensive and up-to-date source of information available about buying property abroad. Whether you want a detached house, townhouse or apartment, a holiday or a permanent home, these books will help make your dreams come true.

Save yourself time, trouble and money!

Order your copies today by phone, fax, mail or e-mail from: Survival Books, PO Box 146, Wetherby, West Yorks. LS23 6XZ, United Kingdom (☎/▤ +44 (0)1937-843523, ✉ orders@ survivalbooks.net, ▣ www.survivalbooks.net).

ORDER FORM

ALIEN'S GUIDES / BEST PLACES / BUYING A HOME / DISASTERS / WINES

Qty.	Title	Price (incl. p&p)*			Total
		UK	Europe	World	
	The Alien's Guide to Britain	£5.95	£6.95	£8.45	
	The Alien's Guide to France	£5.95	£6.95	£8.45	
	The Best Places to Buy a Home in France	£13.95	£15.95	£19.45	
	The Best Places to Buy a Home in Spain	£13.45	£14.95	£16.95	
	Buying a Home Abroad	£13.45	£14.95	£16.95	
	Buying a Home in Britain	£11.45	£12.95	£14.95	
	Buying a Home in Florida	£13.45	£14.95	£16.95	
	Buying a Home in France	£13.45	£14.95	£16.95	
	Buying a Home in Greece & Cyprus	£13.45	£14.95	£16.95	
	Buying a Home in Ireland	£11.45	£12.95	£14.95	
	Buying a Home in Italy	£13.45	£14.95	£16.95	
	Buying a Home in Portugal	£13.45	£14.95	£16.95	
	Buying a Home in Spain	£13.45	£14.95	£16.95	
	Buying, Letting & Selling Property	£11.45	£12.95	£14.95	
	How to Avoid Holiday & Travel Disasters	£13.45	£14.95	£16.95	
	Renovating & Maintaining Your French Home	£13.45	£14.95	£16.95	
	Rioja and its Wines	£11.45	£12.95	£14.95	
	The Wines of Spain	£15.95	£18.45	£21.95	
				Total	

Order your copies today by phone, fax, mail or e-mail from: Survival Books, PO Box 146, Wetherby, West Yorks. LS23 6XZ, UK (☎/▤ +44 (0)1937-843523, ✉ orders@ survivalbooks.net, ▣ www.survivalbooks.net). If you aren't entirely satisfied, simply return them to us within 14 days for a full and unconditional refund.

Cheque enclosed/please charge my Amex/Delta/MasterCard/Switch/Visa* card

Card No. __ __ __ __   __ __ __ __   __ __ __ __   __ __ __ __

Expiry date _____   Issue number (Switch only) _____

Signature _____   Tel. No. _____

NAME _____

ADDRESS _____

_____

* Delete as applicable (price includes postage – airmail for Europe/world).

ORDER FORM

LIVING & WORKING SERIES / RETIRING ABROAD

Qty.	Title	Price (incl. p&p)*			Total
		UK	**Europe**	**World**	
	Living & Working Abroad	£16.95	£18.95	£22.45	
	Living & Working in America	£14.95	£16.95	£20.45	
	Living & Working in Australia	£14.95	£16.95	£20.45	
	Living & Working in Britain	£14.95	£16.95	£20.45	
	Living & Working in Canada	£16.95	£18.95	£22.45	
	Living & Working in the EU	spring 2004			
	Living & Working in the Far East	£16.95	£18.95	£22.45	
	Living & Working in France	£14.95	£16.95	£20.45	
	Living & Working in Germany	£16.95	£18.95	£22.45	
	Living & Working in the Gulf States & Saudi Arabia	£16.95	£18.95	£22.45	
	Living & Working in Holland, Belgium & Luxembourg	£14.95	£16.95	£20.45	
	Living & Working in Ireland	£14.95	£16.95	£20.45	
	Living & Working in Italy	£16.95	£18.95	£22.45	
	Living & Working in London	£13.45	£14.95	£16.95	
	Living & Working in New Zealand	£14.95	£16.95	£20.45	
	Living & Working in Spain	£14.95	£16.95	£20.45	
	Living & Working in Switzerland	£16.95	£18.95	£22.45	
	Retiring Abroad	£14.95	£16.95	£20.45	
				Total	

Order your copies today by phone, fax, mail or e-mail from: Survival Books, PO Box 146, Wetherby, West Yorks. LS23 6XZ, UK (☎/▤ +44 (0)1937-843523, ✉ orders@ survivalbooks.net, 💻 www.survivalbooks.net). If you aren't entirely satisfied, simply return them to us within 14 days for a full and unconditional refund.

Cheque enclosed/please charge my Amex/Delta/MasterCard/Switch/Visa* card

Card No. __ __ __ __ __ __ __ __ __ __ __ __ __ __ __ __

Expiry date _____ Issue number (Switch only) _____

Signature _____ Tel. No. _____

NAME _____

ADDRESS _____

_____

* Delete as applicable (price includes postage – airmail for Europe/world).

OTHER SURVIVAL BOOKS

Survival Books publishes a variety of books in addition to the Living and Working and Buying a Home series (see previous pages). These include:

The Alien's Guides: The Alien's Guides to Britain and France provide an 'alternative' look at life in these popular countries and will help you to appreciate the peculiarities (in both senses) of the British and French.

The Best Places to Buy a Home: The Best Places to Buy a Home in France and Spain are the most comprehensive and up-to-date sources of information available for anyone choosing the best place for a home in France or Spain.

Buying, Selling and Letting Property: The most comprehensive and up-to-date source of information available for those intending to buy, sell or let a property in the UK and the only book on the subject updated annually.

How to Avoid Holiday and Travel Disasters: This book will help you to make the right decisions regarding every aspect of your travel arrangements and to avoid costly mistakes and disasters that can turn a trip into a nightmare.

Renovating & Maintaining Your French Home: The ultimate guide to renovating and maintaining your dream home in France, including essential information, contacts and vocabulary and time and cost-saving tips.

Retiring Abroad: This is the most comprehensive and up-to-date source of practical information available about retiring to a foreign country and will help to smooth your path to successful retirement abroad and save you time, trouble and money.

Wine Guides: Rioja and its Wines and The Wines of Spain are required reading for lovers of fine wines and are the most comprehensive and up-to-date sources of information available on the wines of Spain and of its most famous wine-producing region.

Broaden your horizons with Survival Books!

Order your copies today by phone, fax, mail or e-mail from: Survival Books, PO Box 146, Wetherby, West Yorks. LS23 6XZ, United Kingdom (☎/🖹 +44 (0)1937-843523, ✉ orders@ survivalbooks.net, 🖥 www.survivalbooks.net).